Jossey-Bass Teacher

Jossey-Bass Teacher provides educators with practical knowledge and tools to create a positive and lifelong impact on student learning. We offer classroom-tested and research-based teaching resources for a variety of grade levels and subject areas. Whether you are an aspiring, new, or veteran teacher, we want to help you make every teaching day your best.

From ready-to-use classroom activities to the latest teaching framework, our value-packed books provide insightful, practical, and comprehensive materials on the topics that matter most to K–12 teachers. We hope to become your trusted source for the best ideas from the most experienced and respected experts in the field.

For more information about our resources, authors, and events, please visit us at: www.josseybasseducation.com.

DISCIPLINE
IN THE
SECONDARY CLASSROOM

DISCIPLINE
IN THE
SECONDARY
CLASSROOM

A Positive Approach to Behavior Management

Randall S. Sprick, Ph.D.

JB JOSSEY-BASS™

A Wiley Brand

Library of Congress Cataloging-in-Publication Data

Sprick, Randall S.
  Discipline in the secondary classroom : a positive approach to behavior management / Randall S.
Sprick, Ph. D.—Third edition.
    pages cm
  Includes bibliographical references and index.
  ISBN 978-1-118-45087-1 (paper/dvd)
  ISBN 978-1-118-64027-2 (ebk.)
  ISBN 978-1-118-64013-5 (ebk.)
  1. Classroom management. 2. High school students—Discipline. 3. Problem children—Discipline. I. Title.
  LB3013.S64 2013
  371.102′4—dc23
                                                                                    2013013798

Printed in the United States of America
THIRD EDITION

PB Printing 10 9 8 7 6

THE AUTHOR

Randall Sprick has an undergraduate degree in general education, a master's degree in special education, and a doctorate in curriculum and supervision. He has taught students with emotional and behavioral problems and trained and supervised teachers at elementary and secondary levels. He has taught postgraduate courses on behavior management and behavioral consultation at the University of Oregon.

Dr. Sprick has written numerous articles and books and has developed audio and video in-service programs that address topics such as classroom management, schoolwide discipline policies, playground discipline, and bus behavior. Among the widely used books he has written are:

- *START on Time! Safe Transitions and Reduced Tardiness*
- *Foundations: Establishing Positive Discipline Policies*
- *CHAMPS: A Proactive and Positive Approach to Classroom Management*
- *Teacher's Encyclopedia of Behavior Management: 100+ Problems/500+ Plans*
- *The Administrator's Desk Reference of Behavior Management* (3 vols.)
- *Interventions*
- *ParaPro: Supporting the Instructional Process*
- *Coaching Classroom Management*
- *Behavioral Response to Intervention*
- *Teacher Planner for the Secondary Classroom*

Dr. Sprick is director of Safe & Civil Schools, which provides in-service programs throughout the country. Each year, he and his training staff conduct workshops and classes for more than thirty thousand teachers. His positive and practical approach is helping schools increase safety, reduce classroom disruption, and improve school climate. Districts fully implementing the approach have reduced out-of-school suspensions by up to 86 percent.

Acknowledgments

I extend my gratitude and appreciation for the content suggestions and editorial assistance of Jessica Sprick, Paula Rich, Sara Ferris, Natalie Conaway, Rohanna Buchanan, Susan Isaacs, Laura Hamilton, Jim Whitaker, and Laura Matson. Thanks to the staffs of Pacific Northwest Publishing and Jossey-Bass Publishing for their willingness to link the approach of this book with the Safe & Civil Schools materials. Thanks also to Robin Lloyd, Tracy Gallagher, Bev Miller, Diane Turso, Anitha Mani, and the rest of the Jossey-Bass team for their excellent work throughout the editing and production process. Finally, I thank Marjorie McAneny, senior editor at Jossey-Bass, for being such a gracious, invitational, and professional editor.

How to Use
This Book

This book leaves the decisions to you. There is no part of the book that is a canned program of specific procedures you must implement. Instead, it is more of a toolshed filled with classroom-tested tools and techniques that are made available to you. Consider working through the book with a colleague or even with your entire staff. Note that the DVD that comes with the book includes Peer Study worksheets for each chapter (see the 3 Downloadable Forms and Checklists folder on the DVD). These guides will facilitate sharing of best practice ideas between you and your colleagues. As you work through the book, read each task and think about whether your current classroom management plan addresses the issues it covers. Then determine whether implementing some or all of the suggestions within the task would have a positive benefit on behavior and motivation for your students.

The best way to use this book will vary depending on when you choose to implement it. The early chapters are more for preplanning—that is, determining your teaching plan in advance of the school year. All the tasks in this book can be implemented in any classroom at any time, but coming in fully prepared and with a concrete plan is obviously the ideal situation. Because ideal situations are so rare, this book also describes ways to implement your new skills at any time of the year, or even gradually throughout the year.

- *Beginning in the spring or summer*. Ideally, you will have plenty of time to work through chapters 1 through 8 in sequence before the school year begins. By working through each task and deciding which steps to implement and how, you will build the components of your management plan. Chapter 6 in particular will help you pull all these details together for the first day of school. As the school year approaches, review chapter 9 to completely prepare yourself to take full advantage of the tools offered in this book.

- In some cases, teachers receive a copy of this book as part of teacher induction to a new district. If that is the case and you have only a little time before the students arrive, you can cover the most vital information first: chapter 4 on your classroom management plan, chapter 5 on teaching expectations, and chapter 8 on student motivation. Skim the other chapters to determine other information that might be immediately useful.

- *Beginning in the fall*. The best time to have an impact on student behavior is on the first day of school. Short of that, the first day of second semester is a good time to make some changes if they are needed. Quickly skim through chapters 1 through 6 to identify any suggestions that you think might be of immediate benefit to your classes; then work through the chapters again in more detail, preparing for the next semester. As you have time, work through chapters 6 through 9. During the next summer, work more thoroughly through chapters 1 through 8 to revise your plan and fully prepare for the first day of school.

- *Beginning in winter.* Use the Contents to identify tasks and suggestions that might help address specific problems. Then in late spring, follow the suggestions in the previous section regarding how to prepare for the new school year.

Consult the appendixes as needed to focus on specific topics such as the research behind this book (appendix A), considerations when working with students from different cultural backgrounds (appendix C), and an introduction to the icons available on the DVD for your use in teaching and displaying your classroom expectations (appendix F). First-year teachers should review appendix D. Administrators may wish to review appendix B on schoolwide implementation of Discipline in the Secondary Classroom and appendix E on mapping the contents of this book to the teaching framework outlined in Charlotte Danielson's *Enhancing Professional Practice: A Framework for Teaching.*

No matter when you start using *Discipline in the Secondary Classroom*, keep the DVD handy because it contains blank reproducibles of all the forms shown in the book. You can print the PDFs as needed as you work through the book or fill them out on your computer. The DVD also contains short videos in which I discuss the importance of clearly communicating your classroom expectations and structuring your classroom for student success.

Motivating students is part art and part science. So, too, is classroom management. And both are lifelong learning tasks. When you use the research-based techniques set out in this book, you will reach and teach students who would otherwise be doomed to school failure and a life without much promise of a successful education. Never doubt that you can be the defining difference in a child's life.

Randall S. Sprick

Contents

DVD Contents

These materials are also available online at http://www.wiley.com/go/dsc3e. The password is the last five digits of this book's ISBN, which are 50871.

Video Clips

Introduction
Overview

STOIC

Using the Book

Chapter 5
T in STOIC

Task 2

Task 3

Chapter 8
Task 1 and Task 2

Task 3

Task 4

Bonus Material

Why Bother with a Positive Approach to Discipline?

Schoolwide Implementation of Discipline in the Secondary Classroom

Downloadable Forms and Checklists

Chapter 1
Exhibit 1.2   Sample Letter to Families

Vision Self-Assessment Checklist

Chapter 2
Exhibit 2.2a   Behavior Record Form, 25 lines

Exhibit 2.2b   Behavior Record Form, 35 lines

CHAMPS Icons

This book would never have been possible if it were not for the excellent ideas of hundreds of high school teachers from around North America. During in-service sessions over the past twenty-five years, numerous teachers have openly shared their successful techniques with me. Their ideas and methods have helped me formulate the procedures included in these pages. And so I dedicate this book to these competent and caring professionals who serve such an important role in shaping the future.

Foreword

About eleven years ago, I was part of a project designed to improve the academic outcomes for struggling adolescent learners in some inner-city high schools. Great planning went into the selection of the instructional programs for improving their reading and math performance. We instituted a carefully orchestrated professional development effort to make certain that each of the teachers involved was well prepared to teach the targeted interventions. As the program was launched, we were confident that things were going to go well because of our careful planning and attention to the necessary details.

How wrong we were!

Although some successes in student outcomes were seen, they fell far short of our expectations. Puzzled, we visited with teachers and observed what was happening in many of the classrooms. It soon became clear that many of the classes were out of control: large numbers of students were tardy for class, student behavior during classes was often inappropriate, and the amount of time spent teaching the targeted interventions was limited. In short, when instruction did take place, it didn't reach all of the students and was often compromised because of the poor work environment; teachers were frequently interrupting their lesson to regain control of their class.

In light of the problems that we were facing, I called Randy Sprick to see if he would be willing to problem-solve with us. I knew Randy and had carefully followed his work for over two decades. Over the years, I have talked to countless teachers and administrators throughout North America who have implemented his student motivation and classroom management programs, programs grounded in proactive, positive, and instructional principles. Randy agreed to analyze what was happening in our schools. As a result of that conversation and the programs described in this book that our team subsequently implemented, we experienced a dramatic change in how business was done in those schools. We witnessed firsthand the dramatic effects these methods can have in transforming secondary schools that were once places of chaos and disengaged students to settings of order and safety, where interactions among students and teachers are respectful and students are eagerly and productively involved in the learning process.

Discipline in the Secondary Classroom: A Positive Approach to Behavior Management addresses one of the most pressing needs that secondary teachers face in today's schools: how to effectively motivate and manage adolescent learners so their classrooms can be stimulating, engaging learning environments.

I am convinced that secondary teachers will find this book to be one of the most valuable resources in their teaching toolbox for the following reasons:

- It is grounded in an extensive research base.
- It is hands-on, providing clear, step-by-step instructions for how to implement each procedure.

- It supplies specific examples from actual classroom situations to illustrate each procedure.
- It is principle based.
- It is comprehensive in scope, including all of the necessary components (and accompanying forms and support mechanisms) to be a self-contained management and motivation system.
- It spells out clearly how to introduce and implement the program throughout the school year.
- It is carefully coordinated with a companion volume designed for elementary students: *CHAMPS: A Proactive and Positive Approach to Classroom Management*, Second Edition (Sprick, 2009), thus enabling school districts to implement a systematic approach to student motivation and classroom management across the entire K–12 grade continuum.

This book is the extraordinary resource that it is because of its author, Randy Sprick. Randy has had extensive experience as a teacher, program developer, researcher, writer, and staff developer. One of the most sought-after teachers in the country, he has a deep understanding of the complexities of secondary schools, the needs of adolescents and teachers, and the dynamic that exists among them. The program outlined in this book has been successfully adopted by hundreds of schools throughout North America. I consider Randy Sprick to be one of the brightest and most insightful educators of our time. His mission has been to improve the quality of environments in schools and enable teachers and students alike to thrive. I believe that he has been extraordinarily successful in that quest.

Achieving successful academic outcomes for students is certainly important, but their overall growth, development, and well-being involve much more than academic success. While teachers understand this, they now find themselves in an educational dynamic that does not encourage (and in some cases does not even permit) an emphasis on the nonacademic dimensions of schooling. This book underscores the fact that understanding and addressing factors beyond academics is not only important, it is essential.

Since the passage of the No Child Left Behind Act, schools have focused almost entirely on increasing the academic performance of students. This book provides one of the foundational cornerstones for enabling teachers to be successful in the academic instruction that they provide. It will empower secondary teachers to create the kind of environment and culture in their classroom that will ultimately promote optimal academic outcomes.

This readable book is written with passion, vivid examples, and countless practical suggestions that can be readily implemented. In my more than thirty-five years as an educator, I have relied on the insights and work of many talented educators. This book will add greatly to my abilities as an educator in secondary schools, and it will be a resource I turn to frequently.

Donald D. Deshler
Director, University of Kansas Center
for Research on Learning

Preface

This is the third edition of *Discipline in the Secondary Classroom*. The first edition of this book was published in 1985. Since that time, research continues to confirm that the proactive, positive, and instructional approaches it advocates are far more effective in managing and motivating students than traditional, authoritarian, and punitive approaches. Teacher effectiveness literature has identified that teachers who are highly successful have classroom management plans that

- Include high expectations for student success
- Build positive relationships with students
- Create consistent, predictable classroom routines
- Teach students how to behave successfully
- Provide frequent positive feedback
- Correct misbehavior in a calm, consistent, logical manner

This book translates those broad ideas into specific actions you can take to improve your ability to maintain an orderly and respectful classroom in which students are focused and engaged in meaningful instructional activities.

What's new in this edition? The content has been reorganized to align more closely with the second edition of *CHAMPS: A Proactive and Positive Approach to Classroom Management*, my book for elementary and middle schools. Five parts guide the reader logically and sequentially through the STOIC model (STOIC is explained in more detail in the Introduction and at the beginning of each part):

Structure and organize your classroom.

Teach behavioral expectations.

Observe and monitor students.

Interact positively.

Correct misbehavior fluently.

More information has been added about effectively initiating and maintaining family contacts, using disciplinary referrals, adjusting your management plan for an individual student, and building positive relationships with individual students. New appendixes cover the following topics:

- Professionalism for first-year teachers
- Schoolwide implementation of Discipline in the Secondary Classroom
- The research behind the strategies and techniques in the book

- Working with students who come from cultures different from yours
- Aligning the contents of *Discipline in the Secondary Classroom* with Domain 2 of the teaching framework outlined in Charlotte Danielson's *Enhancing Professional Practice: A Framework for Teaching*
- A guide to three sets of icons provided on the DVD for use in teaching classroom expectations
- Bonus article on DVD only: Why punitive consequences are not as effective as a positive approach to classroom management

In implementation projects throughout the country, my colleagues and I have learned that when clear expectations are directly taught to students, the vast majority of students will strive to be cooperative and do their best to meet those expectations. By implementing the procedures in this book, you will spend less time dealing with disruption and resistance and more time teaching.

Discipline in the Secondary Classroom is part of the Safe & Civil Schools Positive Behavioral Interventions and Supports Model listed in the National Registry of Evidence-based Programs and Practices (NREPP) after review by the Substance Abuse and Mental Health Services Administration (SAMHSA).

Inclusion in NREPP means that independent reviewers found that the philosophy and procedures behind *Discipline in the Secondary Classroom*, *CHAMPS*, and other Safe & Civil Schools books and DVDs have been proven thoroughly researched, that the research is of high quality, and that the outcomes achieved include:

- Higher levels of academic achievement
- Reductions in school suspensions
- Fewer classroom disruptions
- Increases in teacher professional self-efficacy
- Improvement in school discipline procedures

For more information, visit www.nrepp.samhsa.gov.

DISCIPLINE
IN THE
SECONDARY
CLASSROOM

Introduction

Discipline problems in school have always been and continue to be a leading frustration for teachers and, more and more often, a high-level concern for the public. Currently half of new teachers will leave the profession within a few years. Two of the most common reasons given for leaving teaching are discipline problems and lack of administrative support for dealing with discipline. Without foreknowledge of variables that can be manipulated to have a positive influence on student behavior, inexperienced teachers who are less skilled with classroom management are often frustrated and sometimes even terrified by students who misbehave and challenge authority.

There are many obvious and direct links between academic achievement and student behavior. If one student is severely disruptive, the other students in the class learn less than if all students were behaving responsibly. If students are actively or passively resistant, a seemingly simple transition like moving to lab stations, which should take no more than two minutes, can take as long as ten, wasting large amounts of instructional time. A student who is unmotivated will be less engaged in her work and learn less than if she is excited about the content. If all of these examples and more occur every day in every class you teach, you are losing huge amounts of instructional time. By implementing effective management techniques, you can simultaneously increase student engagement and improve academic achievement (Brophy, 1983, 1996; Brophy & Good, 1986; Christenson et al., 2008; Gettinger & Ball, 2008; Luiselli, Putnam, Handler, & Feinberg, 2005; Scheuermann & Hall, 2008; Smith, 2000; Sprick, Booher, & Garrison, 2009).

This book is designed to help you manage student behavior and increase student motivation so that you can focus your time and energy on instruction and student success. This approach is proactive, positive, and instructional:

- *Proactive* means that effective teachers focus on preventing problems instead of constantly dealing with them. Through classroom organization and collecting and using meaningful data, a teacher can modify his or her classroom management plan to make it even more effective.

- *Positive* means that effective teachers build collaborative relationships with students and provide them with meaningful, positive feedback to enhance motivation and performance.

- *Instructional* means that effective teachers directly teach expectations at the beginning of the year, review expectations as necessary throughout the year, and treat misbehavior as an opportunity to teach replacement behavior.

In this book, I refer to this proactive, positive approach as the DSC (Discipline in the Secondary Classroom) approach. Readers who are familiar with the *Safe & Civil Schools* collection of staff development materials, and in particular *CHAMPS: A Proactive and Positive Approach to Classroom Management*, my book for elementary and middle schools, will recognize the overall philosophy and procedures. CHAMPS is an acronym that teachers can use to teach expectations to students—but it has come to mean much more. CHAMPS represents the proactive, positive ideals that every teacher can learn and use to help their students achieve success. DSC takes the CHAMPS approach and translates it for the high school level. (See appendix A for information about the research behind the Safe & Civil Schools series.)

The CHAMPS/DSC approach is based on the following principles and beliefs:

Structure and organize all settings to prompt responsible student behavior. The way a setting is structured has a huge impact on the behavior and attitude of people in that setting.

Teach your expectations regarding how to behave responsibly within the structure you have created. Sports coaches provide a great example of teaching behavior and reteaching as needed to help each individual achieve his or her full potential.

Observe whether students are meeting expectations. (Supervise!) In the short run, this means circulating and visually scanning the classroom. In the long run, this means collecting and analyzing meaningful data on student progress.

Interact positively with students. Provide frequent noncontingent attention to build relationships. Provide frequent, age-appropriate positive feedback to acknowledge students' efforts to be successful.

Correct irresponsible behavior fluently—calmly, consistently, immediately, briefly, respectfully, and (as much as possible) privately.

The acronym STOIC is an easy way to remember these five principles. By manipulating these variables, you can put an effective behavior management system in place, thereby creating a classroom climate that encourages students to be orderly, responsive, engaged, and motivated.

One definition of the adjective *stoic*, from the *Encarta World English Dictionary*, is "tending to remain unemotional, especially showing admirable patience and endurance in the face of adversity." Thus, a stoic teacher is one who is unrattled by student misbehavior and implements research-based strategies (as found in this book) with patience and endurance.

This book is organized into five sections based on the STOIC model.

Section 1: Structure Your Classroom for Success

Chapter 1, "Vision," presents five tasks that set the stage for the remainder of this book by helping you understand the basic principles of behavior and motivation. After working through the tasks, you should have a clear understanding of how behavior is learned and the role that you (and your management plan) can play in shaping student behavior in positive and successful directions.

Chapter 2, "Grading," guides you through six tasks to develop a grading system that will help you teach students that success is an achievable goal. An effective grading system can be more than a simple evaluation tool; it should also be a motivational tool. Many of the students who seem not to care about their grades have never been taught that their behavior directly affects their grades. This chapter will help you teach students that if they change their behavior, they can move from failure to success.

Chapter 3, "Organization," sets out six tasks that show how you can manipulate variables such as schedule, physical setting, the use of an attention signal, beginning and ending routines, and procedures for managing student work. By manipulating these variables, you can create momentum that draws students into mature, responsible, unified, and productive patterns of behavior.

Chapter 4, "Classroom Management Plan," sets out five tasks that will help you assess your students' need for structure and develop a set of classroom rules to address the most likely misbehaviors you will encounter. Once you develop the rules, either on your own or with your students, you will determine a system of appropriate consequences. Examples of different types of corrective consequences that can be implemented in a high school classroom are provided.

Section 2: Teach Expectations

Chapter 5, "Expectations," offers three tasks to help you clarify and then directly teach your expectations for all classroom activities and transitions. You'll choose either the CHAMPS or ACHIEVE acronym to represent the expectations that you will need to teach your students for each major instructional activity and transition: Conversation, Help, Activity, Movement, Participation, and Success (CHAMPS); or Activity, Conversation, Help, Integrity, Effort, Value, and Efficiency (ACHIEVE). When you directly teach these expectations, you are functioning in the same way as an effective sports coach who, before teaching the team content (the plays and patterns of the game), begins the first practice by teaching expectations for how players are to behave during practice and games, on the field and off.

Chapter 6, "Preparation and Launch," provides five tasks designed to pull everything together from the first five chapters. You will form a concise plan that you can easily convey to your students using a three-step process for communicating expectations. Suggestions for and an example of a comprehensive syllabus are included. Steps and suggestions for how to run the first day of school are provided, along with guidance for when to reteach your expectations.

Section 3: Observe Student Behavior

Chapter 7, "Monitor Student Behavior," looks at two tasks. Task 1 explains how circulating around the classroom and using visual and auditory scanning can help you proactively eliminate misbehavior as well as provide you with opportunities to praise students for working hard or for cooperating. Task 2 provides tools and instructions for collecting data. Data on student behavior will help you evaluate how your management plan is working so you can adjust it throughout the year as necessary. Continually improving and refining your management plan will help you continue to encourage your students' success throughout the year.

Section 4: Interact Positively

Chapter 8, "Motivation," guides you through five tasks aimed at increasing student motivation. These tasks include suggestions for building relationships, providing feedback, and monitoring students. Understanding and acting on what motivates your students will enable you to help them succeed.

Section 5: Correct Misbehavior Fluently

Chapter 9, "Proactive Planning for Chronic Misbehavior," acknowledges that no matter how well you plan and implement, chronic behavior problems will still emerge. This chapter first reviews effective correction techniques, then leads you through a step-by-step process for dealing with more difficult chronic behaviors. You will learn how misbehaviors may function for the student and how this understanding can help you end them. Four major types of misbehaviors are addressed: awareness, ability, attention seeking, and purposeful or habitual. Sample intervention plans are suggested for each type.

Appendixes

Following the chapters is a set of appendixes. Appendix A presents information about how the DSC approach is evidence based—the ideas within this book are entirely compatible with more than thirty years of research on how effective teachers manage their classrooms in ways that enhance academic achievement. Appendix B provides information on how to implement the DSC approach schoolwide. Appendix C offers some insight into how to respect and encourage students who come from cultures different from yours. Appendix D offers advice for teachers who may need help navigating through their first year on the job. Appendix E maps DSC tasks to the applicable components of Domain 2 in the framework for teaching presented by Charlotte Danielson in *Enhancing Professional Practice: A Framework for Teaching* (2007). The framework is used by many school systems and educators as a benchmark for successful teaching practice and in some cases may be tied to teacher evaluation processes. This table can be used within staff development sessions or by individual readers to identify aspects of this book that might prove helpful in achieving professional excellence in classroom management. Appendix F is a visual guide to three sets of sixty-six icons included on the DVD that accompanies this book. The icons can be used to teach and display classroom expectations.

Section One

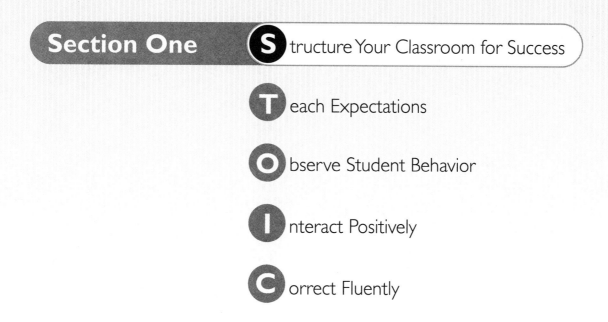

Structure Your Classroom for Success

Teach Expectations

Observe Student Behavior

Interact Positively

Correct Fluently

The way the classroom is structured greatly influences students' behavior, level of motivation, and attitude toward school. The chapters in section 1 offer information on how to develop a clear vision for student behavior, design instruction and evaluation systems, organize your routines and procedures, and develop a systematic classroom management plan.

Chapter 1

Vision

Understand key concepts about managing student behavior

Two concepts form the framework for this chapter: understanding the basic principles of behavior modification and understanding motivation. It is essential to understand these concepts because they form the framework on which you will build your own classroom management plan. Familiarity with these core concepts will also make it easier for you to understand the methods outlined in this book and then adapt them to fit your own teaching style and the specific needs of your students. These core concepts are laid out as tasks you must understand in order to envision your role as a manager of student behavior and motivation (tasks 1 and 2).

The subsequent tasks, like the remainder of this book, provide specific actions you can take to prepare and implement an effective classroom management plan. Task 3 will assist you in clarifying your vision of student behavior and motivation for yourself, your students, and their families. Tasks 4 and 5 will help you achieve and maintain positive relationships with your students and your families. The five tasks are:

Task 1: Understand the basic principles of behavior modification and your role in that process.

Task 2: Understand motivation and the variables that can be manipulated to increase it.

Task 3: Develop and implement Guidelines for Success.

Task 4: Maintain high expectations for students' academic and behavioral performance.

Task 5: Initiate and maintain family contacts.

The Vision Self-Assessment Checklist at the end of this chapter will help you determine which tasks you will need to work on as you build or revise your management plan. A Peer Study Worksheet for this chapter can be found on the DVD in the appendix B folder. It consists of a series of discussion questions that you and one or more of your fellow teachers can use to share information on improving teaching practices. The worksheet also presents a series of activities for use by two or more teachers who want to share information and peer support as they work to improve together.

Task 1: Understand the Basic Principles of Behavior Modification and Your Role in That Process

In order to manage student behavior, you need a solid understanding of how behavior is learned and how it can be changed. This knowledge will allow you to help students become progressively more responsible. If you already have an understanding of behavior analysis, you can simply skim this task for a brief review.

Behavior is learned.

We are constantly engaged in learning that affects our future behavior. For example, if you purchase a car and like the way it handles, rarely need to repair it, and think it was a good value, you are more likely to buy that brand of car in the future. But if the car needs constant repairs, develops annoying rattles, and doesn't seem worth what you paid for it, you are unlikely to buy this brand in the future. (You may even be driven to take up cycling!) Or if you go to a movie based on a friend's recommendation but find it to be a waste of time and therefore a waste of money, you are less likely to trust that friend's movie recommendations in the future. Scenarios such as these are repeated in each individual's life in uncountable, interwoven combinations that create a rich fabric of experience and learning. Simply put, our behavior is influenced by events and conditions we experience—some that encourage certain behaviors and others that discourage certain behaviors (Chance, 1998; Iwata, Smith, & Michael, 2000). Figure 1.1 shows the three main variables that affect behavior.

If you have studied behavioral analysis, you will recognize Figure 1.1 as a simple example of behavioral theory. It is important to understand this model if you are going to manage student behavior successfully. This model suggests that changing behaviors requires focusing on (1) what is prompting a behavior, (2) what is encouraging or sustaining that behavior, and

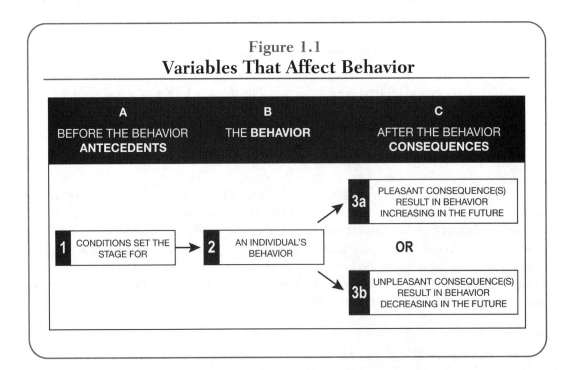

Figure 1.1
Variables That Affect Behavior

A BEFORE THE BEHAVIOR **ANTECEDENTS**	B THE **BEHAVIOR**	C AFTER THE BEHAVIOR **CONSEQUENCES**

1 CONDITIONS SET THE STAGE FOR → **2** AN INDIVIDUAL'S BEHAVIOR

3a PLEASANT CONSEQUENCE(S) RESULT IN BEHAVIOR INCREASING IN THE FUTURE

OR

3b UNPLEASANT CONSEQUENCE(S) RESULT IN BEHAVIOR DECREASING IN THE FUTURE

(3) what might discourage that behavior from occurring in the future. The other important idea to keep in mind as you consider this model is that what may be pleasant consequences for one person could be unpleasant consequences for another. For example, getting a smiley-face sticker for doing good work is likely to be a pleasant consequence for most first graders, and something that will encourage them to work hard in the future. However, the same sticker may very well have the opposite effect on most tenth-grade students. Getting a sticker for doing a good job may be so embarrassing to a tenth-grade student that he or she will be *less* likely to work hard in the future. In this case, the teacher's attempt to reinforce the positive behavior with a sticker actually decreases the probability that the behavior will continue. In behavior analysis, one would say that the sticker served as a punishing consequence.

> ## Note
> The technical language of behavior analysis is based on precise definitions of terms such as *reinforcing consequences, positive reinforcers, negative reinforcers, punishing consequences,* and so on. This book avoids this vocabulary because it is not universally used and understood. Instead, throughout this book, the term *encouragement procedure* will refer to any procedure that is used in an attempt to increase desirable student behaviors and the term *corrective consequence* to any procedure that is used in an attempt to decrease misbehavior.

Any behavior that occurs repeatedly is serving some function for the individual who exhibits the behavior.

As you strive to help students behave responsibly, keep in mind the idea that chronic behavior serves a function (Chance, 1998). Students who consistently behave responsibly have learned that this behavior leads to things they value, such as parental approval, good grades, teacher attention, a sense of pride and accomplishment, increased opportunity, and so on. Their responsible behavior serves a specific function.

This concept applies just as equally to behaviors that are negative or destructive as to behaviors that are positive and productive—which helps explain why an individual student misbehaves when the consequences of that misbehavior seem so unpleasant. Rex is a student in the tenth grade, and his teachers find his disruptive behavior frustrating. A look at his file shows that he has been exhibiting this behavior since middle school. He is frequently sent out of class and assigned detention. His parents are called regularly, and school staff are continually angry and frustrated with him. Yet as unpleasant as these consequences appear to be, Rex is clearly getting some benefit from his irresponsible behavior or he would change it.

In this case, Rex's misbehavior results in immediate consequences that are pleasant for him. When he argues, for example, he gets lots of attention from adults, which gives him a sense of power. In addition, he gets lots of attention from peers for appearing strong and powerful enough to "fight" with his teachers. Rex's irresponsible behavior also allows him to avoid the unpleasant consequences that result when he attempts to exhibit responsible behavior. Rex has academic problems, and when he tries to be compliant and do his work, he usually finds that he can't, which frustrates and discourages him. Rex has discovered that if instead of doing his work, he argues and gets sent out of class, he not only gets adult and peer attention, but also avoids having to demonstrate in public his lack of academic ability.

When a student frequently behaves irresponsibly, it's likely the student hasn't experienced the benefits of responsible behavior enough, or even at all (Horner, Vaughn, Day, & Ard, 1996; Lalli et al., 1999).

Student behavior can be changed.

Although some tendencies and personality traits seem to be present from birth, most behavior is learned—which means it can also be unlearned (Biglan, 1995; Chance, 1998). Consider the following rather exaggerated example.

Picture Dana, a responsible and successful ninth-grade student. Imagine that as of today, Dana stops getting any positive benefits for behaving responsibly. She does her best work but always gets failing grades and critical comments; sometimes other students laugh at her work and class participation and either ridicule her as stupid or ignore her altogether. She tries to be nice to adults and other students, but they are no longer nice in return. She stays on task, but no one ever notices. Her parents show no interest in the fact that she is failing. Adults at school and at home never notice or comment on her independence, her cooperation, or her effort, but they are constantly demanding more and more and pouncing on every opportunity to scold and criticize her. If this were to continue day after day, at home and at school, Dana would probably stop trying, and she might even respond with anger and hostility. If she found that this was a way to get people to notice her, she might develop a sense of satisfaction or self-preservation in acting in an antagonistic and aggressive manner. If this were to continue for months or years, Dana would seem like a very different young woman from the one described at the beginning of the paragraph.

Now think back to Rex who is always argumentative, angry, and getting sent out of class. Imagine that school personnel can create a setting in which he starts experiencing success and good grades, he receives peer recognition for his positive behavior, and he no longer gets so much attention or status for his anger and hostility. If done well, such an environment can create a powerful positive change in Rex (in the opposite way of our example with Dana). Behavior *can* be taught and changed (Langland, Lewis-Palmer, & Sugai, 1998).

To cement the importance of your ability to teach and change behavior, think about a highly motivational sports coach. He will begin the first day of the season by laying out behavioral expectations for the team and then spend the entire season teaching and having the team practice those same behaviors that will lead to the success he wants. A major part of any management plan is direct teaching of the behaviors and routines that will lead to your students' success.

Task 2: Understand Motivation and the Variables That Can Be Manipulated to Increase It

To *motivate* can be defined as "to provide an incentive, to move to action, to drive forward." Understanding motivation will augment your efforts to implement effective motivational procedures with your students (i.e., move them to do their best academically and encourage them to exhibit responsible and successful behavior). The concepts presented here can help you maintain the motivation of students who already follow the rules and do their best on assignments, increase the motivation of students who do nothing or only enough to get by, and motivate responsibility in students who tend to misbehave.

The first concept to understand is this: behavior that is repeated is motivated by something; it does not reoccur if there is no motivation. This concept is always true, regardless of what an individual may think or say about her own behavior. For example, a person may repeatedly complain about his job and even say that he is unmotivated to work, but if he goes to work regularly, he shows that he is in fact motivated in some way to work. Similarly, a person may say she is motivated to paint as a hobby, but if she never gets out her paints and brushes, she is not truly motivated to paint. This does not mean that the man will never lose his motivation to go to work or that the woman will never regain her motivation to paint, only that their current behavior indicates otherwise.

The importance of this concept is that teachers must realize that the student who repeatedly misbehaves is more motivated at the moment to misbehave than to behave and that the student who does nothing is more motivated to do nothing than to work. It means that you, as the teacher, will need to increase these students' motivation to behave responsibly and complete assignments. This book is designed to help you do that.

A second important concept is this: most people are motivated to engage in a particular behavior by a complex mix of intrinsic and extrinsic factors. A person is intrinsically motivated when the pleasant consequences of a behavior are related to the essential nature of that behavior. Thus, a person who is intrinsically motivated to read does so because he likes to learn new things, enjoys a good story, and finds curling up with a book relaxing. The person who is intrinsically motivated to ski does so because she finds the speed exhilarating, the fresh air pleasant, and the feeling of exhaustion at the end of a challenging day gratifying.

> **Note**
>
> If your efforts to increase students' motivation to engage in desired behaviors are ineffective, you will also need to work at decreasing their motivation to engage in undesired behaviors. For specific suggestions, see chapter 9.

Extrinsic motivation occurs when someone engages in a behavior because of pleasant consequences that are not directly related to the essential nature of the behavior. For example, babies tend to utter "mama" and "dada" more frequently than other sounds because of the reactions (e.g., smiles, tickles, and praise) these sounds elicit in the most significant people in their lives. A college student will continue to attend and write papers for a class that she does not like because she wants a certain grade and because doing well in the class will move her toward her desired goal of a degree. A six-year-old child will make his bed to get lavish praise from his mom and dad about how responsible, hard working, and helpful he is.

While some people believe that the only valid kind of motivation is intrinsic motivation and that teachers should not give students praise and rewards of any kind, this book does not adhere to this principle (Cameron, Banko, & Pierce, 2001). This mistaken belief will be addressed in more detail in chapter 6, but it is enough to say that the line between intrinsic and extrinsic motivation is not as distinct as it may seem. Motivation for most behaviors is usually a mix of intrinsic and extrinsic factors. Although the person who reads a lot may do so for the intrinsic rewards of the task, he may also enjoy the compliments he gets for his wide knowledge. The frequent skier may find that in addition to the exhilaration of skiing itself, she also enjoys having others comment on her skill. The baby learning to talk makes "mama" and "dada" sounds because he enjoys making noise, not just because of the reactions of his parents. The college student who attends class and writes papers does so not only because of the grades but also because sometimes the class is genuinely interesting.

This means that when you have students who are unmotivated to work or to behave responsibly, you need to try to enhance their motivation—both intrinsic (e.g., make a science lesson more engaging) and extrinsic (e.g., write an encouraging note on returned homework). You will find suggestions for both in this chapter and chapter 8.

A third important concept has to do with the relationship between one's intrinsic motivation to engage in a task and one's proficiency at that task. The more skilled, comfortable, and proficient a person is with a task, the more likely he or she is to be intrinsically motivated to perform it. A skilled woodworker is more likely to find spending time in a workshop rewarding than the person who has never learned to use tools. Similarly, the skilled musician is more likely to find daily practice intrinsically reinforcing than the person who started learning to play only three weeks ago. In addition, an individual who has experienced success at learning many different skills in the past is more likely to be motivated to try learning something new in the future than someone who has experienced repeated failure. The student who has experienced a lot of academic success is more likely to feel excited about the challenge of a tough course than the student who has failed at academic pursuits in the past.

The key implication of this concept is that in the early stages of learning something new or when learning something difficult, some students (particularly those who have experienced frequent past failure) are not likely to be intrinsically motivated to engage in the behaviors necessary to learn. A further refinement of the concept is the Expectancy × Value theory of motivation. First used by Feather (1982), this theory explains a person's motivation on any given task as a function of this formula:

$$\text{Expectancy} \times \text{Value} = \text{Motivation}$$

In this formula, *expectancy* is defined as "the degree to which an individual expects to be successful at the task" and *value* is "the degree to which an individual values the rewards that accompany that success." The power of this theory is its recognition that a person's level of motivation on any given task is a function of both how much the person wants the rewards that accompany success on the task *and* how much he or she expects to be successful at the task.

Note
The value factor in the formula can include extrinsic rewards (e.g., money, awards, grades), intrinsic rewards (e.g., sense of accomplishment, enjoyment of the task, pride in a job will done), or both. Regardless of the type of value involved, if the expectancy of success is low, motivation will be low.

Many teachers, when trying to ascertain why a student is unmotivated to behave responsibly or complete assignments, tend to ascribe the lack of motivation to issues involving only the value component of the formula: "Nothing seems to motivate him. He doesn't care about getting good grades. He takes no pride in his accomplishments. He doesn't care about free time or positive notes home. I even tried to put him on a point contract where he could earn time on the computer, but he just said he didn't really care about computers. I guess there isn't anything else I can do." What these explanations fail to take into account is that if the

Table 1.1.
Motivation Formula

Expectancy Rate	× Value Rate	= Motivation
10	× 10	= 100%
10	× 0	= 0%
0	× 10	= 0%

student thinks he will not succeed at behaving responsibly or completing assignments (expectancy), his motivation will be very low or nonexistent.

With this equation, both expectancy and value can be calibrated on a scale of 0 to 10, with 0 representing the lowest possible rate and 10 representing the highest possible rate of each. When a value rate and an expectancy rate are multiplied together, they produce a number between 0 and 100, which represents the percentage of motivation a person has for that task. The key implication is that if the rate for either one of the factors is zero, the other factor won't matter—the motivation rate will still be zero (table 1.1).

Another applied aspect of the theory is that the rates for expectancy and value are defined by what a student believes, not what *you*, the teacher, believe. You may know that the student is perfectly capable of being successful if he would simply try. However, if the student believes he cannot be successful (making his expectancy rate low), his motivation will be low to nonexistent (Laraway, Snycerski, Michael, & Poling, 2003). Similarly, if you believe in the value of good grades, but this is not a value that the student has learned, grades will not be a motivating factor in changing behavior or effort.

Whenever a student is not motivated to do something (complete work, participate in class discussions, or behave more responsibly), try to determine whether the lack of motivation stems from a lack of value (intrinsic and extrinsic), a lack of expectancy, or both. To see if you need to increase a student's motivation to complete academic tasks, check whether the student is capable of being successful at them. If the student is not, you may need to modify the tasks so that the student will be able to succeed. *How* you can modify academic tasks is outside the scope of this program, but there are people in your district who can help with strategies for modifying instruction to bring success within your student's reach. Don Deshler and his colleagues at the University of Kansas have spent many years building a variety of resources for improving instruction and increasing the academic success of struggling learners (see exhibit 1.1). For more information on the Center for Research on Learning, go to www.kucrl.org, or read the following:

Deshler, D. D., et al. (2001). Ensuring content-area learning by secondary students with learning disabilities. *Learning Disabilities Research and Practice, 16*(2), 96–108. This article describes the broad array of services that must be available to students with learning disabilities so they can succeed in learning subject area content. It includes a summary of how the Strategic Instruction Model components relate to these requirements.

Schumaker, J. B., Deshler, D. D., & McKnight, P. (2002). Ensuring success in the secondary general education curriculum through the use of teaching routines. In M. A. Shinn, H. M. Walker, & G. Stoner (Eds.), *Interventions for academic and behavior problems II: Preventive and remedial approaches* (pp. 791–823). Bethesda, MD: National Association of School Psychologists. This chapter summarizes key components of an innovative model for providing services to students in general education classes. It includes descriptions of learning strategies and content enhancement routines.

Exhibit 1.1
The Strategic Instruction Model

Drawing on more than twenty-five years of research, the Center for Research on Learning at the University of Kansas has developed the Strategic Instruction Model (SIM), a comprehensive approach to adolescent literacy that addresses the need of students to be able to read and understand large volumes of complex reading materials as well as to express themselves effectively in writing. SIM, used by many state special education departments, thousands of school districts, and four hundred colleges and universities, achieves measurable results by reversing the downward spiral through which so many at-risk and special education students plummet. It integrates two kinds of interventions designed to address the gap between what students are expected to do and what they are able to do. Using a how-to-learn approach, SIM's student-focused interventions, including specific learning strategies, enable students to generalize from one task and situation to others. SIM includes tactics and skills that students use to gain information from texts efficiently, perform more accurately on tests, write more clearly, present written work more attractively, spell more accurately, and perform math operations more efficiently. In short, it enables students to deal more effectively with the process of learning.

SIM's teacher-focused interventions, called *content enhancement routines*, encourage teachers to teach more effectively by helping them think about, adapt, and present their most important content in learner-friendly fashion. Recognizing that academic interventions alone are not sufficient for student success, SIM also includes components that help students create and participate in productive learning communities, develop strong and appropriate social skills, advocate for themselves and their needs in education conferences, envision positive futures for themselves, and plan how to reach their goals.

To date, more than forty instructional programs have been validated through numerous research studies and developed into instructional materials appropriate for teacher use in the classroom.

A schoolwide approach for integrating SIM and other validated literacy programs can be accomplished through the Content Literacy Continuum, a school-reform model developed by the University of Kansas Center for Research on Learning. This model defines a continuum of instructional intensity that serves as a framework for guiding school improvement and professional development.

A network of certified SIM instructors is available to work with teachers and schools to implement SIM programs. SIM is most effective when teachers are afforded sufficient time to plan what and how they are going to teach in a strategic fashion. Teachers must have an opportunity to work with other teachers to coordinate instruction across classes and settings to ensure that critical strategies and behaviors are prompted and reinforced. SIM holds that highly significant change for students or schools occurs only when teachers are armed with numerous interventions to meet the diverse needs of their students.

The Expectancy × Value theory can be a particularly useful way for teachers to think about behavior and motivation. To develop your understanding of this theory, periodically take the time to analyze activities you personally are motivated or unmotivated to do. When thinking about something you are highly motivated to do, identify the value you place on engaging in and completing the activity and the expectancy of success you have before engaging in it. When you think about an activity that you are not motivated to do, see if you can determine what is low: the expectancy rate, the value rate, or both. Try to identify any activities for which you value the rewards but nonetheless avoid doing because your expectancy of success is low. Analyzing your own motivation, or lack of it, will help you develop a deeper understanding of your students' motivations.

As you work through subsequent chapters and analyze your students' motivations, keep the following concepts in mind:

- Your students' behavior will let you know what they are motivated and not motivated to do. You will have to work on increasing their motivation to engage in positive behavior, and possibly on decreasing their negative motivation.

- Use procedures that address both intrinsic and extrinsic motivation when trying to increase positive student behavior.

- Students' motivation to engage in any behavior is related to the degree to which they value the rewards of engaging in that behavior and their expectation of succeeding at it.

Task 3: Develop and Implement Guidelines for Success

In addition to academics, teachers need to provide their students with specific information about attitudes, traits, and behaviors that will help them succeed in school and throughout their lives. Sadly, some students and families believe that school success is not possible for those who don't come from an educated or a well-off family. There are others who believe that school success depends on one's ethnicity. Part of your responsibility as a teacher is to let your students know that everyone can succeed in school and give them guidelines regarding how.

These Guidelines for Success should reflect broad and noble ideals. They should represent what you really hope students will learn from you—not the content, but the attitudes and actions that will help students succeed in your class, the classes they will have in the future, and life in general.

Having these Guidelines for Success is important regardless of the level of structure that may be of most benefit to your students. This can be especially critical if your school or class has a large number of high-needs students. High-needs students often lack the knowledge or motivation to exhibit traits that educators want, need, or expect them to have. Figure 1.2 is an example of schoolwide Guidelines for Success.

When developing your own Guidelines for Success (or goals to strive toward, or whatever else you choose to call them), frame them as brief phrases that describe the attitudes, traits, and characteristics you hope to instill in your students. Identify three to six of these guidelines that you believe are most important for your students to learn and exhibit in your classroom. Note that these guidelines are different from classroom rules. Rules pertain to specific and observable behaviors, and they generally have consequences associated with failing to follow them, whereas your Guidelines for Success are attitudes or traits that you hope to inspire students to strive toward. Rules are like speed limits that you as the teacher will enforce. Guidelines are values that you hope to instill in your students—values that will help them

Figure 1.2
Sample Guidelines for Success

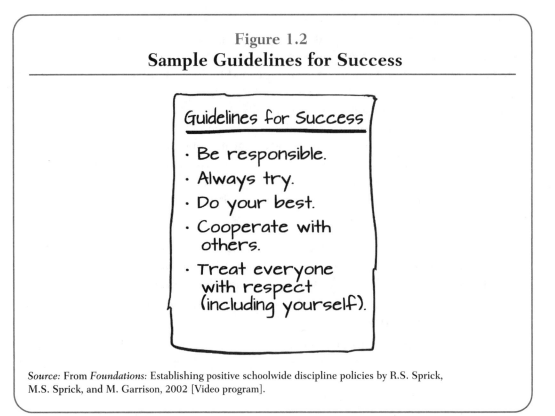

Guidelines for Success

- Be responsible.
- Always try.
- Do your best.
- Cooperate with others.
- Treat everyone with respect (including yourself).

Source: From *Foundations:* Establishing positive schoolwide discipline policies by R.S. Sprick, M.S. Sprick, and M. Garrison, 2002 [Video program].

Note

Optimally, Guidelines for Success are developed and used on a school-wide basis. That is, the entire staff create and agree to post and use a common list of positive traits. Sprick, Howard, Wise, Marcum, and Haykin (1998) provide suggestions on how to involve staff, students, and parents in developing school-wide Guidelines for Success. If your school does not have schoolwide guidelines, plan on developing them for your own class. If your school has already developed and adopted schoolwide guidelines, plan to use them. The advantage of having these guidelines be schoolwide is that students are given consistent messages from all school staff about what is required of them to be successful within the school.

succeed in your class and in all other aspects of life. You can find information on developing specific classroom rules in chapter 5.

Developing your guidelines is just the first step. If students are truly going to learn to exhibit these attitudes, traits, and behaviors, you need to make them an ever-present part of your classroom.

Post your guidelines in a prominent place where everyone can see them. Teach them to students at the beginning of the year. As with your long-range goals, let students' families know what your guidelines are. Using the vocabulary from the guidelines consistently and regularly will help to keep them familiar. For example, you can use the guidelines to prompt motivation and get your students excited about striving for excellence. You should also use them as a basis for providing both positive and corrective feedback to students regarding their behavior:

"Shelly, you have been doing much better about getting homework completed. Thank you for being so responsible."

"Fionna, you need to work quietly. The guideline about treating everyone with respect means you don't disturb others when they are trying to get their work finished."

Plan to put your Guidelines for Success and a brief explanation of their importance in the syllabus that you will distribute to students on the first day of the semester.

Remember that when students do not receive information about these kinds of attitudes, traits, and behaviors at home, the emphasis that school personnel place on their guidelines may provide critical life lessons. If you find that some of your students have had less of a personal context for understanding and operating from your guidelines, plan to provide more instruction on how they can implement them, and be prepared to give those students more encouragement.

> ### Note
> Whether you are starting to work through this book at the beginning of or during the school year, spend some time implementing this task. Guidelines for Success give your students critical information about how they can accomplish what you expect from them—and this is valuable at any point in the year.

Task 4: Maintain High Expectations for Students' Academic and Behavioral Performance

For all your students to succeed, it is essential that you maintain and communicate high and positive expectations. Research has repeatedly demonstrated what we know from common sense: low expectations predict low achievement (Scarborough & Parker, 2003). Your vision of student achievement and performance has an immeasurable impact on your students. It is crucial for you to convey your high expectations for all your students in academics and in personal responsibility.

This is not to suggest that you ignore any problems or difficulties your students may have. Against that, you must still maintain high yet realistic expectations for your students if they are to succeed. The difference is best demonstrated through an example. A student who uses a wheelchair would not be able to do some of the activities required of the other students in gym. It is reasonable to adapt some of the gym activities so that she can participate. Similarly, simply because she is in a wheelchair does not mean that her classroom expectations are any different from those of her peers.

A less obvious example is a student with chronic behavioral and discipline problems in class. If such a student is in a class you teach, it would be naive to think that he will never misbehave, but you must still expect that he can learn to behave responsibly in your class. The goal of this task is forming a belief in the potential success of every student.

Before putting any work into your students, however, you must first evaluate yourself. You must look objectively at your behavior and be sure that the comments you make to your students and to others about your students do not single any of them out or put them down. Even when you make critical comments about a student to another teacher, you are communicating low expectations, and they will come out in other ways. Statements like the following communicate low expectations for students:

"What can you expect from a kid like that?"

"You can't expect any better from a student with that kind of home life."

"They have ADHD, so what can you do?"

"I wish he weren't in my class."

If you find that you have such thoughts or are making such statements, stopping them is the first step to encouraging success in your students. You must believe in their success before expecting it. Try to identify specific negative phrases you are using and make an effort to stop. Then think of phrases you can use that embrace positive qualities about your students instead of negative ones. Try to use positive phrasing in circumstances where previously you would have used negative phrasing.

Even when you start the year with strong, positive expectations for your students, it can be difficult to sustain them. It's easy to get so busy that you don't notice negative thoughts creeping back in. It may be that a particularly trying student or class wears you out, and without realizing it, you lower your expectations. To protect against this, you must check in with yourself regularly, evaluating where you are emotionally with your classes and students. It may help to mark a calendar at intervals to remind yourself to examine your attitude periodically. (There are more specific guidelines for this in chapter 8.)

In addition, once school is in session, make a point of monitoring the kinds of statements you use with your students. Be aware and honestly critical of yourself about the language you use with them, whether it is positive or negative. Watch for statements like these:

"Here, let me give you something easier."

"Grow up!"

"This group will work with me because they've proven they can't work alone."

"What's the matter with you? Use your head."

When one professor was asked, "What do you do with the kid you just don't like?" he wisely responded, "You can't dislike kids on company time." Although you don't have to personally enjoy every student, you do have to maintain a high expectation for every student's success while you're at work. Implementing some of the following suggestions can help you maintain a positive attitude toward your students:

- *Take care of yourself.* Young people are very quick to see hypocrisy, so make sure you're positive with yourself as well as with them. Look to your own attitudes and health. Design a wellness program for yourself that includes exercise and proper nutrition, and make sure you get enough rest. Make time for activities or interests outside school.

- *Maintain a positive and realistic vision of student success.* When problems occur, as they surely will, remind yourself of the vision you have for your students and the success you want them to have. This is especially important when dealing with students who have chronic problems. Setting aside some time to visualize the student being successful can be useful.

- *Be reflective about your plan.* Periodically evaluate your methods to see what is working and what isn't. If you identify something that needs improvement, try something else. Remember that although you may not be able to directly control student behavior, you can control their environment (seating, schedules, interaction) in a way that will have a positive effect on their behavior.

- *Don't take it personally.* If a student misbehaves, try to remain objective. The problem isn't your fault, but you do offer an excellent hope of positively reaching a child. Remind yourself that you're a professional and that eventually every problem can be solved. It may help to remind yourself that the student is likely not singling you out but treats all adults in her life in a similar manner.

- *Make an overt effort to interact positively with every student.* All students should feel that you notice and care about them. Say hi to them, and show an interest in their activities. When you maintain contact with all of your students as individuals, they know that you value them, and that will reduce the likelihood that they will misbehave.

- *Consult with colleagues.* If an individual or group becomes particularly challenging, discuss your concerns with fellow staff members. Be careful not to communicate low expectations, but describe neutrally the problems the student is having. Peer problem solving is a powerful tool for getting ideas about helping your students.

> **Note**
> Whether you are starting in the middle of the school year or at the beginning, make sure you spend enough time on this task to ensure that you have high expectations for every student. If you have low expectations for your students' behavior, they will live up (or down) to those expectations. To implement an effective classroom management plan successfully, you must possess *and* communicate high expectations for every student's success.

All tasks in this chapter are designed to help you develop and maintain a comprehensive student management program. Throughout this book, you will find guidelines on how to continue communicating high, positive expectations to your students. You will find that some methods work better than others with different student groups, and using the approach outlined in this book to the fullest means periodically returning to it and evaluating your methods.

Task 5: Initiate and Maintain Family Contacts

There is no question that when school personnel and families work together to help meet the educational needs of students, the probability of effectively educating those students increases tremendously (Esler, Godber, & Christensen, 2008; Freer & Watson, 1999; Gortmaker, Warnes, & Sheridan, 2004; Henderson & Mapp, 2002; Keith et al., 1998; Rones & Hoagwood, 2000; Sheridan, Kratochwill, & Bergan, 1996). As part of your classroom vision, you should aspire to have your class be a place where you, your students, and your students' families work collaboratively to ensure student success. Building the positive relationships necessary to work collaboratively with families, however, is not always easy. It requires communication, which takes time—and time can be a problem for both teachers and families.

Note

More students than ever before live in one-parent households, in foster care, with grandparents, and in other nontraditional circumstances. It is often inaccurate to refer to "the student's parents," and it is cumbersome to continually refer to "the student's parent(s), grandparent(s), or guardian(s)." Therefore, in most cases the term "student's family" will be used when referring to a student's primary caregivers.

Note

If the families of some (or many) of your students are not English speakers or have limited English, you face an additional challenge. Check with building or district personnel for information about getting assistance in communicating with families in their language. For example, a translator could help with written communications, or an interpreter could be present for telephone calls and at-school events like conferences and open house. If your school is very diverse and there are many different primary languages, it may not be feasible to make adaptation arrangements for all of the languages. However, if half of your students come from Spanish-speaking homes, for example, arranging for important information to be translated into Spanish demonstrates to families the value you place on communicating with them.

Making the effort to communicate with your students' families sends a powerful message that you want to include them in what happens at school. In addition, such efforts increase the probability that an individual student's family will be receptive should you need to inform them about and enlist their assistance in solving the student's behavioral or academic problem (Christenson & Godber, 2001; Miller & Kraft, 2008; Phelan, Yu, & Davidson, 1994). (Information on how to work with families when behavior problems occur appears in chapter 4.) Develop a specific plan for making initial contact with students' families at the beginning of the school year and maintaining contact with them throughout the year. A family contact plan increases the likelihood of communicating efficiently and effectively with your students' families.

Family contacts are especially important when you have a large number of high-need students. Unfortunately, the families of these students may be more likely to feel alienated from the school, and many of those students may come from troubled homes. Because it's also possible that contacts will be more difficult to achieve with families of high-need students, remember that the greater the needs of your students, the greater the need is for you to establish and maintain contact with their families.

Many schools have websites that allow you to post class information and assignments. Students and families can find teachers' e-mail addresses and phone numbers as well as general schoolwide information. In some schools, e-mail is the most common form of communication between families and teachers. However, you can't be sure that all of your students' families have access to a computer or even the knowledge to send e-mail. Electronic communication also tends to be impersonal. If you choose to take advantage of your school's website, be sure to also send home on paper all information and messages you post online.

The more personal you can make both initial and ongoing contacts, the more effective you can be in building friendly and productive relationships with your students' families. Face-to-face contacts are more personal than phone calls, phone calls are more personal than notes, and notes are more personal than form letters. More personal contacts generally require more time than less personal ones. Thus, although it is critical for teachers to establish and maintain contact with their students' families, each teacher will have to determine the nature and amount of contact that is realistically possible for him or her. Obviously a middle school teacher who sees 150 students every day will not be able to have as many, or as personal, contacts with families as a special education teacher who has 12 students.

Initial Contact

Your initial contact with a student's family is their first impression of you, so it's important to make the contact friendly and inviting yet also highly professional. When possible, make initial contact within the first two weeks of school. Given that most high school teachers have large numbers of students, personal contact with every student's family is probably not realistic. Therefore, your main contact will be a letter sent home or a video greeting on the school website.

The purpose of the initial contact is twofold: to begin establishing a productive relationship with the students' families and to give the students and their families important information about you and your vision for the upcoming school year. Provide the following information during your initial contact:

- A welcome indicating that you are looking forward to an exciting and productive year
- Your teaching background ("I have taught for fifteen years, with the last five years at the high school level")
- A statement that you are looking forward to working with the student and getting to know the family
- A statement stressing that you anticipate a very good year
- Your major academic goals for the year
- Your classroom rules and Guidelines for Success
- Information about grading
- When and how the family can contact you when they have questions or want to share helpful information about the student
- When and how you will maintain ongoing communication with them ("My web page address is _____. I will post assignments and grades regularly.")

Exhibit 1.2 provides an example of an orientation letter for families that you can send home on the first day of class. (More information about preparing the letter is given in chapter 6, task 2.) If many of the families speak little or no English, see if you can have your letter translated into their primary languages.

See exhibit 1.2 on the DVD for a customizable version of this letter.

> ### Note
> See "Cultural Competence" (appendix C) for suggestions on working effectively with students and families whose backgrounds are different from yours.

Exhibit 1.2
Sample Letter to Families

Franklin High School • Anytown, USA 55555 • (555) 555-1234

Dear Parents/Guardians,

Hi. My name is Mr. Griffin. I want to take this opportunity to introduce myself and let you know that I am pleased and excited to have your son or daughter in my third-period tenth-grade English class. I am providing the following information so you will know what my expectations are and how your student can be successful in my class. Please take the time to discuss the information here with your son or daughter. Although I am going over this information in class, discussing it at home will be a meaningful way to increase understanding. If you have any questions or concerns, please feel free to contact me.

I believe that if we all work together, your student's success is certain!

The purpose of this class is to teach reading and writing analysis skills that are needed for more advanced work in literature and composition. The major goal of this course is for students to master the integration of reading, writing, listening, speaking, and critical thinking. By the end of the year, students should be able to do the following:

1. Read and understand grade-level material and evaluate an author's arguments and positions.

2. Read and respond to grade-level appropriate literature that represents historically or culturally significant works and be able to conduct in-depth analyses of recurrent themes.

3. Write clear and compelling texts that show point of view and reasoned argument.

4. Use rhetorical strategies of narration, exposition, persuasion, and description of text in both their writing and presentations.

5. Demonstrate competence with standard English-language conventions through their writing and speaking.

6. Deliver coherent presentations that demonstrate solid reasoning with clear and focused objectives.

Classroom Rules

The classroom rules are designed to ensure that no student's behavior interferes with the learning of others:

1. Come to class every day that you are not sick.
2. Arrive on time with your own pencil, paper, and books.
3. Keep hands, feet, and objects to yourself.
4. Follow directions the first time they are given.
5. Stay on task during all work times.

For violations of these rules, I will assign minor penalties.

While I will enforce the rules when necessary, I will be putting more emphasis on teaching students how to be responsible for themselves. I will stress the following traits, which are called **Guidelines for Success.**

Success requires:

Preparation
Responsibility
Integrity
Dedication
Effort

Grading
Below is the information your student has been given about grades:

1. Class participation and how well you follow the rules is worth 20% of your grade.

   - There are 10 possible points per day, for a total of 450 points for the quarter.
   - You will start each day with 8 points, which is 80%, or a low B.
   - Strong effort and application adds 1 point (which I will mark on my record sheet during class).
   - Each rule violation costs 1 point.

2. Your written work is worth 50% of your grade.

3. Unit tests are worth 20% of your grade.

4. The final exam is worth 10% of your grade.

Every Friday, I will provide each student with a weekly grade report that shows his or her current grade in the class as well as any missing assignments. Please check this on the weekend so that if a student is falling behind, we can all work on the problem in the early stages.

Contact Information
The students know that they can always ask me questions in class and can schedule an appointment to talk to me whenever they need help. If you want to contact me, my e-mail is Griffin555@franklinHS.edu. The best time to reach me by phone is during my preparation period (9:15 a.m. to 10:05 a.m.) or after school (3:15 p.m. to 4:15 p.m.) at 555-1234.

Thank you for your time. Please cut off the form below, sign it, and have your student sign to indicate that you have discussed this information. Have your student return the slip below by Monday for a few extra bonus points in the grade book.

Sincerely,
Mr. Griffin

_____

We have discussed this information about how to be successful in Mr. Griffin's third-period class.

Parent/Guardian Signature _____

Student Signature _____

Date _____

Some schools hold an open house a day or so before school starts or early in the fall so students and families can meet their teachers and see their classrooms. If there is any possibility of implementing this wonderful idea at your school, you may wish to encourage it. Families of students who are most likely to have trouble—those with a history of behavioral or academic problems, for example—can especially benefit from attending an open house. Prepare your orientation letter and take this opportunity to personally give it to students and families during the open house. Of course, you will want to be sure that students and families who do not attend also receive the letter in some other manner.

Ongoing Contact

In addition to making initial contact with your students' families at the beginning of the year, you need to maintain contact with them during the year. If families feel that you are making an effort to keep them informed, they are more likely to work with you should their student have a behavioral or academic problem. The key here is to come up with a way to maintain communication without burning yourself out.

Plan to provide positive feedback to families when their child is doing well. Some contact opportunities will arise from regularly scheduled school events such as parent-teacher conferences, open house, and back-to-school night. To keep families informed of major class priorities, activities, and issues, you might want to send them a short newsletter on a regular basis. The school website can be a quick, easy way to get information to lots of people. But again, the Internet is inaccessible for some and impersonal.

Use a class list and some form of coding to keep track of your ongoing contacts with families. For example, you might write "9/22, Ph" and "10/4, Conf" next to a student's name to indicate that you made a phone contact on September 22 and had a face-to-face conference at school on October 4. A written method like this lets you monitor how often and in what ways you have contacted each student's family. It also allows you to see at a glance any families you have not contacted. You might add plus and minus symbols next to your notes about each contact so you can track how frequently you contact a family about positive as compared to negative issues. Try to have contacts about each student's positive behavior outnumber those for any negative behavior. This emphasis on the positive will demonstrate to the family that you have the student's best interests at heart and want to work with the family to help the student be successful in your classroom. This is especially important with your most challenging students. Families of students who struggle may rarely or even never hear positive feedback about their child. These efforts to acknowledge moments of positive behavior or growth can help build families as willing partners who are more likely to be supportive and who may make efforts to help when the student is struggling.

When family contact is necessary because of a problem a student is having, it's important to think about what you want to say and how you are going to say it. This preparation

> **Note**
>
> If you are starting CHAMPS or ACHIEVE during the school year, making initial contact with families will probably be a relatively low priority. However, you should put time and energy into maintaining as much positive contact as you can to build relationships with your students' families. Before the beginning of the next school year, make sure that you have a specific plan for establishing and maintaining contact with families.

will reduce the chance that you will be misunderstood or inadvertently say something insensitive. (Suggestions for handling this type of situation are provided in chapter 4, task 3.)

In Conclusion

To properly integrate the strategies presented in this book and to create and maintain an effective classroom management plan, it is essential to understand the core concepts presented in this chapter. If you are reading this book in the summer, I recommend you return to this chapter for a review before classes begin. The Discipline in the Secondary Classroom approach is highly customizable, allowing you to adapt its concepts and principles to your specific needs, and the more familiar you are with the concepts and strategies behind it, the easier it will be for you to make judgment calls on what practices to retain and what you might be able to do without.

Whenever you have something that works for you, do not feel that it should be immediately discarded simply on the recommendations of this book. If there are aspects of your teaching you wish to retain, you will be the most effective teacher you can be if you add the concepts discussed here to strategies that already work for you.

Vision Self-Assessment Checklist

Use this worksheet to identify which parts of the tasks described in this chapter you have completed. For any item that has not been completed, note what needs to be done to complete it. Then transfer your notes to your planning calendar in the form of specific actions you need to take (for example, "August 17, finish Guidelines for Success, write orientation letter for parents"). A blank worksheet is provided on the DVD.

Task	Notes and Implementation Ideas
☑ *TASK 1: Understand the basic principles of behavior modification and your role in that process.* I have sufficient knowledge of fundamental behavior management principles to effectively help my students learn to behave more responsibly. Specifically: 1. I know why and how to promote responsible behavior by: • Recognizing what is prompting behavior • Recognizing what is encouraging or sustaining a behavior • Recognizing what might discourage a certain behavior in the future and then changing conditions to promote desired behaviors 2. I know why and how to deal with misbehavior by: • Recognizing that any behavior that occurs repeatedly is serving some function for the individual exhibiting the behavior and taking that into account when designing an intervention • Identifying and then modifying any conditions that may be perpetuating the misbehavior • Identifying and then eliminating any positive outcomes that may be resulting from the misbehavior	

☑ *TASK 2: Understand motivation and the variables that can be manipulated to increase it.*

1. I understand that behavior that is repeated is motivated and that motivation is affected by a mix of intrinsic and extrinsic factors. I also understand that intrinsic motivation is related to a student's proficiency at a task. Therefore, I have identified the motivating factors for certain behaviors and modified conditions to:

   - Increase students' motivation to engage in desired behaviors
   - Decrease students' motivation to engage in undesired behaviors

2. Enhanced student motivation using both intrinsic and extrinsic factors.

3. Identified whether students' lack of motivation is related to a lack of value, lack of expectancy, or both.

   - For students who are not motivated because of lack of capability, I have modified tasks so that they can succeed.

☐ *TASK 3: Develop and implement Guidelines for Success.*

I have identified three to six basic attitudes, traits, and/or behaviors that are important in order for my students to succeed in my classroom and in their lives. From them, I have created a set of Guidelines for Success (or "Guiding Principles," "Goals," or something else).

I have posted the Guidelines for Success in my classroom, communicated them to students' families, and included them in my syllabus.

Need to narrow down list of attitudes/traits and phrase them as Guidelines for Success.

☐ *TASK 4: Maintain high expectations for students' academic and behavioral performance.*
 	
I understand the importance of having high expectations for and communicating high expectations to all my students. I will make a conscious effort not to say anything (to students, their families, or others) that would suggest that I have low expectations for any student.
 	
I have identified specific ways I can and will convey my high expectations to students, their families, and others.
 	
I understand the importance of maintaining a positive attitude toward my students. Therefore, I will:
 	
  • Develop a wellness program for myself that includes exercise, proper nutrition, and sufficient sleep
 	
  • Maintain a positive and realistic vision of student success
 	
  • Conduct periodic evaluations of my methods to see what is and isn't working
 	
  • Be objective when dealing with student misbehavior
 	
  • Make an overt effort to value and to interact positively with every student
 	
  • Consult with colleagues to discuss concerns
	Check out new early-morning class schedule at gym.
	
	Once fall schedule is set, add notes to assess methods every six weeks, sooner if problems crop up.
	
	Set up early morning coffee meeting with other math/science teachers. Maybe do the same for ninth-grade homeroom teachers?

☐ *TASK 5: Initiate and maintain family contacts.* I am committed to establishing positive relationships with my students' families as part of my classroom vision. I have a specific plan for how I will make initial contact with my students' families at the beginning of the year. I have a specific plan for how I will maintain ongoing contact with my students' families throughout the year.	*Update start-of-year family letter from last year.* *Remember to send home conference reminder with students.*

Chapter 2

Grading and Instruction

Design instruction and evaluation systems

Mrs. Allen teaches high school biology. She has always enjoyed teaching but finds working with unmotivated students frustrating. She knows that many staff members feel the same way and has heard them complain, "Every year it seems as if I get more and more students who don't care about their grades. They don't even try to pass my courses, and it really doesn't matter to them when they fail. Their parents must not care either."

Motivating students to achieve academic success can be a difficult job. Teachers often work with students who have been neglected or abused and may lack parental support. Drug problems, absenteeism, and general apathy can make it seem as if student motivation is beyond a teacher's reach.

Certainly many factors that affect student motivation are outside your control. You cannot control a student's home life or eliminate drug use. You cannot make each minute of instruction fascinating for every student in your class. Part of every course is going to be hard work. Nevertheless, the way you organize instructional content and evaluate student mastery of that content can play a major role in whether students' expectancy of success is high or low (Harniss, Stein, & Carnine, 2002; Paine, Radicchi, Rosellini, Deutchman, & Darch, 1983). In addition, a well-designed grading system can increase students' motivation to behave in ways that will help them engage with your instructional content. When an effective grading system is paired with effective instruction, even low-performing students are more likely to succeed.

The most unmotivated students tend to consistently get poor grades. These students may view grades the same way many people view the lottery: it would certainly be nice to win, but the odds are stacked heavily against it, so why try? Most students would love to get an A or a B, but many know from experience that their efforts will do little to change their odds. When teachers hand back tests or papers, it is rare to see a student who does not care enough to quickly check his grade. While students may give up trying, they do not usually give up hoping. An effective grading system can teach students that they do have some control over their grades. This chapter will help you design instructional units and grading procedures that will increase your students' expectations of success, which will increase their motivation.

This chapter has six tasks that will help you demonstrate to your students that hard work and appropriate behavior can lead to passing your course and earning the grade they desire:

Task 1: Develop clear goals for each class you teach.

Task 2: Design instruction and evaluation procedures that create a clear relationship between student effort and success.

Task 3: Establish a system to provide students feedback on behavior and effort. Incorporate this into your grading system.

Task 4: Design procedures for students to receive feedback on each aspect of their behavioral and academic performance and to know their current grades.

Task 5: Implement effective instruction practices.

Task 6: Present desired tasks to your students in a manner that will generate their enthusiasm.

Tasks 1 and 2 provide basic suggestions on effective instructional practices. For more information on effective instructional practices with secondary students, explore the strategic instruction model (see exhibit 1.1) developed by Deshler, Schumaker, Lenz, and colleagues at the University of Kansas Center for Research on Learning. You can also visit the University of Kansas website at www.ku-crl.org, or read the following:

Deshler, D. D., Schumaker, J. B., Lenz, B. K., Bulgren, J. A., Hock, M. F., Knight, J., & Ehren, B. J. (2001). Ensuring content-area learning by secondary students with learning disabilities. *Learning Disabilities Research and Practice*, *16*(2), 96–108. This article describes the broad array of services that must be available to students with learning disabilities so they can succeed in learning subject-area content. It includes a summary of how Strategic Instruction Mode components relate to these requirements.

Schumaker, J. B., Deshler, D. D., & McKnight, P. (2002). Ensuring success in the secondary general education curriculum through the use of teaching routines. In M. A. Shinn, H. M. Walker, & G. Stoner (Eds.), *Interventions for academic and behavior problems II: Preventive and remedial approaches* (pp. 791–823). Bethesda, MD: National Association of School Psychologists. This chapter summarizes key components of an innovative model for providing services to students in general education classes. It includes descriptions of learning strategies and content enhancement routines.

The self-assessment checklist at the end of this chapter will help you determine which tasks you will need to work on as you build or revise your management plan. Chapter 2's Peer Study Worksheet in the appendix B folder on the DVD has a series of discussion questions you can use with one or more of your fellow teachers to share information with each other on improving teaching practices. The worksheet also presents a series of activities that can be used by two or more teachers who want to share information and peer support as they work together to improve.

Task 1: Develop Clear Goals for Each Class You Teach

Before school begins, determine what you hope to accomplish with your students by the end of the school year (Colvin & Sugai, 1988; Sprick, Garrison, & Howard, 2002). Identify four to seven major goals that summarize why your class will be a worthwhile experience for your students. Specifically, you need to clarify what skills or knowledge they will develop that they did not have on the first day of school (National Research Council, 2000).

Long-range goals can be a mix of academic and behavioral goals. Academic goals focus on what your students will be able to do differently relative to the content you teach. Behavioral goals focus on the attitudes or traits you hope to instill in your students. Whether your goals are predominantly behavioral or predominantly academic is entirely up to you and what you think your class needs.

Having these long-range goals will help you plan and make decisions on a daily basis throughout the year. For example, if one goal is for your students to be able to plan long-range projects and bring them to completion, plan on devoting time to several long-range projects over the course of the year. If this is not a goal of yours, plan for students to engage in more short daily activities and spend less time and energy on long-range projects.

Sharing your goals with your students and their families at the beginning of the year will let them know what you believe is important and where you hope to guide your students. One effective way to do this is to list your goals prominently within your course syllabus. Detailed information about how to share goals with students initially and throughout the year is covered in detail in chapters 5 and 6. Keeping your long-range goals in mind can be particularly important as you move on into the school year. Teachers can easily get so busy and immersed in daily details that they lose sight of what they are trying to do and what they hope to accomplish. With long-range goals in mind, you can stay focused on your goal and periodically ask yourself if what you are doing on a daily basis is aiding (or hindering) your efforts to help students reach these goals.

The following examples give long-range goals for different grade levels and subject areas:

Ninth-Grade Band: All students will:

- Practice independently for a minimum of four hours a week.
- Perform in the band recital at the halfway point of the semester.
- Prepare an individual recital piece to perform at the end of the semester.
- Demonstrate a marked improvement between the beginning of the semester and the end.
- Demonstrate the capability to complete independent work and practice.

Advanced Placement Literature: All students will:

- Write an in-class essay on an assigned prose passage at the end of the third week.
- Make a team presentation about an assigned author at the end of the sixth week.
- Take a comprehensive, closed-book midterm essay and short-answer exam.
- Write a position paper and make a solo presentation on an author or work of your choice.
- Read the work of four different transcendentalists and present a compare-and-contrast paper on them at the end of the semester.
- Demonstrate the ability to analyze and write clearly about an assigned topic.

Ninth-Grade Math: All students will:

- Demonstrate mastery of the quadratic equation by the end of the second week.
- Perform an equation of the teacher's choice before the class at the end of the fourth week.

- Demonstrate comprehensive mastery of all concepts on the midterm.
- Write a paper on the real-world application of one math technique learned in this class.
- Complete a comprehensive final.
- Demonstrate independent study skills and the ability to analyze problems on your own.

Tenth-Grade U.S. History: All students will:

- Memorize twenty key events in U.S. history, including the year the Constitution was ratified, the beginning and ending years of the Civil War, and the year the United States entered World War II, and be able to place those events on a time line.
- Be able to describe and apply five essential concepts of the U.S. Constitution, including the three branches of government and the First Amendment right to free speech.
- Be able to learn new facts and issues from U.S. history and analyze them using the time line of events and constitutional concepts noted above.
- Learn to take notes from lectures, films, and readings and use them to analyze and synthesize information on tests and projects.
- Learn to study independently and stay on task both in class and with homework.

To develop your long-range goals, consider the following suggestions before identifying your own goals:

- Ask yourself what you want students to know and be able to do at the end of the year that they may not be able to do now. What knowledge, processes, attitudes, behaviors, and traits do you want your students to have? What do you want students to take with them after a year with you?
- Read the school, district, and state standards for your students in the grade levels or subject you teach. Your goals should incorporate these standards.
- Talk to other teachers within your department about the goals they have for their students. Ask your colleagues at the next grade level what they believe students coming into their class will need to be successful.

> **Note**
> These samples of long-range goals are included to prompt your thinking. They are not meant to suggest *your* long-range goals.

> **Note**
> If you are starting to work through this book during the school year, implementing this task should be a lower priority. Before the next semester begins, however, you should give careful thought to what your long-range goals will be.

- If there will be accountability testing, such as Advanced Placement or statewide tests, in your subject, be sure that your goals are connected to this testing so that students can see that striving toward the goals you have identified will help ensure they do well on it.

Include this information in your syllabus, and explain that everything in it is designed to help students achieve success in your class. Clarify that meeting the goals in the syllabus and completing the assigned work will ensure a passing or better grade in the class. Chapter 6 includes an example of a teacher's course syllabus.

Task 2: Design Instruction and Evaluation Procedures That Create a Clear Relationship between Student Effort and Success

This task provides suggestions on how to adapt your goals into small units of instruction. You will also determine the evaluation methods and process you will use to verify that students are learning what you teach them. The goal of this process is to clearly show students the links between learning, doing work and participating, and receiving a passing grade (Brophy, 1998). This should also illustrate that above-average work will result in above-average grades and other goals. First, however, consider what *not* to do.

Two common pitfalls with instruction and evaluation.
Some teachers view all information and concepts they teach as equally important. If this is the case, evaluation can often consist of a random sampling of that information to determine student mastery. Consider an extreme (but true) example of what can happen if a teacher designs an evaluation based on this kind of random sampling. In an undergraduate history course, a college instructor assigns twelve hundred pages of reading. Every three weeks, students are to be tested on a four-hundred-page section of the reading and on three weeks of lecture. The final grade is based entirely on the three tests. Prior to the first test, students are not provided any information that will help them prepare for it. When they ask what information from the text will be important, the teacher tells them, "Everything will be important."

The first test is a single essay question covering a topic that has not been mentioned in class and was discussed on only three pages of the text. Out of fifty students, one receives an A, three receive Bs, fourteen receive Fs, and thirty-two receive Cs and Ds. Students complain that the test was unfair: "How could we know which three pages were important? There is no way to memorize four hundred pages of text!"

The instructor replies, "I tested you on those three pages not because they were the most important but because anyone who knew those three pages would also have learned the material on the other 397 pages." On hearing this reply, half the students drop the class before the second test. Think about the probable attitude and motivation of the students who remain. Keep in mind the Expectancy × Value theory of motivation from chapter 1.

This example demonstrates how a course can seem impossible to some students when important objectives are not made clear to them. Even sophisticated college students may choose not to try when the odds against knowing what to study seem overwhelming.

The instructor made an error in assuming that it was the responsibility of the students to identify what content was important. He felt that his job was only to *give* information. This misconception not only made it impossible for students to know what to study, but also decreased the expectancy of success for many students, and so reduced their motivation.

One skill many academically successful students have is the ability to determine critical objectives. If testing is on random information, they still have a chance to succeed because they start with more background knowledge, are more likely to be adept at remembering information, and are probably skilled at guessing what the teacher will choose to include on the test. Less capable students will have difficulty sorting out critical objectives and less chance of remembering unconnected bits of information. In order to increase motivation for all your students, you need to clarify your instructional objectives and then evaluate students on the basis of only those objectives (Kame'enui & Simmons, 1990).

The other major pitfall of instruction and evaluation is grading on a curve. A major percentage of the final grade should reflect each student's mastery of the course objectives. A failing grade should indicate that a student has not mastered the objectives. Students who master the objectives should receive a C, and students who exceed the objectives should receive an A or a B. Grading on the basis of student mastery of objectives instead of on the curve means that every student has the opportunity to pass. This means that you should avoid grading on the standard curve, which distributes the class's grades according to predetermined percentages. In a standard curve, those percentages are:

2 percent of the students receive an A

14 percent of the students receive a B

68 percent of the students receive a C

14 percent of the students receive a D

2 percent of the students receive an F

Grading on a curve takes all incentive away from lower-performing students. They soon realize that their grades have little to do with how well they master course content and that they have to beat higher-performing students to succeed. No matter how hard they work, their performance will always be evaluated relative to that of another student. If instead they know they can pass a course because they have mastered the course objectives, they will soon learn that they can succeed regardless of their relative position to other students. Your goal should be to provide instruction that gives all students what they need to get a C or better. You would not give away passing grades, but rather give them to students who have earned them.

One of the benefits of organizing a grading system around specific objectives is that students do not have to second-guess what they are supposed to learn (Woodward, 2001). Many students do not know enough about a given subject to identify the most important material to learn, and trying to second-guess their teacher is impossible for them. When students understand a class's objectives, they will know what they are supposed to study. This knowledge increases the likelihood that they will make the effort and so make it easier for you to evaluate their performance. The remainder of this task suggests steps for turning your established class goals into meaningful units of instruction and evaluation.

Break down the semester's content into one- or two-week units of instruction.

If you think of the goals you established in chapter 1 as the final destination of a journey, your units of instruction will be the steps you take to reach that destination. Decide whether you will use the midsemester point for a formal midterm evaluation. If you will not have formal midterm exams, simply divide the content you intend to teach over the entire semester into logical units. Depending on how you build your class, this may be defined for you by curriculum guides or the structure of a textbook you are using. If you plan on giving formal midterms, divide the semester in half, and then divide each half into units.

For students to join you on this journey, they need a vision of the final destination. Remember, though, that this vision can be daunting to some students, particularly those who have experienced failure. Let your students know that their success will come one step at a time, one unit at a time, not all at once.

Determine the percentage of mastery that will be used to determine student grades.

Most teachers use something like the following system:

90 percent or better equals an A

80 to 89.9 percent equals a B

70 to 79.9 percent equals a C

60 to 69.9 percent equals a D

59.9 or less equals an F

Check with your school administration to determine if these breakdowns are already specified by policy or if you can make the choice yourself. Whether you use these percentages or something different, the important thing is to realize that the grade distribution is based on each student's performance, not on the curve. Include this information in your syllabus.

> ## Note
> For simplicity and clarity throughout the rest of this book, it will be assumed you are using the "90 percent for an A" breakdown specified above.

Prior to designing instruction, identify the essential objectives for each unit that you want your students to master and retain for the rest of the semester.

What are you going to hold students accountable for knowing not just for this unit but for the remainder of the semester and on the final if you plan to give one? These essentials may be facts, higher-order processes, operations, or some combination of them.

One way to identify these essential objectives is to begin the process of designing your units of instruction. Start by determining your method of student performance evaluation. In most cases, this will be a test. However, in some cases, the essential objectives may be an evaluation of a product, in which case your first step is to determine the criteria by which you will evaluate the end product. By settling on your final evaluation tool (test or evaluation criteria) first, you can then identify exactly what you want students to know or be able to do and then determine the essential content you will need to teach. If you are using predesigned tests from your district curriculum guide or the textbook publisher, this step means examining what is on that test and editing it as needed.

Break your essential objectives into a manageable number of concepts that are essential for literacy in the subject. If you are basing instruction on a textbook, you may find that many texts present only a few essential concepts and lots of embellishment with interesting but nonessential information. Do not worry if your essentials make up only a small percentage of the content of a given chapter of the book. Plan to teach these essential objectives directly, and provide multiple practice opportunities in daily assignments and homework to help students reach mastery of this content.

These essential competencies will comprise 80 percent of the point value of unit tests and 80 percent of the point value of major assignments and projects. This organizational structure allows you to communicate to students that you will directly teach everything they need in order to get a passing grade for the class. For students who have experienced academic failure in the past, you can use this concept to let them know that you will do everything possible to help all students pass—not by giving away grades but by being direct in telling them the essential objectives and creating lots of practice and feedback opportunities to help them get there. One common concern that some teachers express is, "But I don't want to tell students what will be on the test." However, remember that the essential competencies make up only 80 percent of the point value on the test—you are letting students know everything they need to know to get a high C or the very lowest possible B.

Another advantage of directly teaching the essential competencies is that you can create a challenge for students who want to earn an above-average grade. You will not directly teach the remaining 20 percent of point value on tests and major assignments. To gain this content, students will need to read the textbook carefully and generally demonstrate an above-average mastery of the subject. You can inform students that while you directly teach what is needed to get a high C or low B, they will have to demonstrate performance above and beyond that to earn an A or a high B. Thus, 20 percent of the point value of tests and major assignments can be based on advanced objectives—perhaps content from the textbook, lectures, videos, and other material that students were exposed to but that you did not emphasize or teach directly.

This 80/20 analysis prevents the problem in which a teacher views his or her job as covering 100 percent of the content and testing to see what students have learned. That does not take into account that in most subjects, much of the content is not absolutely essential to literacy in the subject. Read any chapter from any science, health, or social science book, and you will notice that much of the material is not essential to understanding the really important concepts, or "big ideas," and is probably not essential to understanding later chapters of the book.

Some teachers label each test item as either an essential or an advanced objective to demonstrate to students a direct connection to what they do in class and being able to pass the class.

Build cumulative review of essential objectives into subsequent units of instruction.

After the first unit test, provide a one- or two-page summary of the essential objectives covered in that unit of instruction. Let students know that the second unit test will have a review section on the essential objectives from unit 1. Here is one way to do this:

Unit 1

80 percent of the point value covers essential objectives from unit 1.

20 percent of the point value covers advanced objectives from unit 1.

Unit 2

60 percent of the point value covers essential objectives from unit 2.

20 percent of the point value covers advanced objectives from unit 2.

20 percent of the point value covers essential objectives from unit 1.

Unit 3

60 percent of the point value covers essential objectives from unit 3.

20 percent of the point value covers advanced objectives from unit 3.

20 percent of the point value covers essential objectives from units 1 and 2.

Unit 9

60 percent of the point value covers essential objectives from unit 9.

20 percent of the point value covers advanced objectives from unit 9.

20 percent of the point value covers essential objectives from units 1 through 8.

When you follow this structure, students can be taught to study the review sheets you give out at the completion of each unit. Studying these review sheets will prepare them for 20 percent of the point value of each test. If they are correct on most of the essential objectives for the current unit and the essential objectives for past units, they will get a high C—a passing grade. If they want an A or B, they will have to demonstrate above-average mastery of advanced objectives from the current unit. Do not include review items that cover advanced objectives from previous units. You want to demonstrate that you hold them responsible only for keeping track of the essential objectives.

One huge advantage of this cumulative review strategy is that students will perform better on finals and statewide tests. Because they have been reviewing the essential objectives again with each new unit, the information stays fresher in their minds. Most adults do not remember their locker combination from when they were sophomores in high school. You knew this information very well at one time and throughout the year successfully opened that lock hundreds of times. Why don't you remember it now (assuming you are not one of those rare individuals who can remember)? Because it has been years since you needed to use that information, and through lack of use, that information has faded from your memory. Do not let that happen to your essential objectives. Keeping that information fresh in students' minds throughout the semester or the entire year will allow your students to retain the information much better, and for much longer.

Task 3: Establish a System to Provide Students Feedback on Behavior and Effort; Incorporate This into Your Grading System

Highly motivated and academically successful students have learned that their daily performance has a cumulative effect on their grade. They understand that each day's work affects how much they learn, which in turn affects their test performances and their final grade. Academically motivated students can take the long view that their daily efforts will affect their future schooling options and even job opportunities. Less mature and lower-performing students do not understand these relationships. These students may not realize that the reason they are not passing is that they do not work or listen during class.

For example, Mr. Nakamura teaches a sophomore geometry course that he has designed to include lectures, class discussions, and assignments Monday through Thursday. Each Friday, students take a quiz on the week's material. The class discussions and lectures typically focus on the previous day's homework. Mr. Nakamura has designed his schedule to allow students to work on problems independently and then to resolve any difficulties as a group.

During class activities, not all of the students work diligently. Some students work hard each day and take each assignment seriously, and some do not seem to care whether they learn to solve the problems. The students who goof off during class work times do not get out of hand, but they also do not learn the content they are expected to master, and so they perform poorly on quizzes and tests. As the end of the term approaches, many of these students seem legitimately shocked and panicked that their grades are so low. At this point, they are too far behind to raise their grade, and they may have significant difficulty in learning the necessary concepts for success for the remainder of the school year.

Most grading systems in secondary school are structured like those in college. Attendance and behavior do not in themselves affect the grade. The grade is usually based solely on assignments, tests, and quizzes. In this type of system, there is no immediate accountability for goofing off. By the time a student fails a test, it is too late to make improvements. The delayed consequence is too weak to be effective with immature students, who may need more frequent reinforcement to stay on task.

> **Note**
> If your district has policies about whether a percentage of the grade will be based on behavior, effort, and participation, obviously follow your district's policies. If there are no district or building policies, you will need to decide whether behavior or participation should have an impact on grades. Some sources discourage the use of behavioral grading procedures on the grounds that a grade should reflect only students' mastery of standards. However, this is not a well-researched topic. Using behavior, effort, or participation, or some combination of these, as a component in your students' grades will be more of a philosophical decision based on whether you feel a portion of the grade for behavior, effort, or participation will contribute to or detract from students' mastery of the course standards.

The benefit of including a behavior component in the academic grade is that it places ongoing emphasis on how effort and appropriate participation will influence course mastery and the grade earned. Without this immediate, daily feedback, many students do not connect the impact of poor behavior with negative school outcomes until it is too late to turn around their grade, earn necessary credits, and learn important academic concepts.

If you decide not to include behavior or participation as part of the academic grade, an alternate approach is to create a separate grade for "citizenship" or "employability skills." However, many students (especially those who are more immature and irresponsible) tend to take these grades less seriously or do not make the connection between their behavior, success, or failure in mastering standards and the corresponding academic grade. More suggestions for how to implement or modify a behavioral or effort grading component are included in the remainder of this task.

An effective grading system at the secondary level must teach less sophisticated students the skills that more sophisticated students learn on their own. The grading system must demonstrate to the students that daily work and attention have a cumulative effect on their grades. Less motivated students in the typical secondary classroom must be taught to evaluate the long-term consequences of their daily actions. This can be accomplished by basing a percentage of their final grade on behavior and effort. This will help students learn appropriate classroom behavior and that what they do in class each day is an important part of earning their final grade (Lam, 1995).

Some districts have a policy that prohibits teachers from using behavior in class as a criterion for grading. If that is the case, look closely at the policy to find out if its intent is to restrict you from lowering a student's grade because of misbehavior. If so, you may still be able to use a system that partly bases a grade on behavior by saying that your class objectives involve teaching students the overall behaviors they need to be successful in any educational setting. For example, in a chemistry class, the abilities to stay on task, follow directions, and follow safety rules are critical factors for success. This same argument can be used to justify grading on behavior and effort in more traditional academic classes like English and history. By including behavior and effort as part of grading, you demonstrate to students that learning independent study skills, knowing how to listen, and taking responsibility for assignments and materials have a direct relationship to success and good grades. These behaviors are necessary for all of their future educational and professional endeavors and are therefore important objectives. Your district may agree that because these behaviors represent sound educational objectives, it is reasonable to base a percentage of each student's grade on them.

If district policy prevents you from incorporating behavior and effort into your grading system, find out if you can run a parallel system of providing a weekly behavior and effort score that affects the academic grade only when a student is just below the cutoff for receiving a higher grade. If this is acceptable to the district, you can modify the system described in the remainder of this task so that it comes into play only when a student is no more than 2 percent below the cutoff for the next higher grade. Then you can establish criteria like the following:

> **Note**
> Some high school teachers and college professors track verbal participation in class. For example, each time a student speaks up in class by participating in a discussion or verbally answering a question, the student gets a point added to his or her academic grade for the day. This type of system, however, can be unfair to shy, quiet students. In addition, it can encourage each student to say something each day just to get checked off for speaking in class. The system described in this chapter for evaluating behavior and effort is different: students are given points for both the degree to which they follow the rules and demonstrate significant effort. These effort points could be for verbal participation, but could also be given for cooperating, demonstrating respect, actively participating in activities, and so on.

- If you are 1 percent or less away from the next highest grade but have 80 percent or more of the behavior and effort points, you move up to the next grade.

- If you are 2 percent or less away from the next highest grade but have 90 percent or more of the behavior and effort points, you move up to the next grade.

If even this moderate influence of behavior and effort on the course grades is unacceptable in your district, you should still implement systematic feedback on behavior and effort like the system described in the remainder of this task. Instead of affecting student grades, however, behavior and effort points will have to count toward something else. To reinforce these ideas, there must be a positive motivator and a negative motivator—for example, evenings without homework or free time for the positives, and extra homework or loss of a privilege for the negatives. The planning steps that follow assume you will base a percentage of the academic grade on behavior and effort. Adapt these procedures as necessary to ensure that you follow the policy guidelines of your district.

Planning Step 1: Establish a Grade Percentage for Classroom Behavior or Effort

To teach students that daily effort affects their final grade, establish a set percentage of the final grade for classroom performance. The exact percentage should vary from class to class according to two factors.

Subject.

Some subjects must have grades that are based heavily on competency. For example, students in a ninth-grade writing class must demonstrate competency in basic writing skills to pass the course. If too high a percentage of the grade is based on behavior and effort, a student could potentially pass the class without demonstrating mastery of the basic course objectives. For this type of class, do not allocate more than 10 percent of the total possible points for behavior and effort. In a chorus class, it might be appropriate to base as much as 50 percent of the grade on behavior and effort. This gives credit to students who work hard, even if they are not exceptionally talented.

If you are working with students who are not yet demonstrating consistent maturity and self-motivation, base a larger percentage of the grade on class performance. The lower the maturity level and motivation of your class, the more the grade percentage should depend on behavior. In general, this means that ninth-grade classes should have a higher percentage of the grade affected by behavior than a twelfth-grade class, and introductory or remedial classes should have a higher percentage affected by behavior than Advanced Placement classes.

Course level.

The level of student experience with a given subject should affect how much of their grade is based on behavior and effort. Students beginning a new skill should have a higher percentage of the grade based on classroom effort than those with experience whose grade may be more based on mastery of course content. When students acquire a new skill, effort will determine whether they move beyond the beginning stages. It is during this time that students need

Table 2.1.
Differing Percentages for Behavior and Effort

Type of Class	Estimated Level of Student Maturity	Behavior and Effort Percent
Introductory Drafting	Mixed	40 percent
Advanced Composition	Highly motivated, excellent skills	5 percent
Remedial English	Poorly motivated, low-performing	20 percent
Biology	Mixed	20 percent
Intermediate Band	Some mix, primarily motivated	30 percent
Advanced Art	Highly motivated	20 percent
Twelfth-Grade History	Mixed	10 percent

the most encouragement. As they gain proficiency in any skill area, that skill becomes more intrinsically reinforcing. For example, beginning string students need encouragement as they learn to read and play notes. Advanced string students are able to enjoy their own ability to play complex pieces and interpret music.

Table 2.1 provides several examples of classes and the kinds of percentages that might be reasonable to assign for behavior and effort.

Determine in advance what percentage of the final grade your students can earn for daily behavior and effort in class. Throughout the term, you will need to monitor and record student behavior. Be sure to inform students about the behavioral-grading component at the start of the semester, rather than after problems occur, so that students know what to expect. If you implement this procedure without letting students know that their class behavior has an impact on their academic grade, it becomes an unfair and arbitrary system.

Planning Step 2: Determine the Approximate Number of Total Points Students May Earn During the Term

Count the units of study you hope to cover during the term, working from the district text or a district curriculum guide. Next, using the number of units you hope to cover, estimate the number of tests, assignments, and projects students will be doing during the term. Although you are projecting what you hope to accomplish during the term, these preplanning steps should not lock you into a system. By estimating the number of tests, assignments, and projects students will be graded on, you can prepare the students for how you plan to evaluate them. You do not have to plan the assignments or write out your tests in advance. You can adjust the number of assignments and tests as you work to meet the needs of your students.

Assign point values to the tests, assignments, and class projects. The point value of each type of work will vary according to the organization of your course and how you want to balance the points for different tasks. Once you have assigned approximate point values, add them together to get an approximate number of work points that students may earn during the term.

Planning for a history class might look something like this:

Nine Units Covered in the Nine-Week Term

8 unit tests, 100 points each	800 points
8 quizzes, 25 points each	200 points
16 homework assignments, 20 points each	320 points
Final exam	200 points
1 term paper	200 points
Total work points	**1,720 points**

Planning Step 3: Determine the Approximate Number of Total Points Based on Behavior and Effort

Using the total work points from step 2 and the percentage of the grade that will be based on behavior and effort from step 1, determine the approximate number of points possible based on behavior. Using the history example, there are 1,720 work points. If this teacher wants the behavior portion of the grade to have about a 10 percent influence on the grade, she takes 10 percent of 1,720 to find that approximately 172 points should be possible for behavior and effort. She could then divide this number by the number of weeks in the term to determine how many behavior points are possible for each week—in this case, 19.11. Because she does not want to bother with fractional points, she will round up or down. For ease, this teacher will inform students that they can earn up to 20 points each week for behavior and effort. This information should be included in your syllabus. See the example in exhibit 2.1.

Note

You may note that in exhibit 2.1, the teacher wanted behavior and effort to be about 10 percent of the grade, but she ended up with 1,900 possible points and only 180 for behavior and effort, which is less than 10 percent. There are formulas for doing this more accurately that you can figure out on your own, but in most cases, it is perfectly acceptable for the point values for behavior and effort to be slightly less than the original percentage you estimated for this category.

Exhibit 2.1
Grading Information

Nine Units Covered in the Nine-Week Term

8 unit tests, 100 points each	800 points
8 quizzes, 25 points each	200 points
16 homework assignments, 20 points each	320 points
Weekly behavior/effort, 20 points each	180 points
Final exam	200 points
Term paper	200 points
Total points possible	**1,900 points**

Planning Step 4: Design an Efficient System for Monitoring and Recording Daily Classroom Behavior Points

To understand that daily performance affects their final grade, students need to see that their daily behavior is being monitored and recorded. (Exhibit 2.2 shows an example of a sheet that can be used to quickly note any information related to a student's classroom performance. A blank version of this is provided as exhibit 2.2a on the DVD; exhibit 2.2b on the DVD provides ten additional lines to list students.)

Exhibit 2.2
Behavior Record Form

Date ____10/14____ Reminders _____

Name	Fri.	Mon.	Tues.	Wed.	Thurs.	Total
Andersen, Gina	dd	CC	dA	d		14
Bendix, Frank	C	C	AA	B	B	20
Bigornia, Brad	o		A		A	16
Collias, Zona	t	B tt	ttt		CB	12

Codes:

off-task	o	doing your best (effort)	A
talking (at the wrong time)	t	be responsible	B
disruptive	d	respect/cooperation	C

The Behavior Record Form in exhibit 2.2 provides space to record each student's behavior during the week. It can be used to note attendance, assignments, behavior, classroom performance, and weekly point totals. At the bottom of the form is a place for a code. For this, first identify three or four positive traits or behaviors you wish to encourage at a classwide level. These will likely have several points in common with your Guidelines for Success. Then identify the three or four particular misbehaviors that represent rule violations you wish to address and reduce at a classwide level. For each positive and each negative behavior, assign a code that you will use to record occurrences of that behavior

---

Table 2.2.

Sample of Codes for Behavioral Grading

Misbehavior	Code	Positive Trait	Code
Off-task	o	Doing your best (effort)	A
Talking (at the wrong time)	t	Be responsible	B
Disruptive	d	Respect/cooperation	C

---

on your record sheet. Table 2.2 shows an example. Once you complete the codes, enter an alphabetical list of student names for each class you teach. Thus, if you teach five classes, you will have a different sheet for each class.

Notice that the form begins with Friday of one week through Thursday of the following week. That way, you can calculate and post the grades on Friday to show your students how they did on the previous five days. Posting these grades on Monday may be too much of a delay and can reduce the interest of some of the less mature students in the behavior and effort score.

Keep the behavior record form readily accessible at all times, especially when you are circulating throughout the classroom monitoring student behavior during independent work and cooperative group activities. Some teachers keep forms for each class on a clipboard; others use a notebook. Throughout the period, students should see you using the record form. If a student comes in tardy, you can quickly mark an L for late. If a student needs to be reminded to get to work, note an *o* for off-task next to the student's name. Immediate notation of these negative behaviors will teach students that they are immediately accountable for their actions every day. (See exhibit 2.2 for a partially filled-in sheet.) When students excel, you can record an *A* for effort or a *C* for cooperation on the form. You will have to determine when you start using this system how publicly you wish to acknowledge student behavior. When a student receives an *A*, will you announce it in front of the class, or will you tell the student later on, privately? (For additional information on giving students positive feedback without embarrassing them, see chapters 6 and 8.) Consistently using the behavior record form during class will allow you to record behavior grades as they happen without cutting into your class time.

> ## Note
>
> If you are working with low-performing students in a remedial setting of any kind, consider giving behavior and effort grades daily instead of weekly. This increased immediacy in feedback will help motivate students who may have given up. The major disadvantage to this is the amount of time required. Therefore, use daily grades only with smaller classes. With a smaller class, assigning and recording daily performance grades should take only two or three minutes at the end of each period. A system of this type can also be incorporated into any behavior plan a student may have, such as a behavior card.

Each time you record a positive behavior, add 1 point to that student's current total for the week. Each time you record misbehavior, subtract 1 point from that student's current total. Because you are unlikely to be able to give each student enough positive marks to get all of them into the A or B range, determine a number of points that each student will start with at the beginning of each five-day period. This should be approximately mid-C level—in our example, 15 points. Inform students that every week they start with 15 points and will move up or down from there based on the feedback you give them and the marks they receive during the week. In exhibit 2.2, if you start with 15 and subtract 1 point for each lowercase letter and add 1 point for each uppercase letter, you come out with the total in the far-right column. The one exception in the example in exhibit 2.2 is Frank Bendix. He has six positives but receives only 20 points—not 21. Inform your students that no matter how many positive marks they receive, they will not get more points than the total possible, in the same way that if an essay is worth 100 points, they won't get a score of 110 no matter how many positive comments are written in the margins.

Planning Step 5: Determine the Impact of Excused and Unexcused Absences on Your Grading of Behavior and Effort

Determine how you will deal with students who are not in class. Obviously a student who is not in class cannot be evaluated on behavior and effort. However, you do not want to have a system that penalizes students who have legitimate absences. Below are some recommendations for you to consider:

- *Unexcused absences.* An unexcused absence removes the student from the learning environment, causes her to fall behind, and can distract other students. There must be a negative consequence equal to all the points that could have been earned with the student's presence. Thus, if 20 points are possible for the week, students should be penalized 4 points for each day they have an unexcused absence.

- *Excused absences.* Students who have an excused absence will be allowed to earn back the credit they missed. Note that they will not automatically earn performance points on the days they are gone. Instead, they will have an opportunity to do extra credit to make up the lost class time. This procedure is not designed to penalize students who are ill; rather, it is designed to demonstrate how valuable class time is. When students miss class time, they also miss learning. Thus, a small extra-credit assignment must be completed to compensate for the lost time. Students will learn that they are accountable for making up missed time. This procedure also applies to students who miss class because of involvement in sports, student government, and other extracurricular activities. You are not discouraging students from participating in other activities; you are holding them accountable for class time. A student who is pulled out regularly for special services of some type, such as English Language Learning or speech therapy, should not be required to make up the participation points that he or she missed.

- *Sent out of class.* A student who is sent out of class has lost the opportunity to earn performance points for the class period and will lose points based on the remaining amount of class time missed. A student who misses half the class will lose half the behavior points for that day, in addition to any other behavior coding recorded before the removal.

Exceptions can be made for students who are out of school with a serious or long-term illness. If a student is out of class for an extended period of time, award performance points as regular work is made up.

Not all administrations will allow you to require makeup work for behavior and effort points in the event of an absence. If this is the case, make sure your grading policies and behavior and effort points reflect this. You should make the other requirements balance without using excused absences as a criterion for points.

Planning Step 6: Assign Weekly Performance Points and Provide Feedback to Students

Every Thursday, your Behavior Record Form will have all the information you need to determine the student's weekly performance points. Simply follow these steps:

1. Begin with the number of points students can earn for average performance.
2. Add the appropriate number of points for each notation of excellence.
3. Subtract the appropriate number of points for each notation of inappropriate behavior.
4. Record the total number of points earned on the behavior record form.

The first few weeks will be a period of adjustment as you get used to regularly noting performance, but as you continue, the task will become automatic. After some practice, you will be able to scan the performance sheet and quickly take in totals. Noting behavior in class should not take extra time once you get used to it, and totaling and awarding the points each week should take no more than five minutes.

When students enter class on Friday, give them their weekly performance points for the previous five-day period and inform them that the new five-day period has just begun. If they do not receive the point totals before they go home for the weekend, the mental connection between their performance and their grades will weaken. Students need frequent and consistent feedback, especially with the implementation of a system to encourage them to follow the rules and give their best effort. There are several ways to give individual students information about their points while maintaining an element of confidentiality:

- If you are using a computerized grading program, print out each student's current grade status, using student numbers for confidentiality.
- Post the sheet on which you have totaled the previous week's points, using a coded number to cover the student names on the far left. This may take a few more days to implement, and it would be best to use something only the student knows (like the last four numbers of his or her Social Security number). Once you have created a form with codes instead of names, the procedure should not take any longer than any other method. Some students may share their numbers with each other and defeat the coding method, but if this is their choice, it does not negate your effort to respect students' confidentiality.
- If you have a class with more behavioral concerns or class size is small, the best way to give feedback is a personal form for each student that breaks down the totals of the

weekly performance points. This provides the students with the most immediate and direct information. It also keeps the process private for each student. The drawback of this method is that it will take longer than five minutes to prepare these for every student in your class.

When you have logged the performance score in your grade book, file the Behavior Record Form. Keeping these records can be useful for several reasons, the most important being to provide answers to any questions about a student's grade. The record sheets provide detailed information about a student's behavior and motivation. This information is useful in conferences with students, parents, and administrators. It can also be helpful in determining a special education placement or in any formal hearings or meetings about a particular student.

Keeping the Behavior Record Forms on file can also provide you with valuable information about revising your teaching methods with a particular group. For example, if you are concerned about off-task behavior in your seventh-period class, you can look at the record forms for the past four weeks to track the problem. If there are many o's (for "off task") marked on the sheet, you should be concerned and make a plan of action. You may want to consider giving your class more structure. If there are steps in this book that you have not taken, explore them. Talk with colleagues who may have a similar group of students and find out what steps they have taken. You should be able to use the record sheet to get a sense of how your class is doing as a whole, not just to evaluate students on their own.

Summary of Behavior Feedback Within Grading Systems

By including a behavior and effort grade, your grading system will become more than a simple evaluation tool. It will become a systematic monitoring device that demonstrates to students that they are accountable for their efforts each day and that their efforts will result in a better grade at the end of the term ("Teachers favor standards," 1996).

For Example

An exciting variation on behavior and effort grading comes from the Academy of Irving Independent School District in Irving, Texas. The academy is a high school in which students are graded on employability skills (ES). (The following information was provided by Patrick Martin, lead special education teacher, and Robin Wall, principal.) The academy is a school of choice where entrance selection is made based on a lottery system; a student who fails to maintain the required grade could potentially be returned to his or her home campus. The ES grade is based on a rubric developed in conjunction with business leaders. The skills measured are:

- Keeps appointments on time
- Completes assignments on time
- Exhibits professionalism in the areas of courtesy, appropriate language, and dress

- Works toward achieving individual and group goals
- Adheres to the ethical use of technology in regard to property, privacy, and appropriateness

The grading scale for these five areas runs from 1 ("rarely does any of these") to 5 ("always does these"). Each of the five areas is graded individually. Let's say that a student receives a 3 in each of the five areas. At this point, the total score is 15. That number is then multiplied by 3, to arrive at 45, and then added to 25 for a graded score of 70. Each grade level has a passing score that must be achieved in order for the student to be invited back the following academic year. The score is 70 for freshmen, 80 for sophomores, and 85 for juniors and seniors.

At the beginning of the school year, each parent and student receives a briefing regarding the academy's expectations and performance criteria. What we have noted is that the grades in academic subjects closely parallel the ES grade. It is unusual for a student to have a high ES grade and be low academically. The underlying philosophy for the program is that the skills needed to succeed in academics are the same skills employers want and employees need for success in the adult working world.

Task 4: Design Procedures for Students to Receive Feedback on Each Aspect of Their Behavioral and Academic Performance and to Know Their Current Grades

The first part of this task is obvious but difficult: get graded work back to students as quickly as you can. The longer a student waits between completing a task and getting feedback on it, the less the student will apply the feedback academically. The longer the delay, the less impact (good or bad) a grade will have. In addition, you want students to know their current status in your class at all times. It is imperative that students be able to track their own grades so that they can measure the effect their effort has on their grade performance. If you are using a computerized grade program, you can and should easily print out current grades and assignment status on a weekly basis.

If you are not using a computerized system, you can teach students to keep a grade sheet. Two different options are shown in exhibits 2.3 and 2.4.

For the first, you can give students a grading sheet with spaces for them to record points for each scored piece of work in your class. In task 3 you identified the approximate number of tests, assignments, and class projects students would complete during the term and the number of points each would be worth. List this information on a student grading sheet with spaces for students to record work points, weekly performance points, and point totals. A sample is shown in exhibit 2.3.

Exhibit 2.3
Student Grading Sheet

CLASS PERIOD *American History*
STUDENT *Estaban Perez*

TESTS

1 Score _84_ /100 points			
2 Score _77_ /100 points			
3 Score _83_ /100 points			
4 Score _88_ /100 points			
5 Score _85_ /100 points		Total _417_ / 500 points

QUIZZES

1 Score _18_ / 20 points
2 Score _16_ / 20 points
3 Score _16_ / 20 points
4 Score _17_ / 20 points
5 Score _17_ / 20 points   Total _84_ / 100 points

TERM PAPER

Score _164_ /200 points   Total _164_ / 200 points

HOMEWORK

1 Score _10_ / 10 points
2 Score _8_ / 10 points
3 Score _10_ / 10 points
4 Score _9_ / 10 points
5 Score _7_ / 10 points
6 Score _9_ / 10 points
7 Score _5_ / 10 points
8 Score _7_ / 10 points
9 Score _9_ / 10 points
10 Score _10_ / 10 points   Total _84_ / 100 points

WEEKLY PARTICIPATION

Week 1 Score _19_ / 20 points
Week 2 Score _17_ / 20 points
Week 3 Score _14_ / 20 points
Week 4 Score _18_ / 20 points
Week 5 Score _17_ / 20 points
Week 6 Score _16_ / 20 points
Week 7 Score _18_ / 20 points
Week 8 Score _18_ / 20 points
Week 9 Score _20_ / 20 points
Week 10 Score _19_ / 20 points   Total _176_/ 200 points

FINAL SCORE _925_ /1,100 points

The benefit to this grade-tracking method is that students have a visual idea of what tests, quizzes, assignments, homework, and participation will be given throughout the term and how much each is worth. By prompting students to use the Student Grading Sheet each time you return an assignment, you are reminding them about what is coming next and can prompt them if they have missing scores. The downside is that students do not have a cumulative record of their grade until all of the scores have been given. Students will not have an overall sense of their letter grade or percentage until the end of the grading period unless you also use another method. For some students, this inability to see how their grade changes daily or weekly removes some of their motivation to strive for higher grades until it is too late and they realize the grade they want is unattainable.

Another option for students to use to track their grades is the Assignment and Grade Tracking Log (a sample follows as exhibit 2.4; see the DVD for a blank reproducible of this form), which provides a running record of scores for all assignments as they are returned to students. Students calculate their cumulative grade and can easily see how each score affects their percentage and letter grade.

You will need to demonstrate and teach students how to record scores on this form using the following steps:

- For each assignment you return, students record the date the assignment was due and the assignment name.

- In the Points Earned and Points Possible column, students record the grade they received on the individual assignment. For example, if the assignment had a total of 15 points possible and the student earned 13 points, the student would record 13/15.

- In the Total Points Earned column, students record the accumulated points they have earned throughout the semester. They then add the score from the previous Total Points Earned (one row above) to the Points Earned for the new assignment. For example, the student earned 18 of 20 points on the first assignment of the year. She earns 24 out of 30 points on the next assignment. She records that score and a new Total Points Earned of 42 (18 + 24).

Exhibit 2.4
Assignment and Grade Tracking Log

Due	Assignment	Points Earned/ Points Possible	Total Points Earned/ Total Points Possible	Current Percentage	Current Letter Grade
9/8	Homework	18 / 20	18 / 20		
9/12	Quiz 1	24 / 30	42		

- In the Total Points Possible column, students record the accumulated points possible for all assignments throughout the semester. They add the score from the previous Total Points Possible (one row above) to the Points Possible for the new assignment. In our example, the student now adds the total points possible for Quiz 1 (30) to the previous Total Points Possible (20), for a total of 50.

Exhibit 2.4
(continued)

Due	Assignment	Points Earned/ Points Possible	Total Points Earned/ Total Points Possible	Current Percentage	Current Letter Grade
9/8	Homework	18 / 20	18 / 20	90%	
9/12	Quiz 1	24 / 30	42 / 50	84%	

- In order to determine the current percentage, students will divide the total points earned by the total points possible, multiply by 100, and round to the tenths place. In our example, the student divides 42 by 50 = 0.84, then multiplies 0.84 by 100 = 84%. She records this as her Current Percentage.

Exhibit 2.4
(continued)

Due	Assignment	Points Earned/ Points Possible	Total Points Earned/ Total Points Possible	Current Percentage	Current Letter Grade
9/8	Homework	18 / 20	18 / 20	90%	A
9/12	Quiz 1	24 / 30	42 / 50	84%	B

- Finally, students record their current letter grade, applying the current percentage to your letter-grading scale, which should be provided in a visual format somewhere in the room. The student records a letter grade of B, because 84% is a B on her teacher's grading scale.

The maturity and level of sophistication of your students will serve as a guide for determining how much prompting you must give them to record their grades. A typical ninth-grade class may have many students who will need to be taught how to keep this sheet in an easy-to-find place in their notebook and how to track their grades. Each time they receive a grade, they should record it. It may be necessary to warn students that you will conduct periodic spot checks to be sure they have kept their grading sheets up to date. If many students in the class have low skills, motivation, or maturity, you may need to reinforce students by awarding bonus points for keeping their sheets up to date. If your students are fairly sophisticated (with a low-structure need), the grading sheet may simply be a useful tool for them. Hand out the sheet at the beginning of the term, and let students know that you will occasionally check to see if they are properly recording their grades. A grading sheet will be a useful tool for all students, especially because you can use it to illustrate your grading plan. You may need to make some minor adjustments if you decide to add or remove assignments as the term progresses, but the students will have a clear outline of their activities and the relative grade values for different assignments.

> ## Note
> Many students, especially those who are less proficient in math, may need ongoing assistance in using this tracking log. Each time you return an assignment, demonstrate and guide the recording of scores until all students are able to perform this procedure with ease. By doing this as a teacher-directed group activity, you will also prompt all students to participate and view grade tracking as a routine part of classwork. If you fade the guided portion of this procedure once students are proficient, be sure to continue to circulate and periodically check how individual students are doing with completing the log. This will ensure that students are following through with tracking grades and are using the appropriate steps to complete the log.

Task 5: Implement Effective Instructional Practices

Your grading system must be paired with effective instructional techniques in order to maximize student success. Instructional practices are an integral part of effective behavior management practices. A teacher who implements dull instruction, presents unclear tasks, or assigns work that is consistently beyond the ability of some of her students—even if she does everything else well in terms of behavior management—is likely to have some students who appear unmotivated, disruptive, or hostile. Effective instruction prevents a great deal of misbehavior, mostly because students who are highly engaged in meaningful tasks do not have time to misbehave (Skiba & Peterson, 2003). In addition, it can have a snowball effect: when students are successful, their sense of accomplishment can be so satisfying that they are more motivated to behave responsibly.

All teachers must learn to ask themselves whether a behavior problem might be caused, at least in part, by an instructional problem. While it is beyond the scope of this program to comprehensively cover effective instruction (the topic is far too broad and complex), what follows are brief descriptions of some factors related to effective instruction that can significantly influence student behavior.

Teacher's Presentational Style

Teacher behavior can be a big factor in the behavior of students. Students are more likely to pay closer attention to a teacher who is dynamic, clear, humorous, and excited in class than to a teacher who is confusing or boring, or talks in a monotone. To understand how important a factor teacher presentation can be, you need only think back to how you felt about the interesting (as opposed to boring) teachers you had in high school or college.

Although some teachers are naturally better presenters than others, every teacher can and should strive to make presentations more interesting to students. A reasonable goal to set is to be a slightly better presenter every year. Look at the following suggestions, and pick one or two that you will practice and work to improve over the course of this year:

- Vary your tone of voice to avoid monotony.
- Vary the intensity of your presentation; do not always act excited or calm.
- Use humor; try to make at least some part of every lesson fun or funny.
- Clarify the purpose of the lesson. Make sure students know what they are supposed to be learning and why it's important.
- Clarify the information you present. Zero in on the key concepts students need to understand; the more direct you are, the better.

Actively Involving Students in Lessons

Don't talk too much at any given time. When you speak for more than a few minutes without getting students involved in some way, students who are less motivated will start to tune you out. Some simple strategies can keep students engaged, even during teacher-directed lessons:

- Ask questions.
- Initiate brainstorming.
- Give students tasks to work on in pairs.
- Present small tasks for students to work on independently.
- Have students volunteer personal examples.
- Give mini-quizzes.
- Set up role plays.
- Use visual aids.
- Present guided practice of tasks that students will work on later.

Ensuring High Rates of Student Success

All students learn faster when they get predominantly correct answers on both oral and written tasks. While it is true that students should be challenged with difficult tasks, it's also true that they will get discouraged over time when they constantly face tasks on which they make a lot of errors. You should try to provide clear enough instruction and frequent enough practice opportunities to ensure that students will get approximately 90 percent correct on most tasks (Kame'enui, Carnine, Dixon, Simmons, & Coyne, 2002).

In situations where you know that students are likely to make a high number of errors, plan to provide more directed instruction. You can do this whether you are working with students in small groups (while the others work independently) or with the whole class. Consider the following example involving a whole-class math lesson. Your original plans may call for about fifteen minutes of teacher-directed instruction and thirty minutes of independent work. During the teacher presentation portion, you realize that many students are confused and do not seem to understand. If you stick with your plan, many students are likely to make a lot of errors, and some will become discouraged. Several students may seek your help during the independent work period. Because many students are confused, a better approach is to change your plan. Instead of giving thirty minutes of independent work, you might say, "Class, because this is such a difficult assignment, I am going to walk you through the first ten problems. Anyone who wants to work ahead may do so, but I invite anyone who is still confused to do them together with me. Watch me do item 1, then copy what I have done." As you proceed through the task, you can gradually release responsibility. For example, have students complete two problems before coming back as a group to check the correct answer and review the procedure, then four problems, and so on.

Providing Students with Immediate Performance Feedback

When students practice a task, they need to receive information on the parts of it they are doing correctly and the parts they are doing incorrectly—as quickly as possible. If students hand in an assignment on a new math concept but you do not get their corrected papers back to them for a week or more, they will learn little. A student who is making mistakes needs to know it as soon as possible in order to learn from those mistakes and avoid imprinting them in memory. During an oral class exercise, you should provide this kind of performance information to students immediately. Feedback about correct and incorrect responses during guided practice in class also should be immediate. When you assign written tasks that are to be done independently, be sure to correct the papers within one or two days and then go over the corrected papers when you return them—for example: "Class, look at the papers I just handed back. Quite a few people had trouble with question 5. Let's look at why. When you do a problem like this, keep in mind that ..."

Task 3 in chapter 1 discussed the importance of high expectations on the part of the teacher. When high expectations are combined with effective instruction, students soon see that if they apply themselves, they can be successful.

Task 6: Present Desired Tasks to Your Students in a Manner That Will Generate Their Enthusiasm

Consider a sports coach who is particularly good at motivating her players. In addition to teaching the necessary skills, she brings a great deal of passion to her interactions with the players. Think about what an effective coach says to players during the game, after the team has won ("You did great, but don't get overly confident, because next week we face the Cougars and they may be even tougher than the team we just beat"), and after the team has lost ("Yes, we lost, but you played a great game and we can learn from the mistakes we made—we just need to work even harder next week"). The actions of an effective coach are designed to inspire the players and motivate them to try their hardest.

This task has four specific strategies you can use, alone or in combination, to increase students' intrinsic motivation. By presenting tasks and behaviors in a manner that will generate student enthusiasm, you can help push your students toward success (Hamre & Pianta, 2001; Stronge, 2002).

Explain how an activity will be useful to students.

Most people are more motivated to work on a task that has a clear and important purpose than on one that seems like meaningless busywork. Therefore, whenever possible, tell your students why you assign the tasks you give them. For example, when presenting a new math skill, you might emphasize how the skill will help them solve certain types of problems. When discussing an important historical event, you might emphasize how the event has relevance to current events in the country being studied. If you are trying to get your class to work harder toward one of your Guidelines for Success, you can stress how following the guideline will help them be more successful individually and help make the whole classroom a better place for everyone.

Obviously your explanations need to be age appropriate. With high school students, it is imperative to communicate what the expected outcome will be and how the task will be useful to them. It may not be necessary to provide this kind of explanation for everything you ask your students to do, but you should plan on doing it fairly often, especially for classes that require more than the typical amount of work or have more inquisitive students.

Provide a vision of what students will eventually be able to do.

Students should be aware of the long-term benefits of full and active participation in your class. Each student who follows your directions and works hard at the tasks you assign should know what he will be able to do at the end of the year that he was not able to do at the beginning. The benefits may involve academic skills, study skills, social skills, or a mix of all three. Your long-range classroom goals (see task 1 in this chapter) may provide examples to your students of what they will be learning. You can show your students at the beginning of the semester what they will be able to accomplish or understand once they have learned what you have to teach them.

Relate new tasks to previously learned skills.

Whenever you introduce a new skill or topic, tell students how the new subject relates to those they have previously learned. Students should not feel that you are presenting hundreds of unconnected skills or concepts. They need to understand how what you ask them to do at any one time relates to what they are working on over time. In this way, they can see how what they have already mastered is useful in understanding new skills or topics. When you combine this strategy with the two previous suggestions, you will ensure that students have a continuing sense of where they have been and where they are going. Relating new information to old also helps students make connections to what they are learning and thus increases the likelihood that they will remember new information.

Rally student enthusiasm, especially for challenging tasks.

Many students will not find it easy to get motivated to do something new or hard. This is where you must make a point of emulating that highly motivating coach. Don't be afraid to give some variation of the "Win one for the Gipper" speech (a famous pep talk given by coach Knute Rockne to the Notre Dame football team before a particularly challenging game, made famous by the 1940 movie *Knute Rockne, All American* starring Ronald Reagan as George Gipp). A classroom example might resemble the following hypothetical speech given two days before a unit test in science:

> Class, in two days we have the unit test in science. This is a tough unit, but I know that you can do it. You can learn these important concepts. I want you to do three

things in the next two days that will help you get a good score on this test. First, work to pay attention in class. We are going to be reviewing the essential information you need to understand in these next two days, so keep focused. Second, any time you don't understand something we are reviewing, speak up! There are no stupid questions. If you are unsure what to ask, just ask me to give more information, and I'll explain the idea again in a different way.

Third, decide right now how much you are going to study tonight and how much are you going to study tomorrow night for this test. How many minutes are you going to study? Decide—right now! Now add fifteen minutes to that number. If you were thinking that you would study zero minutes, add fifteen minutes—so you will study at least fifteen minutes tonight and fifteen minutes tomorrow night. If you planned to study thirty minutes each night, make it forty-five minutes. Remember, the more you study, the more you learn, and the more you learn, the better you will do on this test!

Generating enthusiasm for the tasks you assign can boost student motivation. Always encourage motivated behavior from your students. As self-help author Zig Ziglar once put it, "People often say that motivation doesn't last. Well, neither does bathing—that's why we recommend it daily."

In Conclusion

An effective grading system is more than an evaluation tool; it is an instructional and motivational tool as well. A properly designed and implemented grading system can encourage students to try their best every day (Detrich, 1999). An increase in daily motivation increases the chance that students will keep up with course work and learn to demonstrate mastery of course objectives. When students discover they can be successful in your class, they will remember their success. This will increase the likelihood that they will try to succeed in the future.

Grading Self-Assessment Checklist

Use this worksheet to identify which parts of the tasks described in this chapter you have completed. For any item that has not been completed, note what needs to be done to complete it. Then transfer your notes to your planning calendar in the form of specific actions you need to take (for example, "October 10, finish determining the percentage of mastery used to determine student grades"). A blank worksheet is on the DVD.

	Task	Notes and Implementation Ideas
☑	*TASK 1: Develop clear goals for each class you teach.*	
	I have developed and written down four to seven major goals (instructional and/or behavioral) that I want to accomplish with all my students by the end of the school year.	
	I have identified specific ways in which I will use these goals to guide lesson planning and decision making throughout the year.	
☐	*TASK 2: Design instruction and evaluation procedures that create a clear relationship between student effort and success.*	*Need to set objectives and grading for British and World Lit. Rest of fall schedule done.*
	I have determined the evaluation methods and processes I will use to verify that students who are learning what I am teaching can clearly see the link between learning, doing work and participating, and receiving a passing grade.	
	In order to increase motivation for all my students, I have clarified my instructional objectives and will evaluate students only on the basis of those objectives.	
	I have made sure my students understand my class objectives so that they will know what they are supposed to study, thus increasing the likelihood they will make the effort. Moreover, I have organized my grading system so that a student who meets specific objectives will pass. It is not based on a curve. I have done the following to help me establish my goals in units of instruction and evaluation:	

- Broken down the semester's content into one- or two-week units of instruction
- Determined the percentage of mastery that will be used to determine student grades
- Identified the essential objectives for each unit that I want my students to master and retain
- Built cumulative review of essential objectives into subsequent units of instruction

TASK 3: Establish a system to provide students feedback on behavior and effort. Incorporate this into your grading system.

I understand that my grading system must demonstrate that daily work and attention have a cumulative effect on grades. I need to teach less-motivated students that learning independent study skills, knowing how to listen, and taking responsibility for assignments and materials have a direct relationship to success and good grades. I will accomplish this by basing a percentage of their final grade on behavior and effort.

I have done the following to assist me in accomplishing this:

- Established what percentage of the final grade will be for classroom behavior and effort, taking into account the subject, course level, and maturity and self-motivation of the students
- Determined the approximate number of total points students may earn for tests, assignments, and class projects during the term

Discuss adding behavior component for Freshman Composition grade with department head.

- Determined the approximate number of total points students may earn for behavior and effort
- Designed an efficient system for monitoring and recording daily classroom behavior points (using the Behavior Record Form)
- Determined the impact on students' grades that not being in class will have, making sure not to penalize excused absences
- Planned to total points on the Behavior Record Form weekly and give them to students

---

☐ *TASK 4: Design procedures for students to receive feedback on each aspect of their behavioral and academic performance and to know their current grades.*

I understand the importance of getting grades back to students quickly and the importance of them knowing their current status in class at all times so that they can measure the effects their effort has on their grade. Therefore, if I am using a computerized grade program, I will print out current grades and assignment status on a weekly basis. Otherwise I will use a student grading sheet to prompt students to record their grades.

Make copies of the Assignment and Grade Tracking Log to hand out on first day.

☑ *TASK 5: Implement effective instructional practices.*

I understand that instructional style has a significant impact on student behavior. I have identified one or two aspects of my presentation style that I will work to improve over the course of the year.

I have made plans to improve my presentational style by:

- Varying the tone of my voice to avoid monotony
- Varying the intensity of my presentation so I am not always excited or always calm

- Using humor
- Clarifying lesson purpose
- Clarifying information

I have made plans to actively involve students in lessons. Following are strategies I can use:

- Asking questions
- Giving students tasks to work on in pairs
- Presenting small tasks for students to work on independently
- Giving mini-quizzes

TASK 6: Present desired tasks to your students in a manner that will generate their enthusiasm.

I understand that presenting tasks and behaviors in a manner that generates student enthusiasm will help motivate my students to try their hardest. I can do this by:

- Explaining how an activity will be useful to students
- Providing a vision of what students will eventually be able to do
- Relating new tasks to skills students have already learned
- Rallying student enthusiasm, especially when the task is challenging

Chapter 3

Organization

Prepare routines and procedures

Picture two different college classes. One has an organized professor who starts class on time, uses class time efficiently, and clearly states the requirements for assignments and their due dates. The other class has a disorganized professor who never starts on time. He is often sorting his notes or PowerPoint slides until ten minutes into class. Then he takes up class time to talk about things that interest him, not the class topics. His students are never clear on what their assignments are or when they're due. In which of these classes would you do better? Never doubt that a teacher's organization affects his students. If he is clear and motivated, his students are likely to be as well (Moran, Stobbe, Baron, Miller, & Moir, 2000; Simola, 1996).

The six tasks presented in this chapter will help you organize your classroom in a manner both efficient and likely to prompt responsible behavior on the part of your students. Whenever possible, you should complete the tasks before the school year begins so that you have a solid organizational structure in place from the start (Bell, 1998; Schell & Burden, 1985). In addition, once you have finished the tasks, the essential information should be included in your course syllabus. (See chapter 6.) If you are starting this chapter during the school year, address the tasks one at a time and implement them gradually so as not to make too many changes to your classroom routine at once.

Six tasks are presented and explained in this chapter:

Task 1: Arrange the schedule of activities for each class period to maximize instructional time and responsible behavior.

Task 2: Arrange the physical space in your classroom to promote positive student-teacher interactions and reduce disruptions.

Task 3: Decide on a signal you can use to immediately quiet your students and gain their full attention.

Task 4: Design efficient, effective procedures for beginning and ending the class period.

Task 5: Design efficient, effective procedures for assigning, monitoring, and collecting student work.

Task 6: Manage independent work periods.

At the end of this chapter is a worksheet for you to complete. The Self-Assessment Checklist will help you determine which tasks, or parts of tasks, your classroom management plan will need. In addition, the Peer Study Worksheet for this chapter on the DVD presents a series of discussion questions that you can use with one or more fellow teachers to share information on improving classroom management practices.

Task 1: Arrange the Schedule of Activities for Each Class Period to Maximize Instructional Time and Responsible Behavior

How you schedule activities within a class period and through the week can have a tremendous influence on student behavior (Kame'enui & Simmons, 1990; Tanner, Bottoms, Caro, & Bearman, 2003). For example, the teacher who schedules independent work for the last half of the last period of the day may find that students engage in high rates of off-task behavior because they are fatigued and restless. During the last half-hour of the school day, you will keep students more engaged if you schedule only brief independent work tasks and implement more interactive and teacher-directed tasks. This may even mean that if you have two classes of freshman English, one first period and one seventh period, you will teach the same content in both classes, but the schedule and type of activities you use may be different in the two periods. An effective schedule provides enough variety that students will be able to stay focused on any task. It also takes into consideration your skill at keeping students on task and the maturity of your students.

The information in this task is designed to help you evaluate and change your schedule to ensure that it promotes effective student behavior. (See exhibit 3.1.) Along with specific scheduling suggestions, this task also identifies specific times of the day during which students are more prone to irresponsible behavior and what you can then do to increase productive behavior. To begin evaluating your schedule, list the subjects you teach and the length of your class periods. Then list the activities that typically occur during each class and the amount of time each activity takes. Finally, list whether the activities are independent or directed by you. The end result should be a schedule that lays out each period like this:

2 minutes	Independent warm-up exercise and attendance
5 minutes	Teacher-directed review of previous concepts
10 minutes	Teacher-directed introduction of new concepts
8 minutes	Teacher-directed guided practice, working on assignment
20 minutes	Independent work or cooperative tasks (depending on task)
5 minutes	Teacher-directed corrections and guided practice to help students identify errors or misunderstandings

The level of structure your class requires has a direct impact on how you approach scheduling. If you determine that your students are likely to be successful with a low-structure management plan, you may not need to attend closely to daily schedule issues. Low-structure students are more likely to be able to stay on task for extended periods and should be able to begin class with an independent or cooperative (as opposed to teacher-directed) activity. If your class requires a medium- or high-structure plan, carefully consider the information in this task and use it to get the most out of your daily schedule.

Exhibit 3.1
Level of Structure

Throughout the remainder of this book, there are frequent references to the level of structure that you will use in your classes. *Structure* refers to the degree of orchestration of student behavior and the predictability of the classroom environment. For example, when considering structure as you create your schedule of activities for each class period, consider that in a high-structure class, students require shorter periods of independent work with more frequent check-ins and periods of teacher-directed instruction or guided practice. When left to work independently for long periods of time, the class becomes chaotic, students stop working, and you will spend more time managing behavior. In a low-structure class, students may be able to work independently for thirty minutes at a time. The low-structure approach requires greater maturity on the part of the students to ensure safe and responsible completion of the assigned activity.

Your classroom management plan may be tightly or very loosely structured, depending on the collective needs and maturity of your students as well as on your own personal style. In chapter 4, you will evaluate the level of structure needed in each of your classes, considering your students' level of maturity and needs as well as your own preferences. As you complete the tasks in this chapter, keep the following considerations in mind:

- Are your students more or less mature?

- Self-motivated or unmotivated?

- High or low achieving?

- Do they have higher risk factors that may make school more difficult or a lower priority for them?

- What is your personal tolerance for noise, movement, and multitasking?

The answers to these questions will guide you as you proceed with making decisions in this chapter about scheduling, arranging the physical space, and the other organizational considerations. In general, levels of structure will correspond to the following considerations:

- *High structure:* Required for students with high risk factors, lower maturity, frequent misbehaviors, less self-motivation, or several of these; also required if you have personal needs for a calm, orderly setting

- *Medium structure:* Some balance between the tight orchestration of high structure and the more freewheeling nature of low structure

- *Low structure:* Used only in classes where students are highly mature, are able to handle responsibility and independence appropriately, and are generally more proficient with the subject matter or have low risk factors, or both

Create a balance of teacher-directed, independent, and group tasks.

Your goal is to balance the kinds of activities your students are doing. Especially watch for a tendency to schedule too much of a good thing. For example, if you like students to work in cooperative groups and feel strongly that they learn the most by working in this way, you may inadvertently schedule group activities for too much of your class period. Similarly, if you prefer teacher-directed activities (lectures, discussions, and demonstrations), you may tend to not schedule enough time for independent work and group tasks.

Look at your daily schedule and estimate the approximate percentage of class time your students spend on various activities. You may find your schedule looks something like the following:

40 percent teacher directed

35 percent independent work periods

25 percent cooperative groups

There are no absolute rules on balance in the classroom. A technology class would have far more independent work, while a history class would have more teacher instruction. Look closely at what type of task takes up the highest percentage of your class time, and honestly ask yourself if that task is appropriate for the class or if it represents too much of a good thing.

Whenever students engage in one type of task for too long, behavior problems can result. When teacher-directed instruction goes on too long, students tend to become inattentive. When they have to sit and do independent work for an extended period, they may get bored and stop working.

There are no absolute rules about how long is too long or how much is too much, but a good rule of thumb is to keep all activities under thirty minutes. The amount of time depends in part on your skills and talents as a teacher. A teacher who designs clear, interesting, and fun independent assignments can successfully engage students for longer periods. A teacher whose presentation style is dynamic, organized, and humorous can sustain student attention for longer periods of teacher-directed instruction. If you have found in the past that student behavior deteriorates as a particular activity progresses (e.g., students do well at the start of independent work but get increasingly off-task after about fifteen minutes), schedule shorter time periods for that type of activity.

If you teach in ninety-minute blocks, pay particular attention to keeping each activity to a reasonable length of time. Instead of longer activities, you should schedule more activities within the period — for example:

3 minutes	Independent warm-up exercise and attendance
7 minutes	Teacher-directed review of previous concepts
10 minutes	Teacher-directed introduction of new concepts
10 minutes	Teacher-directed guided practice, working on assignments
15 minutes	Independent work
5 minutes	Teacher-directed correcting and clarifying
5 minutes	Introduction to cooperative exercise
15 minutes	Cooperative group task
5 minutes	Teacher-directed clarification
10 minutes	Independent work
5 minutes	Teacher-directed introduction to homework

Schedule independent work and cooperative group tasks so that they immediately follow teacher-directed tasks.

Teacher-directed instruction is an excellent way to generate classroom momentum, whereas starting class with independent projects can result in lower rates of on-task behavior. Starting the period by reviewing previous concepts, introducing some new concepts or skills, and then moving students into independent work or cooperative tasks allows you to clarify what students should be working on, sets out cohesive and clear expectations for on-task behavior, and maintains the momentum that you create at the beginning of class (Kame'enui & Simmons, 1990).

There are exceptions to this rule. For example, a common approach is to have students work on review exercises or a challenge problem as soon as they enter the classroom while you take attendance and deal with other housekeeping tasks. This strategy usually involves brief (two to five minutes) independent or cooperative activities and is a structured part of the daily routine. This can be a highly effective practice. Another exception may be a class in which students work mainly on extremely clear and highly motivating independent tasks—a computer lab, for example.

As you develop your daily schedule, remember that in general, teacher-directed instruction is the best way to begin class; therefore, avoid beginning class with a long period of independent work time. Also keep in mind that for a class that needs high structure, brief periods of independent work are more likely to result in high rates of on-task behavior than an independent work time that lasts more than twenty minutes.

Implementing these suggestions as you schedule daily activities is an excellent way to reduce the likelihood of irresponsible student behavior. Another way is to identify and address the specific activities and times of day during which students typically exhibit the most distraction or misbehavior. For problem activities or times, make a point of diligently teaching students what your expectations are and how to meet them. What follows are times that are particularly troublesome for many teachers, along with some suggestions for addressing the increasing irresponsible behavior during those times.

The last hour of the day   Students (and teachers!) tend to be tired by the end of their day. Students are more likely to be distracted at this time, so you should avoid scheduling too much independent work then. This can be an effective strategy even if you teach several units of the same class at different times. If you teach two classes of tenth-grade English—one first period and one seventh period—it would be reasonable to begin the first class with twenty minutes of teacher-directed instruction and then assign students to work on a long-range project for thirty minutes. Students in the last class would find it more difficult to stay on task for such an extended independent work period. You would be better off giving fifteen minutes of teacher-directed instruction, then fifteen minutes of project work, and then five more minutes of teacher-directed instruction before fifteen minutes of guided practice on a specific aspect of the project to end the class. You would cover the same amount of information as you did in the first period, just split into more distinct sections.

The last five minutes of a class period   Try to end each class period with a few minutes of teacher-directed instruction. If you schedule independent work time during the last part of the class, students will begin to take advantage and let their work slide as the clock winds down. The more they get away with this behavior, the more time they will waste, and ultimately the last fifteen minutes of your class may be wasted altogether. By scheduling the last class activity as a teacher-directed task, you set a precedent that class time is used only for class work. This should not be complicated. If you have students work in groups during the second half of class, you can monitor their progress and make corrections. As the period draws to a close, you can get everyone's attention and discuss any common mistakes: "Class, for these last fifteen minutes, we'll be working on this problem. We'll finish by looking at the problem together. Before you leave, I'll give you the homework assignment for tonight. While you're working, keep in mind ..."

In addition to giving students feedback or information about the current task, you can use those final minutes to review homework expectations or remind your students about long-range projects: "Class, do not forget that you should be done with your outline for the projects by Wednesday, and tomorrow is the last day to get your permission slips in for the field trip."

If you do not end the class with teacher-directed instruction, your students may begin to act as if independent work time is free time. Another example of how to accomplish this is to use the last three to five minutes to draw names and have the students answer pop questions for bonus points. This can be an enjoyable and fast-paced way to keep students focused on the academic subject right up to the end of the period.

A well-designed schedule ensures that students experience a varied and balanced range of activities within class. If students are kept engaged with activities that are scheduled for reasonable lengths of time, they will behave responsibly. If they are required to engage in the same type of activity too often or for extended periods, they may become bored, distracted, and even disruptive.

Task 2: Arrange the Physical Space in Your Classroom to Promote Positive Student-Teacher Interactions and Reduce Disruption

Note

Teachers may not always have control over the physical layout of their classroom environment. If you teach in a classroom that isn't yours, have inherited fixed student desks or other permanent fixtures, or have a large class in a small space, adapt the principles in this task as best as you can.

The physical organization of the classroom has a significant influence on student behavior. For example, if student desks are arranged in a manner that makes it difficult for you to circulate throughout the room, student behavior is likely to be less responsible than if the room is arranged so that you can easily be among the students. This task covers the four aspects of a classroom's physical arrangement that you can address to increase responsible student behavior. If you have a high-structure classroom management plan, carefully consider how you can implement all four aspects of physical space presented in this task. Well-designed physical space can prevent a wide array of potential behavioral problems.

The basic rule regarding physical arrangements is this: change what you can, and make the best of what you can't. If you must teach English in a science lab, you will have to put more energy into teaching your students to stay on task than you would if they worked at individual desks. Manage the aspects of the physical space over which you have no control by manipulating other variables, such as teaching more expected behaviors and monitoring student behavior more closely.

To whatever extent you can control the physical space in which you teach, consider the following suggestions.

Make sure you have easy access to all parts of the room.

One of the most effective behavior management strategies a teacher can implement is to circulate through the class as often as possible. To this end, however you organize the desks and chairs in the class, make sure you're able to move around them freely.

When students are working independently or in groups, your proximity will have a moderating effect on their behavior. As you circulate, you will be able to provide corrective feedback to students who are off-task, give positive feedback to students who are using their work time well, and answer the questions of students who need assistance. If, while you are assisting a student, you notice another student who is off-task, you should be able to go directly to that student. This will keep the students aware of your proximity, which will keep their behavior in check.

If you are unable to change the layout to provide this easy access to all parts of the room (e.g., if you share a room with another teacher), carefully consider where you place your students who struggle the most with behavior, academic skills, or effort. Assign these students to parts of the room you can get to without any difficulty, making it easier to use proximity control, give quiet corrections, or provide additional check-ins and assistance.

Arrange desks to optimize the instructional tasks that the students are most likely to engage in.

Following are descriptions of common arrangements for desks, with information about their relative pros and cons:

Desks in Rows, Front to Back (Figure 3.1)

- Excellent if you frequently schedule whole-class instruction or have students do tasks at the board
- For occasional cooperative learning activities, students can be trained to move quickly into and out of groups of four
- Allows students to interact, but the spaces between desks will help keep off-task conversation down
- Directs student attention to the front of the room
- Allows easy circulation among students
- Effective for medium- to high-structure classes

Desks Side to Side (Figure 3.2)

- Excellent if you use frequent whole-class instruction where you have students do tasks for which they must see the board
- For occasional cooperative learning activities, students can be trained to move quickly from the rows into groups of four and back to the rows when the cooperative activity is completed
- Allows more student interaction, which is helpful for group study but can result in off-topic conversations
- Directs student attention to the front of the room

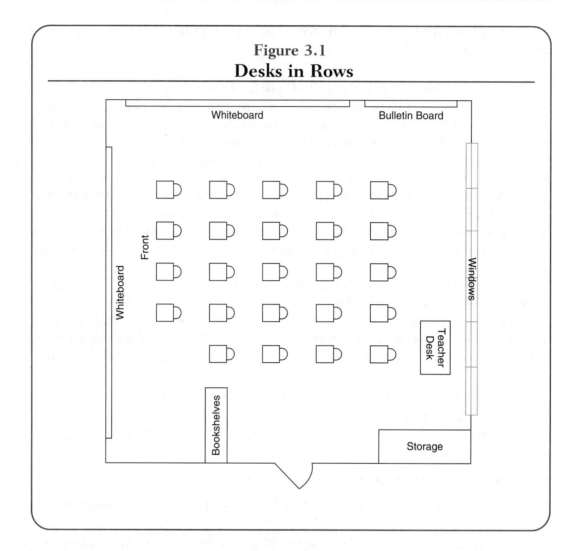

Figure 3.1
Desks in Rows

- Best for a low- to medium-structure classroom
- May be necessary for larger classes
- Grouping desks in rows of three creates aisles for easy access

Desks in Clusters (Figure 3.3)
- Allows easy circulation and access to all students at any time
- Excellent if you schedule frequent cooperative learning tasks
- If students are easily distracted, the small groupings may draw attention away from activities
- Requires some students to turn in their seats to see the board for teacher-directed instruction
- May lead to off-topic conversation due to student proximity
- Best for low-structure classes; clusters may prompt inappropriate student interaction in a class that needs high structure

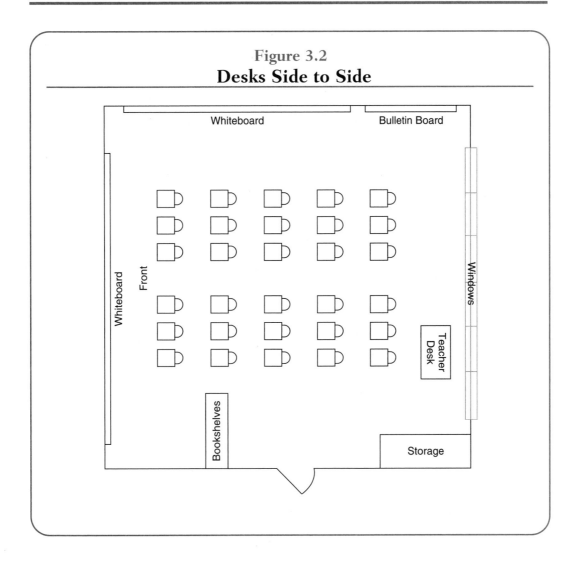

Figure 3.2
Desks Side to Side

Desks in U-Shape (Figure 3.4)

- Excellent for class discussion and teacher-directed instruction with student participation
- Excellent for teacher proximity and circulation
- Does not lend itself to group activities
- Inefficient use of space; may not be useful for labs and small group instruction, for example
- Cannot be used with a large class
- U shape may require breaks to allow easier student circulation—for example, to the teacher's desk or the exit
- Best for classes that need low to medium classroom structure; can be adapted to work for a smaller high-structure class if the teacher is committed to circulating and giving frequent feedback

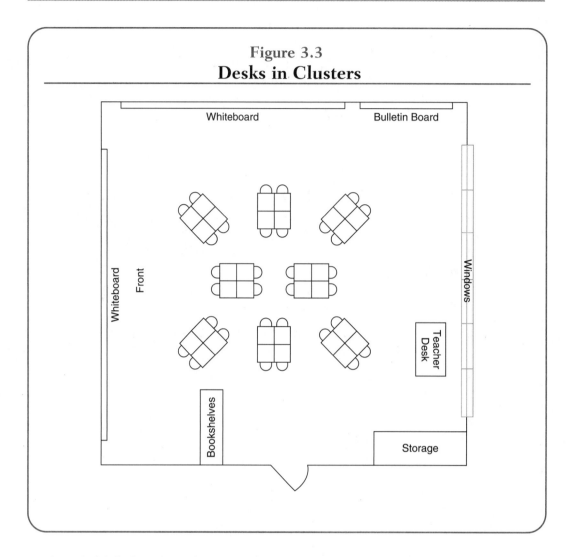

Figure 3.3
Desks in Clusters

Desks in Modified U-Shape (Figure 3.5)

- Excellent for class discussion and teacher-directed instruction with student participation
- Excellent for teacher proximity and circulation
- Students can move quickly into groups of four
- Can be used with a large class
- Good option for classrooms with double desks
- Breaks in U-shape allow easy student circulation
- Best for classes that need low to medium classroom structure; can be adapted to work for a smaller high-structure class if the teacher is committed to circulating and giving frequent feedback

As you consider what arrangement you want for your classroom (one of these five or one of your own), keep in mind the tasks your students will be participating in and the level of classroom structure they will require.

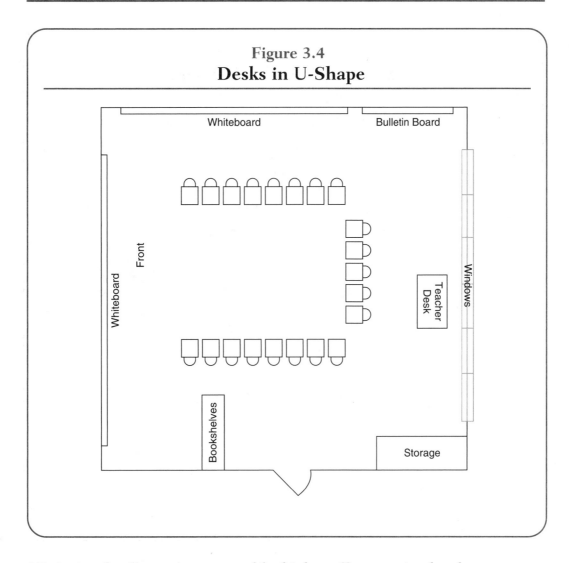

Figure 3.4
Desks in U-Shape

Minimize the disruptions caused by high-traffic areas in the class.
There are a number of legitimate reasons that students need to move about the classroom during the day. Any time students are out of their seats, however, there is greater potential for misbehavior. When setting up your classroom, give thought to high-traffic areas. As much as possible, you should keep desks away from the areas where students will do the following:

- Get supplies
- Sharpen pencils
- Turn in work
- Have small group instruction
- Use lab stations

If you can't avoid having student desks near one or more of these high-traffic areas, you will need to teach students how to be in these areas without distracting other students.

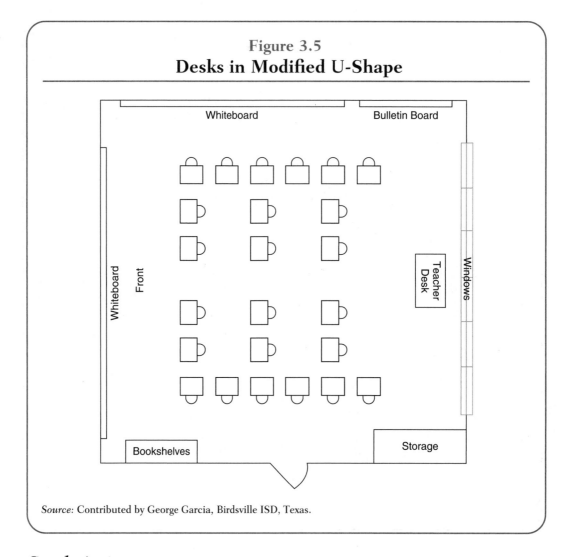

Figure 3.5
Desks in Modified U-Shape

Source: Contributed by George Garcia, Birdsville ISD, Texas.

Conclusion.
Arrange the physical space in your classroom to prompt responsible behavior from students. One way to accomplish this is to make sure there is easy access from any one part of the room to any other part of the room so that you can circulate unpredictably among students and so that students can move about without disturbing each other. In addition, desks and traffic patterns should be arranged in a manner that takes into account the major types of instructional activities you use and the level of structure needed in your classroom management plan. Your goal is a physical environment that is comfortable and functional for you and your students.

Task 3: Decide on a Signal You Can Use to Immediately Quiet Your Students and Gain Their Full Attention

Getting and holding students' undivided attention is an important management tool for any teacher. Just as a conductor uses a baton to gain the attention of the orchestra, so you need a signal to draw your students' attention to you so that you can give directions or provide instruction.

An attention signal is useful at many times and in many situations. Imagine a class of twenty-eight students working in small groups. As the teacher monitors her class, she realizes that her students do not fully understand their assignment. Using a well-practiced signal, she can get her class's attention in less than five seconds. After briefly clarifying the directions and answering any new questions, she can then return them to their small group work. Without a well-practiced signal, it is likely to take the teacher several minutes of yelling over the noise of the class to get their attention. It is even possible that not all of the students will hear and understand the correct assignment if the class never really quiets down.

> ### Note
> Whether your class requires a low-, medium-, or high-structure classroom management plan, an attention signal is an important behavior management strategy for any class with more than fifteen students. Regardless of the structure level your class requires, you need a way to get students to make the transition from active and potentially noisy group activities to activities that demand the attention of the whole class.

To implement this task successfully, first identify what you will use as a signal. One effective method is saying in a firm, loud voice (but without shouting), "Class, your attention please," while at the same time swinging your right arm in an arc (from nine o'clock to twelve o'clock on a clock face). Then hold your hand in the twelve o'clock position until all students have also raised their hands. This prompts each student to stop talking, look at you, and raise his or her own hand until all students are quiet and looking at you with their hands raised (see figure 3.6).

Figure 3.6
Attention Signal

"Class, your attention please."

This signal has several advantages. First, it can be given from any location in the room. Second, it can be used outside the classroom, in the hall, or even on a field trip. Third, it has a visual and an auditory component, so students who miss one component may notice the other. A fourth advantage of this signal (and others like it) is its ripple effect: students who miss the signal will see the reactions of other students and thus be aware of the signal without having to see it themselves.

Some teachers find that high school students may consider raising their hands as part of the signal process to be beneath them. If you think this might be the case, you can let students know that they do not have to raise their hands, but it becomes their responsibility to make sure that all students around them (e.g., the other students in their small group) are aware that the signal has been given. In this way, the teacher will be able to get the attention of the entire class without requiring raised hands. If this adaptation is not effective, go back to requiring raised hands until students can become quiet without a need to raise their hands.

Regardless of the signal you use, you must be able to get the attention of the entire class within five seconds. To this end, you must teach students the signal and how to respond to it from the first day of class. (Information on when and how to teach your attention signal is provided in chapter 6.)

Task 4: Design Efficient, Effective Procedures for Beginning and Ending the Class Period

How you start and end each class period has a significant influence on the climate of your classroom. Established procedures for beginning and ending class will foster an inviting and supportive atmosphere (Reddy, Rhodes, & Mulhall, 2003). The more efficiently you use the time you have, the more you communicate to your students that time in your class will not be wasted. This will make a difference in student behavior (Burnette, 1999; Harlan, 2002). Consider the following two scenarios.

Teacher A begins the day by warmly greeting students as they enter the classroom. She has previously taught students that when they enter the room, they are to take their seats immediately, take out any required materials, and begin working on the challenge problem written on the board. Students who do not have their materials do not interrupt the teacher while she is greeting students because she taught them specific procedures for dealing with this situation. When the bell rings, the students continue to work on the challenge problem while the teacher takes attendance. Within one minute of the bell ringing, the teacher has taken attendance, secured the attention of the class, and started teaching. In the next ten minutes, two students enter late, but she does not stop teaching. Her students know her tardiness procedures, which are designed to ensure accurate record keeping without disrupting class. Suggestions on how to achieve this kind of efficiency are provided later in this task.

The situation is different in Teacher B's class. As students enter the class, the teacher is seated at his desk trying to finish last-minute preparations for the lesson. Some of the students take their seats, while others socialize in groups. When the bell rings, Teacher B looks up from his work and acknowledges that students are there by saying, "Quit talking and sit down. It's time to begin class." After two minutes of nagging, the students are finally in their seats and reasonably quiet. He instructs students to get out their materials and then spends several minutes assisting students who are not prepared, all the while telling them to be more responsible. Five minutes after the bell rings, the teacher finally begins teaching. In the next five minutes, two more students arrive. Both times the teacher stops teaching to determine if the tardiness is excused or unexcused and to fill out the necessary paperwork. Each incident requires him to stop teaching as he deals with the late individual.

Note that Teacher A spends only one minute on attendance, materials, and tardiness procedures, and even during that minute, students are engaged in an instructional task. Teacher B spends over ten minutes on attendance, materials, and tardiness. Students who arrive on time with all of their materials are forced to sit and do nothing while the teacher deals with these procedures. In both scenarios, some students did not have their materials and two arrived late, things that will happen to every teacher. The difference is that Teacher A anticipated these problems and has taught her students procedures for handling them so that all of her class time is used efficiently.

Task 4 addresses how to begin and end class with a positive tone and how to maintain maximum time for instructional activities. There are eight goals related to beginning and ending class, each supplied with suggestions on how you can best implement them.

> **Note**
> If you need a medium- or high-structure classroom management plan, you should address all the issues outlined in this task. In particular, it will be important for you to be in your classroom (or in the hall near your door) when students enter. Plan to keep students occupied from the moment they enter the room. For a low-structure class, you may be able to let students occupy themselves for a minute or two between their arrival and engagement in an instructional task.

As always, if your methods are working for you, remember that this book presents you only with a potential alternative. If your class already begins and ends in an organized manner, there is no reason to change your methods. If you are struggling, try these suggestions in addition to consulting your colleagues on the methods they use.

Entering Class

Goal: Students will feel welcome and will immediately go to their seats and start on a productive task.

Greeting students as they enter your classroom helps them feel welcome and reduces classroom behavior problems. A brief greeting communicates to students that you are aware of and interested in them not just as students but as individuals. Learn student names as soon as possible. Using a student's name as you greet her demonstrates a level of respect and communicates that you are aware of this person as a valuable individual. One high school physics teacher took a digital photograph of each row of students on the first day of class and had students write their names on a seating chart. By the end of the week, he was calling each student by name in each of his six classes: "Charlene, how did things go at the choir concert last night?" In addition, greeting students as they enter provides a subtle but powerful message that you are aware of the students and what they are doing from the minute they enter class, not just when the bell rings.

When possible, greet students at the door. Although you can greet students while seated at your desk, the effect is not as powerful as being at or near the door as they enter. Greeting students at the door also allows you to assist in supervising the hallway. High schools in which most teachers are at their doorways between classes have fewer problems with misbehavior in the halls, and as a result, students are calmer and ready for instruction when they enter class. If you are supervising the hall outside your room, you can greet your students before they even enter the class.

Have a task that students can work on as they arrive. This gives them something to do while they wait for the bell to ring and while you take care of any attendance or housekeeping tasks in the first minutes of class. Having students work on a daily task like this communicates to them that every minute in class should be used as efficiently as possible.

Keep the task short—one that will require only three to five minutes of work from students. It should be a review task that students can perform independently, but it should also be instructionally relevant, not just busywork. For example, math teachers might give a short daily quiz on the previous night's homework assignment, and language arts teachers might have students work in their journals or do a short writing exercise.

When you have finished taking attendance, give the students feedback on the correct responses for their short task and have them trade with a neighbor for correction. Then collect the papers so that you can later record the grades and note the students' involvement. If this initial task does not count toward students' grades, they will soon stop completing the task.

Opening Activities

Goal: Students will be instructionally engaged while you take attendance.

When the bell rings and as students work on the assigned task, use a seating chart rather than calling out names and having students reply to determine who is present and who is not. This eliminates the need for you to read a boring litany of names every day and allows students to continue focusing on the work they are doing. Seating charts are also extremely important for substitutes to use, as lengthy attendance procedures with substitutes can easily lead to a breakdown in classroom control and result in lost instructional time.

> ### Note
>
> If tardiness is a chronic problem in your school, a schoolwide program should be considered. If possible, mention to the administration that tardiness should be addressed. *START on Time!* (Sprick, 2004), a DVD-based in-service program, has reduced tardiness in some high schools up to 96 percent.

If you have a low-structure class and students are mature enough to stay focused and highly responsible when they choose their own seating arrangement, it is still important to have a seating chart so that valuable instructional time is not wasted each day on attendance. If students are always in different places, you will need to take more time to assess who is present and absent than if you can just look at the vacant desks to know who is missing. Have students choose their seats; then create a seating chart that will be used for the next two- to four-week period. This still rewards students for their maturity and responsibility without creating a dramatic loss of time each day.

Goal: You will develop procedures for dealing with tardiness.

This goal will:

- Ensure that students who are tardy do not disrupt class or take your attention away from teaching.
- Allow you to keep accurate records of excused and unexcused tardies.
- Let you assign consistent corrective consequences for unexcused tardiness.

One recommended procedure for dealing with tardy students is to place a three-ring binder with forms like the reproducible Record of Tardies (shown in exhibit 3.2) on a table or shelf near the door to the classroom. (See the DVD for a blank reproducible of this form.)

Exhibit 3.2
Record of Tardies

Names	Excused or Unexcused? If your tardy is excused, attach the excuse slip from the attendance office or a note from the excusing teacher.	
First Period		
Kendall Ludwigson	☐ Excused	☒ Unexcused
Devon Porter	☒ Excused	☐ Unexcused
Eduardo Sanchez	☐ Excused	☒ Unexcused
Second Period		
	☐ Excused	☐ Unexcused
	☐ Excused	☐ Unexcused
	☐ Excused	☐ Unexcused
Third Period		
Janitra Warren	☒ Excused	☐ Unexcused
	☐ Excused	☐ Unexcused
	☐ Excused	☐ Unexcused
Fourth Period		
	☐ Excused	☐ Unexcused
	☐ Excused	☐ Unexcused
	☐ Excused	☐ Unexcused
Fifth Period		
Cedar Bromwell	☐ Excused	☒ Unexcused
Ethan York	☐ Excused	☒ Unexcused
	☐ Excused	☐ Unexcused
Sixth Period		
	☐ Excused	☐ Unexcused
	☐ Excused	☐ Unexcused
	☐ Excused	☐ Unexcused
Seventh Period		
	☐ Excused	☐ Unexcused
	☐ Excused	☐ Unexcused
	☐ Excused	☐ Unexcused

During the first week of school, train your students that when they are tardy, whether excused or not, they are to enter the classroom quietly without interrupting you or the other students in the class, put their name in the box for the appropriate period, indicate excused or unexcused, attach the excuse if they have one, and then quietly take their seat.

Each day before students arrive, make sure that a new page is showing with the correct day and date filled in at the top. Attach paper clips to the page so students with excused tardies can attach the excuse paperwork.

When a student enters late, do not stop what you are doing. Visually monitor to make sure that the tardy student goes to the notebook and writes something. If the student does not go to the notebook, provide a verbal reminder: "Paul, before you sit down, put your name in the notebook by the door and indicate whether you have an excused or unexcused tardy. Now class ..."

Later in the period, when the class is engaged in independent work or cooperative groups, check the information on the tardy student in the notebook. Record the information in your grade book, and follow any schoolwide procedures for reporting unexcused tardies to the attendance office. Check the excuse notes to verify them. If you need to talk to a student about being tardy, do so then, while the rest of the class is occupied. Following these procedures prevents the tardy student from getting attention or interrupting your lesson.

There should be corrective consequences for unexcused tardies. If your school does not have such a policy, develop your own and inform students of it on the first day of school. An example policy is below, although the severity of individual consequences will depend on how much authority you have:

Two unexcused tardies in a semester: family notification (notification occurs for each subsequent incident)

Four unexcused tardies: after-school detention

Six unexcused tardies: half-day in-school suspension

Goal: Announcements and other housekeeping tasks will not take up too much time.

Strive to begin instructional activities as soon as the period begins. Therefore, plan to spend no more than a minute or two on announcements and housekeeping. Activities that are not directly related to the subject of the class should be reserved for advisory or homeroom periods.

Materials

Goal: You should have procedures for dealing with students who do not have materials or are otherwise unprepared.

This goal will:

- Ensure that a student who does not have the necessary materials can get them in a way that does not disrupt instruction.
- Establish penalties that will reduce the likelihood students forget materials in the future.
- Reduce the amount of time and energy that you spend dealing with this issue.

First, make sure that you clearly communicate to students exactly what materials you expect them to have each day in your class (e.g., two writing instruments, a binder with a divider, lined notebook paper, and the textbook). This information should be communicated verbally to students and in writing to their families as part of a syllabus or letter that goes home on the first day of class. At the end of each period during the first week, remind students what materials they should have when they return to class the next day.

Next, develop procedures that will allow a student who lacks any of the necessary materials to get what he or she needs to participate in the lesson *and* receive a mild consequence designed to reduce the probability that the student will forget materials again. For example, you might inform students that they should try to borrow the missing material from another student (a pencil or some paper) without involving you or interrupting instruction. Explain further that all students who have their materials will gain one point toward their behavior or participation grade for the week. (See chapter 2 for proper application of this strategy.)

If you anticipate that there will be times when students need to go to their lockers to get materials, include procedures that minimize the teaching time you will lose to fill out hall passes. For example, you could inform students that if they have to go back to their locker for materials after class has begun, it will count as being tardy. Tell them that you will give them a hall pass that they must fill out for you to sign. That way, while the student is filling out the pass, you can continue with your other teaching responsibilities. Having the student fill out the pass reduces your involvement with this student from two or three minutes to only thirty seconds or so. Remember never to let more than one student at a time leave class to go back to his or her locker.

If you ask other teachers in your building how they deal with students who do not have materials, you will probably hear a wide variety of procedures. Some teachers just give away pencils and lend books without any penalty. Others impose a cost in the form of a point fine or other consequence. There is no one right answer; the important thing is to decide in advance how you will deal with this very common occurrence. If you aren't sure whether your planned procedure is fair or appropriate, ask your administrator for feedback. Some administrators, for example, may not want teachers to impose penalties, and there may be other limitations on policies regarding students without materials or tardiness.

It's important that during the first few days of class you inform your students how you will respond if they do not have their materials. For high-structure classes, you should start conducting a materials check daily: "As you are working on the challenge problem, I want to check that you came to class with all your materials. Put your spare pencil, your notebook, and your textbook on your desk. While you are working, I'll come around and check." If any students are missing one or more of the required materials, provide a gentle but firm reminder about the importance of being responsible for bringing their materials every day.

After the first couple of weeks, conduct intermittent spot checks of materials. Any students who do not have what they need should receive a minor corrective consequence (e.g., losing one point from their participation grade), while students who have all their materials might receive one bonus point. If you plan to do this, be sure to inform students on the first day of class that you may conduct spot checks for the first few weeks of school.

When a student does come unprepared to class, do not get upset or frustrated; simply follow through consistently with the procedures you have implemented. Remember that you don't want these procedures to usurp too much of your instructional time. If you start feeling frustrated because you are spending too much time dealing with students who have forgotten materials, ask colleagues for ideas on how to streamline your procedures so that you can keep your focus on instruction.

Dealing with Students Returning after an Absence

Goal: Students who have been absent can easily catch up on missed assignments without greatly involving you.

An excellent way to deal with absent students is to set up two baskets in the classroom—one labeled "Absent, Missed Assignments" and the other labeled "Absent, Due Assignments"—that you keep in a consistent location. Any time you give students an assignment or a handout, put that same material in a folder for any students absent that day. The folder should have the date and the class period clearly marked on it. Place these folders in the "Absent, Missed Assignment" basket.

Teach students that when they return after an absence, they should look in the folders for the dates they missed. This way, they can find out all the tasks they missed and get any handouts they might need without interrupting you.

The basket marked "Absent, Due Assignments" can be used in two ways. When a student returns on Tuesday from an absence on Monday, he can turn in any assignment that had been due on Monday to the "Absent, Assignments Due" basket at the same time he is picking up the folder from the "Absent, Missed Assignments" basket. When the student completes the work assigned on Monday (the day he was absent), he will also return that work to the "Absent, Assignments Due" basket. A system like this will save you time and interruptions, but will work only if you keep the baskets up to date and remind students who return from being absent to collect what they missed and hand in anything that was due.

As a general rule, students should have the same number of days to complete a missing assignment as the number of days they were absent. Thus, the student who returns Tuesday from being absent on Monday would have until the next day to turn in the work assigned Monday and due on Tuesday. If the student did not return until Thursday, he would have until the following Tuesday, three school days following his return, to turn in his missing assignments.

Decide whether you will allow students to make up assignments they missed as a result of unexcused absences. If you do not have a policy, ask your building administrator whether students should be allowed to make up missed assignments from unexcused absences. Defer to his or her judgment.

End of Class or Period

Goal: Your procedures for wrapping up the period will:

- *Ensure that students do not leave the classroom before they have organized their own materials and completed any necessary cleanup tasks*
- *Ensure that you have enough time to give students both positive and corrective feedback and to set a positive tone for ending the class*

Leave enough time at the conclusion of each class to ensure that things end on a relaxed note. How much time this entails will vary. For example, in a math class, one minute will probably be sufficient; in an art class, it may take up to ten minutes to get all the

> **Note**
>
> At the beginning of the year, plan to leave a little extra time at the end of class until you determine precisely how much time is needed for these wrap-up activities.

supplies put away and the room ready for the next class. Allow time for reminders about homework, upcoming tests, permission slips for field trips, and so on. Avoid trying to do all this in too brief a time, or you may inadvertently demonstrate a franticness and sense that you are somewhat disorganized and out of control.

When students have finished organizing and cleaning up, give the class as a whole feedback on what they are doing well and what may require more effort on their part. This is especially important during the first six weeks of school but is also useful intermittently throughout the school year: "Class, I want to let you know that the way you have been using class time demonstrates a high level of responsibility. You should be very proud of how well you are all functioning as a group. One thing that a few people need to manage more effectively is remembering homework. Tomorrow you have a science assignment due. Make a decision right now about when you are going to work on that assignment."

Dismissal

Goal: Students will leave the classroom when you dismiss them, not by the bell.

On the first day of school, and periodically thereafter, remind your students that they are not to leave their seats when the bell rings. Explain that the bell is the signal to *you* and that you will excuse them when they are reasonably quiet and all final tasks have been completed. If you let students run for the door when the bell rings, it sets a precedent that your instructional control ends then. By reserving the right to excuse the class, you can judge whether you should excuse the whole class at once or by rows or table clusters. As a general rule, higher-structure classes should be excused by rows, and lower-structure classes can be excused as a group. However, if you excuse as a group, let the students know that if they rush out of the room or crowd the door, you will start excusing them by rows.

The beginning and ending of class periods play major roles in setting the climate of the classroom. Opening and dismissal routines that are welcoming, calm, efficient, and purposeful demonstrate to students that you are pleased to see them and that you care so much about class time that not a minute will be wasted. Calm and efficient dismissal brings organized closure and sets a tone for your class for the following day.

Task 5: Design Effective, Efficient Procedures for Assigning, Monitoring, and Collecting Student Work

An all-too-common frustration for teachers is dealing with students who do not complete assigned work. The problem is often compounded by the fact that students who do not complete assignments will not achieve mastery of skills they need to complete future assignments. In addition, without seeing their work, you will be unable to track their progress. If you can increase the likelihood that students will complete their assignments, they will learn more and you will be less frustrated.

This task addresses procedures for managing student work. Implementing well-designed and well-organized strategies for assigning, monitoring, and collecting student work will (1) let students know that you put a high value on their completing work, (2) prompt more responsible student behavior regarding assigned tasks, and (3) help you effectively manage student work without taking unreasonable amounts of time (Lynn, 1994).

If you are new to the school, find out what policies your school has before you start implementing your own homework policies. Check with the administration, your

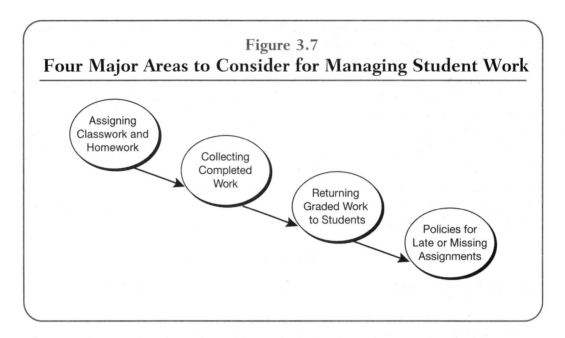

Figure 3.7

Four Major Areas to Consider for Managing Student Work

department chair, or a colleague to see what rules are already in place. High schools often create schoolwide policies on late work and makeup work, and may have standing rules on assigning work. Some schools are also implementing a policy to monitor when other classes assign major projects like term papers so that they do not overlap. This enables your students to focus more on one class at a time, instead of potentially having to turn in three big projects in a week.

There are four major areas to consider in relation to managing student work (see figure 3.7). The rest of this section gives some considerations and suggestions for each area.

Assigning Classwork and Homework

The first step toward greater student work return is to create a system that allows students to track their assignments. Students should have a consistent place to look (e.g., on a board or an assignment sheet) to find out what their assignments are. It is not enough simply to tell students what their assignments are or to write them out during the lessons. These methods do not create the necessary permanent place for students to check when they need to know what they should be working on or may have missed. If there is no set place where students can check their assignments, a student who forgets an assignment will have no choice but to ask you or another student for the information. When assignments are left on the board or recorded on an assignment sheet, the student can easily check to determine what he needs to do.

In keeping with this, also teach students to keep their own records of assigned work so that when they get home, they will know what they need to do. If you decide to put assignments on the board, teach students to copy the assignments onto a sheet that they keep in a consistent place in their notebook. If you give out a weekly assignment sheet, students should be taught to keep the assignment sheet in a consistent place in their notebooks. Be specific: tell students exactly how and where to record the information. Show them an example and, especially at the beginning of the year, monitor whether they are following through—for example: "Class, we have a couple of minutes before the bell. Open your notebooks to the page immediately after the divider for this class. I want to see that you have the weekly assignment sheet in the correct place."

If you give both short-term daily assignments and long-term assignments (e.g., a term paper), make sure they note both assignments. Daily reminders about a long-term task will help students remember that they should be working on the task on an ongoing basis, not putting it off to the last minute. This is also an opportunity to remind students what part of the assignment they should have completed at any given time: "Remember that your projects are due in one week, so by Monday you should have your outline and your first draft completed."

Figure 3.8 shows how you might use board space for recording assignments.

A permanent record of daily assignments is especially useful if you have determined that your students need a high-structure classroom management plan. It is essential, then, to establish a way for a student to find out what assignments were missed during an absence. Refer to task 4 for more information on how best to approach this.

Note

If your school does not have a study skills curriculum, you might want to suggest that your staff consider *Advanced Skills for School Success* by Anita Archer and Mary Gleason (2003). This program for grades 7 to 12 is designed in four modules, each addressing one area of school performance that is of immediate use to students in meeting school demands: school behaviors and organization skills, completion of daily assignments, effective reading of textbooks, and learning from verbal presentations and participating in discussions.

Figure 3.8
Sample of Assignments on Board

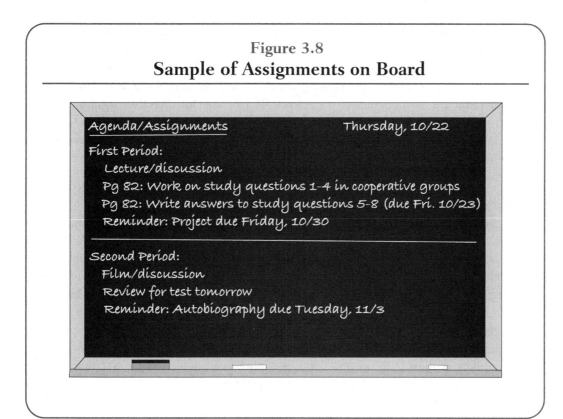

Agenda/Assignments   Thursday, 10/22

First Period:
  Lecture/discussion
  Pg 82: Work on study questions 1-4 in cooperative groups
  Pg 82: Write answers to study questions 5-8 (due Fri. 10/23)
  Reminder: Project due Friday, 10/30

Second Period:
  Film/discussion
  Review for test tomorrow
  Reminder: Autobiography due Tuesday, 11/3

While helping students keep track of their assignments in a particular place, also monitor their study habits. Just as you should encourage them to make steady progress on long-term projects instead of doing them all at once, you should watch to see which students are more likely to let work go unfinished. Encourage those students in particular to stay on top of their assignments, being sure to acknowledge any successes.

Collecting Completed Work

Give some thought early on to the method you will use to collect homework. Whenever possible, collect the work personally from each student: "Class, put your homework on the upper-right-hand corner of your desk. While you are working on the challenge problem on the overhead, I will come around and collect it." The biggest advantage to this procedure is that you know immediately when students have not completed the work (and your students will know you know). If a student does not have his or her homework, take that moment to reemphasize to him or her that work completion is an important aspect of responsible behavior in your class. Do not accept excuses, but let the student know that she will need to speak to you later. It is important to doubly use this time by having your students work on a current project while you collect their completed assignments.

Because this allows you to give students immediate feedback about their work, it is most effective in a classroom where you are using a high-structure plan. Another benefit for high-structure classes is that this procedure does not require students to leave their seats, which can lead to lost time, irresponsible or unsafe behavior, and a loss of instructional control. Personally collecting completed work does have the drawback of being time-consuming for you. If you require only a low- or medium-structure classroom management plan, you may prefer a less hands-on way of collecting homework and monitoring completion.

Having students turn in their work, having a student helper collect it, or having students place their work in a basket are all less time intensive, but lack the advantage of the personal contact that your collecting the work has and may lead to disruptions with less responsible students. Even if students don't see a grade for a day or two, seeing you take the completed work and knowing you have it, instead of knowing you'll get it eventually, is a much more powerful reminder of the value of their work. If you are not directly collecting student work in your classes and you have been unhappy with the percentage of completed work, experiment with directly collecting your students' work. You may find the rate of completion will improve.

Consider having students check off completed tasks.
If you give students a daily or weekly assignment sheet or have them use an assignment notebook, consider adding a place for them to check that they have completed a task. Another option is to display a wall chart similar to the reproducible form shown in exhibit 3.3 on which students can check off completed tasks. (A blank reproducible of exhibit 3.3 is provided on the DVD with two formats: exhibit 3.3a is as shown here, and exhibit 3.3b is a long form for larger classes, with ten additional lines for student names.) This is *not* an official record and does not take the place of your grade records. It is simply an opportunity for students to put closure on their tasks. It is also a quick way for them to verify whether they are on top of their assignments. You should, however, make sure such a display is not used by any students to show off or brag about their marks.

Exhibit 3.3
Completed Assignments Checklist

Class Period _Algebra 1_   Week of _11/3_
  Directions: When you turn in an assignment, put your initials in the space next to your name under that assignment.

Name	Page 44, 1–15	Page 44, 16–27	3.3 Work-sheet	Page 57, 1–10, 12, 15		
Abbott, Chelsea						
Allan, Aquene						
Boardman, Jim						
Chavez, Graciela						
Chung, Lisette						
D'Antonio, Gus						
Franklin, Toby						
Herrera, Felipe						
Isaacs, Juliana						
Kung, Sue						
Martinez, Hector						
Patel, Arman						
Pelayo, Jorge						
Potter, Kort						
Ruiz, Stacy						
Sakamoto, Aki						
Tanner, Uri						
Ju, Quoc						
Wright, Kennedy						

Teaching students to use a check-off procedure can also give you an opportunity to teach them about self-reinforcement. Encourage them to tell themselves they have been responsible when they check off each completed assignment.

Returning Graded Work to Students

Just as students are expected to be on time turning in their work, you must be timely with grading it and returning it to them. For simple homework and in-class assignments, return it the next day whenever possible. This will keep students actively aware of their progress and allow them to work on problem areas when the tasks are still relatively fresh in their mind. In addition, timely return gives students a chance to learn what they are doing wrong before moving on to more advanced work, which often builds on the previous work.

Because you expect a reasonable level of neatness from your students on their written work, you must hold yourself to the same standard. Anything that is complex or difficult to communicate should be covered in person, not in a note you write in the margin. Legibility is essential as well: feedback serves no purpose if students can't read it.

It is vital that grades be kept as confidential as possible. Do not post the grades with student names on the check sheet or anywhere else public. Your students will find out about each other's grades quickly enough without your help. Respect the fact that some of your students will not want to share their grades or may be embarrassed. Put letter grades on the back pages of assignments or return work face down. To facilitate the latter, write each student's name on the back of the papers where you can see it.

Finally, do not waste class time by having students wait while you return graded work. Have them do some in-class work or talk about the assignment you are returning. This is a perfect time to address problems that most of your students had trouble with or to answer questions that were raised by the work.

An extra procedure for classes that need high structure.

In addition to ensuring that all students receive regular and ongoing feedback about their grades, you may consider giving the class feedback on the quality of their homework as a class. If you want to increase the rates of homework completion, you might use a wall chart or an overhead to track the percentage of the class that returns any given assignment. This gives you the opportunity to emphasize daily the importance of taking responsibility for completed homework. Divide the number of completed assignments by the number of students, and chart the number so your students can see over time how many of them are finishing their homework.

In addition to emphasizing the importance of responsibility, this procedure may create some healthy peer pressure because the students will see the effect their homework completion has on the whole class. If you need to give them a further incentive, you can tie a percentage of completion to a reward: when they reach a certain completion percentage, they can have a period of free time or a day without homework.

Late or Missing Assignments

The last major consideration regarding management of student work is how you will deal with late and missing assignments. Some teachers choose to have no penalty for late work: students can hand in anything at any time. Other teachers do not allow students to turn in any assignment late: a late assignment receives zero points. Some form of middle ground between these two extremes is probably the best option. When there is no penalty, some students will turn in everything late, possibly even handing in all assignments on the last day of the term. If students are allowed to do this, it is unfair to you (you should not have to stay up all night at the end of every grading period) and to the students (they can learn that they do not really have to pay attention to due dates). An extreme "if it's late, it's a zero" policy does not take into account that an occasional late assignment is likely for even the most responsible student. Exhibit 3.4 shows a sample policy that might be implemented by a high school science teacher.

> ## Exhibit 3.4
> ## Sample Late Assignments Policy
>
> - Any assignment that is turned in late will receive an immediate 10 percent penalty (e.g., a 100-point lab will have 10 points deducted from whatever score you earn).
> - No assignment will be accepted beyond one week late.
> - Students who have more than ____ late or missing assignments will have their families informed.
> - No more than four late assignments will be accepted during the quarter.

In most classrooms, a large percentage of a student's time will be spent on written work. The way you manage assignments and work periods will have a big impact on how responsible students will be for managing and completing their written tasks. If you effectively manage student work, the students will be more likely to complete their work, thus giving them the practice they need on essential instructional objectives. In addition, when students complete their work, you will be able to track whether they are achieving mastery of those objectives and judge whether additional instruction is necessary (McLean, 1993).

> ### Note
> The details of and criteria used in a policy reflect the decisions of individual teachers. The important point is to develop a policy that works for you and to inform students and their families about the policy at the beginning of the term or year.

After taking the time to develop the policies and procedures you plan to use for managing student work, you should be able to summarize this within the syllabus that you provide students on the first day of class. Chapter 6 has a syllabus template and an example of a syllabus that include the policies and procedures covered in this chapter.

Task 6: Manage Independent Work Periods

The following suggestions focus on how to design efficient and effective procedures for scheduling and monitoring independent work periods. In chapters 4 and 5, we provide additional information on how to clarify and directly teach your behavioral expectations regarding independent work periods.

When students are expected to work without direct teacher supervision, off-task behavior can easily result. There is more potential for off-task behavior, which can lead to inappropriate horseplay and disrespectful interactions among students, when students are working independently than during any other type of activity. Your goal should be to keep students on task and actively engaged in their work. The following suggestions can help minimize off-task behavior during independent work periods.

Be sure that any independent work you assign can be done independently by your students.

If you assign students tasks that they cannot complete, you set them up to fail. When students have to do work that is beyond their ability, they are likely to:

- Do the work but fail because they don't understand it
- Not do the work and fail because they didn't complete the assignment
- Do the work, but deal with feeling and looking helpless because they ask for help day after day from you or peers

Over time, many students slip into the second option because when they do nothing, at least they look tough or bored instead of stupid and helpless. Following are suggested steps you can take to ensure that all students can complete the independent work you assign (Babkie, 2006; Barbetta, Nornona, & Bicard, 2005; Gettinger & Ball, 2008; Howell & Nolet, 2000; Simonsen, Fairbanks, Briesch, Myers, & Sugai, 2008):

> **Note**
>
> If students are struggling with reading and a reading intervention group can be put in place, a useful tool is *REWARDS (Reading Excellence: Word Attack and Rate Development Strategies)* (2005a) for grades 4 to 12 and *REWARDS Plus* (2005b) for grades 6 to 12 by Anita Archer, Mary Gleason, and Vicky Vachon.

- Modify assignments to meet the needs of the lower-performing students in the class. For more information on modifying instruction for such students, see Intervention B: Academic Assistance in *Interventions: Evidence-Based Behavior Strategies for Individual Students* by Randall Sprick and Mickey Garrison (2008).
- Provide alternative assignments for some of the students.
- Work together on the assignment with a few students in a small group while the rest of the class works independently (Ysseldyke, Thurlow, Wotruba, & Nania, 1990).
- Have students work in pairs or cooperative groups so they can help each other (Delquardri et al., 1986; Simmons, Fuchs, & Fuchs, 1995; Spencer, 2006). Do not overuse this strategy, or your higher-performing students may get tired of helping others do their work. Consider setting up the groups yourself—who works with whom—to avoid having low-performing students choose to work together and be unable to perform the required tasks.
- Use computer-assisted instruction (Clarfield & Stoner, 2005; Silver-Pacuilla & Fleischman, 2006).
- Provide students with guided notes (Sweeney et al., 1999).

Schedule independent work times in a way that maximizes on-task behavior.

The subject of scheduling to maximize on-task behavior and minimize off-task behavior was discussed in task 1 of this chapter. The following information summarizes the suggestions in task 1 on how to improve student engagement during independent work periods:

- Do not schedule long periods during which students are expected to stay on task while working independently. There is no magic rule about how long students can stay focused, but in general, having students work on the same task for more than thirty minutes without some change in routine will result in high rates of off-task behavior. For students in high-structure classes, it is advisable to keep independent work periods to no more than ten to fifteen minutes. Then return to a teacher-guided activity for at least a few minutes before requiring more independent work.

- Schedule independent work periods to follow some form of teacher-directed instruction.

- Arrange for independent work periods that occur at the end of the day to be shorter than those that occur at the beginning of the day.

- Create immediate accountability during independent work time. Walk between the desks and follow the students' progress, in particular keeping an eye on those most likely to become distracted.

Develop a clear vision of what student behavior should look and sound like during work times.

This suggestion is covered in detail in chapter 5. For now, remember that if you do not clarify and teach exactly what you want from students, some students are likely to assume that behaviors such as chatting in groups and moving about the room are okay during independent work times. Once you have a vision of the behaviors you want students to exhibit (and, correspondingly, the behaviors you do not want them to exhibit), teach students to meet those expectations (Barbetta et al., 2005; Emmer, Evertson, & Anderson, 1980; Greenwood, Hops, Delquadri, & Guild, 1974; Lewis & Sugai, 1999; Marshall, 2001; Mayer, 1995; Simonsen et al., 2008).

Provide guided practice on tasks and assignments—that is, work with students in a teacher-directed activity for the first 10 to 50 percent of an assignment.

Guided practice is important because it increases the chance that students will have the skills or knowledge needed to complete the task successfully. Guided practice can also create behavioral momentum. That is, when you guide students through the first part of a task, a portion of the task is already completed by the time you say, "Now do the rest of the assignment on your own [or in groups]." Without guided practice, when you say, "Get to work on your assignment," students face a blank piece of paper. For many students, the hardest part of doing assigned tasks is getting started. Guided practice increases work completion because it ensures that students have started their work, and likely understand it, before the independent part of the class period begins (Council for Exceptional Children, 1987; Rosenshine, 1983).

The structure level that your group management plan calls for should determine how often you use guided practice. The more structured your classroom environment is, the longer you should guide the work before letting your students work independently.

For Example: Guided Practice

When teaching a math lesson, you might start by reviewing previously taught concepts, then introduce the day's new concept, then work through the first several exercises of the math assignment, and finally turn students loose to work on the remainder of the assignment independently or in groups.

If there are thirty problems in the assignment, you might model and lead students through the first six.

"Watch me do the first two problems on the overhead and copy what I do." Then you demonstrate and explain.

"On the next two problems, I'll do the first half, and you do the second half of the problem." You demonstrate the first part and let students do the second part. Correct the problems and answer student questions or reteach based on student mistakes.

"Now do the next two problems on your own. Stop when you finish problem 6 so we can correct." Let all students do two problems while you monitor their performance. Then model or have individual students demonstrate the correct answer. Answer questions and provide any additional instructions.

If students are doing well, you can then assign the remaining problems as independent work. If many students are having problems, continue to work through the problems together until you are sure students understand the concepts and processes.

Develop a specific system that enables students to ask questions and get help during independent work periods (Scheuermann & Hall, 2008; Trussell, 2008).

It is important that students have a clear and efficient way to ask questions and get help as they do independent work. Notice that the following suggestions do not require students to raise their hands. This is deliberate. Although hand raising is perfectly acceptable during other activities like teacher-directed instruction, there are some problems with a traditional hand-raising procedure during independent work:

- It is physically difficult to keep a hand in the air for the three to five minutes it may take you to respond.
- The student is necessarily off-task while waiting for your help because he or she is unlikely to continue working with one hand raised in the air.
- Hand raising tends to draw more attention to a student, which may discourage some students from asking for help.

When students have a question about how to do something, they may feel that they cannot continue with their work until the question is answered. If you have not structured a way for students to ask questions, get answers, and get help when necessary, you will have higher rates of off-task behavior. For independent work periods in which you (or another adult—a coteacher or paraprofessional) are available to answer questions, develop and teach your students to use a predetermined visual signal rather than hand raising when they need assistance. You can have students put an upright book (not the book they need for the assignment) or a flag or sign on the corner of their desk. (See figures 3.9 and 3.10.)

Another way students can indicate they need assistance is to write their name on the board, along with the question or problem number they need help with. If several students

Figure 3.9
Flag as Signal for Needed Teacher Help

Figure 3.10
Upright Book as a Signal for Needed Teacher Help

have a question about the same item, you can gather those students together and provide assistance at one time instead of helping each one individually: "Sandra, Mark, and Dani, please come to my desk so we can figure out problem number 5." A caution with this procedure is that it requires students to get out of their seats. The students who will have the most questions are often the same ones who are most likely to misbehave if they are frequently out of their seats, so this procedure may be inappropriate for high-structure classes or if you have a few students who have significant behavioral challenges.

With the signals described here (or some variation), students can be trained to unobtrusively put up their signal, mark the question or problem they need help with, and continue working on other problems.

For independent work times when you are not available (perhaps you are working with a small group while other students work on independent assignments), you should devise strategies for students to ask and help each other. Be sure that students understand that talking is permitted only to get needed help on assignments. Implement this type of strategy gradually and with your supervision until you feel your students are responsible enough to continue assisting each other on their own.

In Conclusion

The day-to-day operation of your class may make the difference between success and failure for many of your students. It is one thing to have a plan and an entirely different thing to follow that plan on a day-to-day basis. Taking advantage of these procedures, laying them out for your students, and sticking to them will help your students succeed and will also help you maintain a better classroom environment. Each of the items in this chapter should be summarized for students on your comprehensive syllabus. (Writing a syllabus is covered in chapter 6, task 1.) A clear syllabus will be a cornerstone of your curriculum. With a proper syllabus and frequent reference to the policies it sets out, your students will not be able to complain they were unaware of something when it has clearly been presented to them on more than one occasion.

Organization Self-Assessment Checklist

Use this worksheet to identify which parts of the tasks described in this chapter you have completed. For any item that has not been completed, note what needs to be done to complete it. Then transfer your notes to your planning calendar in the form of specific actions you need to take (e.g., "September 5, finish arranging desks in the classroom"). A blank worksheet is provided on the DVD.

	Task	Notes and Implementation Ideas
☑	*TASK 1: Arrange the schedule of activities for each class period to maximize instructional time and responsible behavior.* I have evaluated my schedule by listing the subjects I teach and the length of class periods. Then I listed typical activities and the amount of time those activities take. I have used this information to: • Arrange my daily schedule to include a reasonable balance of teacher-directed work, independent work, and cooperative group activities • Arrange my daily schedule so that no one type of activity (e.g., teacher-directed work, independent work, or cooperative groups) lasts too long • Schedule independent work and cooperative group activities to immediately follow teacher-directed tasks I have identified and taken steps to address those times of the class or day when students are likely to misbehave, such as: ◦ Last hour of day ◦ Last five minutes of class	

☐	**TASK 2:** *Arrange the physical space in your classroom to promote positive student-teacher interactions and reduce disruptions.*
	
	I have arranged the physical space in my classroom in such a way to create a comfortable and functional space. I have achieved this by:
	
	   • Arranging desks in my classroom so that I can easily circulate throughout the room
	
	   • Arranging desks in my classroom to optimize the most common types of instructional activities students engage in and to reflect the level of structure my students require
	
	   • Arranging desks so they are not near high-traffic areas so that disruptions caused by activity in those areas will be kept to a minimum
		Waiting for room assignment for Spanish 3. May need to adjust desk arrangements for Spanish 1 if class size goes up.

☑	**TASK 3:** *Decide on a signal you can use to immediately quiet your students and gain their full attention.* I have identified an age-appropriate attention signal to use that has both auditory and visual components so that I can gain my students' full and immediate attention at any time during class. I have taught my students this signal and how to respond to it.	

TASK 4: Design efficient, effective procedures for beginning and ending the class period.

I understand that setting procedures for beginning and ending class allows me to use class time more efficiently and communicates to students that time in my class will not be wasted:

1. I have identified how I will begin class and the school day in a way that makes students feel welcome and has them going immediately to their seats to work on a productive task.

2. Students will be instructionally engaged while I take attendance.

3. I have set up procedures for dealing with tardiness that will ensure that tardy students will not disrupt class or greatly involve me.

4. I will not waste valuable class time by spending more than a minute or two on announcements and housekeeping tasks.

5. For dealing with students who do not have necessary materials or are otherwise unprepared, I have procedures that:

   • Ensure students can get needed materials in a way that does not disrupt instruction
   • Establish reasonable penalties to reduce the likelihood the students will forget materials in the future
   • Reduce the amount of time and energy I have to spend dealing with this issue

6. I have identified how I will deal with students returning after an absence so that they can easily find out what assignments they have missed and get any handouts and returned papers in a way that does not greatly involve me.

7. I have developed procedures for wrapping up at the end of the school day or class period that:

- Ensure students will not leave the classroom before they have organized their materials and completed any necessary cleanup tasks
- Ensure I have enough time to give students both positive and corrective feedback and set a positive tone for ending class

8. I have developed dismissal procedures that ensure students will not leave the classroom until they have been dismissed by me (not by the bell).

TASK 5: Design efficient, effective procedures for assigning, monitoring, and collecting student work.

I understand that implementing well-designed and well-organized strategies for assigning, monitoring, and collecting student work will let students know that I put a high value on their completing work, prompt more responsible student behavior regarding assigned tasks, and help me effectively manage student work without taking unreasonable amounts of time.

I have designed procedures for assigning classwork and homework that ensure students can easily find out information about the tasks they have been assigned.

I have developed procedures for students to check off completed tasks.

I have developed procedures for how I will return graded work to ensure that it is returned in a timely, legible, and confidential fashion.

I have designed efficient and effective procedures for dealing with late and missing assignments.

☑ TASK 6: *Manage independent work periods.*

As I set up my independent work periods, I will make sure that I do the following:

- Only assign independent work that I know students can do independently.

- Schedule independent work times in a way that maximizes on-task behavior (see task 1).

- Establish a clear vision of what student behavior should look and sound like during independent work times.

- Arrange to provide guided practice on tasks and assignments that I expect students to do independently.

- Develop a specific system for how students can ask questions and get help during independent work periods.

Chapter 4

Classroom Management Plan

Plan to encourage responsible behavior and to respond consistently to student misbehavior

By developing a classroom management and discipline plan before the school year begins, you set the stage to deal productively with the range of behaviors, both positive and negative, that students will exhibit in your classroom (Alberto & Troutman, 2006; Brown, 1998; Emmer, Anderson, & Worsham, 2003; Emmer, Evertson, & Anderson, 1980; Marshall, 2001; Scheuermann & Hall, 2008; Trussell, 2008).

An effective management and discipline plan is not a canned program or a static entity. It is a framework that supports a variety of rituals, routines, rules, consequences, and motivational techniques you can use to ensure that students are academically engaged and emotionally thriving. Though your plan should be in place before the school year begins, you will adjust your initial plan to meet the changing needs of your classes as the year progresses. Your plan will be somewhat different on the first day of school, the twentieth day of school, the day a new student comes to class, and the last day of school.

A system of rules and consequences provides specific information about what behavior is acceptable and what is not (Metzger, 2002). Unacceptable behavior leads to consequences. Consider an interstate highway. Simply telling people they need to drive safely isn't specific enough to provide guidance or clear enough to be enforceable. Therefore, most jurisdictions identify a specific speed deemed appropriate, and that speed is posted and enforced.

Posting rules and enforcing consequences does not guarantee compliance, but it does help manage the frequency and intensity of misbehavior. To return to the driving metaphor, assume the posted speed is 70 miles per hour, but it is reduced to 60 miles per hour through an urban area with a lot of on- and off-ramps. If the speed weren't posted, some drivers would continue at 70 miles per hour simply because they were unaware of the increased risk in the urban setting. The posted speed limit provides those drivers with the information they need to be compliant. Of course, some drivers will exceed that speed, but if they drive at 80 miles per hour in the 70 miles per hour zones, they may slow to 70 miles per hour in the 60 miles per hour zones. Thus, the posted rules reduce the number of drivers exceeding the limit and reduce the magnitude of the misbehavior of other drivers. In addition, once the drivers know the rules, the presence of a police car on the side of the road or in the next lane prompts careful following of the rules, which is why teacher monitoring of student behavior is also important (it is discussed in detail in chapter 7).

The most important and basic concept of this chapter is that preplanning your response to misbehavior will make your corrections more effective. This is true for both early-stage misbehavior and more chronic rule violations. By developing and mentally rehearsing the application of corrective consequences to various misbehaviors, you reduce the probability that you will be rattled, frustrated, or upset by student misbehavior (Spaulding, 1978).

Another concept to keep in mind as you work through this chapter is that traditional behavior management has typically consisted of trying to "make" students behave through reactive and punitive solutions such as administrator-assigned consequences. While reactive and punitive procedures are not bad or wrong and are necessary to teach students the boundaries between acceptable and unacceptable behavior, consequence-driven solutions have been shown to be the weakest variable you can manipulate to create behavioral change.

In this chapter, you will learn how to effectively design and deliver consequences, increasing the likelihood that you can address the vast majority of misbehaviors in your classroom without turning to administrator-assigned consequences. While consequences such as office disciplinary referrals and suspensions may be necessary in some cases (e.g., severe chronic misbehavior or when student safety is threatened or harmed), these consequences should be reserved for the most extreme circumstances. The more often they are used, the less likely they are to be effective, and they are often reinforcing for your more difficult students. ("Why Bother with a Positive Approach to Discipline?" in the Bonus Material folder on the DVD has more information on why punitive consequence often has limited effectiveness, especially with the most at-risk or behaviorally difficult students.) By clearly defining rules and consequences in your classroom management plan, you will create the foundation for appropriate behavior in your classroom, allowing you to manage the vast majority of student misbehavior in your own setting. Chapter 9 will help you in the event that individual students or a group of students are not responding to your classroom management plan and other efforts to promote responsible student behavior.

There are five tasks in this chapter:

Task 1: Adjust the structure of your management plan based on your needs and the needs of your students.

Task 2: Identify and post three to six classroom rules that will be used as the basis for providing positive and corrective feedback.

Task 3: Develop a plan for correcting early-stage misbehaviors.

Task 4: Develop consequences for rule violations.

Task 5: Know when and when not to use disciplinary referral.

Task 1: Adjust the Structure of Your Management Plan Based on Your Needs and the Needs of Your Students

The level of structure in your classroom management plan refers to the degree that you will need to orchestrate class activities and transitions and be hands-on throughout class to ensure the success of your students. To determine the level of structure necessary, at the end of this task you will evaluate your needs (exhibit 4.1) and the needs of the students you will be teaching (exhibit 4.2).

If you have a high need for structure (e.g., if you prefer minimal background noise and very orderly movement), you will be encouraged to have a highly orchestrated management plan, even if your students can responsibly handle a less structured setting. And if you personally have quite a bit of tolerance for noise and movement, you can reflect more on the needs of your students. The level of structure required for successful classroom management is determined largely by the risk factors of your student body. If you have large numbers of immature students or students who struggle with the course content, the risk factors are likely high and you will need a more structured class environment. If your classes have predominantly mature and independent students, you will be able to follow a more loosely structured plan.

Bear in mind that it is always better to err on the side of high structure. In general, research has shown that classrooms with more structure typically promote increases in appropriate academic and social behaviors (Simonsen, Fairbanks, Briesch, Myers, & Sugai, 2008). If the risk factors of your class are high and your management plan is not sufficiently structured with tightly orchestrated activities and transitions, student behavior will become problematic (Barbetta, Norona, & Bicard, 2005; Huston-Stein, Friedrich-Cofer, & Susman, 1977; Martella, Nelson, & Marchand-Martella, 2003). For example, although it is always a good idea to begin instruction quickly at the start of class, student behavior can deteriorate quickly in a class with higher risk factors when the beginning of class is not particularly structured. If your students have nothing to do for the first five minutes because you are taking attendance or getting class materials organized, they are likely to be talking and wandering out of their seats. This will make it much more difficult to get them under control when you are finished. For a high-structure class, it is much more advisable to begin instruction immediately after the bell rings, then provide a short assignment and take attendance once students demonstrate that they are engaged and working.

Consider Your Needs

Reflect on your personal style. Are there issues that you need to address in order to be comfortable in the classroom? For example, what is your tolerance for noise? A teacher with a high tolerance for noise still needs to teach students appropriate noise levels, but these levels might be higher than in some classrooms. This teacher is also unlikely to be rattled by activities where the noise level rises, such as in cooperative groups. For a teacher with a low tolerance for noise, this same level of activity in a class of thirty or more students without a high and clearly defined structure may provoke a feeling of chaos and concern that the class is spiraling out of control. The teacher may begin turning to increased punitive consequences or exhibit a level of stress and frustration that is not productive to the class environment. The difference here is not the behavior of the students but the needs and perception of the teacher. The teacher who knows he has a low tolerance for noise needs to create a management plan that will directly teach and ensure that students keep the noise level to a minimum. He must plan to monitor and provide feedback to students about the level of noise that is acceptable. This is especially true during activities such as cooperative groups and lab activities.

Complete the questions in exhibit 4.1 (a blank reproducible of this exhibit is on the DVD). This survey is not a scientific instrument, but rather a good way to reflect on the type of classroom setting you need in order to thrive as a positive and energetic force. There are no right answers to these questions. Assign yourself a score on a scale between 0 and 20 for each question. Plan to be honest with yourself about yourself.

Exhibit 4.1
Classroom Management and Discipline Planning Questionnaire

Read each question. Then assign yourself a score from 0 to 20, where 0 represents the answer on the left of the scale and 20 the answer on the right.

1. What is your tolerance for background noise?

I love to have
conversations in crowded,
noisy restaurants.

Holiday music in
department stores drives
me crazy after about 30 minutes.

0 1 2 3 4 5 6 7 8 9 10 11 12 13 14 ⑮ 16 17 18 19 20

2. What is your tolerance for individual voices (volume, pitch, whiny, mumbling, and so on)?

No style seems to bother
me—even when there are
several at once.

Some voices are like
fingernails on a chalkboard.

0 1 2 3 4 5 6 7 8 9 10 11 ⑫ 13 14 15 16 17 18 19 20

3. What is your tolerance for interruption?

I would be fine working as a
receptionist—managing
phones, people, and equipment.

When the phone
rings twice during dinner,
I want to scream.

0 1 2 ③ 4 5 6 7 8 9 10 11 12 13 14 15 16 17 18 19 20

4. What is your tolerance for background movement?

I thrive on the hustle and
bustle of downtown in a large
city during the holiday season.

I prefer to relax by
the side of a lake.

0 1 2 3 4 5 6 7 ⑧ 9 10 11 12 13 14 15 16 17 18 19 20

5. What is your ability to multitask without becoming flustered?

I love to do
three things
at once.

I do not like to
talk to anyone while
I am collating papers.

0 1 2 3 ④ 5 6 7 8 9 10 11 12 13 14 15 16 17 18 19 20

Total score __42__

- If you scored a total of 20 or less on this survey, you may be fine in any type of setting. As long as your students can responsibly handle low structure, you can establish a management plan that is less orchestrated. Proceed to the next section on determining your students' needs to see if this kind of low-structure management plan will address the needs of your students, or if they will need a medium- or high-structure plan.

- If you scored 21 to 59 on this survey, you probably do best in classrooms that are medium to high structure. You require some level of calm, orchestration, and predictability in order to feel under control and that your classroom is running smoothly. Proceed to the next section to determine the level of structure needed for your students in order to prompt responsible behavior and effort.

- If you scored 60 or more on this survey, you probably need more structure, even if your students can handle a less structured setting. If noise, interruption, and multitasking make you nervous or put you on edge, structure you classroom to keep these factors to

> **Note**
>
> In general, most teachers can plan for different classes using the same level of structure. However, if you know you will be teaching groups with highly different needs and risk factors throughout the day, plan to complete the students' needs evaluation for each group. For example, if you teach three periods of freshman remedial math classes and two periods of AP Calculus, these two distinct groups will likely require different levels of structure.
>
> In some cases, you may teach periods with the same material and grade level, but one class has highly mature and responsible students and the other has many immature students with behavioral concerns. In these instances, you will need to assess each group for the required level of structure.

a minimum so you can stay calm and positive. You may wish to complete the student needs survey simply out of interest, but regardless of the results, plan to implement a high-structure management plan.

Consider Your Students' Needs

The second consideration in determining the structure level of your management plan is the risk factors and needs of your students. Exhibit 4.2 helps you evaluate these factors (a blank form of this reproducible is on the DVD). An example of something that influences the level of structure your students need is the number of students in your class: you probably need a more structured management plan for a class of thirty students than for a class of fifteen. If you have significant numbers of immature or emotionally needy students, the risk factors are higher, so you need a more tightly structured plan. If your class is composed of predominantly mature and independent students, the risk factors are lower; a more loosely structured plan may be perfectly adequate.

Exhibit 4.2
Management and Discipline Planning

1. For each question, circle the number under the statement that best answers the question. When you are unsure about the answer to a question, circle the middle number.
2. Total the scores for all items. You should have a number between 0 and 120.
3. Use the scale at the end of the form to determine the most appropriate structure level for your classroom management plan.

Questions 1 to 6 relate to the population of the entire school:

1. How would you describe the overall behavior of students in your school?	Generally quite irresponsible. I frequently have to nag and/or assign consequences.	Most students behave responsibly, but about 10 percent put me in the position where I have to nag and/or assign consequences.	Generally responsible. I rarely find it necessary to nag and/or assign consequences.
	10	(5)	0
2. What percentage of students in your school qualify for free or reduced lunch?	60 percent or more	10 to 60 percent	Less than 10 percent
	(10)	5	0
3. What percentage of students in your school typically move in and/or out of the school during the course of the school year?	50 percent or more	10 to 50 percent	Less than 10 percent
	(10)	5	0
4. How would you describe the overall attitude of students toward school?	A large percentage hate school and ridicule the students who are motivated.	It's a mix, but most students feel okay about school.	The vast majority of students like school and are highly motivated.
	10	(5)	0
5. How would you describe the overall nature of the interactions between students and adults in your school?	There are frequent confrontations, which include sarcasm and/or disrespect.	There is a mix, but most interactions are respectful and positive.	The vast majority of interactions are respectful and positive.
	10	(5)	0
6. How would you describe the level of interest and support provided by the parents of students in your school?	Many parents are openly antagonistic, and many show no interest in school.	Most parents are at least somewhat supportive of school.	The majority are interested, involved, and supportive of what goes on in the school.
	10	(5)	0

Questions 7–11 relate to students in your class this year. Use your most difficult class, or if you are doing this before the school year begins, simply give your best guess.

7. What grade level do you teach?	Ninth grade **20**	Tenth grade **5**	Eleventh or twelfth grade **(0)**
8. How many students do you have in your class?	30 or more **(10)**	23 to 30 **5**	22 or fewer **0**
9. What is the reputation of this group of students from previous years? For example, if you teach tenth grade, what was the reputation of these students as ninth graders?	This class is going to be awful. **10**	It's a mix, but most students work hard and cooperate. **(5)**	This group is very hard working and cooperative. **0**
10. How many students in your class have been identified as severely emotionally disturbed (SED)? Note: This label varies from state to state.	Two or more **10**	One **(5)**	Zero **0**
11. Not including students identified as SED, how many students have a reputation for chronic discipline problems?	Three or more **10**	One or two **5**	Zero **(0)**

Total: _60_

If your total score is:	Your risk factors are:
0 to 30	*Low,* which means your students can probably be successful with a classroom management plan that involves low, medium, or high structure. The level of structure can be defined by your teaching style.
31 to 60	*Medium,* which means that for your students to be successful, your classroom management plan should involve medium or high structure.
61 to 120	*High,* which means that for your students to be successful, your classroom management plan should involve high structure. Regardless of your personal preference or style, your students will probably benefit from a detailed, systematic, and organized classroom management plan.

Identify the Level of Structure You Will Use

In the previous chapter and as you progress through the remainder of this book, you will find references to how tasks will be implemented differently depending on your and your students' needs for structure. Use table 4.1 to determine which level of structure is indicated based on your responses to the previous two exhibits. Find the column that describes the level of structure indicated for your needs, then find the box that meets the row that corresponds to the level of structure needed for your students.

If your needs indicate medium structure, for example, and your students' needs indicate high structure, you would find where the Medium column and the High row intersect. High structure is indicated for your management plan.

Note that the only time low structure is indicated is when you have identified that both your needs and those of your students are low. Also remember that if your plan indicates low or medium structure, you can always begin with a higher level of structure. However, the reverse is not true: your students will likely struggle if you implement a management plan with lower structure than is indicated by either your or your students' needs.

Apply the level of structure to your management plan.
Use the following information as you implement tasks in this book:

- If you have a class that needs high structure, implement all of the tasks in this book.

- If you have a medium-structure class, implement most of the tasks in this book, except for those that your students clearly do not need. You may decide to implement them in a somewhat less orchestrated or teacher-directed fashion than may be needed with a high-structure class.

- If you have a low-structure class, you can implement only the tasks you believe will be needed to motivate your class and ignore any procedures that you feel will be unnecessary to ensure effective use of instructional time.

Err on the side of being too highly structured. This rule applies especially to the beginning of the year. By starting the school year in a highly structured way, you increase the likelihood that students will engage in high levels of academic engagement and appropriate behavior later in the year (Emmer et al., 1980; Evertson & Emmer, 1982). In addition, you can easily move to less structure if you find your class to be highly responsible.

Table 4.1.
Determining the Best Structure to Meet Your and Your Students' Needs

		Your Needs		
		Low	Medium	High
Your students' needs	Low	Low	Medium	High
	Medium	Medium	Medium	High
	High	High	High	High

For example, in your end-of-class routine, it is more structured to excuse students by rows or table than to simply say, "Class, you are excused. See you tomorrow." During the first two weeks of school, you excuse the class by small groups. You find that these students are a highly respectful and responsible group, so you compliment them for their maturity and explain that their positive behavior means you are comfortable releasing them as a whole class. You state that you know they will respect physical safety and use quiet voices. This procedure has provided an opportunity to acknowledge and reward the students for their positive behavior.

Now imagine that on the first day of school you excuse the entire class at the same time, assuming that this group of students will handle the procedure appropriately because of their grade level or the type of class being taught. The students in fact are loud and unruly. The next day you are required to enforce a more highly structured dismissal, which is more difficult because students expect the previous day's procedure. You are also taking away a more student-directed procedure, which can be perceived as unfair or punitive by your students.

Make adjustments as the year progresses.

Plan to evaluate your students' need for structure at various times throughout the year—for example, how well students are meeting your expectations sometime during the fourth or fifth week of school and again after winter and spring breaks. If a significant number of students are not meeting expectations, you may need to move to a higher level of structure and organization (Barbetta et al., 2005; Simonsen et al., 2008). During the last month of school, student behavior predictably deteriorates somewhat. Rather than relaxing your structure, it is probably better to increase it at that time.

Task 2: Identify and Post Three to Six Classroom Rules That Will Be Used as a Basis for Providing Positive and Corrective Feedback

Posted classroom rules communicate to students that you have specific expectations. Therefore, your rules should provide objective descriptions of the behaviors you expect from students and inform them that certain behaviors are unacceptable and will result in corrective consequences (Malone & Tietjens, 2000; McLeod, Fisher, & Hoover, 2003). Because these rules should serve as the basis for implementing consequences for the most frequent misbehaviors, you must develop them in such a way that if students follow the rules, the most likely misbehaviors will not occur. This means that before you develop your classroom rules, you need to identify the misbehaviors that you think are most likely to occur. To do this, following our guidelines for brainstorming the most common behaviors you see in your classroom will help you determine the most frequent misbehaviors to consider as you develop your rules. The list you develop will also help guide your thinking with other tasks as you develop your management plan.

Begin by brainstorming the common misbehaviors you see in your classroom. Include the range of behaviors that occur: arguing, physical horseplay, pencil tapping, blurting out, students out of their seats at inappropriate times, students arriving to class without materials, passive work refusal, and so on. Be as specific and descriptive as possible. Rather than just putting "disruptive behaviors" or "defiance," explain what common disruptions and acts of defiance occur.

If it is the middle of the year, consider your current students and the behaviors that prevent your classroom from running as smoothly as you would like. You may wish to list only the misbehaviors from your most problematic class because it is probably more manageable to start tweaking your management plan in one setting before applying the strategies and skills in other settings.

If it is the summer or the beginning of the school year and you do not yet know your students and the common misbehaviors they demonstrate, consider classes from previous years and the misbehaviors you would have liked to have seen corrected from the very beginning of the year. Think about the grade and the typical developmental level of students in your classes. Also consider your schedule and whether there are specific routines, procedures for managing work, and other activities or transitions that seem to be associated with an increase in inappropriate behavior. If you are new to the school or have never taught a particular class or grade level before, you may find it useful to speak to another teacher who has taught similar classes to find out the most frequent concerns. List the common misbehaviors in exhibit 4.3 (see the DVD for a blank reproducible of this form).

Exhibit 4.3
Common Misbehaviors in My Class

List the common misbehaviors you have identified:

Off-topic talking: Before class starts, students chat. Takes a few minutes to get them all focused on class. Small groups also tend to lose focus on work and instead talk about other things.

Arguing: A few students are always trying to get me to reduce the amount of homework, cancel quizzes, extend deadlines, etc.

Missing materials: Has been a problem at the start of each semester.

After completing your list, cross out any behaviors that only one or two students exhibit. After your rules are in place, you may want to address these misbehaviors using the tools and strategies in chapter 9. Your classroom rules and other components of your management plan should provide the foundation for a productive and efficient classroom. Your management plan will be designed to keep things running smoothly the majority of the time for the majority of your students. Therefore, the rules should address the misbehaviors that more students commonly exhibit in a particular class or grade level. Naturally, a small number of students may need more individualized planning. However, you may also notice that the adjustments to your management plan will create a significant positive effect even with the most difficult students. As your classes begin demonstrating more appropriate behavior and effort as a whole, you may observe that the students who chronically misbehave also begin demonstrating appropriate behavior. They see more consistent modeling of the right thing and are less frequently drawn off track by a classroom that is chaotic or by peers who are out of control.

Once you have brainstormed misbehaviors, begin thinking about three to six rules that will cover the majority of the listed misbehaviors. You should have no more than six rules; if you have too many rules (e.g., one for each misbehavior you have listed in exhibit 4.3), students will not be able to keep track of them. In addition, a long list of rules sets a negative and adversarial tone when you present them to the students. Therefore, the rules should be broad enough to cover multiple misbehaviors that are similar. You do not need a rule for every possible misbehavior that might occur—only those that are the most likely to occur, such as off-task behavior, minor disruptions, or not having materials.

Here is a sample set of rules:

1. Come to class every day that you are not seriously ill.
2. Arrive on time with paper, pencil or pen, textbook, and a notebook with a divider for science.
3. Keep hands, feet, and objects to yourself.
4. Follow directions the first time they are given.
5. Stay on task during all work times.

Use the remaining guidelines in this task to develop your three to six classroom rules.

Decide who will help develop the rules.

The first decision is whether you are going to develop the rules yourself or work them out with your students. This decision is really a matter of style and expediency; both teacher-designed and student-designed rules have high correlations with teacher effectiveness (Emmer et al., 2002). An advantage of student-developed rules is that the process itself may give students a greater sense of ownership in the classroom. There are disadvantages as well—for example:

* No rules are in place for the first day of school.
* It may be difficult keeping track of multiple sets of rules if you teach more than one class.
* Students may not come up with the rules you feel you need to have an orderly classroom.

If you have not involved students in rule development before, it is probably best to design the rules yourself. However, if you like the idea of involving students and have been successful doing so in the past, you certainly should feel free to continue. Regardless of the process used to develop the rules, be aware that when you discuss rules with the students, you need to involve the class in a discussion about why the rules are needed to ensure that misbehavior does not interfere with anyone's success in the classroom. Later in this chapter, there is more information and examples of how to involve students in this discussion.

If you will develop rules with your students, plan some rules or concepts ahead of time that are nonnegotiable for you—those that need to be included in some form. Then you can work with students to develop the wording of the rules that cover those topics or say something like, "We will include these two rules because they are essential for our classroom to function effectively, and now we will work together to develop the rest." Another possibility is to brainstorm possibilities with students and tell them that you will take their list and recommendations and make the final decision about which rules to include.

State the rules positively.

Positively stated rules communicate both high expectations and an assumption of compliance, and they set a positive tone. They also put the attention and focus on the positive behavior rather than have students think about what they shouldn't be doing. An example of a positively stated rule is, "Stay on task during work times" rather than "No side conversations during work times."

One or two of your rules may be impossible to state positively, for example: "No food or drink in the computer room." If this is the case, one or two negatively stated rules are acceptable, but make sure that most rules are stated positively.

Be aware that if you allow students to help develop classroom rules, you will have to guide the group in coming up with a manageable number of positively stated rules. Some groups of students will tend to develop a laundry list of negatively stated rules. Thus, you may want to start by having the class brainstorm possibilities, then state each in positive terms (if possible), and then select a set of the three to six most important rules.

Rules should be specific and refer to observable behaviors.

Given that rules will be enforced with the application of consequences, you need to have rules that describe specific behaviors, not attitudes, traits, or conclusions. "Arrive on time with all of your materials" is specific and observable. "Be responsible" is not. "Stay on task during all work times" is observable. "Always do your best" is not. Nonspecific rules like "Be responsible" can have different meanings to different people and will create strife if you enforce a behavior you found to be irresponsible that your class did not.

Your classroom rules should be different from your Guidelines for Success, which are more global goals. An exhortation like "Do your best" is something you want students to strive toward rather than a rule. It is too broad, subjective, and open to interpretation to be a rule that has consequences tied to it. While you may have a discussion with a student about your perception that she is not doing her best, you are not going to impose penalties on her for not doing so. Rules must be specific because infractions of those rules have consequences. The rules are specific behavioral expectations that you will enforce with reasonable consequences. Guidelines for Success are more like beacons pointing your students toward the lifelong traits you wish to inspire in them.

Rules must be applicable.

The rules you post must be applicable throughout the class period. "Keep hands, feet, and objects to yourself" can apply throughout the entire class period. "Raise your hand before speaking" may apply only to teacher-directed instruction, and you would not expect students to do this when working in cooperative groups. Therefore, "Raise your hand before speaking" should not be posted as a rule, but it may be taught as one of your classroom expectations specific to teacher-directed instruction (see chapter 5 for more details). A rule that may not apply to the entire class period, such as, "Arrive on time with all your materials," can be kept if there is no portion of the class period that invalidates it. Although "Arrive on time with all your materials" focuses only on the beginning of class, it is a rule that affects the entire class period. If you believe a rule like this is important to have posted, include it on your list.

Post the rules in a prominent, visible location.

Certainly include the rules in your syllabus, but posting them in the classroom creates even more of a sense of permanence and importance. Posting also enables you to point to them whenever they are discussed and allows you to be brief in some of your reminders about minor violations. If during a teacher-directed portion of a lesson, for example, students are getting restless and off-task, you can give a quick reminder as you point to your rules, such as, "Class, rule 5! Please stay focused on the lesson."

When you have to speak to an individual student about a rule violation, point or refer to the rules as you speak to him or her. The act of orienting the student's attention to the rules reduces the sense of negative personalization—that you are attacking the student—and implies that you are simply enforcing the classroom rules. In addition, the act of indicating the rules decreases any intense eye contact between you and the student. This make-eye-contact, break-eye-contact pattern can also reduce the possibility that the student will argue with you about the rules.

Plan to teach your rules using a variety of formats.

Once you have your classroom rules, you need to teach students what the rules are and how they can demonstrate that they are following them (Mendler & Curwin, 1999). Whether or not students were involved in developing the rules, it is essential to engage them in an age-appropriate discussion of why each rule is needed. These steps involve more than just reading the rules to the students and telling them why they need to follow them, which for many students is unlikely to sink in and may set an adversarial tone. The best way to help students understand your rules is to demonstrate specific behaviors that are examples of following and not following the rules. Then students can contribute their thoughts about why that rule is necessary and helpful to their education.

Through the use of positive and negative examples, you can teach students to understand your interpretation of the rule and how you will make judgments about whether a particular behavior breaks a rule. You might sit at a desk and show your students what you think not paying attention looks like in contrast to what paying attention looks like. Can they slouch down in their chairs? Put their head on the desk? Fidget or doodle? Students may not know what *irresponsible* looks or sounds like, especially when another teacher may have accepted a far wider range or a drastically different set of behaviors for what is responsible or irresponsible. Therefore, teaching students *your* rules and the line between acceptable and unacceptable behavior may require teaching some things that you feel are unnecessary, but it is better to overteach than underteach. This kind of direct teaching and modeling of your rules will help make a concept that might be abstract more concrete and easily understood. It might even make it fun.

Following are other suggestions for ways that you might teach or clarify your rules, as well as suggestions for providing a rationale for each rule.

Create scenarios of some behaviors that follow the rules and some that violate the rules. Place them on a worksheet or activity cards. Have students work individually, in partners, or in groups to discuss whether each scenario is an example or nonexample of following the rules and to what degree the rule was broken if it is a nonexample.

Act out examples and nonexamples of following the rules. Have students give thumbs up and thumbs down for nonexamples. Make sure to demonstrate extreme behaviors as well as ones that are more subtle and require more consideration and judgment from the students. If you wish to make this more complicated and advanced for students, have them rate the examples and nonexamples, holding up one finger if the example was perfectly appropriate, two fingers for appropriate but could have been more respectful or overt, three fingers for mildly inappropriate, and four fingers for extremely inappropriate. You could model a student's reaction when you direct him to sit in his assigned seat and he reacts in one of the following ways:

- Says, "Make me," and doesn't go to his seat.
- Goes to his seat but scowls and doesn't say anything.
- Goes to his seat after saying "Okay."
- Begins going to his seat but takes the longest route and says "hi" to others on the way.
- Goes to his seat and within a minute gets out again.
- Mutters "stupid teacher" and walks to his seat.
- Asks, "Why can't we sit somewhere else today?"

The students then judge whether the student follows the rule of "Follows directions without arguing."

For each rule, have students create a list of reasons why it will be helpful to the class as well as important later in life with work or other aspects of their lives.

This can be done individually, in partners, in small groups, or with the whole class. For example, ask students to brainstorm why the rule "Come to class every day that you are not seriously ill" is important for class and for later life. Guide students to think about things like:

"It is important so we don't miss important information in class."

"We need to come to class to earn credits."

"If you skip or are absent a lot in a job, you will get fired. We are developing habits for work."

Use real-life examples to provide a rationale for each rule and engage in a discussion about why each rule is needed.

Explain to students that they will encounter rules throughout their lives. When they are driving, they will need to follow the rules or get ticketed and possibly lose their license. One common rule is to drive on the right side of the road. Ask students why this rule is important. They will come up with responses like, "To keep people safe," "So people don't run into each other," and "Because if everyone just drove on either side, traffic would be even more crazy than it already is." Explain that your classroom rules are like the rule of driving on the right side of the road. They are designed to keep people safe, make sure that no one is interfering or getting in the way of someone else's learning, and keep the instruction and class activities running as smoothly as possible.

Task 3: Develop a Plan for Correcting Early-Stage Misbehaviors

Early-stage behaviors are those that are not yet a pattern. Student violation of a rule at the beginning of the year and any other time it appears that students are violating a rule because they may not understand it should be addressed as an early-stage misbehavior. This must be dealt with differently from when a student is knowingly or intentionally violating a rule. Once a particular misbehavior has become habitual, it is past the early stage and is more difficult to correct.

This task includes a list of potential corrective consequences for early-stage misbehaviors. For an early-stage misbehavior, the correction must be instructional more than a consequence or punishment (Lovitt, 1978; Sponder, 1993). To return to the speeding analogy, if the speed limit on a stretch of highway is changed, the highway patrol on that section of highway probably would not issue tickets on the first day of the new law; rather, they would issue warnings for a period of time. Once the highway patrol was certain that the new speed limit was widely known, they would begin to ticket normally. In the next task, information will be provided on the type of consequences you might use when the students know and understand the rules and should receive a consequence that comes with a cost—the type of consequence drivers receive for exceeding the speed limit on a section of highway in which the speed limit has been posted and in force for more than a week or two.

The basic rule for early-stage misbehavior is to try the easy solution first. In general, the easiest correction strategies are simply to give the student information about what he or she should be doing at that moment. If you try a simple correction strategy and it works, the problem is solved. If the misbehavior continues over a period of days or weeks, you are no longer working with an early-stage problem, and you need to look at the situation more systematically and analytically.

What follows is a series of correction strategies that are appropriate for early-stage misbehaviors. These are especially useful in the first week of school, when a new student arrives, or when a new behavior occurs that is not covered by your classroom rules. If you take the time to familiarize yourself with these strategies, you will be prepared to respond effectively to an early-stage misbehavior.

Proximity

The proximity correction strategy is based on the same rationale as having highway patrol officers on the roadways. Most people, even those who tend to exceed the speed limit, are more likely to follow the speed limit when a police officer is near. In the classroom, proximity simply involves moving to where the misbehavior is. The misbehavior is likely to cease as you get near because your proximity will prompt the students to stop exhibiting the misbehavior and start exhibiting the desired behavior. The more you move throughout your room in unpredictable ways, the better able you will be to correct misbehavior through proximity (Marzano, 2003).

If you are presenting a lesson and a couple of students begin talking to each other rather than listening to you, for example, you might start walking over to that part of the room while continuing to present the lesson. If the students quit talking while you are on the way, continue the lesson from where you are, and then move to a different place in the room or back to the front. After a few minutes, make eye contact with the students who had been talking. The eye contact after they are behaving appropriately communicates that you notice and acknowledge the appropriate behavior and is less potentially embarrassing to the students than a public compliment.

Ideally proximity can work both passively and actively. The example shows how moving around the class can prevent misbehavior. Moreover, if your students are aware of your tendency to patrol the class or move about during your lessons, they will be much less likely to misbehave given the chance that you may be nearby.

Gentle Verbal Reprimand

To use a gentle verbal reprimand is simply to go over to the student or students engaged in misbehavior and quietly tell them what they should be doing at that moment. If the two students in the scenario do not stop talking as you move in their direction, you might say to them, without drawing undue attention, "Johanna, Alexander, if you have something to say, you need to raise your hand and wait to be called on."

Effective verbal reprimands have the following features:

- They are short. They cause only a brief interruption in the lesson.
- They are given when you are physically near misbehaving students, not from across the room.
- Their tone and content are respectful.
- They are clear and unequivocal.
- They state the expected behavior rather than accusing the student of misbehavior.
- They are given in a way that creates the impression of privacy. They should be heard without making the students feel they are on display and without making the rest of the class feel that a secret is being told.

Discussion

Sometimes you may need to talk with a student about misbehavior in a way that is more detailed and lengthy than a reprimand. If a student makes a disrespectful comment as you are presenting a lesson, for example, you may want to talk with the student about the importance of treating others with respect. Discussions are usually best if they occur at a neutral time. There are several reasons that having a discussion immediately after a misbehavior tends to be ineffective: you leave the rest of the class waiting, you give the misbehaving student immediate attention that can be affirming, the student may be defensive, and you are likely to be somewhat frustrated or angry at that moment. It is far more effective to wait until later, when the class is engaged in independent work or even after class, and then privately speak with the student. During your meeting, be sure to discuss with the student better ways that he or she could handle similar situations in the future. If you feel a misbehavior warrants a longer discussion but needs to be addressed immediately, say something like, "Nathan, that was disrespectful. We will discuss this after class."

Family Contact

An important and potentially effective early-stage correction procedure is family contact. When making contact with the family about misbehavior, keep the following suggestions in mind:

- Provide an objective description of the behavior, not a judgment about the student.
- Suggest that it would be useful for the family to discuss the behavior with the student and communicate the expectation that the student will behave more responsibly in the future.
- Avoid implying that the student should be punished at home or that the family should make the student behave.

- Create a sense that you and the family can work as partners in helping the student reduce misbehavior and succeed in your class.

Exhibit 4.4 illustrates a format you may use to prepare for a call to a family (a reproducible of this form is on the DVD). The handwritten text is a possible way to present each part of the call.

Be aware that it is also important to have positive, or at least neutral, contact with the family so that when they hear from you, it isn't always about the child's problem behavior.

Exhibit 4.4
Early-Stage Problems—Family Contact

1. Introduce yourself and provide an appropriate greeting:

Hello, Mrs. Thompson? This is Mr. McLemore, Rasheed's teacher. How are you today? I'll bet that new baby is keeping you very busy. How is she doing? May I take just a moment of your time?

2. Inform the family that you are calling about a problem:

I am calling because I wanted to speak with you about a problem that has been going on at school.

3. Describe the problem (avoid labeling or passing judgment on the child):

For the last two days, Rasheed has not been doing his work in class. He sits at his desk and stares out the window, talks with his neighbor, and plays with his pencil. When I remind him to get to work, he will work if I am standing right there, but as soon as I go to do something else, he quits working again. Today he didn't finish any of his assignments.

4. Describe why the behavior is a problem, keeping the focus on the student, not on yourself or the other students. Emphasize that you know the student can be successful:

I am concerned because Rasheed is a very able student. I don't want him to develop the bad habit of wasting class time. To succeed at school, he will need to learn to keep his attention on his work.

5. If appropriate, ask whether the family has any insight into why the behavior may be occurring. If they share with you, adjust the remainder of this call based on what you learn:

One of the reasons I am calling is to find out if you know of anything that might be bothering Rasheed or that could be distracting him from his classwork.

6. Make suggestions about how the family might help the child:

I am not calling so that you will punish Rasheed. I am just concerned about him and hope you will talk to him about the problem. I know that he is capable of being successful in my class, but he has to keep his attention focused and do his work. Please tell him I called and that I look forward to seeing him tomorrow. I will call you in a few days to let you know how he is doing. Feel free to call me as well. The best time to reach me is between 3:30 and 4:00 any afternoon but Tuesday.

    Date of this contact: *September 27*

    Notes on the contact: *Mrs. Thompson couldn't tell me any particular reason that Rasheed has been so inattentive the last two days. She said she would talk to him, find out if anything is wrong, and encourage him to pay attention to his work.*

Humor

Humor can be a powerful and effective way to respond to misbehavior, especially with older students. For example, consider a situation in which a student makes a smart-aleck comment on the second day of school as you are presenting a lesson. If you are quick-witted enough, you might be able to respond to the student's comment in a way that will make the student himself laugh, and a tense moment will be diffused. However, you should not use sarcasm or ridicule. The sensitive use of humor brings people closer together. Sarcasm or ridicule makes a student feel hostile and angry that you made a joke at his expense.

If you do use humor in response to a misbehavior, you should plan on talking to the student later to make sure that he understands that his behavior was not acceptable and that he knows you expect him to behave more responsibly in the future. In addition, you can check to see that you did not embarrass the student with your humorous comment.

For example, in a situation similar to the one above, you might say something like this:

Thomas, today in class you made a comment, and then I made a joke out of what you said. First, I want to make sure that I did not embarrass you. Good, I'm glad I didn't. I owe it to all students to treat them as respectfully as I expect them to treat me. If I ever do anything that feels disrespectful to you, please come and talk to me about it. Now, I need to remind you to raise your hand when you have something to say in class and make an effort to see that your comments are respectful. I appreciate humor in the classroom, and I suspect that you will be someone who will not only contribute to our lessons, but also get us to see the humor in different situations as well. Thanks for taking the time to talk to me. I'm looking forward to seeing you in class tomorrow.

Restitution

The goal of restitution is for a misbehaving student to learn that if her behavior causes damage, she needs to repair that damage. A student who is rude to a guest speaker, for example, should be required to apologize to the guest speaker in writing, on the telephone, or in person. If you use this strategy, try to make it clear to the student that what you are asking her to do (in this case, apologize to the guest speaker) is not punishment but reparation—an attempt to repair any damage that might have been done on her part.

Conclusion

Whichever correction strategy you use to respond to an early-stage misbehavior, be sure that when the students who engaged in the misbehavior behave responsibly, you give them positive feedback. Students need to see that you notice positive behavior more than negative behavior (McLeod et al., 2003; Ridley & Walther, 1995). Also, remember that if one or more of these strategies do not solve the problem quickly, you will need to develop and implement an intervention plan that is based on a more thoughtful analysis of the misbehavior (see chapter 9).

Task 4: Develop Consequences for Rule Violations

When you are sure that students understand your rules, plan to move from informative early-stage correction techniques to consequences that impose a penalty for breaking a rule. These consequences need to be preplanned with certain considerations in mind, or there is a high probability that you may inadvertently reinforce misbehavior (Lovitt, 1978). Many consequences, for example, fall into traps that actually increase the likelihood of repeat misbehavior, such as giving the student too much attention, providing the student with a feeling of power if you lose emotional control, or allowing the student to escape something aversive.

The following suggestions can help you choose and implement effective corrective consequences that will help students learn that engaging in misbehavior has a cost associated with it. Give a lot of thought to what the consequence for each rule violation should be and how to implement each consequence effectively using the suggestions in this task. Look at the list of common misbehaviors you developed in exhibit 4.3 to help determine preplanned consequences for your most frequent rule violations. Identify what should happen if a student does not arrive on time with all materials, for example, or appropriate consequences for tardiness and speaking out of turn (Ma & Willms, 2004).

Remember that the consequences in your classroom management plan are designed to address and prevent the vast majority of student misbehaviors. Some students may exhibit chronic misbehavior outside of what is addressed by these procedures. Refer to the strategies in chapter 9 to address these chronic misbehaviors. However, the strong foundation you develop in this chapter for implementing rules and consequences with your students will help ensure that techniques for chronic misbehavior remain individualized and manageable rather than becoming unwieldy strategies you need to implement with your whole class.

> **Note**
>
> If you developed classroom rules with your students, this step should involve student input as well. If you developed rules by yourself, you can decide whether to involve students in determining consequences.

Plan to implement the corrective consequence consistently.

If corrective consequences are going to reduce purposeful or habitual misbehavior, they must be implemented consistently. When you implement a corrective consequence only some of the time, the consequence, no matter how severe, is not likely to change the behavior. In fact, it may even make things worse than if there were no consequence at all. Any time a student violates a rule and does not receive the designated consequence, he is likely to feel a great sense of satisfaction. Getting away with misbehavior can be great fun, and the student may find he likes to see how frequently he can engage in the behavior and not get caught.

Teachers tend to implement corrective consequences based on an accumulation of misbehavior. Teacher emotion, not a series of rules, controls classroom consequences.

What the student got away with five times might be the last straw the sixth time, but the consequence will seem to come from out of the blue to the student. While this is understandable behavior on the part of the teacher and can happen to anyone, it will not create a disciplined environment in the class. To change purposeful or habitual misbehavior, you need to define specific behaviors that are not acceptable and then implement corrective consequences for them every time, regardless of how you feel about the behavior.

Your goal here is to develop clear expectations of what behaviors are unacceptable so that you can be consistent with your students. If you are concerned about disruptions, specify the precise behaviors you consider disruptive and connect the concept of disruption to one of the positively stated rules. As always, be sure to identify positive examples of nondisruptive behavior and class participation.

Make sure the corrective consequence fits the severity and frequency of the misbehavior.

When deciding on the corrective consequence that you will implement, make sure to choose one that matches the severity of the problem (Wolfgang & Glickman, 1986). Choose a consequence that fits even the mildest example of the rule violation. All too often, teachers pick a consequence that is so harsh they are unwilling to implement it when the occasion arises. For example, a teacher who says, "Now, LaVona, stop that because I do not want to have to give you a detention," is demonstrating inconsistency. In this case, she is letting the student get away with it, but in some cases she may not. The consequence should be mild enough that you will be comfortable implementing it every time a student exhibits an irresponsible behavior. When determining the severity of a consequence, err on the side of making consequences too mild because you may not follow through if the consequence is too harsh.

Whatever corrective consequence you choose, plan to implement the consequence in the same way for all the behavior within that category and with any student who violates that rule. In other words, if you have decided to deduct a point, all disruptive acts should result in a loss of one point. Do not create a situation in which some disruptive acts cost one point and some cost three points. You will find yourself having to explain why you feel the acts are of different severities and deserve different penalties. If you decide to use time owed as a consequence for a student who tends to be disrespectful, have each infraction equal the same amount of time owed (for example, fifteen seconds owed after class). Do not issue fifteen seconds in some instances and several minutes in others. Again, if you err on the side of consequences that are too mild, you are much more likely to follow through than if the consequences are too harsh. Also, keep in mind that a student may exhibit the behavior several times, and if the consequence is fairly severe, say, a detention, you probably cannot assign several detentions to the same student in one class period. But if the student is disruptive three times, you can impose fifteen seconds for each incident.

Plan to implement the consequence unemotionally.

Some students have learned that there is a high probability that they can make adults frustrated, hurt, or angry. For some students, this is virtually an invitation to do so as often as they can. If you get angry when correcting a student, your anger may reinforce the student's misbehavior. When a student is seeking a sense of power, seeing an adult frustrated or exasperated can be highly satisfying. For this student, getting an adult angry on a regular basis can provide a huge sense of power and control. You must strive to implement corrective consequences unemotionally so your reactions do not give any students the idea that they can have power over you by misbehaving.

One way to prepare yourself to deliver a calm, unemotional response is to mentally role-play how you would handle specific misbehaviors in your classroom. Think of situations that have recently occurred in your classroom and your list of common misbehaviors (exhibit 4.3). Consider situations in which you may have responded with a frustrated, upset response or any situation in which a power struggle ensued. Then visualize an unemotional response to each situation, thinking about how you would deliver corrections or consequences calmly and quickly. You could also role-play scenarios with a colleague by describing the student's misbehavior and having the colleague act it out, with you acting out your preplanned response. Certain student misbehaviors, like defiance, trigger an emotional response from most people, and without preplanning and practice, you may find it difficult to counter the instinct to react with anger, frustration, or disappointment. Visualizing and role playing will help you build automaticity so that you do not have to think as hard about how to deliver an appropriate response when the situation presents itself.

Plan to interact with the student briefly at the time of the misbehavior without arguing.

When any student breaks a rule, your interaction with that student should be brief. Simply state the rule and the consequence: "Lucy, the rule is to stay on task during work times. You will owe thirty seconds after class." A common mistake is to explain and justify. The student may ask you for such information. Resist doing so. Any explanations should already be self-evident from your instruction because you have pretaught your rules and consequences. The reasons for the consequence can be analyzed in a later conversation with the student.

Sometime during the first few days of school, let the students know that if anyone ever wants to speak to you about something they think is unfair, they can make an appointment to see you before or after school. Once you have made this clear, simply remind any student who tries to argue that he can make an appointment to see you; then resume teaching. It is imperative not to let your students draw you into explaining your actions, consequences, or reasoning. That transfers the power to them and lets them know that they can disrupt class by misbehaving and making you explain yourself.

Although keeping interactions brief may be a difficult habit to get into, you will find that it allows you to keep your focus where it belongs: on teaching and providing positive feedback to all students who are meeting your expectations. The frequency of your positive feedback must far outweigh your negative feedback. Think about the consequence you plan to use for a targeted misbehavior. If you cannot imagine implementing that consequence without lengthy explanations or negotiations at the time of the misbehavior, consider a different consequence.

The following sections contain descriptions of effective corrective consequences that you can implement in a high school classroom. Each description includes a brief explanation of the consequence and how to

> **Note**
> *Never* use a corrective consequence that humiliates or ridicules the student, and avoid using academic tasks as corrective consequences (such as extra math homework or writing an essay). You do not want students to associate academic work with punishment!

use it. When using corrective consequences, be sure to assign them consistently and calmly, interacting with the student as briefly as possible (Orange, 2005).

Loss of Point

If you use the behavior grading procedures presented in chapter 2, you have already set your class up so that certain infractions result in the loss of a point. In this system, each student starts the beginning of the week with a preestablished number of points—say, fifteen out of a total weekly possible of twenty. Then during the week, each singled-out example of positive behavior adds a point and each rule violation subtracts a point from the student's total.

One of the biggest difficulties for high school teachers, as compared with elementary teachers, is that there are relatively few corrective consequences that the teacher can implement. One advantage of behavior grading is that you now have a mild corrective consequence that can be implemented consistently for low-level misbehavior that would otherwise be absent from your menu of possible consequences.

Here are some reminders of the essential features that are described in detail in chapter 2:

- Check with your administrator to determine if this system can be a component of the academic grade or if it must remain separate.
- Each time an infraction occurs, inform the student of the infraction and the loss of a point.
- Make sure that all students get feedback on the total number of points they earned for the week.

Time Owed

When a student misbehaves and you have to intervene, some of your time is wasted. Therefore, a reasonable corrective consequence is to have the student lose time from an activity he or she values (e.g., instead of being dismissed with his classmates at the end of the period, he has to wait an additional fifteen seconds). Time owed is an appropriate and effective corrective consequence for misbehaviors that occur frequently, such as disruptions, talking during lessons, name-calling, or disrespectful behavior, because of its compounding nature.

Although fifteen seconds might sound almost silly, it is actually a pretty long time for an adolescent who wants to be in the hall talking with friends between classes. The brief nature of the consequence also allows it to be assigned more than once in a class. If the immediate corrective consequence was several minutes, you could not issue it to any student more than once a class. You may need to establish a policy that if the maximum of time owed is reached, another penalty will be issued, such as detention. You could inform students in advance that each time you have to remind a student about a rule violation, he or she will owe fifteen seconds, but at the fourth infraction, you will make a parental contact and assign an after-school detention.

It is important that the time owed not be paid in such a way that it interferes with the student's time with another teacher. If keeping students after class for more than one minute will delay a student from getting to his or her next class promptly, you should plan to keep any student for no more than one minute.

Finally, you must decide what to have the student do while paying this time owed. As a general rule, you should have the student do nothing. For a first offense, you may wish to use the time to discuss the misbehavior and ways the student can behave more responsibly in the future. Do not do this regularly, however, as the one-on-one interaction time with you may become reinforcing to the student and actually serve to perpetuate the misbehavior.

Time-Out

Many people think that the purpose of a time-out is to send the student to an aversive setting. This is not the case. The actual purpose is to remove a misbehaving student from the opportunity to earn positive reinforcement. The goal is to communicate to the student that if he engages in a misbehavior, he will not get to participate in the interesting, productive, and enjoyable activities that will continue without him. The obvious implication here is that instruction and classroom activities need to be interesting, productive, and enjoyable. Following are descriptions of two different types of time-outs that some high school teachers have implemented effectively. Of course, if you think these procedures seem unlikely to be effective with your high school students, you should follow your instinct and use another consequence.

> **Note**
>
> Any time-out given should be relatively short. The goal is for the student to think about the appropriate behavior while missing an interesting, productive, and enjoyable activity, then quickly rejoin instruction. For an in-class time-out, it is recommended to keep the time-out to five minutes or less, and time-outs in another classroom should be no more than ten minutes.

Time-out in class.

In this option, you establish an area in a low-traffic part of your classroom. It can be as simple as having a chair off to the side of the room. Let students know that if you ask them to go to this time-out area, you are doing it instead of sending them out of the classroom. Also let students know that if they go quietly to this area and complete their time-out without further disruption, they can rejoin the class with no additional consequences. However, make sure students understand that if they refuse to go, disrupt others on the way, or continue to disrupt the class, you will have no choice but to remove the student from class and write a disciplinary referral. If you are concerned that your students may view this consequence as too elementary, consider using a sports example such as hockey: a player who breaks a rule is given a time-out in the penalty box.

Time-out in another class.

For students who are likely to misbehave during an in-class time-out (e.g., a student may try to get other students to laugh at her while she is in time-out), it may be necessary to assign the student to time-out in another class. To do this, you need to find a teacher with a room near yours who has a class with fairly mature students.

A student who misbehaves in your room would be sent to the classroom of the other teacher, who should have a prearranged spot for a time-out student (e.g., a chair in a low-traffic area of the class) and should have already warned his or her class to ignore the student when he enters. The time-out teacher should not be required to stop teaching class or interact with the misbehaving student. The idea behind this procedure is simply that the student is less likely to show off for students in a class he does not know.

Restitution

Restitution, which was presented as a correction strategy for early-stage problems in task 2, can also be effective with chronic misbehaviors when they involve damage to property or social relationships. If a student engages in behavior that causes damage, a logical consequence is that the student has to repair the damage. A logical consequence for a student who writes on desks is to spend some time cleaning them. (You may not be able to have the student use chemicals such as a disinfectant, but he can certainly use water, a sponge, and a little effort.) When in doubt, check with your administrator to see if parent permissions need to be obtained or if there are other district rules about things like use of cleaning supplies and gum scraping. When restitution is used with ongoing misbehavior, the amount of the restitution should increase with successive instances. Thus, if a student wrote on a desk, you might have him wash the desk. If he did it a second time, you would have him wash his desk and several others.

Detention

Detention is usually a schoolwide system that involves assigning a student to spend an established amount of time (say, forty minutes) in a nonstimulating setting. Most schools that use detention have their detention periods after school, before school, or during lunch. When it is used as a schoolwide procedure, any teacher can assign any student detention. Detention is often structured so that the students are required to do academic tasks during the detention period. One problem with detention is that students may find it reinforcing if they are assigned to detention with friends. Like any other corrective consequence you try, keeping records can be helpful. If you are repeatedly assigning the same student to detention across a period of time, this corrective consequence is not working for that student, and you should modify your correction plan accordingly.

Demerits

Demerits are negative points that, when accumulated, result in a negative consequence or the loss of a privilege. They can be used to soften a predetermined consequence that might otherwise be overly harsh for a single misbehavior. If the consequence for talking in class is after-school detention (which would be rather harsh for a single instance), for example, the teacher is likely to respond to that behavior inconsistently, sometimes ignoring the behavior and sometimes threatening ("If you keep talking, I am going to have to give you a detention"), then finally giving the detention.

The use of demerits might allow the teacher to set up a more consistent policy. The teacher might tell students that each time he has to speak to a student about talking in class (or any other minor disruption), that student receives a demerit. If a student gets four demerits within one week, he or she will receive an after-school detention. The teacher is much more likely to intervene every time there is disruptive behavior if he is issuing a demerit instead of a detention.

If you can use the loss of a point consequence or the fifteen seconds of time owed after-class consequence (or both), you probably do not need to use the demerit system as well. However, if you cannot use either of those corrective consequences, demerits can be an adequate way to consistently correct mild misbehavior.

Many teachers use a system of tracking demerits on the board or other public posting. In fact, public posting of demerits may escalate the behavior of some students and can contribute to a negative, punitive, or hostile climate. It is recommended that teachers record demerits in a more private manner, such as on a clipboard or with a record on the student's desk.

Office Referral

Referring a student to the administration should be used only in cases of the most severe misbehaviors, such as physically dangerous or illegal behaviors. In some cases, as you are addressing chronic misbehaviors with strategies in chapter 9, it may be necessary to send a student to an alternate location because her behaviors are so disruptive you are unable to conduct your class; however, this should be used infrequently and only as an interim solution while other interventions are being put in place. If you think this will be necessary or if you think there may be other behaviors for which you might want to send a student to the office, discuss these circumstances with an administrator ahead of time so that he or she can coordinate a plan for when the student is sent to the office.

Task 5: Know When and When Not to Use Disciplinary Referral

Severe misbehavior may require involving the school administrator in charge of discipline. This may be the principal or an assistant principal. Regardless of who this person is, as a teacher you must know his or her expectations about what types of behaviors you should handle on your own and what types warrant sending a student to the office—known as an ODR (office disciplinary referral). Also be sure you know how to write a disciplinary referral.

If the administrator has clarified her expectations during an in-service and you feel you understand her position, you may disregard the suggestions below. However, if you are at all unclear, make an appointment with the administrator to discuss the following issues.

Find out precisely what types of behaviors you should refer the first time they occur. Should you refer physically dangerous acts, for example? The answer will probably be yes, but what exactly is a physically dangerous act? You do not want to refer a student for a first-time infraction only to have the administrator ask, "What did you try before you resorted to ODR?"

You should also be clear on the broad categories of behaviors that can result in ODRs. Find out the administrator's recommendations about each of the following categories and examples. Should they be handled with an ODR the first time they occur, or should you handle them with your classroom-based consequences and parental contacts? There is no right answer to what warrants an ODR and what does not. The key is that both you and the administrator are in agreement. You should discuss whether the following would warrant an ODR.

Physically Dangerous Acts

- One student hits another student.
- One student pushes a student in line, but no one is hurt.
- Two students are in a slugging fight.
- Two students are arguing, and one pushes the other.
- One student pulls a chair out from under another student.
- A student is tipping over desks.
- A student is throwing books.

Insubordination

- A student makes a rude comment.
- A student directs an obscenity at the teacher.
- A student makes a disparaging remark about an assignment or about the teacher, but there is no obscenity.

Threats

- A student threatens to damage materials.
- A student threatens violence toward another student or an adult.
- A student threatens to bring a weapon.

Refusal to Follow Directions

- A student says, "I am not going to . . .," but actually complies.
- A student says, "I am not going to . . .," and does not comply.

Classroom Disruption

- A student is tapping a pencil.
- A student is screaming.
- A student is telling jokes.
- A student is pounding on his desk.

Find out exactly what kind of referral form should be used in the event you do need to send a student to the office. Be sure to use objective language to describe the incident that led to the referral. The administrator needs an objective description in concrete terms that explains what you saw and heard that prompted you to refer the student. The referral form should not contain responses that are based on jargon, labels, or judgments, all of which are conclusions about, rather than observations of, events. Conclusions can be biased depending on whether you are having a good day, whether you like the student, or even whether you have unconscious prejudices about ethnicity, gender, age level, or other issues.

Table 4.2.
Objective versus Nonobjective Descriptions

Objective Description	Jargon/Label/Conclusion (Nonobjective Description)
Kindra was pounding on her desk. When I asked her to stop, she loudly shouted, "You fat, ugly b___."	Kindra was obscene and obnoxious.
During a cooperative group activity, Allen and Alfonso were disagreeing. As I made my way to that part of the room, Allen got out of his seat, grabbed Alfonso by the shirt, and threw him to the floor. I was able to intervene at that point.	Allen attacked Alfonso.
James was out of his seat, pulling students' hair and knocking work off their desks. When I told him to go to his desk and sit down, he kept running around the room, refusing to go to his seat. I repeated the instruction three times.	James's ADHD is out of control, and I can't take it anymore!

Remember also that most schools send a copy of the ODR home, so anything written on the ODR will be viewed by the student's parent or guardian. Make sure that your language describing the situation and the student remain appropriate and respectful, even if you are extremely frustrated and upset. Objective descriptions of misbehavior are more likely to promote positive parent involvement and support than nonobjective statements, especially those that indicate frustration and anger.

Table 4.2 shows the differences between objective and nonobjective descriptions of the same event that resulted in an office referral.

Nonobjective responses tell very little about what actually took place. In some cases, as in the example about James, they tell more about the teacher than what the student actually did. In other cases, like the example about Allen, the nonobjective description could describe a number of different actions, from pushing to punching to using a weapon. The administrator would not know how to address this student's behavior without immediately following up with the staff member on the severity of the misbehavior. The goal here is to ensure that you and the administrator are on exactly the same page. In some schools, teachers do not feel supported by administrators with regard to disciplinary issues, and the administrator feels that teachers should handle more behaviors on their own without involving administration. When teachers and administrators feel this way, the implication is that there is some miscommunication about the details of implementing ODR.

Exhibit 4.5 is a sample referral form taken from *Foundations: A Positive Approach to Schoolwide Discipline* (Sprick, Garrison, & Howard, 2002; see the DVD for a blank reproducible of this form).

Exhibit 4.5
Behavior Incident Report Form

Student *Jayden*　Gender: F ☐ M ☑　Grade Level *10*
Date *12/4*　Class Period *2*　Location *Algebra 1, Room 24*
(If classroom, indicate subject of class)

Moderate (Paper Goes to Office)
☑ Chronic misbehavior (e.g., late to class, late homework, late classwork, disruption)
☐ Not following direction (but eventually complies)
☐ Disrespect to an adult (low-grade)
☐ Name calling, put-downs, or mild behavior that might be gender or racially based
☐ Other _____
_____
_____

Severe (Student Goes to Office)
☐ Illegal (e.g., threats, weapons, drugs, assaults)
☐ Physically dangerous
☐ Not following direction (even when direction is written)
☐ Gross insubordination
☐ Gender, racial, or other gross teasing
☐ Other _____
_____
_____

Description of problem/situation: *Jayden was ten minutes late to class (this was the third time in the past two weeks). He was also unprepared with books and materials.*

Action taken by referring adult:

☐ Use a one-liner (e.g., "That is not OK. Keep your hands to yourself.")
☐ Instructional/verbal correction (e.g., for minor disrespect)
☑ State that you will follow up (e.g., "We'll talk later.")
☑ Parental contact
☐ Have student demonstrate or practice the rule

☐ Off-limits or otherwise restrict activity
☐ Stay with supervisor
☐ Assigned school-based consequence (e.g., detention)
☐ Restitution
☐ Other _____
_____
_____

Referring adult *Mr. Apo*
Action taken by administrator:

Note that this referral form includes a place where the teacher can provide a referral for a moderate infraction: the student stays in the classroom but the referral form goes to the office. Ask your administrator if your school has provision for a referral in which the student is not removed from class but administrative or counseling staff are given an incident report. The teacher can use this type of referral when a student's behavior may warrant a more serious, collaborative response and keeping a record of the misbehavior, but is not so severe as to warrant removing the student for an ODR.

In Conclusion

Classroom rules should be designed in advance to correct the most common misbehaviors. Your three to six rules should be specific, observable, and stated positively. Design the consequences that you will assign for violations of these rules. Clear rules and consistent corrective consequences will reduce, and eventually eliminate, most classroom misbehavior. Teaching your students these rules and consequences is fully addressed in chapter 7, and responding to chronic misbehavior after these steps are in place is covered in chapter 9.

Classroom Management Plan Self-Assessment Checklist

Use this worksheet to identify which parts of the tasks described in this chapter you have completed. For any item that has not been completed, note what needs to be done to complete it. Then transfer your notes to your planning calendar in the form of specific actions you need to take (e.g., " August 25, finish identifying classroom rules that will be used as a basis for providing positive and corrective feedback"). A blank worksheet is on the DVD.

	Task	Notes and Implementation Ideas
☐	**TASK 1: Adjust the structure of your management plan based on the needs of your students.** I have filled out the Management and Discipline Planning worksheet (exhibit 4.1) and carefully considered all factors, especially the needs of my students, to determine whether my classroom management plan needs to involve high, medium, or low structure. I have noted in my planning calendar times throughout the year to reevaluate the level of structure my classroom needs. Specifically: • During the fourth or fifth week of school, I will conduct CHAMPS or ACHIEVE versus Daily Reality Rating Scales (chapter 7, Tool A). • Shortly after winter vacation, I will conduct the CHAMPS or ACHIEVE versus Daily Reality Rating Scales (chapter 7, Tool A).	*Start with high structure for all classes. Use results from Tool A after first month to determine whether to move to medium structure.*
☐	**TASK 2: Identify and post three to six classroom rules that will be used as a basis for providing positive and corrective feedback.** I understand that posted classroom rules communicate to students that I have specific expectations. I have identified three to six positively stated rules that describe specific observable behaviors I expect students to exhibit and specific observable behaviors I expect them not to exhibit. In creating my rules, I have considered the following:	*Be sure to include rules in each class syllabus. Poster is ready to tape to front whiteboard. Also have slide to display before start of class.*

- Who will have input into the rules
- That rules will be applicable
- Where rules will be posted (i.e., in a prominent, visible location)
- How I will teach my rules (e.g., using positive and negative examples)

TASK 3: Develop a plan for correcting early-stage misbehavior.

I understand that early-stage behaviors are those that are not yet a pattern, and that corrective consequences should be more instructional than punitive. I have a repertoire of information-giving corrective strategies to use with early-stage misbehaviors that includes:

- Proximity
- Gentle verbal reprimand
- Discussion
- Family contact
- Humor
- Restitution

When implementing any early-stage corrective strategy, I am careful to always treat students with dignity and respect.

TASK 4: Develop consequences for committing rule violations.

I understand that I need to impose penalties for rule breaking when it is no longer an early-stage misbehavior. I know that if I do not plan in advance what my response will be, there is a high probability that I may inadvertently reinforce the misbehavior. I have used the following suggestions to help me choose and implement effective corrective consequences:

Need to finalize list of consequences before start of school.

- The corrective consequence needs to be implemented consistently.
- The corrective consequence must fit the severity and frequency of the misbehavior.
- The consequence must be implemented unemotionally.
- I will interact only briefly with the student during the time of the misbehavior and consequence.

The following are potential corrective consequences I can use:

- Loss of point
- Time owed
- Time-out in class
- Time-out in another class
- Restitution
- Detention
- Demerits
- Office referral

TASK 5: Know when and when not to use disciplinary referral.

I know what behavior warrants sending students to the office according to my principal or assistant principal's guidelines, and what situations I should handle in my own classroom.

I know how to write an objective disciplinary referral.

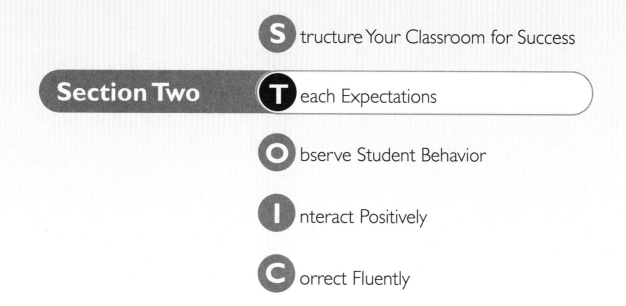

S tructure Your Classroom for Success

Section Two **T** each Expectations

O bserve Student Behavior

I nteract Positively

C orrect Fluently

Once you have structured your classroom for success, the next step is to directly teach students how to behave successfully in your classroom (Barbetta, Norona, & Bicard, 2005; Evertson & Emmer, 1982; Moskowitz & Hayman, 1976; Simonsen, Fairbanks, Briesch, Myers, & Sugai, 2008). Teaching expected behavior involves far more than simply telling students what you expect on the first day of school. You will teach students to strive toward your vision and your Guidelines for Success. You will also teach them the details of how to function successfully in your classroom. Chapter 5 introduces the CHAMPS and ACHIEVE acronyms and guides you through clarifying and then teaching either Conversation, Help, Activity, Movement, Participation, and Success (CHAMPS) or Activity, Conversation, Help, Integrity, Effort, Value, and Efficiency (ACHIEVE) for all major instructional activities and transitions. Chapter 6 provides information on how to prepare for the first day of class, communicate your expectations, build a class syllabus, monitor student behavior, and give positive and corrective feedback.

Chapter 5

Expectations

Plan to teach students how to be successful

The school and teacher effectiveness literature has consistently shown that successful teachers are very clear with students about exactly how they expect them to behave during the school day (Cotton, 1999; Kame'enui, Carnine, Dixon, Simmons, & Coyne, 2002). Many teachers think that by developing classroom rules and classroom procedures, they have prepared everything they need to orient students to their classroom. Rules and procedures are certainly essential, but they do not provide details on what behaviors are expected and not expected of students in each type of classroom activity (D. M. Baer, 1999). You want your students to behave one way during lectures, a different way during independent work periods, and still a different way during cooperative group activities. If you don't know or don't clearly communicate behavioral expectations to students, then the students have to guess at what constitutes responsible behavior. The problem with this is obvious when you consider the most common student misbehaviors:

- Talking too much or too loudly or about the wrong things
- Demanding attention by following the teacher around or calling out to the teacher
- Doing math when they should be working on science or socializing when they should be cleaning up
- Doing work together that they should do on their own, or copying another student's work, or copying source materials without giving credit
- Wandering around the room or sharpening pencils when they are supposed to be listening to the teacher
- Monopolizing classroom discussions or not participating at all
- Disrupting lessons or sitting and doing nothing during work periods

You can avoid most of these problems by clearly defining for yourself and then communicating to your students how you expect them to behave during each activity and transition that occurs during the typical class period. If you do not, your students won't know whether their behavior is acceptable. For example, are they allowed to sharpen their pencils during cooperative group times, ask other students for help during a work period, or ask you questions while you are taking attendance?

Keep in mind that the answers to these kinds of questions will be different for different teachers. The important thing is that you know what *your* answers are. That is why the first two tasks in this chapter are designed to help you specifically define your behavioral expectations for students during major classroom activities (e.g., teacher-directed instruction, independent seat work, class discussions, cooperative group work) and common transition times (switching from one subject to another, getting textbooks open to a particular page, correcting papers). The foundation for completing these tasks is the CHAMPS acronym, which is designed to help you clarify the major behavioral expectations for each activity and transition in your classroom (Sprick, Garrison, & Howard, 2002; McCloud, 2005):

C — Conversation

H — Help

A — Activity

M — Movement

P — Participation

S — Success

The issues incorporated in CHAMPS and the basic questions to be addressed for each issue are included within task 1. The CHAMPS acronym has been used successfully by many high school teachers to clarify expectations. Some teachers are understandably concerned that their students may consider the CHAMPS acronym to be too elementary. To accommodate this concern, this chapter also introduces a more sophisticated acronym, ACHIEVE:

A — Activity

C — Conversation

H — Help

I — Integrity

E — Effort

V — Value

E — Efficiency

The basic questions to be addressed for each issue within this acronym are included in task 1. Samples and blank templates for both CHAMPS and ACHIEVE are included to assist you in deciding which model to use and to facilitate your planning for the first day of school.

Defining your expectations with precision is critical if you hope to have a positive and productive classroom. However, defining expectations alone is not sufficient. You also have to effectively communicate your expectations to your students. Thus, the third task in this chapter has to do with designing lessons to teach students the expectations you have defined. Teaching expectations is the first step in a three-step process for effectively communicating expectations to students: teaching expectations, monitoring student behavior during activities and transitions, and giving students feedback about their implementation of the expectations (National Research Council, 2000). This three-step process is summarized in figure 5.1. (Detailed information about how to apply this three-step communication process is presented in chapters 7 and 8.)

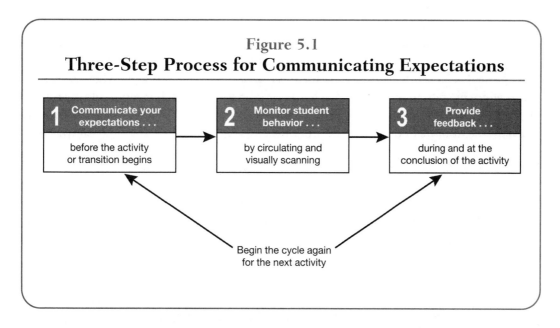

Figure 5.1
Three-Step Process for Communicating Expectations

1 Communicate your expectations . . .	2 Monitor student behavior . . .	3 Provide feedback . . .
before the activity or transition begins	by circulating and visually scanning	during and at the conclusion of the activity

Begin the cycle again for the next activity

The three tasks described in this chapter are designed to ensure that you will be ready for the first day of school with clear expectations and lessons for teaching those expectations to students.

At first glance, this may seem too elementary for high school students. However, think about effective high school or college coaches. Coaches start the first practice by going over the basic expectations: "Attend every practice and game if you are not physically sick." Successful coaches drill their athletes in the sport's fundamentals throughout a season, teaching and reteaching the basics as necessary. If students need instruction to know how to function as a member of a basketball team, then it is reasonable to assume they need instruction on how to function responsibly in a chemistry class (Bell, 1998; Paine, Radicchi, Rosellini, Deutchman, & Darch, 1983; Sprick, Garrison, & Howard, 2002).

> **Note**
> Even if you are starting this program partway into the school year, it is critical that you attend to the tasks in this chapter. Clarifying and teaching expectations is especially useful for any activities and transitions during which student behavior has been consistently problematic.

Three tasks are presented and explained in this chapter:

Task 1: Define clear and consistent behavioral expectations for all regularly scheduled classroom activities.

Task 2: Define clear and consistent behavioral expectations for the common transitions, both within and between activities, that occur during a typical school day.

Task 3: Develop a preliminary plan, and prepare lessons for teaching your expectations to students.

The focus of this chapter is on student behavior in individual classrooms. However, one other related area needs to be addressed: student behavior in the school's common areas.

Although this important consideration is not specifically covered in this program, students need to know the behavioral expectations for common area settings (hallways, cafeteria, restrooms, bus waiting areas, buses, assemblies) and with substitutes. If your school has not clarified schoolwide expectations for these areas, ask your principal what you should teach your students about responsible behavior in these settings. For more information on defining and teaching behavioral expectations for common area settings, you may want to preview one or more of the following programs:

Sprick, R. S. (1994). *Cafeteria Discipline: Positive Techniques for Lunchroom Supervision* [Video]. Eugene, OR: Pacific Northwest Publishing. *Cafeteria Discipline* provides guidance to a school's staff in how to organize the cafeteria, teach students appropriate cafeteria behavior, and train supervisors to circulate, praise good behavior, and correct misbehavior.

Sprick, R. S. (1994). *START on Time! Safe Transitions and Reduced Tardiness* [Multimedia program]. Eugene, OR: Pacific Northwest Publishing. *START on Time!* supplies information on how to develop and implement procedures for supervising halls and restrooms as a unified staff, teach students appropriate hallway behavior, and dramatically reduce tardiness.

Sprick, R. S., Garrison, M., & Howard, L. (2002). *Foundations: Establishing Positive Discipline Policies* [Video]. Eugene, OR: Pacific Northwest Publishing. *Foundations* guides a school-based leadership team to involve the entire staff in implementing a proactive and positive approach to managing student behavior. This three-volume set teaches data-driven decision making, how to set priorities, and how to increase student and staff motivation.

Task 1: Define Clear and Consistent Behavioral Expectations for All Regularly Scheduled Classroom Activities

The first step in defining your behavioral expectations for classroom activities is to make a list of the major types of activities your students will engage in on a daily (or regular) basis. Your list might include topics like these:

Opening/attendance routines	Class meetings
Teacher-directed instruction, lecture	Tests/quizzes
Discussion	Labs/stations
Independent work	Peer tutoring sessions
Cooperative groups	Cushion activities
Partner work	

The idea is to identify specific activities or categories of activities for which you will have different behavioral expectations. For example, you may choose not to list teacher-directed instruction and discussion as different items if your expectations for student behavior are exactly the same in both. However, you would list them as two separate items if you require students to raise their hand before speaking during teacher-directed instruction but allow students to speak up whenever they wish as long as they do not interrupt anyone else during discussions. You will likely have the same classroom activities, and thus the same set of expectations, among classes within the same subject area and level (e.g., the same activities for all foreign language sections) but different expectations for other subjects you teach or different age or skill levels, such as a freshman English class and a junior/senior AP Literature class. You may also need to have different expectations for two classes that require a drastically different level of structure. For example, one of your freshman classes is highly mature and responsible (low structure) and your other class has mainly at-risk students who have a tendency to misbehave (high structure). You may design two different sets of expectations to address the needs of these different groups.

Use exhibit 5.1 to list your major classroom activities (see the DVD for a blank reproducible of this form). Note that you may have different expectations for different subjects you teach.

Exhibit 5.1
Classroom Activities List

Teacher: Ms. Rivera   School Year: _____

List each major activity or category of activity that will occur during a typical day in your classroom. Create a separate item for every activity or category during which you will have **different** behavioral expectations.

Subject 1: Spanish 1, 2

Major Activities

- Lecture
- Class discussion
- Conversation (Teams)
- Conversation (Pairs)
- Language lab
- Independent work
- Presentations
- Oral quizzes/tests
- Written quizzes/tests

Subject 2: Contemporary Issues

Major Activities

- Lecture
- Class discussion
- Video viewing
- Team projects (multimedia presentation, debate)
- Library/computer lab research
- Tests
- Independent work

Subject 3: World Literature

Major Activities

- Lecture
- Independent work tasks
- Group discussions
- Reading together
- Computer lab research/writing
- Presentations
- Quizzes
- Tests

Once you have identified your major classroom activities, either the CHAMPS or the ACHIEVE acronym can serve as your guide to developing behavioral expectations for students for each separate activity. Below is an explanation of each term of the acronym and some of the ways that you will strive to clarify for students for each instructional activity. Later in this task, you will find reproducible worksheets for CHAMPS and ACHIEVE, respectively, that you can use to clarify your expectations. Pick either CHAMPS or ACHIEVE as an approach; using both might be too much of a good thing!

CHAMPS guides you in clarifying the following:

C—Conversation	Under what circumstances, if at all, can students talk to each other during the activity? If they can talk during this activity, with whom can they speak, about what, and for how long?
H—Help	How do students get their questions answered during the activity? How do they get your attention? What should they do while they are waiting for your help?
A—Activity	What is the task or objective? What is the end product?
M—Movement	Can students move about? If so, for what reasons? Do they need your permission? What routes should they take?
P—Participation	What does the expected student behavior look or sound like? How do students show they are fully participating? What behaviors would indicate they are not participating?
S—Success	Success comes from following the expectations. Alternatively, some teachers and schools choose to have the **S** stand for Special Considerations, which can be a catch-all for any expectations that do not fit the other categories of the CHAMPS acronym.

ACHIEVE guides you in clarifying the following:

A—Activity	What is the activity that is being defined (a lecture or a cooperative group, for example)?
C—Conversation	Under what circumstances, if at all, can students talk to each other during the activity? If they can talk during this activity, with whom can they speak, about what, and for how long?
H—Help	How do students get their questions answered during the activity? How do they get your attention? What should they do while they are waiting for your help?
I—Integrity	What are your expectations regarding students doing their own work and avoiding copying work or plagiarizing sources? When is collaboration appropriate or inappropriate?
E—Effort	What does appropriate student work behavior during the activity look or sound like? How do students demonstrate their full participation? For classes needing high structure, identify under which circumstances, if any, students can move about during the activity. For example, can they get up to sharpen a pencil?

| V—Value | How will participation in this activity be of value to students? Explain to your students how their efforts will contribute to their success in your class. |
| E—Efficiency | What tips or suggestions can you give students for getting maximum benefit from this activity? |

> **Note**
>
> With the ACHIEVE acronym, there is no specific movement category. Therefore, it is easy to forget to address whether movement is allowed, for what reasons, and with what parameters. Make sure to include movement criterion in the "E—Effort" section of your expectations for each activity, especially in high-structure classes.

The details are important. The more specific you can be in your own mind about exactly what you expect from students, the more clearly you will be able to communicate those expectations to your students. In addition, the more specific your expectations are, the more consistent you are likely to be in enforcing them (Deno, 1985). Exhibit 5.2 sets out a simple method for explaining noise levels appropriate to a classroom setting. You may choose to post these levels in your room as a memory aid to students and use them when describing appropriate volume levels for talking and working within your CHAMPS or ACHIEVE expectations.

Exhibit 5.2

Levels of Conversation

Level 0	Silence
Level 1	Whisper
Level 2	Soft conversation
Level 3	Presentational
Level 4	Outside

When defining your behavioral expectations, pay close attention to the level of structure your students need. The greater the level of structure your students require, the more tightly you will need to define your expectations to reduce the probability that students will make irresponsible behavioral choices. For example, with a class needing high structure, you should have narrowly defined guidelines about when and how it is acceptable for students to sharpen their pencils (e.g., okay during independent work but not okay during teacher-directed instruction). For a class needing only low structure, it is reasonable to have a broad guideline that permits pencil sharpening at any time.

Also keep in mind that it's always easier to ease up on highly structured procedures gradually than to try to implement more structure because students are making poor choices. The more leeway you give students with things like the amount of conversation allowed during activity and how much movement is acceptable, the more this may prompt irresponsible behavior. For example, at the beginning of the year when you don't know your students, it is probably not advisable to allow student-to-student talking during work periods. Some groups of students may not be able to make responsible decisions about how much to talk and on what topics. Two or three weeks into the year, after you've had a chance to see how your students typically behave, you might revise your expectations: "Class, starting today, if you have a question and I'm not available, you can quietly ask the person next to you, get the question answered, and then get right back to quiet independent work."

Similarly, you might start the year by handing out textbooks to all students at their desks while they write down the assignment in their planner. Structuring the procedure in this way limits the amount of student movement and reduces one transition, but it requires more effort on your part. If students demonstrate that they are highly responsible and mature, you could change this procedure during the year so that one person from each row silently gets the textbooks from the bookshelf and students pass them down the row. This procedure requires more student responsibility and maturity in order to complete the transition with little wasted time.

Note

The completed examples that follow show CHAMPS and ACHIEVE expectations for a variety of classroom activities. Each activity includes both a high- and low-structure example to demonstrate how a teacher would accommodate for structure level in designing expectations. These completed examples have been provided as models only; there is no intent to imply that you should use the expectations included on them.

Exhibits 5.3 and 5.4 show CHAMPS and ACHIEVE expectations for a variety of classroom activities. Each activity includes both a high- and low-structure example to demonstrate how a teacher would accommodate for structure level in designing expectations. Exhibit 5.3 on the DVD is a reproducible template of a CHAMPS classroom activity worksheet, and exhibit 5.4 is a reproducible of an ACHIEVE classroom activity worksheet. Make multiple copies of whichever form you decide to use. Then document your behavioral expectations by filling out one worksheet for each major type of activity you identified in Exhibit 5.2. The completed worksheets will provide the content for your lessons to teach your students about your behavioral expectations. (Specific information on teaching your expectations is covered in chapters 7 and 8.)

Exhibit 5.3a
CHAMPS Classroom Activity Worksheet
Example 1a: High-Structure Class

Activity: *Teacher-directed instruction*

CONVERSATION

Can students engage in conversation with each other during this activity? *No*

    If yes, about what?

    What voice level? *0*

    With whom?

    How many students can be involved in a single conversation?

    How long can the conversation last?

HELP

How do students get questions answered? How do students get your attention? *Silently raise hand for public question (one that pertains to class activity). Private question (one that does not pertain to activity, such as restroom), wait until I am circulating nearby, then raise hand.*

If students have to wait for help, what should they do while they wait? *Keep hand raised without waving and wait silently.*

ACTIVITY

What is the expected end product of this activity? (This may vary from day to day.) *Working on tasks and activities presented by the teacher, verbal and written responses to teacher-presented tasks.*

MOVEMENT

Can students get out of their seats during the activity? *Yes*

    If yes, acceptable reasons include:

Pencil *No*
Drink *No*

Restroom *Yes (but not in first 10 minutes of class)*
Hand in/pick up materials *No*

Do they need permission from you? *Any leaving of seat must have permission. For restroom, must fill out hall pass in planner in advance and place open on desk. I will look for this while I circulate, but will not grant permission while I am giving whole-class instructions. Students will have eight allowed restroom passes throughout the term.*

PARTICIPATION

What behaviors show that students are participating fully and responsibly? *Looking at teacher or materials being discussed. Raising hand with something to say about the activity. Answering questions when called on or signaled to. Having all needed materials out. Writing or performing other action as directed by teacher.*

What behaviors show that a student is not participating? *Talking to another student. Getting out of seat without permission. Looking somewhere or using item other than directed. Not raising hand or raising hand for something off topic. Not following teacher directions. Not answering when signaled, not performing directed action, or not having needed materials.*

SUCCESS

Exhibit 5.3b
CHAMPS Classroom Activity Worksheet
Example 1b: Low-Structure Class

Activity: *Teacher-directed instruction*

CONVERSATION

Can students engage in conversation with each other during this activity? *Yes*

    Voice level: *1*

    If yes, about what? *To ask to borrow materials or look at notes*

    With whom? *Peers sitting directly next to, in front of, or behind*

    How many students can be involved in a single conversation? *Only two*

    How long can the conversation last? *No more than 20 seconds*

HELP

How do students get questions answered? How do students get your attention? *Wait until natural break in discussion or lecture, then ask question, saying, "Excuse me" (hand raising not necessary). Or raise hand silently when there is a break.*

If students have to wait for help, what should they do while they wait? *Keep hand raised without waving and wait silently.*

ACTIVITY

What is the expected end product of this activity? (This may vary from day to day.) *Working on tasks and activities presented by the teacher, verbal and written responses to teacher-presented tasks.*

MOVEMENT

Can students get out of their seats during the activity? *Yes*

    If yes, acceptable reasons include:

Pencil *Yes*	Restroom *Yes*
Drink *Yes*	Hand in/pick up materials *Yes*

Do they need permission from you? *No, except for restroom. No more than two students should be out of their seat at one time, so wait if others are moving. For restroom, ask for permission.*

PARTICIPATION

What behaviors show that students are participating fully and responsibly? *Looking at teacher or materials being discussed. Raising hand with something to say about the activity. Answering questions when called on or signaled. Having all needed materials out. Writing or performing other action as directed by teacher.*

What behaviors show that a student is not participating? *Talking to another student off topic. Wandering around classroom without purpose or when more than two people are out of seat. Looking somewhere or using an item other than directed. Not following teacher directions. Not answering when signaled, not performing directed action, or not having needed materials.*

SUCCESS

Exhibit 5.3c
CHAMPS Classroom Activity Worksheet
Example 2a: High-Structure Class

Activity: *Group activity*

CONVERSATION

Can students engage in conversation with each other during this activity? *Yes*

Voice level: *Up to level 2 (so only your group can hear you)*

If yes, about what? *Only the assignment you are working on (if finished, begin following independent work procedures — no talking)*

With whom? *Only with students you are working with*

How many students can be involved in a single conversation? *Those assigned to the activity with you*

How long can the conversation last? *Throughout activity, until signal is given*

HELP

How do students get questions answered? How do students get your attention? *Put out sign that says, "We need help, but are still working."*

If students have to wait for help, what should they do while they wait? *Continue to work on the rest of the assignment. If unable to continue, each student will work on other classwork or read independently.*

ACTIVITY

What is the expected end product of this activity? (This may vary from day to day.) *Working on tasks and activities presented by the teacher, verbal and written responses to teacher-presented tasks.*

MOVEMENT

Can students get out of their seats during the activity? *Yes*

If yes, acceptable reasons include:

Pencil *No*	Restroom *Yes (but not in first 10 minutes of class)*
Drink *No*	Hand in/pick up materials *No*

Do they need permission from you? *Any leaving of seat must be with teacher permission. For restroom, must fill out hall pass in planner in advance and place open on desk. I will look for this while I circulate, but will not grant permission to more than one student at a time. Students will have eight allowed restroom passes throughout the term.*

PARTICIPATION

What behaviors show that students are participating fully and responsibly? *Looking at paper or others in group. Writing or doing what task requires — everyone must have a role and contribute. Talking only with those in group and only on assigned topic. Staying with group and in seat until finished. When group thinks it is finished, begin silent independent work and place "We are done/teacher check" sign on desk.*

What behaviors show that a student is not participating? *Not working with group — working independently, not contributing, monopolizing activity. Not writing or doing what task requires. Talking with others outside of group. Leaving group or moving around class. When finished, talking or doing things outside of silent, independent work.*

SUCCESS

Exhibit 5.3d
CHAMPS Classroom Activity Worksheet
Example 2b: Low-Structure Class

Activity: *Group activity*

CONVERSATION

Can students engage in conversation with each other during this activity? *Yes*

> Voice level: *Up to level 2 (so only your group can hear you)*

> If yes, about what? *About the assignment you are working on. When finished, on work for this or other classes*

> With whom? *Only with students you are working with (or one person from another group with a question about the activity)*

> How many students can be involved in a single conversation? *Those assigned to the activity with you (or one person from another group for a question)*

> How long can the conversation last? *With your group, throughout the activity until signal is given (with question, only as long as getting question answered requires)*

HELP

How do students get questions answered? How do students get your attention? *One person can ask a student from another group. If that group member cannot answer, the student will silently walk and place the group name/number on the board in the "Help" section.*

> If students have to wait for help, what should they do while they wait? *Keep working on the rest of the assignment. If unable to continue while waiting, work on other classwork but remain with group.*

ACTIVITY

What is the expected end product of this activity? (This may vary from day to day.) *Working on tasks and activities presented by the teacher, verbal and written responses to teacher-presented tasks.*

MOVEMENT

Can students get out of their seats during the activity? *Yes, but no conversation during movement*

> If yes, acceptable reasons include:

Pencil *Yes*	Restroom *Yes*
Drink *Yes*	Hand in/pick up materials *Yes*

Do they need permission from you? *Only for restroom.*

PARTICIPATION

What behaviors show that students are participating fully and responsibly? *Looking at paper or others in group. Writing or doing what task requires — everyone must have a role and contribute. Talking only with those in group and only on assigned topic. Staying with group until finished. Moving quickly and silently wherever needed for drink, pencil, etc. When group thinks it is finished, begin working on other class work while one student puts group name/number on board in "We are done/teacher check" section.*

What behaviors show that a student is not participating? *Not working with group — working independently, not contributing, monopolizing activity. Not writing or doing what task requires. Talking with others outside of group (not on help topic). Leaving group or moving around class without acceptable reason. When finished, talking or doing things outside of classwork.*

SUCCESS

Exhibit 5.3e
CHAMPS Classroom Activity Worksheet
Example 3a: High-Structure Class

Activity: Individual written tests

CONVERSATION

Can students engage in conversation with each other during this activity? *No*

    Voice level: 0

    If yes, about what?

    With whom?

    How many students can be involved in a single conversation?

    How long can the conversation last?

HELP

How do students get questions answered? How do students get your attention? *Flip cover of folder from green to red side that says, "I need help, but I'm still working." Folders are propped up on your desk to shield your test from view of others.*

    If students have to wait for help, what should they do while they wait? *Continue to work on the rest of the test.*

ACTIVITY

What is the expected end product of this activity? (This may vary from day to day.) *Silently work on written test. When finished, sit quietly and read or work on other classwork.*

MOVEMENT

Can students get out of their seats during the activity? *No*

    If yes, acceptable reasons include:

Pencil	Restroom
Drink	Hand in/pick up materials

Do they need permission from you? *No permission granted during test*

PARTICIPATION

What behaviors show that students are participating fully and responsibly? *Looking at own paper. Writing or doing what task requires. Not talking or leaving seat for any reason.*

What behaviors show that a student is not participating? *Looking at another student's paper or materials other than test. Talking to another student or getting out of seat. Not working on task.*

SUCCESS

Exhibit 5.3f
CHAMPS Classroom Activity Worksheet
Example 3b: Low-Structure Class

Activity: Individual written test

CONVERSATION

Can students engage in conversation with each other during this activity? *No*
> Voice level: 0
> If yes, about what?
> With whom?
> How many students can be involved in a single conversation?
> How long can the conversation last?

HELP

How do students get questions answered? How do students get your attention? *Walk silently to board and write name under "Help." Then return to seat.*

> If students have to wait for help, what should they do while they wait? *Continue working on the rest of the test.*

ACTIVITY

What is the expected end product of this activity? (This may vary from day to day.) *Silently work on written test. When finished, sit quietly and read or work on other classwork.*

MOVEMENT

Can students get out of their seats during the activity? *Yes, but no conversation during movement or looking at other students' materials. Only one student out of seat at a time.*

> If yes, acceptable reasons include:

Pencil *Yes*   Restroom *No*
Drink *No*   Hand in/pick up materials *Yes*

Do they need permission from you? *No*

PARTICIPATION

What behaviors show that students are participating fully and responsibly? *Looking at own paper. Writing or doing what task requires. Not talking. If out of seat, going straight to destination without talking or looking at anyone else's work, then returning to seat. When finished, working on silent activity at desk.*

What behaviors show that a student is not participating? *Looking at another student's paper or materials other than test. Talking to another student. Getting out of seat without purpose or while another student is moving. Not working on task.*

SUCCESS

Exhibit 5.3g

CHAMPS Classroom Activity Worksheet
Example 4a: High-Structure Class

Activity: Individual seatwork

CONVERSATION

Can students engage in conversation with each other during this activity? No

    Voice level: 0

    If yes, about what?

    With whom?

    How many students can be involved in a single conversation?

    How long can the conversation last?

HELP

How do students get questions answered? How do students get your attention? Flip textbook or binder upright on desk and mark/write question for when teacher gets to you.

    If students have to wait for help, what should they do while they wait? Continue working on the rest of the assignment. If you cannot move on, take out independent practice packet and complete as much as possible until teacher is able to help. Mark the time and place you started and time and place you stopped.

ACTIVITY

What is the expected end product of this activity? (This may vary from day to day.) Complete assigned work. When finished, work on independent practice packet. Mark the time and place you started and time and place you stopped.

MOVEMENT

Can students get out of their seats during the activity? Yes

    If yes, acceptable reasons include:

Pencil Yes

Drink Yes

Restroom Yes (total of five restroom passes a term)

Hand in/pick up materials No: teacher will hand back materials while you work. When finished, leave assignment turned over on desk and teacher will pick up.

Do they need permission from you? Yes. Follow expectations for help. Granted only when no one else is out of seat — teacher will list in order if multiple people ask at one time. Only granted once a period per student.

PARTICIPATION

What behaviors show that students are participating fully and responsibly? Looking at own paper. Writing or doing what task requires. Not talking.

What behaviors show that a student is not participating? Looking at another student's work or somewhere other than work. Not doing task. Talking or walking around the room.

SUCCESS

Exhibit 5.3h
CHAMPS Classroom Activity Worksheet
Example 4b: Low-Structure Class

Activity: Individual seatwork

CONVERSATION

Can students engage in conversation with each other during this activity? *Yes*

> Voice level: *2 or below*

> If yes, about what? *Only for question on assigned work*

> With whom? *Only a student you sit next to*

> How many students can be involved in a single conversation? *Two students*

> How long can the conversation last? *Only a minute, then back to silent*

HELP

How do students get questions answered? How do students get your attention? *Ask student you are sitting next to. If that student is unable to help, get teacher attention by raising your hand and saying your name out loud. Keep hand up until you see teacher write your name down on clipboard. Students will be helped in order.*

> If students have to wait for help, what should they do while they wait? *Continue working on the rest of the assignment. If unable to continue, work on vocabulary notes/homework.*

ACTIVITY

What is the expected end product of this activity? (This may vary from day to day.) *Complete assigned work. When finished, work on independent practice packet. Mark the time and place you started and time and place you stopped.*

MOVEMENT

Can students get out of their seats during the activity? *Yes*

> If yes, acceptable reasons include:

Pencil *Yes, if no one else is using*

Drink *Yes, as long as doesn't create a line*

Restroom *Yes. if no one else is using. Sign name on list at door.*

Hand in/pick up materials *Yes*

Do they need permission from you? *No*

PARTICIPATION

What behaviors show that students are participating fully and responsibly? *Looking at paper. Writing or doing what is required. Talking only under allowed circumstances.*

> What behaviors who that a student is not participating? Looking somewhere other than at work. *Not doing task. Getting out of seat too many times, wandering around room, or taking too many restroom breaks in a term. Talking outside allowed circumstances.*

SUCCESS

Exhibit 5.4a
ACHIEVE Classroom Activity Worksheet
Example 1a: High-Structure Class

Achieve—To succeed in something!

ACTIVITY

(e.g., lecture, labs, independent work, tests, cooperative groups): lecture, Q&A

CONVERSATION

Can students talk to each other? No

    Voice level: 0
    If so, about what?
    To whom?
    How many can be involved
    How long should conversations last?

HELP

How should students get questions answered during this activity? How should students get your attention? Silently raise your hand and wait to be called on — only on topics relating to lecture or to ask for pencil stub. Ask questions about anything you don't understand.

INTEGRITY

What are your expectations for students working together, quoting sources, and so forth? In other words, define what you consider to be, for example, cheating or not cheating, plagiarizing or not plagiarizing. All information in lectures is open for sharing. If you get behind in notes, raise your hand and ask me to repeat and slow down, or you can ask to look at another student's notes or my notes during independent work or after class.

EFFORT

What behaviors demonstrate active participation? Sit up and act interested!! Eyes on the presenter, overhead screen, board, handout, or your own notes. Write notes on material from board or screen. No talking unless called on. Remain in seat.

What behaviors demonstrate a lack of participation? Slouching, head down, fidgeting with items or doing something unrelated to the class (reading, doing other work, writing notes, texting). No eye contact with presenter. Not responding to questions or directions — "Off the bus!" Talking with other students.

VALUE

How would active participation be of benefit to students? Lecture content will help you understand all other activities in class. Lecture notes will guide you to essential course content and help you study for tests and complete assignments successfully. Appropriate participation in this and other activities is 20% of grade. Learning to take good notes is an important skill for students who want to go to college.

EFFICIENCY

Can you provide tips to increase student productivity? Don't worry about writing everything I say. If I tell you to write or if I put something on the board, write it in your notes. This is what will be tested. Immediately put all handouts, lecture notes, and assignments in correct section of notebook. Record all due dates in your planner and calculate your grade each time an assignment is returned — this will be spot checked periodically as part of your participation grade.

Exhibit 5.4b
ACHIEVE Classroom Activity Worksheet
Example 1b: Low-Structure Class

ACTIVITY

(e.g., lecture, labs, independent work, tests, cooperative groups): *Lecture, Q&A*

CONVERSATION

Can students talk to each other? *Yes*

    Voice level: *1*

    If so, about what? *When asking to look at notes*

    To whom? *A neighbor*

    How many can be involved *Two*

    How long should conversations last? *No more than a minute*

HELP

How should students get questions answered during this activity? How should students get your attention? *Raise your hand and wait to be called on. Ask questions about anything you don't understand in the material.*

INTEGRITY

What are your expectations for students working together, quoting sources, and so forth? In other words, define what you consider to be, for example, cheating or not cheating, plagiarizing or not plagiarizing. *All information in lectures is open for sharing. If you get behind in notes, quietly ask to look at another student's notes or raise your hand and ask me to repeat and slow down.*

EFFORT

What behaviors demonstrate active participation? *Sit up and act interested!! Eyes on the presenter, overhead screen, board, handout, or your own notes. Write notes on material from board or screen. Only get out of seat if needed to sharpen a pencil or use the restroom — use sparingly.*

What behaviors demonstrate a lack of participation? *Doing something unrelated to the class (reading, doing other work, writing notes, texting). No eye contact with presenter. Not responding to questions or directions — "Off the bus!" Talking off topic with other students.*

VALUE

How would active participation be of benefit to students? Lecture content will help you understand all other activities in class. *Lecture notes will guide you to essential course content and help you study for tests and complete assignments successfully. Learning to take good notes is an important skill for students who want to go to college.*

EFFICIENCY

Can you provide tips to increase student productivity? *Take good notes — essential content and what I write on the board. This is what will be tested. Immediately put all handouts, lecture notes, and assignments in correct section of notebook and use to guide studying.*

Exhibit 5.4c
ACHIEVE Classroom Activity Worksheet
Example 2a: High-Structure Class

ACTIVITY

(e.g., lecture, labs, independent work, tests, cooperative groups): *Class discussion*

CONVERSATION

Can students talk to each other? *Yes, but only with the "discussion ball"*

   Voice level: *3*

   If so, about what? *Only the topic under discussion*

   To whom? *To the group — no side conversations*

   How many can be involved? *One at a time when you have the "discussion ball"*

   How long should conversations last? *Each person's contribution should be no more than 2—3 minutes, then let someone else have the floor*

HELP

How should students get questions answered during this activity? How should students get your attention? *Raise your hand (open) and wait to be called on for any on-topic questions or comments. I will pass you the discussion ball. Raise your hand (closed fist) for an individual question, like using the restroom, and I'll come to you while the discussion continues.*

INTEGRITY

What are your expectations for students working together, quoting sources, and so forth? In other words, define what you consider to be, for example, cheating or not cheating, plagiarizing or not plagiarizing. *If you are stating something you heard or read, credit the source.*

EFFORT

What behaviors demonstrate active participation? *Sit up. Make eye contact with the person speaking. Join discussions verbally at least once per week. Following expectations for joining the conversation and getting permission to get out of seat.*

What behaviors demonstrate a lack of participation? *Slouching or head down. No eye contact or acknowledgment of speaker. Never speaking. Not listening to what others are saying. Talking out of turn or side conversations. Moving from seat without permission.*

VALUE

How would active participation be of benefit to students? *The exploration of ideas during discussion activities will help prepare you for essay questions on unit tests and will help you formulate your own understanding of the course content. When we have a class discussion, it indicates an important topic that will be tested.*

EFFICIENCY

Can you provide tips to increase student productivity? *If you think of something to say about what someone else said, use a discussion starter, such as, "Jamal had a really good point that I'd like to expand on . . ." or "I have a different perspective from Susan. I think . . ." Keep comments respectful. Disagree with ideas, not people, and honor others' ideas even if you don't agree with them.*

Exhibit 5.4d
ACHIEVE Classroom Activity Worksheet
Example 2b: Low-Structure Class

ACTIVITY

(e.g., lecture, labs, independent work, tests, cooperative groups): *Class discussion*

CONVERSATION

Can students talk to each other? *Yes, but only when you have the floor*
> Voice level: *3*
> If so, about what? *Only the topic under discussion*
> To whom? *To the group — no side conversations*
> How many can be involved? *One at a time, wait for logical pauses*
> How long should conversations last? *Evaluate if you are "playing monopoly" — that is, monopolizing the conversation. Are you talking too much?*

HELP

How should students get questions answered during this activity? How should students get your attention? *Ask any on-topic question or make a comment any time there is a logical break. If you cannot get the floor, raise your hand and I will get it for you.*

INTEGRITY

What are your expectations for students working together, quoting sources, and so forth? In other words, define what you consider to be, for example, cheating or not cheating, plagiarizing or not plagiarizing. *If you are stating something you heard or read, credit the source.*

EFFORT

What behaviors demonstrate active participation? *Sit up. Make eye contact with the person speaking. Join discussions verbally at least once per week. Get up as needed for drink, restroom, etc., but only one person at a time.*

What behaviors demonstrate a lack of participation? *Slouching or head down. No eye contact or acknowledgment of speaker or disrespectful acknowledgement. Never speaking. Not listening to what others are saying. Leaving class for an unreasonably long "restroom" or "drink" break.*

VALUE

How would active participation be of benefit to students? *The exploration of ideas during discussion activities will help you formulate your own understanding of the course content. When we have a class discussion, it indicates an important topic that might be tested.*

EFFICIENCY

Can you provide tips to increase student productivity? *If you think of something to say about what someone else has said, keep comments respectful. Disagree with ideas, not people, and honor others' ideas even if you don't agree with them.*

Exhibit 5.4e

ACHIEVE Classroom Activity Worksheet
Example 3a: High-Structure Class

ACTIVITY

(e.g., lecture, labs, independent work, tests, cooperative groups): *Cooperative groups*

CONVERSATION

Can students talk to each other? *Yes — that's the whole idea!*

  Voice level: *2*

  If so, about what? *Only the assigned task or questions*

  To whom? *Only members of your group*

  How many can be involved *Three to four*

  How long should conversations last? *Until the task is completed or the time is finished. Watch the projected timer.*

HELP

How should students get questions answered during this activity? How should students get your attention? *Try to answer within the group. If everyone in the group has the question, one member of the group can raise his or her hand until I write the group name on my clipboard. I will come to each group on the clipboard in order. While waiting, the group should continue working on the task, or get out independent seatwork if stuck.*

INTEGRITY

What are your expectations for students working together, quoting sources, and so forth? In other words, define what you consider to be, for example, cheating or not cheating, plagiarizing or not plagiarizing. *Each person should contribute to the discussion or task completion. If you are shy and don't want to talk, offer to take notes. If you don't like writing, be the timekeeper and contribute ideas. Everyone must contribute.*

EFFORT

What behaviors demonstrate active participation? *Talking to the group, listening, recording responses, looking at source material. Sit up and make eye contact. Remain with the group until the task is finished, and do not move out of seat without permission. When finished with task, work on independent work and have one person raise their hand to get my attention for review.*

What behaviors demonstrate a lack of participation? *Never talking, talking off topic or to other groups, working on other assignments before you are finished and I have reviewed the work, not contributing ideas and work. Getting out of seat without permission.*

VALUE

How would active participation be of benefit for students? *All tasks will have a graded project. These tasks will also give you information or processes that will help you succeed with other assignments or tests and deepen your understanding of the content.*

EFFICIENCY

Can you provide tips to increase student productivity? *If your group gets right to work, you can have more time on the task and/or finish before the time is complete. Assign "jobs" at the beginning of the task so that every group member has a role. Share the workload.*

Exhibit 5.4f
ACHIEVE Classroom Activity Worksheet
Example 3b: Low-Structure Class

ACTIVITY

(e.g., lecture, labs, independent work, tests, cooperative groups): *Cooperative groups*

CONVERSATION

Can students talk to each other? *Yes — that's the whole idea!*

　　Voice level: *2*

　　If so, about what? *Only the assigned task or questions*

　　To whom? *Only members of your group unless the group has a question — then follow "help" expectations*

　　How many can be involved? *Three to four in group, one to one if group has a question*

　　How long should conversations last? *Until the task is completed or the time is finished. Watch the projected timer.*

HELP

How should students get questions answered during this activity? How should students get your attention? *Try to answer within the group. If everyone in the group has the question, one member of the group can go to another group to ask. If that group is unable to answer, the group member can come and get me.*

INTEGRITY

What are your expectations for students working together, quoting sources, and so forth? In other words, define what you consider to be, for example, cheating or not cheating, plagiarizing or not plagiarizing. *Each person should contribute to the discussion or task completion. Find a role you are comfortable with and make an equal contribution.*

EFFORT

What behaviors demonstrate active participation? *Talking to the group, listening, recording responses, looking at source material. Sitting up and making eye contact.*

What behaviors demonstrate a lack of participation? *Never talking, talking off topic or to other groups, doing other work.*

VALUE

How would active participation be of benefit to students? *Some tasks will have a graded project. Other tasks will give you information or processes that will help you succeed with other assignments or tests and deepen your understanding of the content.*

EFFICIENCY

Can you provide tips to increase student productivity? *If your group gets right to work, you can have more time on the task and/or finish before the time is complete. Share the workload.*

Exhibit 5.4g
ACHIEVE Classroom Activity Worksheet
Example 4a: High-Structure Class

ACTIVITY

(e.g., lecture, labs, independent work, tests, cooperative groups): *Independent work*

CONVERSATION

Can students talk to each other? *No*
    Voice level: 0
    If so, about what?
    To whom?
    How many can be involved
    How long should conversations last?

HELP

How should students get questions answered during this activity? How should students get your attention? *Place book upright on desk — facing away from you if it is not the book for the class. Keep working on other parts of the task.*

INTEGRITY

What are your expectations for students working together, quoting sources, and so forth? In other words, define what you consider to be, for example, cheating or not cheating, plagiarizing or not plagiarizing. *Do your own work. Ask me if you need help, but do not ask someone else or copy someone else's work. Copying is not OK.*

EFFORT

What behaviors demonstrate active participation? *Reading, writing, or doing what the task requires. Eyes on your own work. If finished, work silently on tasks from this or other classes or read. Remain in seat unless I give permission. Have only needed materials on your desk or in your hands.*

What behaviors demonstrate a lack of participation? *Doing nothing, sleeping, doing work from another class before work on this task is complete, talking to others, out of seat without permission. Having non-task-related materials out, looking at places other than your work.*

VALUE

How would active participation be of benefit for students? *Time to work in class reduces the amount you must do as homework, and you can identify questions you may have while I am available to help, so you don't get stuck later. All assignments have point values.*

EFFICIENCY

Can you provide tips to increase student productivity? *Avoid being distracted — have only the materials needed for the task. Connect your mind to the task and get it done in a fraction of the time it would require if you let your mind wander to other things. When you complete one task or question, move immediately to the next.*

Exhibit 5.4h

ACHIEVE Classroom Activity Worksheet
Example 4b: Low-Structure Class

ACTIVITY

(e.g., lecture, labs, independent work, tests, cooperative groups): *Independent work*

CONVERSATION

Can students talk to each other? *Yes*

    Voice level: *1 (whisper or very quiet conversational level)*

    If so, about what? *Only to get help on assigned work*

    To whom? *Anyone close*

    How many can be involved? *No more than three people total*

    How long should conversations last? *No more than a couple of minutes*

HELP

How should students get questions answered during this activity? How should students get your attention? *Ask another student or me if I am nearby and unoccupied. If I am busy, place an open book upright on the desk and keep working on other parts of the task.*

INTEGRITY

What are your expectations for students working together, quoting sources, and so forth? In other words, define what you consider to be, for example, cheating or not cheating, plagiarizing or not plagiarizing. *Do your own work. Help with a few questions from peers is fine, but copying is not OK.*

EFFORT

What behaviors demonstrate active participation? *Reading, writing, or briefly and quietly answering a question about the task. If finished, read or work on tasks from other classes.*

What behaviors demonstrate a lack of participation? *Doing nothing, sleeping, doing work from another class before work on this task is complete, talking off topic.*

VALUE

How would active participation be of benefit to students? *Time to work in class reduces the amount you must do as homework, and you can identify questions you may have while I am available to help, so you don't get stuck later. All assignments have point values.*

EFFICIENCY

Can you provide tips to increase student productivity? *Avoid being distracted — stay focused on the task. Connect your mind to the task and get it done in a fraction of the time it would require if you let your mind wander to other things.*

Task 2: Define Clear and Consistent Behavioral Expectations for the Common Transitions, Both within and between Activities, That Occur during a Typical School Day

In between the activities that take place during the class period, there are also transitions, or times when students make a transition from one task to another during an activity (e.g., in a math lesson, you present teacher-directed instruction and then students transition by getting out their math books to work independently). Transitions are often problematic in terms of student behavior, and poorly managed transitions are troublesome because of their potential for student misbehavior and because they end up consuming valuable instructional time (Dawson-Rodrigues, Lavay, Butt, & Lacourse, 1997). When you clearly define and communicate your expectations for transitions, you will have well-managed and efficient transitions.

As with classroom activities, the first step in defining behavioral expectations for transitions is to list the major transitions that typically occur during any given class period (exhibit 5.5 shows an example; a reproducible form is on the DVD). Be sure to identify all the specific transitions and categories of transitions for which you will have different behavioral expectations. A list of transitions might include the following:

- Before the bell rings
- After the bell rings
- Getting out paper, pencil, and writing the heading on your paper
- Getting a book out and opening to a particular page
- Moving to and from locations such as lab stations
- Putting things away (clearing their desks)
- Handing in work (e.g., after an in-class assignment or a quiz)
- Trading papers for corrections
- Cleaning up after project activities
- Leaving the classroom at the end of the class period
- Handing things out (e.g., an assignment sheet or art supplies)
- Handing things back (e.g., graded papers)
- Opening and dismissal routines (expectations for these transitions were discussed in chapter 3)

Teachers of specialized subjects such as music, art, physical education, and technology are likely to have types of transitions not listed above. Special education teachers with a self-contained classroom will have a greater variety of transitions during the day than a general education teacher: they may have the same students all day and have additional transitions with students who are in general education classes part of the day.

Exhibit 5.5

Transitions List

Teacher: *Mr. Lin*   School Year: _____

List each common transition or category of transitions that occur during a typical week. Create a separate item for every transition (or category) during which you will have different behavioral expectations. If you teach different subjects during the day, think about whether there are some transitions that may occur in that subject, but not in the other subjects you teach. List transitions for each subject separately.

Subject 1: *Computer Science*

Transitions

- *Arriving to computer lab*
- *Logging onto computer/starting needed software*
- *Getting out textbook*
- *Turning in assignments/homework*
- *Passing out handouts/assignments*
- *Saving work/closing programs on computer*
- *Leaving computer lab*

Subject 2: *Biology*

Transitions

- *Entering class*
- *Handing in homework/lab reports*
- *Getting out textbook*
- *Pairing up for lab work*
- *Getting out lab materials*
- *Cleaning up after lab work*
- *Passing out handouts/assignments*

Subject 3: *English 1*

Transitions

- *Arriving to class*
- *Getting materials out — textbook, notebook, pencil*
- *Getting book and turning to correct page*
- *Handing in assignments/homework*
- *Passing out assignments/worksheets*
- *Breaking into teams*
- *Turning to partners*
- *Leaving class*
- *Preparing to take quiz/test*

Once you have your list of transitions, use the CHAMPS acronym as a guide for defining your behavioral expectations for the important issues. If you are using ACHIEVE, the full acronym is too involved for every transition. Therefore, if you are using the ACHIEVE acronym to clarify instructional expectations, the transition worksheets that follow do not use the acronym. Make copies of the CHAMPS transition worksheet template (exhibit 5.6) or the ACHIEVE transition worksheet template (exhibit 5.7), both on the DVD, for all of the transitions on your list. Be thorough: remember that the more detailed you are, the more clearly you will be able to communicate your expectations to students and the more consistent you are likely to be in implementing your expectations. (Information on teaching expectations to students is covered in task 3 in this chapter and in chapters 4 and 8.).

Following are completed CHAMPS transition worksheet (exhibit 5.6) and ACHIEVE transition worksheets (exhibit 5.7) for a variety of transitions. These completed examples are models only and are not meant to imply that the expectations on them should be your expectations.

Level of structure and expectations for transitions.

The more structure your class requires, the more specific and tightly orchestrated you need to make your expectations for transitions. For a low-structure class, you probably don't need to specify the routes students are to take to get to lab stations. For students needing high structure, include the expectation that students need to take the most direct route and keep their hands, feet, and objects to themselves so they do not disturb students who are working at their seats or take up valuable class time due to traffic jams or horseplay.

Exhibit 5.6a
CHAMPS Transition Worksheet
Example 1a: High-Structure Class

Transition: Getting a book out and opened to a particular page — for example, for guided practice on problems during a math lesson

CONVERSATION

Can students engage in conversations with each other during this transition? *No*

   Voice level: 0

   If yes, clarify how (so that they are keeping their attention on completing the transition).

HELP

How do students get questions answered? How do students get your attention?

No questions during this time unless you do not have a book. If you need a book, silently raise hand.

If students have to wait for help, what should they do while they wait? *Keep hand raised while I pass out books.*

ACTIVITY

Explain transition. What will be different afterward (e.g., change in location, use of different materials)? Include time criteria (how long it should take). *Teacher will tell (and write on the board) the book and the page number. Within 10 seconds, all students will have the book open to the correct page and should be silently waiting. If you do not have book, raise hand and I will pass one to you. I will keep a record, and if you need to borrow a book more than twice in a semester, I will dock one participation point for each subsequent time you are not prepared with your book.*

MOVEMENT

Does the transition involve movement? *No*

   If yes, what kind of movement is allowed for the transition?

   Can students get out of their seat during this transition for any other reason (e.g., to sharpen a pencil)? *No*

PARTICIPATION

What behaviors show that students are participating in the transition fully and responsibly?

As soon as the instruction is given, students will silently open their books and wait for further instructions. If you didn't hear the page number, look on the board — I will always write it in the same place.

What behaviors show that a student is not participating appropriately in the transition?

Asking, "What page?" Talking, wasting time (e.g., taking too long to turn to the page or fiddling with other materials), repeatedly coming to class without book.

SUCCESS

Exhibit 5.6b
CHAMPS Transition Worksheet
Example 1b: Low-Structure Class

Transition: *Getting a book out and opening to a particular page — e.g., for guided practice on problems during a math lesson*

CONVERSATION

Can students engage in conversations with each other during this transition? *Yes*

    Voice level: *1*

    If yes, clarify how (so that they are keeping their attention on completing the transition).

Allowed only if you need to ask to look on with a neighbor's book because you do not have your book. Quietly whisper the request to your neighbor and quietly move chair if necessary so you both can see the book.

HELP

How do students get questions answered? How do students get your attention? *Raise hand silently.*

    If students have to wait for help, what should they do while they wait? *Keep hand raised.*

ACTIVITY

Explain transition. What will be different afterward (e.g., change in location, use of different materials)? Include time criteria (how long it should take). *Teacher will tell (and write on the board) the book and the page number. Within 10 seconds, all students will have the book open to the correct page and should be silently waiting. If you do not have book, you can ask to look on with a neighbor. If this happens too often or with too many students, I will start keeping track of who is unprepared and periodically dock points.*

MOVEMENT

Does the transition involve movement? *No*

    If yes, what kind of movement is allowed for the transition?

    Can students get out of their seat during this transition for any other reason (e.g., to sharpen a pencil)? *Yes, you may sharpen pencils if necessary, but only after your book is open to the correct page.*

PARTICIPATION

What behaviors show that students are participating in the transition fully and responsibly?

As soon as the instruction is given, students will silently open their books and wait for further instructions.

What behaviors show that a student is not participating appropriately in the transition?

Asking "What page?" Talking (other than asking quietly to share book), wasting time (e.g., taking too long to turn to the page or fiddling with other materials), repeatedly coming to class without book.

SUCCESS

Exhibit 5.6c

CHAMPS Transition Worksheet
Example 2a: High-Structure Class

Transition: Handing in papers (homework, tests, etc.)

CONVERSATION

Can students engage in conversations with each other during this transition? Yes

    Voice level: 1

    If yes, clarify how (so that they are keeping their attention on completing the transition.)

Only for the purpose of saying "Excuse me" and "Thank you."

HELP

How do students get questions answered? How do students get your attention? Raise hand silently.

    If students have to wait for help, what should they do while they wait? Keep hand raised.

ACTIVITY

Explain transition. What will be different afterward (e.g., change in location, use of different materials)? Include time criteria (how long it should take). Pass papers to the next person and so on in the direction the teacher indicates. Last person in row will straighten the papers. Teacher will collect the stacks from each row. Collecting papers should take no longer than 30 seconds.

MOVEMENT

Does the transition involve movement? No

    If yes, what kind of movement is allowed for the transition?

    Can students get out of their seat during this transition for any other reason (e.g., to sharpen a pencil)? No

PARTICIPATION

What behaviors show that students are participating in the transition fully and responsibly? Have the item to be turned in prepared on desk with name and period complete (teacher will give 10 seconds for students to make sure their assignment is ready to turn in). If it is a class assignment or homework and your work is incomplete, put it in your homework folder to complete that night rather than holding up the process by trying to finish it. Students will collect papers from the person next to them. Talk only to say "excuse me" if student next to you does not immediately take the stack of papers. Pay attention so everyone gets papers in quickly. Wait to get a drink or sharpen pencil after you have passed the papers.

What behaviors show that a student is not participating appropriately in the transition? Talking for any other reason than one given above. Not having your paper prepared (trying to complete or copy work, writing name or other information once passing papers has begun). Getting out of seat before papers pass you. Not paying attention so passing papers takes longer than 30 seconds.

SUCCESS

Exhibit 5.6d

CHAMPS Transition Worksheet
Example 2b: Low-Structure Class

Transition: Handing in papers (homework, tests, etc.)

CONVERSATION

Can students engage in conversations with each other during this transition? Yes

   Voice level: 1

   If yes, clarify how (so that they are keeping their attention on completing the transition.)
Only for the purpose of saying "Excuse me" and "Thank you"

HELP

How do students get questions answered? How do students get your attention? Raise hand silently.

   If students have to wait for help, what should they do while they wait? Keep hand raised.

ACTIVITY

Explain transition. What will be different afterward (e.g., change in location, use of different materials)? Include time criteria (how long it should take). Pass papers to the next person and so on in the direction the teacher indicates. Last person in row will straighten the papers, then place the stack in the "Turned In" box for that class period.

MOVEMENT

Does the transition involve movement? Yes

   If yes, what kind of movement is allowed for the transition? Only last person in each row out of seat to turn in papers. Students will go straight to the box and straight back to seats.

   Can students get out of their seat during this transition for any other reason (e.g., to sharpen a pencil)? After you pass your papers to the next person, you may get up if needed to get a drink or sharpen a pencil (as long as there is no line).

PARTICIPATION

What behaviors show that students are participating in the transition fully and responsibly? Have the item to be turned in prepared on desk with name and period complete (teacher will give 10 seconds for you to make sure your assignment is ready to turn in). If it is a class assignment or homework and your work is incomplete, put it in your homework folder to complete that night rather than holding up the process by trying to finish it. Collect papers from the person next to you. Only talk to say "excuse me" if student next to you does not immediately take the stack of papers. Pay attention so everyone gets papers in quickly.

What behaviors show that a student is not participating appropriately in the transition? Talking for any other reason than one given above. Not having your paper prepared (trying to complete or copy work, writing name or other information once passing papers has begun). Getting out of seat for any reason. Throwing papers to next person. Rudely getting neighbor's attention by poking or saying something other than "excuse me" and "thank you." Not paying attention so passing papers takes longer than 30 seconds.

SUCCESS

Exhibit 5.6e
CHAMPS Transition Worksheet
Example 3a: High-Structure Class

Transition: *Getting out supplies (paper/pencil, etc.)*

CONVERSATION

Can students engage in conversations with each other during this transition? *No*

Voice level: 0

If yes, clarify how (so that they are keeping their attention on completing the transition).

HELP

How do students get questions answered? How do students get your attention? *Raise hand silently.*

If students have to wait for help, what should they do while they wait? *Keep hand raised.*

ACTIVITY

Explain transition. What will be different afterward (e.g., change in location, use of different materials)? Include time criteria (how long it should take). *Teacher will tell (and write on the board) what supplies are needed. Within 10 seconds, students will have the supplies out and should be waiting silently. If other materials are needed, teacher will pass out these supplies once students are working.*

MOVEMENT

Does the transition involve movement? *No*

If yes, what kind of movement is allowed for the transition?

Can students get out of their seat during this transition for any other reason (e.g., to sharpen a pencil)? *No*

PARTICIPATION

What behaviors show that students are participating in the transition fully and responsibly? *As soon as the instruction is given, get supplies out quietly and wait for further instructions. Be prepared for this by making sure you have supplies in the morning.*

What behaviors show that a student is not participating appropriately in the transition? *Asking, "What do we need?" Talking. Wasting time (looking for supplies in a messy bag). Getting out of seat for any reason. Not coming to class with needed supplies (for first few times, student may raise hand and ask to borrow supplies, but after two times, this will cost one participation point).*

SUCCESS

Exhibit 5.6f
CHAMPS Transition Worksheet
Example 3b: Low-Structure Class

Transition: *Getting out supplies (paper/pencil, etc.)*

CONVERSATION

Can students engage in conversations with each other during this transition? *Yes*

Voice level: *1*

If yes, clarify how (so that they are keeping their attention on completing the transition).
You may ask to borrow material from another student seated next to you.

HELP

How do students get questions answered? How do students get your attention? *Write your name on the board under "Question."*

If students have to wait for help, what should they do while they wait? *Get out all other materials and begin working when instructed.*

ACTIVITY

Explain transition. What will be different afterward (e.g., change in location, use of different materials)? Include time criteria (how long it should take). *Teacher will tell (and write on the board) what supplies are needed. Within 10 seconds, students will have the supplies out and should be waiting silently. If other materials are needed, teacher will assign a few students to pass them out while others begin working.*

MOVEMENT

Does the transition involve movement? *No*

If yes, what kind of movement is allowed for the transition?

Can students get out of their seat during this transition for any other reason (e.g., to sharpen a pencil)? *Yes. You may move to sharpen a pencil or get pencil stub from back of classroom, or to write your name on board to signal help is needed.*

PARTICIPATION

What behaviors show that students are participating in the transition fully and responsibly?
As soon as the instruction is given, get supplies out quietly and wait for further instructions. Be prepared for this by making sure you have supplies in the morning.

What behaviors show that a student is not participating appropriately in the transition?
Asking, "What do we need?" Talking. Wasting time (looking for supplies in a messy bag). Getting out of seat for any reason other than to write your name on board for help or to sharpen pencil.

SUCCESS

Exhibit 5.6g

CHAMPS Transition Worksheet
Example 4a: High-Structure Class

Transition: *Beginning class*

CONVERSATION

Can students engage in conversations with each other during this transition? *No*

Voice level: 0

If yes, clarify how (so that they are keeping their attention on completing the transition.)

Students should be silent once they enter the classroom.

HELP

How do students get questions answered? How do students get your attention? *Write name on board under "Question." This will signal to me that I need to come and speak to you once everyone is working on the warm-up activity.*

If students have to wait for help, what should they do while they wait? *Work on warm-up once bell rings if possible. If not, wait quietly until I can answer your question.*

ACTIVITY

Explain transition. What will be different afterward (e.g., change in location, use of different materials)? Include time criteria (how long it should take). *When you enter the room, silently go to your seat and get out all needed materials (listed on board). You may sharpen a pencil or get needed supplies. Then begin working on the warm-up activity. By the time the bell rings, all students should be seated, with all needed supplies out, and working on the warm-up activity.*

MOVEMENT

Does the transition involve movement? *Yes*

If yes, what kind of movement is allowed for the transition? *Only what is needed to move directly to desk, sharpen pencil, or get other necessary supplies.*

Can students get out of their seat during this transition for any other reason (e.g. to sharpen a pencil)? *Yes, to sharpen pencil, get a drink, or get supplies.*

PARTICIPATION

What behaviors show that students are participating in the transition fully and responsibly?
Moving directly to your desk. Sharpening pencil or getting other necessary supplies. Beginning warm-up as soon as supplies are ready. Not talking except to greet teacher on entering.

What behaviors show that a student is not participating appropriately in the transition?
Continuing to react to a situation that occurred in the hallway. Moving around the room without a purpose. Not getting out needed materials. Not working on warm-up activity once seated with materials. Talking when inside the classroom. Continuing to move around the room or being unprepared once bell has signaled beginning of class.

SUCCESS

Exhibit 5.6h
CHAMPS Transition Worksheet
Example 4b: Low-Structure Class

Transition: *Beginning class*

CONVERSATION

Can students engage in conversations with each other during this transition? *Yes*

    Voice level: *Up to 2*

    If yes, clarify how (so that they are keeping their attention on completing the transition.)
You should be silent until seated at your desk. Once there, you can talk quietly with nearby students until the bell rings.

HELP

How do students get questions answered? How do students get your attention? *For a short question, come ask me. For a longer one, write your name on the board.*

    If students have to wait for help, what should they do while they wait? *Work on warm-up once bell rings if possible. If not, wait quietly until I can answer your question.*

ACTIVITY

Explain transition. What will be different afterward (e.g., change in location, use of different materials)? Include time criteria (how long it should take). *On entering the room, get prepared for class by getting out needed materials, sharpening pencils, turning in work, and sitting down. When the bell rings, immediately begin the warm-up activity.*

MOVEMENT

Does the transition involve movement? *Yes*

    If yes, what kind of movement is allowed for the transition? *Only what is needed to move directly to desk, sharpen pencil, or get other necessary supplies.*

    Can students get out of their seat during this transition for any other reason (e.g., to sharpen a pencil)? *Yes, to sharpen pencil, get a drink, or get supplies.*

PARTICIPATION

What behaviors show that students are participating in the transition fully and responsibly?
Moving directly to your desk. Sharpening pencil or getting other necessary supplies. Talking quietly at your desk until the bell rings, then getting to work immediately on the warm-up activity.

What behaviors show that a student is not participating appropriately in the transition?
Continuing to react to a situation that occurred in the hallway. Moving around the room without a purpose. Not getting out needed materials. Talking loudly or across the room. Continuing to move around room or being unprepared. Not starting warm-up once bell has signaled beginning of class.

SUCCESS

Exhibit 5.7a
ACHIEVE Transition Worksheet
Example 1a: High-Structure Class

ACHIEVE Transition Expectations

Transition: *Ending the class*

Describe the transition. What will be different after the transition? *Students will prepare for departure from class. All materials will be cleaned up and put away. Homework for the night will be recorded on assignment sheet and organized in homework folder. Students will be in assigned seats prior to the bell ringing. The instructor will dismiss the class by rows, not the bell.*

How long should this transition take? Be specific. *No more than three minutes.*

Can students speak to each other or you? *Yes (to me but not to each other)*

If so, for what reasons and how (voice level, permission, how many students, etc.)? *Students may raise hand to ask about assigned homework once all materials are put away. For any other question, see me after class is dismissed.*

Can students move during this transition for any reason? *Only if directed by teacher.*

If so, for what reasons and how (do they need permission)? *Students should move only if I give instructions to put away materials in a certain location. This will never involve the whole class; only those students who are called on to collect materials from other students and put them away.*

What behaviors indicate a student is participating appropriately? *Cleaning up your area and putting away all materials used during class. Remaining in seat unless asked by me to collect materials from others. Raising hand to ask a quick question or make an appointment to see me. Staying seated silently until I dismiss your row.*

What behaviors indicate a student is not participating in this transition appropriately? *Talking to other students. Talking to me without raising hand or about something other than homework or an appointment. Leaving materials out. Shoving materials, homework, etc., into binder or bag without organizing in folder and recording work. Getting out of seat for any reason. Leaving class with the bell or before row is dismissed.*

Exhibit 5.7b
ACHIEVE Transition Worksheet
Example 1b: Low-Structure Class

Transition: *Ending the class*

Describe the transition. What will be different after the transition? *Students will prepare for departure from class. All class materials will be cleaned up and put away, and personal materials will be organized and recorded. Students will be in assigned seats prior to the bell ringing. I (not the bell) will dismiss the class.*

How long should this transition take? Be specific. *No more than three minutes.*

Can students speak to each other or you? *Yes*

If so, for what reasons and how (voice level, permission, how many students, etc.)? *You may talk quietly at your desk with another student once all materials are put away and assignments recorded, until I give the attention signal. You may raise your hand to ask me a quick question or make an appointment to see me.*

Can students move during this transition for any reason? *Yes* If so, for what reasons and how (do they need permission)? *Only to put away class materials or get a missing assignment from the assignment box.*

What behaviors indicate a student is participating appropriately? *Cleaning up area and putting away all materials used during class. Remaining in seat unless putting materials away or getting missing assignment. Talking quietly when finished but paying attention for signal. Staying in class until I dismiss you.*

What behaviors indicate a student is not participating in this transition appropriately? *Leaving materials out. Going to someone else's desk or out of seat for reason other than those listed above. Talking loudly or to someone who is not seated nearby. Not paying attention to signal or leaving class before I dismiss you.*

Exhibit 5.7c
ACHIEVE Transition Worksheet
Example 2a: High-Structure Class

Transition: *Moving from lab stations back to seats*

Describe the transition. What will be different after the transition? *Each student will help group clean up lab station according to preassigned roles (wash beakers/other, throw away unneeded materials, put away materials, wipe down table/floor). When area is cleaned and materials put away, group will sit silently with hands raised. When all students have finished and teacher gives direction, students will move from station to their assigned seats.*

How long should this transition take? Be specific. *No more than 4 minutes.*

Can students speak to each other or you? *Yes (to me but not each other)*

If so, for what reasons and how (voice level, permission, how many students, etc.)? *Students may raise hand before the cleanup portion of the transition begins to ask a question (where does something go?). Once I give the direction for cleanup to begin, there will be no talking unless I say so.*

Can students move during this transition for any reason? *Yes*

If so, for what reasons and how (do they need permission)? *Students move only to complete their assigned cleanup role, then return to their station. When teacher gives direction for whole class to return to seats, students move promptly to their assigned seats. No other movement is necessary or allowed.*

What behaviors indicate a student is participating appropriately? *Completing assigned cleanup role. Waiting silently with hand raised once station is clean. Moving quickly and quietly to assigned seat when signal is given.*

What behaviors indicate a student is not participating in this transition appropriately? *Talking with other students. Talking to me once movement begins. Not cleaning up your area and doing your part. Not keeping hand raised when finished cleaning. Not moving or moving to the wrong seat when directed to leave station.*

Exhibit 5.7d
ACHIEVE Transition Worksheet
Example 2b: Low-Structure Class

Transition: *Moving from lab stations back to seats*

Describe the transition. What will be different after the transition?

Each student will help group clean up lab station. When area is cleaned and materials put away, group members will move back to their regular seats.

How long should this transition take? Be specific. *No more than 4 minutes.*

Can students speak to each other or you? *Yes*

If so, for what reasons and how (voice level, permission, how many students, etc.)? *Come to me to ask a question about where something goes or something else about the transition. When you are seated back at your seat, you can talk quietly to others nearby until I give the attention signal.*

Can students move during this transition for any reason? *Yes*

If so, for what reasons and how (do they need permission)? *Students move only to complete cleanup, check in with group at lab station to see that all is cleaned, then move promptly to their seats. No other movement is necessary.*

What behaviors indicate a student is participating appropriately? *Helping with cleanup, then going back to regular seat. Paying attention when talking quietly for teacher's attention signal.*

What behaviors indicate a student is not participating in this transition appropriately? *Talking to other students during cleanup. Not cleaning up your area and doing your part. Not paying attention for signal. Not moving or moving to the wrong seat when directed.*

Exhibit 5.7e
ACHIEVE Transition Worksheet
Example 3a: High-Structure Class

Transition: *Moving into cooperative groups or lab stations*

Describe the transition. What will be different after the transition? *Each student will move from his or her desk to cooperative group or appropriate lab station.*

How long should this transition take? Be specific. *No more than 1 minute.*

Can students speak to each other or you? *No*
If so, for what reasons and how (voice level, permission, how many students, etc.)?

Can students move during this transition for any reason? *Yes*

If so, for what reasons and how (do they need permission)? *Move directly to the group location or station when signaled to do so. Check syllabus if you do not remember which group/station you are assigned to for the month.*

What behaviors indicate a student is participating appropriately? *Moving silently and directly to assigned location. Checking syllabus for assigned location if you don't remember. Taking needed materials (assignment, pencil, etc.). Sitting silently until next direction is given.*

What behaviors indicate a student is not participating in this transition appropriately? *Talking. Staying at desk. Going to someone else's group or station. Asking which station you are assigned to (not checking syllabus for assigned location). Not taking needed materials to group. Moving for any reason other than to get to assigned location.*

Exhibit 5.7f
ACHIEVE Transition Worksheet
Example 3b: Low-Structure Class

Transition: *Moving into cooperative groups or lab stations*

Describe the transition. What will be different after the transition? *Each student will move from his or her desk to cooperative group or appropriate lab station.*

How long should this transition take? Be specific. *No more than 1 minute.*

Can students speak to each other or you? *Yes*

If so, for what reasons and how (voice level, permission, how many students, etc.)? *You may ask me a quick question or make an appointment to see me. You may chat quietly during the transition as long as it does not take longer to get to your group. Once in group, you should be talking only about the assignment.*

Can students move during this transition for any reason? *Yes*

If so, for what reasons and how (do they need permission)? *You may move during the transition to sharpen a pencil or get other necessary supplies.*

What behaviors indicate a student is participating appropriately? *Move directly to assigned location or for other acceptable reasons, like sharpening a pencil. Check syllabus for assigned location or ask a peer if you have forgotten your group location. Take needed materials (assignment, pencil, etc.). Get to work immediately when seated.*

What behaviors indicate a student is not participating in this transition appropriately? *Talking that distracts from purposeful movement to group. Staying at desk. Leaving needed materials at desk. Going to someone else's group or station. Wandering around the class. Not beginning assigned work when in group.*

Exhibit 5.7g

ACHIEVE Transition Worksheet
Example 4a: High-Structure Class

Transition: *Preparing for a test*

Describe the transition. What will be different after the transition? *Each student will immediately put everything away except for a writing instrument and blank paper.*

How long should this transition take? Be specific. *20 seconds*

Can students speak to each other or you? *No*

If so, for what reasons and how (voice level, permission, how many students, etc.)?

Can students move during this transition for any reason? *No*

If so, for what reasons and how (do they need permission)?

What behaviors indicate a student is participating appropriately? *Clear everything from your desk except for the above materials. If you do not have a needed item or need to sharpen your pencil, raise your hand and keep it in the air until I write your name down. I will get to each name once all tests are handed out and students begin working. Keep test face down until I give the signal to turn it over.*

What behaviors indicate a student is not participating in this transition appropriately? *Talking after the transition begins (this is the beginning of the test period). Leaving a textbook, notes, sweatshirt, or any materials other than pencil and blank paper on your desk. Moving about the room without permission. Turning your test over before my signal.*

Exhibit 5.7h
ACHIEVE Transition Worksheet
Example 4b: Low-Structure Class

Transition: *Preparing for a test*

Describe the transition. What will be different after the transition? *Each student will immediately put everything away except for a writing instrument and blank paper.*

How long should this transition take? Be specific. *20 seconds*

Can students speak to each other or you? *No*

If so, for what reasons and how (voice level, permission, how many students, etc.)?

Can students move during this transition for any reason? *Yes*

If so, for what reasons and how (do they need permission)? *Only to sharpen your pencil or get a pencil stub out of the cup in the back of the room.* What behaviors indicate a student is participating appropriately? *Clear everything from your desk except above materials. Move only to sharpen a pencil or get one from back of room, keeping eyes off others' work. Immediately begin test once everything is put away.*

What behaviors indicate a student is not participating in this transition appropriately? *Talking after the transition begins (this is the beginning of the test period). Leaving a textbook, notes, sweatshirt, or any materials other than pencil and blank paper on your desk. Moving about the room for reasons other than above. Dawdling to put away materials, or not beginning test immediately once materials are put away.*

Task 3: Develop a Preliminary Plan, and Prepare Lessons for Teaching Your Expectations to Students

As important as it is for you to define for yourself exactly how you expect students to behave during various classroom activities and transitions, identifying expectations alone is not enough. If students are going to be able to meet your expectations, you also need to communicate those expectations to students clearly and thoroughly (Deno, 1985; Martin, 1989). Effectively communicating expectations can be accomplished through the three-step process introduced earlier in this chapter (shown in figure 5.1).

> **Note**
> Detailed information on the second and third steps in the communication process—monitoring student behavior and giving students feedback on their implementation of the expectations—is presented in chapters 7 and 8.

The first step in the communication process is teaching your expectations to students. To do this effectively, develop a preliminary plan for how you will teach students and then prepare lessons that you will use to teach them. The remainder of this task addresses those two issues.

Develop a preliminary plan for how you will teach your expectations.

Your plan for how you will teach your expectations should reflect answers to these three basic questions:

- How detailed do your lessons need to be?
- How long do you anticipate having to actively teach the lessons?
- What is the best way to organize the content?

When answering these questions, consider the complexity of the expectations you have defined, your own teaching style, and the age and sophistication of your students. For example, in settings with mature and responsible students (a class that needs only a low-structure behavior plan), it may be sufficient to simply verbalize your expectations on the first day of school, provide short verbal reviews on the second and third days, and thereafter use only occasional reminders. With difficult students (a class that needs a highly structured management plan) or in a setting with dangerous chemicals or equipment, you should probably plan to teach your expectations using visual displays, demonstrations, and perhaps even actual practice every day for at least the first ten days of school, and then with relatively frequent reminders in subsequent weeks.

If you find you need to provide frequent corrections on your expectations for a given activity or transition, this is a sign that you need to continue teaching your expectations until students can meet them. The general rule is that students should be able to meet your expectations without needing corrections or consequences for a minimum of three days in a row. Although this may feel frustrating or redundant (if you find yourself thinking, *How many times do I have to tell them?*), remind yourself that your expectations are unique to your classroom, so it may take students some time to become automatic with your routines and procedures. Also remind yourself that some things that are not acceptable in your room may be acceptable or even encouraged by a teacher that some of your students have in the class period before coming to you. By taking enough time in the beginning to teach your expectations, you will save time, energy, and frustration in the long run by not having to constantly respond to misbehavior.

If a verbal presentation alone will work with your students, you may not need to prepare any lessons; you can just have your CHAMPS or ACHIEVE worksheets handy. However, when you anticipate that repeated teaching will be necessary, vary the instructional approach you use to keep students' attention (Kame'enui et al., 2002; Stone, 2002). If you believe your class will need high structure, plan on preparing lessons that have maximal variety and include student involvement so that you reduce the probability that students will get bored and ensure that students will fully understand the expectations.

Plan to teach expectations for each activity and transition immediately before students perform the activity or transition rather than teaching multiple sets of expectations at one time. With infrequent activities such as tests, you may need to periodically simulate mini-quizzes and test activities that are less about testing student knowledge on the subject matter and more about having students practice test-taking expectations. This will help ensure that students follow expectations during the actual test.

Another consideration when developing your teaching plan is how you will organize the content for students. You may not want to actually use the CHAMPS or ACHIEVE acronym when teaching your expectations. However, one advantage of using the acronym is that it can be a useful way to communicate that there is consistency regarding what students have to know to behave responsibly (Chance, 1998; Kame'enui & Simmons, 1990). Although the specific expected behaviors might be different between, say, cooperative groups and teacher-directed instruction, students will learn that the issues you consider to be important (conversation, help, integrity, effort, value, and efficiency) are the same from one activity or transition to another; that is, you have definite thoughts about each of those categories. Without the acronym as an anchor, students may feel cast adrift among hundreds of unconnected expectations. Another advantage of using either the CHAMPS or ACHIEVE acronym is that the content is already neatly organized for you; all you have to do is use the worksheets that you completed to help you clarify your expectations.

One final advantage is that if either acronym has been adopted schoolwide, students come to expect each teacher to clarify how these expectations will be defined for each class. When you use the acronym, lesson preparation for students can be as simple as writing your expectations in bold letters on the worksheet itself, then reproducing a transparency of each activity sheet. More ideas for visual displays of your expectations are provided later in this chapter.

> ## Note
> Regardless of whether you use the CHAMPS or ACHIEVE acronym with your students, you should use it when defining your expectations to ensure that you cover all important aspects of student behavior.

Prepare lessons for teaching your CHAMPS or ACHIEVE expectations.

Preparing these lessons in addition to academic lessons may seem overwhelming. However, the amount of time required to clarify your expectations fully is slight in comparison to the time you will have to spend correcting misbehavior throughout the year if you do not.

As you begin to prepare lessons, keep in mind that you will teach the lesson for a particular activity or transition immediately before it occurs. Also keep in mind that the two main components that must be included in all lessons on expectations are presenting the expectations to students and verifying that students understand those expectations. Depending on what you determined when you developed your teaching plan, you may also want to include the following elements as part of your presentation:

> **Note**
>
> When developing your plan for teaching expectations (i.e., deciding how detailed your lessons will be, anticipating how many days you will actively teach the expectations, and choosing how you will organize the content), it is better to overplan than underplan. Err on the side of more lessons and more detailed lessons than you might need because it is always easier to condense (or eliminate) some of what you have than it is to scramble to create new lessons once school has started.

- Some kind of textual or graphic visual display (e.g., overhead transparency, flip chart, flip notebook, bulletin board) of expectations for each activity
- Actual demonstrations of the expected behaviors (by you, by students)
- Opportunities for students to practice and rehearse the expected behaviors

Given the amount of detail involved with most classroom expectations (which you may have noticed when you completed your CHAMPS or ACHIEVE worksheets), it is important that you structure your lessons so that they inform but do not overwhelm or intimidate students. Following are brief discussions of the various means of embellishing the way you present (explain) your expectations.

Visual displays. Using a visual display as part of your presentation of expectations has several advantages. It can be used to summarize key expectations and make the lesson more graphic for students. A visual display represents a permanent record of the expectations to which students can refer if they have any questions. It also provides a concrete object to which you can draw students' attention, both when you are explaining the expectations and as a prompt during an activity should students not be following them. If you decide to use a visual display, you will have to make further decisions about which kind to use.

Decide whether your displays will be text or picture based. The DVD that accompanies this book has 198 visuals for you to choose from—three different icons for 66 CHAMPS expectations such as "CONVERSATION: Talk quietly with anyone in your group" and PARTICIPATION: Listening/Answering/Asking" (see the sample icons in figure 5.2). The three versions of the icons are:

Version 1: Graphic. Black-and-white graphic symbols

Version 2: Sentence strip. Text-only icons

Version 3: Road sign. Text-based street signs in different shapes and colors.

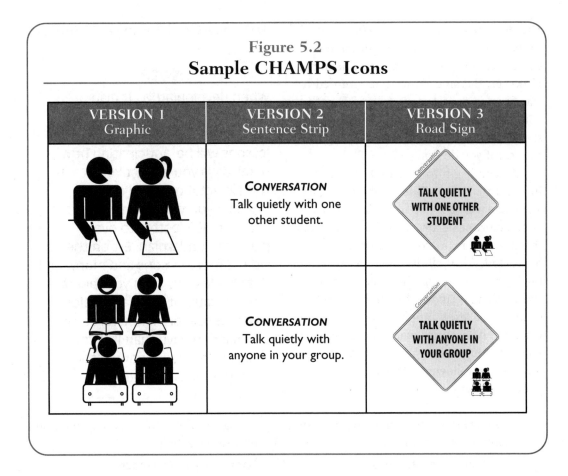

Figure 5.2
Sample CHAMPS Icons

VERSION 1 Graphic	VERSION 2 Sentence Strip	VERSION 3 Road Sign
	CONVERSATION Talk quietly with one other student.	*Conversation* **TALK QUIETLY WITH ONE OTHER STUDENT**
	CONVERSATION Talk quietly with anyone in your group.	*Conversation* **TALK QUIETLY WITH ANYONE IN YOUR GROUP**

Each icon is available on the DVD as a PDF file that you can size to meet your needs (see appendix F for more details). A list of the icons and thumbnails of all the different versions can also be found in appendix F.

Once you have selected the icons that are appropriate for your class (artistic teachers may wish to design their own), determine how you will use them to create classroom displays. Note that you can copy and insert the icons into Word documents and PowerPoint slides. See the instructions on the DVD for more details.

Among the most useful of the many forms for presenting visual displays of your expectations are document cameras, slides, flip charts, notebook flip charts, and bulletin boards.

Document camera, smart board, or other visual display technology.   Immediately prior to an activity or transition, place your visual display on the document camera or display it on the screen or smart board and use it as the focus for a short lesson on how students are expected to behave. If you do not otherwise need the visual display space, you can leave the expectations showing on all or part of the screen during the activity or transition.

You can use this approach regardless of how you have decided to organize your lesson content. That is, you could create a document or transparency on which you list your expectations or on which you have placed a T-chart of "Looks Like/Sounds Like." A particularly simple solution is to use the various worksheets you completed as part of task 1. Simply write your expectations for major activities and transitions in bold letters on the activity or transition worksheet and keep a copy or transparency of each one handy. Then you can place a tab on each sheet that indicates what the transition is (figure 5.3). By staggering the tabs on the right-hand side of each of these documents when they are in a

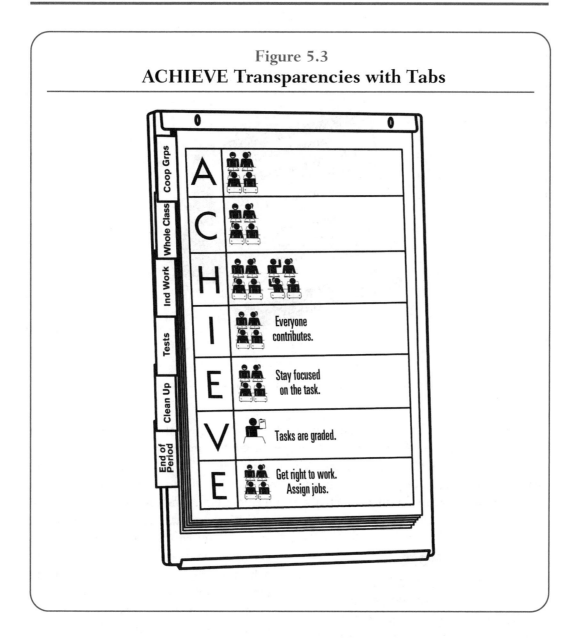

Figure 5.3
ACHIEVE Transparencies with Tabs

stack within a file folder, you can have immediate access to each sheet without having to sort them physically. To teach your expectations before an activity or transition begins, pull the appropriate document and display it.

If it is easier, you can also create a low-tech way of displaying your expectations. Figure 5.3 shows how expectations can be displayed using a flip chart with each page labeled with an index tab so you can quickly flip to the page you need as you change from activity or transition to the next.

Slides.   Using the worksheets you completed in task 1, create PowerPoint slides that convey your expectations for each activity and transition. Insert them as appropriate into your class presentation. Keeping your slides clearly labeled and organized on your computer will help you find and reuse them in the future. As with the document camera, you can leave the slides on display during the activity or transition.

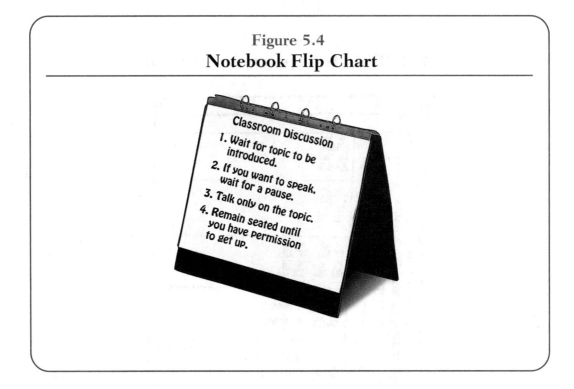

Figure 5.4
Notebook Flip Chart

Flip charts.   On each page of the flip chart, put the expectations for one activity or transition (figure 5.4). (Again, you can organize the content in any way that is comfortable for you—with the CHAMPS or ACHIEVE acronym, as a T-chart, or simply as a list of major expectations.) Keep the flip chart in a location that all students can see easily. As you are about to begin a particular activity or transition, flip to the page for that activity or transition and have students follow along as you describe the activity or transition and what your expectations for student behavior are. When you get to the point that you no longer have to review your expectations with students, you can simply flip the chart to the correct page and point to the list of your major expectations for that activity or transition.

There are other options for organizing the content of your expectations. One is to simply list the three or four main expectations you have for each activity or transition. This option might be appropriate if you have students who need only a low-structure management plan. Another possibility is to organize your expectations into T-charts of "looks like/sounds like" descriptors. Exhibit 5.8 shows a sample T-chart for teacher-directed instruction and class discussions that might be used by a history teacher who conducts interactive lessons involving frequent discussion opportunities. T-charts are appropriate for classes needing medium to high structure because of the amount and nature of detail they provide.

Note

You can use either a full-size flip chart or a notebook flip chart (figure 5.4), which is a large three-ring binder that can be set up on your desk or a file cabinet. In order to find the page for a particular type of activity quickly, plan to have tabs staggered as in the transparency example in figure 5.3.

Exhibit 5.8

T-Chart Sample: Expectations for Teacher-Directed Instruction and Discussions

Looks Like	Sounds Like
Eyes on speaker, overhead, or your own notes	Only one voice at a time can be heard
Everyone looks as if they are listening to the speaker	Presentation voice is used when you are the speaker
Hands raised before speaking	Questions and comments from the speaker relate to the lesson
Notes being taken on essential points	No other noise than writing or turning a page of your notes if you are not the current speaker
Everyone in seat except speaker	
If someone disagrees, she or he raises hand to become the speaker — no nonverbal expressions of disagreement	All verbal participation sounds respectful — even when you are disagreeing

---

Visual displays, whether they are on overhead transparencies, flip charts, notebook flip charts, or bulletin boards, can include text only, graphic icons only, or some combination of text and graphics. Again, the decision depends on the complexity of your expectations, the age and sophistication of your students, and, to a lesser extent, how you have chosen to organize the content of your expectations.

Demonstrations.

Some aspects of behavioral expectations may be clearer to students if they are demonstrated. One way to do this is for you to model (i.e., act out) both positive and negative examples of what you expect. For example, when teaching students what active participation during independent work periods should look and sound like, you might want to model the right way and the wrong way for students to demonstrate participation (McLeod, Fisher, & Hoover, 2003). You can even ham it up a bit. If you use modeling, it's a good idea to provide a couple of positive models, that is, the right ways to demonstrate participation. Then give the negative models, showing the most likely wrong ways students might misbehave. End by briefly reprising the positive models. By beginning and ending with positive models, you reduce the chance that students will mistakenly view the negative models as the way to do things.

You may also wish to involve students when modeling expectations. Students at all school levels enjoy participating in role-play situations, in which student volunteers demonstrate one or more aspects of the expectations. The advantage of having students do the role-playing is that they become more actively involved in the lesson. Ask for a couple of volunteers, and have them demonstrate a positive model of one or more aspects of your expectations. With low-structure groups, you may have the students demonstrate one or more negative examples, but with high-structure groups, you should be the only person modeling negative examples. You do not want students who struggle with appropriate behavior to have extra practice in demonstrating negative behavior in your class. Just as when you model the expectations, be sure the students' final role plays demonstrate positive examples.

Verification.

Regardless of exactly how you teach your expectations, you should probably ask students a few questions about them before you start an activity or transition. The answers students give (or fail to give) will help you determine whether you have adequately explained the essential information. If students can answer your questions, you are probably ready. If they seem unsure or are unable to answer the questions at all, go over the information again more thoroughly. Plan on reteaching the expectations until students know what you expect of them.

Do not ask for volunteers to answer the questions. Students who do not know the answer are unlikely to volunteer, so you will not get accurate information about whether all students understand the expectations. A more effective approach is to ask the question in a true/false or yes/no format and have students give a thumbs-up if the statement is an example of following expectations and a thumbs-down if not, or a 1 for following expectations and a 2 for not. For example, say something like, "During teacher-directed instruction, you can get out of your seat without permission to get a drink of water." Students respond by giving a thumbs-up if this is true and a thumbs-down if false. This procedure is most effective when you teach students to give the signal with their hand close to their chest so that it is not in the air and visible to other students.

Another approach is to ask the question first, give everyone time to think, and then assign individual students to answer. The question should be specific and use wording similar to that used in the teaching phase—for example, "Everyone get ready to answer a few questions. During the time we will be working in cooperative groups, can you choose to work on an independent project? If so, what are the reasons? [Pause] Jared, please answer." While this approach is random, it allows you to sample the understanding of individual students only, so it may be more effective when combined with a whole group method as described in the previous paragraph.

Level of structure and lessons to teach expectations.

The greater the level of structure needed in your classroom, the more detailed you are going to have to be when teaching your expectations and the more time you should plan to spend explaining and reviewing your expectations. If your expectations are relatively simple and your students relatively sophisticated, it might be enough to tell them the expectations before an activity begins. If your expectations are complex or students are less mature, your lessons should be more involved—perhaps using the CHAMPS or ACHIEVE acronym, visual displays, modeling, practice, and verifying student understanding. The goal is to ensure that your lessons communicate to students exactly what behaviors you expect from them.

Remember that students should be able to effectively meet your expectations for an activity or transition for at least three days before you begin fading from direct teaching to brief reminders and infrequent prompts. Also note that if you do not reteach when students fail to meet your expectations, there is a tacit implication that what they did the day before was perfectly acceptable. Therefore, any time that student behavior is slipping, return to teaching your expectations before the activity in subsequent days until students again meet them for three consecutive days.

In Conclusion

Your students will never know what you expect of them until you find a way to communicate it to them. Once your students understand what you expect them to achieve, you will be a big step closer to helping them in that success. Making sure that your expectations are achievable and well communicated are the first two steps in making this happen. When it does, you will find yourself working with your students instead of working against them.

Expectations Self-Assessment Checklist

Use this worksheet to identify which parts of the tasks described in this chapter you have completed. For any item that has not been completed, note what needs to be done to complete it. Then transfer your notes to your planning calendar in the form of specific actions you need to take (e.g., "September 30, finish listing major classroom activities"). A blank worksheet is on the DVD.

	Task	Notes and Implementation Ideas
☐	*TASK 1: Define clear and consistent behavioral expectations for all regularly scheduled classroom activities.*	*Completed for geometry and trigonometry classes. Still need to do for homeroom period and new statistics and probability elective.*
	I have made a list of the major classroom activities and/or categories of activities that will take place during a typical day for which I have different behavioral expectations.	
	For each activity (or category), I have defined in detail my behavioral expectations for students using the CHAMPS acronym. For each activity (or category), I have considered the level of class structure my students need as I addressed the following issues and questions:	
	◦ **Conversation**	
	How much and what type of conversation among students is allowed?	
	◦ **Help**	
	How are students to request help, and what should they do while they are waiting for help?	
	◦ **Activity**	
	What is the activity, task, or assignment students will be engaged in? What is its purpose? What is the expected end product?	
	◦ **Movement**	
	How much and under what circumstances can students move about?	

- **Participation**

  What student behaviors show active and responsible participation, and what student behaviors show lack of appropriate participation?

- **Success (or Special)**

For each activity (or category), I have defined in detail my behavioral expectations for students using the ACHIEVE acronym. For each activity (or category), I have considered the level of class structure my students need as I addressed the following issues and questions:

- **Activity**

  What is the activity that is being defined?

- **Conversation**

  Under what circumstances can students talk to others, how long, and with whom?

- **Help**

  How do students get their questions answered? How do they get my attention? What should they do while they're waiting for help?

- **Integrity**

  What are my expectations regarding students' own work? When is collaboration appropriate or inappropriate?

• **Effort**

  What does appropriate student work behavior during the activity look or sound like? How do students demonstrate full participation?

• **Value**

  How will participation in this activity be of value to students?

• **Efficiency**

  What tips or suggestions can I give students for getting the maximum benefit from this activity?

☐ *TASK 2: Define clear and consistent behavioral expectations for the common transitions, both within and between activities, that occur during a typical school day.*

I have made a list of all the common transitions and categories of transitions (within and between activities) that will take place during a typical day.

For each transition (or category), I have defined in detail my behavioral expectations for students using the CHAMPS acronym. For each transition (or category), I have considered the level of class structure my students need as I addressed the following issues and questions:

• **Conversation**

  How much and what type of conversation is allowed?

• **Help**

  How are students to request help, and what should they do while they are waiting for help?

Same as task 1: need to do for homeroom and stats.

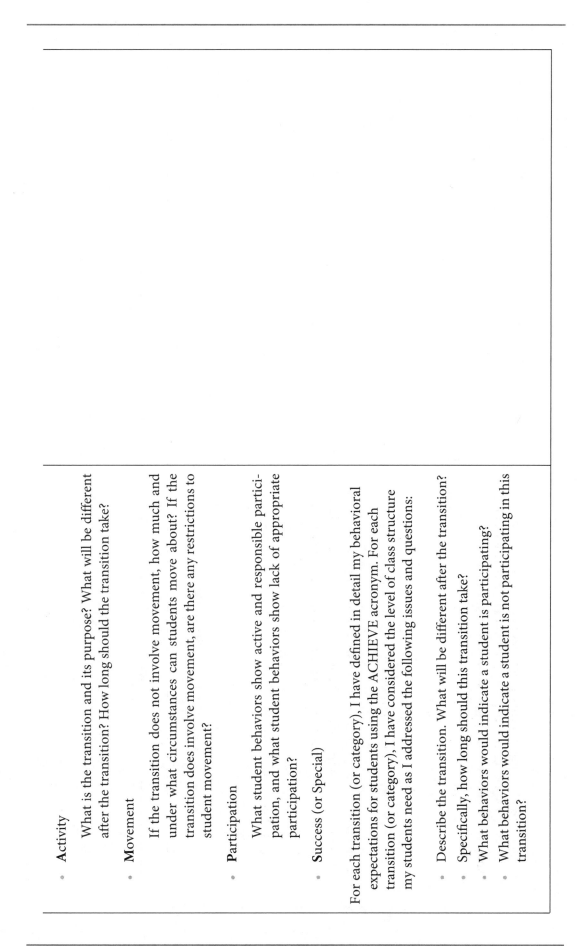

- **Activity**

    What is the transition and its purpose? What will be different after the transition? How long should the transition take?

- **Movement**

    If the transition does not involve movement, how much and under what circumstances can students move about? If the transition does involve movement, are there any restrictions to student movement?

- **Participation**

    What student behaviors show active and responsible participation, and what student behaviors show lack of appropriate participation?

- **Success (or Special)**

For each transition (or category), I have defined in detail my behavioral expectations for students using the ACHIEVE acronym. For each transition (or category), I have considered the level of class structure my students need as I addressed the following issues and questions:

- Describe the transition. What will be different after the transition?
- Specifically, how long should this transition take?
- What behaviors would indicate a student is participating?
- What behaviors would indicate a student is not participating in this transition?

☐

TASK 3: Develop a preliminary plan, and prepare lessons for teaching your expectations to students.

Based on the needs of my students, I have developed a preliminary plan to teach my CHAMPS or ACHIEVE expectations for activities and transitions. In developing my plan, I considered the following questions:

- How detailed do my lessons need to be?
- How long do I anticipate having to actively teach the lessons?
- What is the best way to organize the content?

Based on my plan, I have prepared CHAMPS or ACHIEVE lessons that I will use at the beginning of the school year to communicate behavioral expectations to students. In developing my plan, I considered the following:

- Visual displays
- Demonstrations
- Verification
- Level of structure and lessons to teach expectations

Geometry: Spend first week or two reviewing slides before each activity and transition.

Trig and stats: Quick review on first day; after that, displaying the slide may be enough.

Chapter 6

Preparation and Launch

Pull it all together for the first day

In this chapter, you will make sure that your classroom organization is complete and that you can smoothly implement the first day of school. The five tasks in this chapter will help you build your class syllabus, prepare your class to make a positive first impression, prepare and implement effective behavior management strategies on the first day of school, fade your teaching of the expectations, and plan to reteach them.

Most students are somewhat apprehensive about their first day, and putting them at ease will go a long way toward influencing your relationship with them for the coming year. Keep in mind that your students have a lot more on their minds than just your class. They are concerned that other students won't like them, that they may be ignored, that they will be noticed for the wrong reasons, or that their clothes may not look right. The more you do to help your students feel safe and comfortable, the greater the likelihood is that they will feel a sense of appreciation and loyalty to you (Brophy, 1998; Stronge, 2002).

By following the tasks in this chapter, you should be fully prepared for your first day of class and beyond. Your students will notice, too. They should leave their first class with you knowing that you are interested in them, that you care about them, and that you have high expectations for them. They should leave knowing that you will be firm and fair with them and believing that they can succeed in your class.

There are five tasks in this chapter:

Task 1: Finalize your classroom management plan, and prepare to communicate that plan to your students.

Task 2: Complete your preparations for the first day.

Task 3: Implement your plan for the first day.

Task 4: Gradually decrease the amount of time you spend teaching expectations, procedures, and routines.

Task 5: Mark on your planning calendar particular times when you will reteach your expectations.

Task 1: Finalize Your Classroom Management Plan, and Prepare to Communicate That Plan to Your Students

Review your implementation of the essential concepts from chapters 1 through 5 by comparing your plan against your syllabus. Exhibit 6.1 shows a completed class syllabus for a highly structured class of ninth-grade students (see the DVD for a blank reproducible of this form). Although you might not provide a handout to your students that includes this much detail, you need to know in advance what your procedures and policies are going to be (Baron, 1992; McLeod, Fisher, & Hoover, 2003), and it is recommended that your syllabus be as comprehensive as possible to prevent confusion and other issues in the future. Use the template as a guide for designing the handout you will give to students on the first day of class. If you have followed each task in the preceding chapters, much of this information is probably already at hand. This template provides an example of how to organize and present information on grading, rules, expectations, and procedures. As you put everything together and compare it to the syllabus, you may find some sections where you are uncertain of your policies or procedures.

Exhibit 6.1
Class Syllabus

Example for a Ninth-Grade Remedial Reading Skills Class

Welcome to Expanding Academic Opportunities
Teacher: Mrs. Hernandez

Classroom Goals
By the end of this class, you will be able to:

- Read long multisyllable words.
- Use strategies to understand and analyze what you read. These strategies include:

  Paraphrasing

  Visual imagery

  Self-questioning

- Learn to use new vocabulary words.
- Read aloud smoothly and with expression.
- Write complete sentences and well-organized paragraphs.
- Learn study strategies so you can take reading tests with confidence and perform well on those tests.
- Learn to self-manage and stay on task with class work and homework.

Accomplishing this will require cooperation. Think of this class like a sport such as basketball or track. You will have to work hard independently, but you will also have to work effectively with other students and with me.

Guidelines for Success

Winners make their own luck. They achieve.
   It takes:

Preparation

Responsibility

Integrity

Dedication

Effort

to be successful!

Classroom Rules

Winners know the rules and follow them.

1. Come to class every day that you are not sick.
2. Arrive on time with your own pencil and paper.
3. Keep hands, feet, and objects to yourself.
4. Follow directions the first time.
5. Stay on task during all work times.

Activities

Winners participate and strive to ACHIEVE. The ACHIEVE approach will teach you exactly what you have to do during each type of classroom activity. For now, just be aware that each activity below will include very specific information for you about how to be successful in this class.

Large-Group Activities
- Teacher-directed instruction

Station Activities
- Partner fluency practice
- Mastery checks with teacher (Parents: Mastery checks involve each student reading to me so I can monitor progress. These will occur about every two weeks.)
- Partner vocabulary practice
- Computer practice
- Independent practice: Writing activities

Notice the word *practice*. These activities are practice for you to improve your skills, just like an athlete, dancer, or musician does.

Grades

Winners know that you have to keep score. Your grades for each of the coming nine weeks will be based on the following:

1. 50 percent of your grade will come from your class participation and how well you follow the rules. There are 10 possible points per day, for a total of 450 points for the quarter.

   - You will start each day with 8 points, which is 80 percent, or a low B.
   - Strong effort and application will add 1 point. I will mark additional points earned in my grade book throughout class.
   - Each rule violation costs 1 point.

2. Your written work is worth a total of 30 percent.

3. Your performance on mastery checks is worth 20 percent.

Classroom Procedures

Entering the Classroom

1. Be in the room and seated at your desk before the bell rings.
2. Have your folder and writing implement ready.
3. Begin work on the activity that is on the board or on your desk.
4. Quietly work on this activity until I signal for your attention.

Tardy to Class

If you are in the classroom and seated before the bell rings, you are on time. If you enter after the bell rings or are wandering around the classroom 10 seconds after the bell, you are tardy and will lose 1 behavior point. When you are tardy, enter the room silently. Write your name and reason for being late on the clipboard by the door (attach an excused note if you have one), then immediately join in whatever activity the class is doing. All tardies are reported to the attendance office according to school policy.

Paper and Pencil

If you do not have a pencil, I keep golf pencils and stubs available on my desk. Please return them when you are finished and donate pencils that you no longer intend to use. There is also extra notebook paper on my desk. Use it when you need to and replace it when you bring your own.

Daily Assignments

Each of you will have a folder with your name on it on the counter by the door. A weekly assignment sheet will be in this folder every Monday. This sheet will outline the tasks you will work on during the week.

Turning In Assignments

Turn in your completed work by putting it in the tray labeled "Period Two," which is on the counter by the door.

Returning Assignments

Graded work will be returned to your folder.

Finding Out Grade Status in Class

A grade printout will be placed in your folder every week. This will show your current grade in the class, any missing assignments, and a progress report showing your current reading level.

Your Responsibilities after an Absence

Any time you are absent, you will view a video of the large-group activities you missed. You may do this during your study hall or before or after school. You will also need to complete independent practice and vocabulary assignments for the days missed. You will have the same number of days to make up your work as the number of days you were absent. If you were absent on Monday and Tuesday, you will have to finish your makeup work and turn it in on Friday. *Always be in class unless you are seriously ill!*

Communication Procedures with Parents or Guardians

Show your weekly grade printout to a parent or guardian each week. You will get 3 bonus points for each week you return a weekly grade printout with a parent or guardian's signature.

Ending Class

One minute before the end of class, I will ask you to return to your assigned seats for final announcements. You will be excused by rows, *after* the bell rings.

Consequences for Classroom Rule Violations

If you violate a rule, you may be assigned a consequence. Depending on the frequency and severity of the misbehavior, you may receive one or more of the following consequences:

- Loss of a behavior point
- Parental contact
- Change in seating assignment
- Time owed after class
- Detention
- Office referral

If you ever feel that the enforcing of rules and consequences is unfair, you have the right to make an appointment with me to discuss the situation. I will be as neutral as I can in hearing your complaints or comments.

Consequences for Code of Conduct Violations

If you break a rule that is covered by the Code of Conduct in your student handbook (possession of illegal substances, abuse, etc.), I must refer the situation to the office for the administrator to make decisions on parent contacts, police involvement, and other matters. This is part of my job, and not my decision. If you violate a Code of Conduct rule, it will be handled out of class.

In addition to completing your classroom plan, give some thought to how you will communicate the plan to your students (Harlan, 2002). One easy way to accomplish this is to provide a comprehensive syllabus to students that they can keep in their notebook. Be aware that simply giving students the syllabus on the first day, whether you read it as a group or have students read it on their own in class or as homework, is unlikely to result in their knowing your policies and procedures.

The syllabus functions as a reference tool, making it easy to remind students about your policies, but you will still need to explicitly teach the components of your classroom plan. Each day during the first week of school, teach some portion of the syllabus in detail. If you are concerned that this may be overwhelming to students, you might instead provide a one-page overview on the first day of school and then one more page each subsequent day for the first week. This way you will cover a small amount of information at a time, but still cover everything necessary before getting too far along in the class (Bell, 1998; Lovitt, 1978).

Task 2: Complete Your Preparations for the First Day

In this task, you will complete your unique preparations for the first day of school: developing a modified schedule for the first day, making a sign to help students find your room, preparing an activity for students to work on when they enter your room, and creating an orientation handout for parents and guardians.

Develop a modified class schedule for the first day of school.

In chapter 3, task 1, you developed a well-thought-out schedule for each of your classes. You will need to modify that schedule for the first day of school to ensure that you include the unique tasks and activities that must occur on the first day. Your goal is to make it as close to a typical day as possible while still including activities that accomplish such important first-day functions as helping students feel comfortable; communicating your classroom goals, rules, guidelines, and expectations; communicating any schoolwide rules and expectations; and dealing with logistics such as distributing textbooks.

Before you create your first-day schedule, find out from your school administrator whether you need to take into account any schoolwide activities such as assemblies or testing. Be sure to schedule the first few minutes of the class period for going over your goals, classroom rules, Guidelines for Success, and other essential information from your syllabus. Other activities you may need to address are distribution of books, assignment of storage space, and otherwise getting your students settled in. Plan to allow more regular time for each activity on the first day in order to acquaint students with how you do things. Chapter 5, task 3 presents detailed information on how to introduce and communicate your expectations to students.

Exhibit 6.2 shows a sample first-day schedule as it might be posted on the board.

Exhibit 6.2
Sample First-Day Schedule

Ninth-Grade Science (Periods 1, 3, and 6)

10 minutes	Welcome, goals, and rules
10 minutes	Grading and homework
15 minutes	Activity to identify what you know about science (not graded!)
10 minutes	Tips for succeeding in this class
5 minutes	Wrap-up and dismissal

Make a sign that identifies your room.

Create an easy-to-read sign displaying your name, grade level, subject, and room number that you can place in the hall near your door to help students find your room. Be sure to put it in print large enough that students can see the information from a distance; your students are likely to be self-conscious about looking as if they do not know what they are doing. A clear sign will keep them from having to go from door to door looking at room numbers or teacher names. Don't block the sign as you greet incoming students by the open door!

Prepare an initial activity for students to work on when they enter the room.

Having an initial activity serves several important functions. First, it gives your students something to do while they wait for the bell to ring. This can reduce the self-consciousness that some students will feel if they don't have a friend in the class to talk to. Second, having an activity to work on keeps students who know each other from grouping together. Without an activity, students may become so engrossed in their own activities that when the bell rings, you will have to interrupt and try to get them into their seats so that class can begin. Having students occupied with an activity gives you the added benefit of being able to focus on greeting all your students as they enter. Finally, this initial task communicates the expectation that when students are in your class, they will be actively engaged, not just free to do what they want (Paine, Radicchi, Rosellini, Deutchman, & Darch, 1983).

Choose any task that students can do independently—that is, with no assistance from you. Ideally it should be reasonably short and educational. Don't forget that students who enter the room first will have longer to work on the task than students who don't enter until just before the final bell. Exhibit 6.3 provides an example. (See the DVD for a blank reproducible of this form.) Plan to have this or a similar activity on a sheet you can hand to students when they enter or that is visible on the board or overhead.

Create an orientation handout for parents and guardians.

Your comprehensive syllabus may contain too much information for parents to review. You can pare it down to a one-page handout that you ask students to share with their parents or guardian. Have the parents or guardian sign and return it. Review the orientation letter example presented in chapter 1, task 5. This could include your goals, the Guidelines for Success, grading information, and homework expectations. Also include information about how and when parents can contact you if they have questions, suggestions, or concerns. Be sure to let them know your preferred contact method, like e-mail, and a backup method, such as telephone during specific hours.

Although you are not likely to get all of these back, families that are taking an active interest in their child's high school experience will value the fact that you make an effort to contact them. To increase the likelihood that students will show the form to a parent or guardian, you can offer bonus points for its return. For example, you could include something under where the parent signs that says, "5 bonus points if this signed form is returned by tomorrow, Tuesday, August 23; 4 points if returned by Wednesday; 3 points by Thursday; 2 points by Friday. 1 point will be given if this is returned at any time during the second week of school." This must also be clearly explained to the students so they are aware of their involvement in the process.

Exhibit 6.3
Sample First-Day Worksheet

Welcome to Room 19, Mr. Jacobi's Science Class!

For my records and to help you learn as much as possible from this class, please fill out this form while waiting for class to begin.

Name: *Carlos Yturra*

Name of parent or guardian: *Enrique and Janice Yturra*

Address: *1972 Oak St.*

Your phone number: *555–1212*

E-mail address:

Please identify which type of classroom activity you think helps you learn most effectively:

Lecture [ ] Hands-on Labs [x] Cooperative Groups [ ] Independent Study [ ]

Explain why: *Everything makes more sense when I get to do it myself.*

Identify two things for which you like to receive public praise and two things for which you would prefer to get feedback in a more private manner.

Public praise: *getting an answer right, looking good*

More private feedback: *work that needs improvement, grade problems*

The procedures suggested in this task have been designed to completely organize the first class you spend with your students and help put your students at ease from the moment they arrive in your classroom. Implementing these procedures will help you head into your first day feeling confident, organized, and prepared to motivate your students toward responsible behavior.

Task 3: Implement Your Plan for the First Day

The first day of school is an important one for both you and your students. When it is managed well, students will leave your classroom thinking that though you expect a lot from them, you will be there for them while you also push them. They should also leave with the feeling that your class will be exciting and fun, not intense or dreary. Your goal is to conduct each period on the first day of school in a manner that will make your students feel welcome and help them learn to behave responsibly from the beginning (Lewis & Sugai, 1999; Reddy, Rhodes, & Mulhall, 2003). The following strategies will help you succeed in doing just that.

Greet the students individually as they enter your room.

Arrange to be near the door so you can greet each student as he or she enters. Ask the students their names and introduce yourself. Then instruct them to take their seats and start on the task you have prepared—for example, filling out the information form you hand them as they enter. Continue greeting other entering students. By the time the bell rings, all students should be in their seats and quietly working on the task. Being at the doorway sets an inviting tone and allows you to supervise the students in your room while also assisting in the supervision of hallway behavior.

Get students' attention as soon as the bell rings.

Use your attention signal (raise your hand and say, "Class, your attention please"—see chapter 3, task 3) to get students to turn their focus to you. Although students will not yet know your signal, it is likely to be effective because students will be working quietly at their seats. If students look at you, thank them for their attention, and explain that whether or not they have completed their task, they should put their pencils down and turn their attention to you. If students fail to give you their attention, repeat the signal and wait with your hand up until everyone is quiet and looking at you. Even if this takes several minutes, which it should not, simply maintain the visual aspect of the signal and wait quietly. Resist the urge to shout at the students to get their attention. If you start shouting for your students' attention at the beginning of the year, you set that as a threshold and are likely to have to shout at them from then on.

Communicate the essentials in the first ten minutes.

Once you have the full attention of all students, introduce yourself again, and tell them one or two personal or interesting things about yourself, without going into great detail. Then describe your long-range goals for the year, both academically and behaviorally—for example:

> Thank you for giving me your attention. Please put your pencils down for now—you will be able to complete the form later in the period. My name is Mr. Younce [you may want to write your name on the board], and I will be your English teacher this year. Over the year we will get to know each other better, but for now I'll just tell you a couple of things about myself. I have two children of my own. They are both older than you: my daughter is twenty and my son is eighteen. My hobby is bicycling, and I have cycled as much as a hundred miles in a single day. I look forward to getting to know you all this year. I would also like to share with you some of the things we will accomplish together throughout this year. It is my job to help prepare you not just with skills for reading, writing, and speaking, but also with habits that will help you be successful in any job you choose. So some of my goals for this year are that you learn to . . .

Next, hand out your syllabus and explain to your students that this is a guide for how to succeed in your class. Let students know that you will be covering all of this information in the next few days. Explain your major goals, your Guidelines for Success, and the classroom rules. As you share this information, involve your students—for example: "Raise your hand if you have an idea about why I have a rule that says 'Stay on task'—regardless of the type of activity."

At the conclusion of this first ten minutes, students should have a preliminary sense of who you are, what you expect of them, and what they will learn in your class. Do not spend more than ten minutes on this orientation. If you talk too much or provide too many details, many students will get overwhelmed or tune you out.

Teach your attention signal.

Demonstrate the signal you used earlier to get your students' attention and tell them why the signal will be important:

> I appreciate how well all of you are keeping your attention on me while I'm speaking. During class when you are working at your seats or in groups or at one of the lab stations, there will be times when I need you to stop what you are doing and give me your attention. At those times, I will say, "Class, your attention please," while I am making this big circular motion with my arm. Then I will hold my hand in the air. When you hear me say those words or see me make that motion, stop whatever you are doing, stop talking, look at me, and raise your own hand. Raising your hand will help get the attention of other students who might not have seen or heard my signal. Stopping immediately when I give the signal is very important. There will be many times when we will all need to start an activity together. This way, even if you are all doing something different—working at your seats, at the lab stations, or at computers—I can give the signal and everyone will be quiet and paying attention within five seconds. Then we can begin the next activity, and no individuals or small groups will be wasting class time. I'm going to show you my signal one more time and do it for five seconds. This is how quickly I expect the whole class to be quiet and looking at me.

Demonstrate the attention signal while counting five seconds. Then provide opportunities for the students to practice the signal. Give students a quick (no more than one minute) getting-to-know-you question to prompt discussion with someone seated near them, or provide another quick discussion starter. Tell students that the goal of this exercise is to see how quickly and appropriately they can respond to your attention signal. Once students have begun discussing the prompt with one another, give the signal. If students follow it appropriately and within the time limit given, move on with other instruction. Continue to provide frequent opportunities for brief discussion tasks that end with using the attention signal throughout the period and rest of the week. Also provide feedback about how students are meeting expectations for the attention signal.

If students do not meet your expectations for the attention signal at any point, reteach both the rationale for the signal and the expectations for responding to the signal. Then have students demonstrate it appropriately multiple times. Be relentless in having students adhere to this signal! If you allow them to slip on any part of these expectations, it can add significant time to each transition and each time that you need to regain student attention.

Orient students to the posted first-day schedule and begin using the three-step process for communicating your expectations.

Start by giving students a clear idea of what the class period is going to be like. Then for each activity throughout the class, use the three-step process for communicating expectations. This cycle, which was introduced in chapter 4, is summarized in figure 6.1 and then explained.

Step 1: Communicate Your Expectations

Teach students what your expectations are for the activity that will follow. Just before students engage in any activity or transition, use the lessons you developed (see chapter 5, task 3) to prepare students for what you expect during that activity or transition. It's important to note that you will teach your expectations for each activity or transition immediately before it occurs. You do *not* want to teach the expectations for more than one activity at a time (Brophy & Good, 1986; Sponder, 1993).

Be prepared to spend as much time as necessary at the beginning of an activity to ensure that students understand what you expect of them. If the lesson you have prepared involves modeling or practicing a behavior, you will need to allow more time than if you are simply going to describe your expectations. For example, if you have scheduled a fifteen-minute teacher-directed instructional period, it is possible that on the first day, you may have to spend three to seven of those fifteen minutes explaining and modeling your expectations. In other words, be prepared to spend anywhere from 20 to 50 percent of the time scheduled for a given activity on teaching your expectations for that activity during the first days of class. Some teachers may feel that they do not have time to do this because there is so much content to cover; however, time spent teaching expectations early is time you will save in later weeks reviewing this information over and over and dealing with misbehaviors because students do not know and are not following your expectations.

Step 2: Monitor Student Behavior

The only way to track how well students are meeting your behavioral expectations is for you to monitor their behavior in some way (Deno, Espin, & Fuchs, 2002; Ysseldyke & Christenson, 1987). This is the second step for effectively communicating your expectations. Two of the most useful and efficient ways to monitor student behavior during an activity or transition are to circulate among students and scan all parts of the classroom. These two essential strategies will allow you to know exactly what is going on at all times. You can then use this information to help make sound decisions about the type and frequency of feedback you should provide students concerning their behavior. Circulating has another benefit: your physical presence will reduce student misbehavior. It's human nature: your proximity makes the likelihood of getting away with something much lower, which in turn makes misbehaving much less attractive. Circulating and scanning are discussed in detail in chapter 7, task 1.

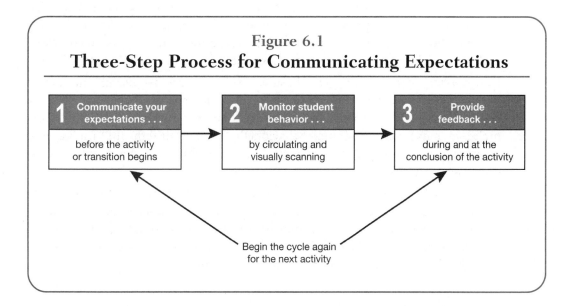

Figure 6.1
Three-Step Process for Communicating Expectations

1 Communicate your expectations . . .	**2** Monitor student behavior . . .	**3** Provide feedback . . .
before the activity or transition begins	by circulating and visually scanning	during and at the conclusion of the activity

Begin the cycle again for the next activity

Step 3: Give Students Feedback on Their Implementation of Expectations

The third step in the process of effectively communicating your behavioral expectations is giving students, both individually and as a class, clear information about the degree to which they behaved as expected for a particular activity or transition. Provide positive feedback when students are meeting expectations and corrective feedback (calmly, immediately, and consistently) when they are not. Specific positive feedback serves two vitally important functions: it gives students specific information about what they are doing correctly, and it gives them adult attention when they are behaving responsibly. Corrective feedback also serves two vitally important functions: it lets students know that you are monitoring their behavior, and it communicates that you are serious and consistent about your expectations for student behavior (Colvin & Sugai, 1988; Rosenshine & Stevens, 1986).

As you monitor students during an activity or transition, notice examples of students who are meeting your expectations and examples of students who are not. Both represent opportunities for you to continue to teach students how to meet your behavioral expectations by giving them positive and corrective feedback.

Positive feedback.

Providing positive feedback is covered in more detail in chapter 8, but it is also addressed briefly here because of its importance in creating behavioral change. To set students up for success, it is critical that you provide frequent positive attention to what they are doing right rather than just provide feedback on the things they need to work on. For example, if most students in class are meeting expectations in the first week of school, pay special attention to complimenting and acknowledging these positive efforts. Effective teachers strive to provide positive feedback at least three times more often than they provide negative feedback. Here are a few tips on providing effective positive feedback:

- *Give feedback that is accurate.* Do not provide positive feedback unless the individual or class has actually exhibited responsible behavior. When you tell a student that he has been responsible when he has not, you ruin your credibility and lead students to think, justifiably, that your positive feedback means nothing.

- *Give feedback that is specific and descriptive.* Tell the student or group exactly what they are doing that is responsible and important: "Alex, Maria, Travis, you are keeping your attention focused on your work. That is a very important part of being successful in this class." Avoid rote phrases like, "Good job," "Nice job," or "Well done."

- *Give feedback that is contingent.* Positive feedback provides useful information on important behaviors. Inform students how the positive behaviors they are demonstrating will contribute to their success and the success of the class. Also, praise students for demonstrating behaviors that are new or difficult: "Tanika, your comments in class today were insightful and contributed to the quality of class discussions. Thanks."

- *Give positive feedback immediately.* Immediacy is important because students need to know when they are doing something correctly. In addition, not getting any attention for meeting expectations will lead students who are starved for attention to demand attention through misbehavior. Positive feedback is most effective when it occurs immediately after the behavior you are trying to encourage.

- *Give positive feedback in a manner that fits your style.* The specific manner in which you give positive feedback does not matter. What is important is that you are specific and sincere. If you have a bubbly, happy personality, your positive feedback should be true to that form. If you are a more serious person, your positive feedback should be given in a more serious manner.

Corrective feedback.

When students exhibit behavior that does not meet your expectations for that activity, you *must* correct the inappropriate behavior. To give the most effective correction, consider each instance of not meeting expectations as an instructional opportunity. Think of a student's behavioral errors as similar to errors he or she might make in math. Most math errors are a function of students' not fully understanding a particular concept or all the steps in a particular process. Effectively correcting those errors involves reteaching the concept or steps. If students fail to meet your behavioral expectations, you should first determine if they understood what the expectations were or if they did not know how to meet them. If the answer to either of those questions is yes, you will need to reteach what your expectations are and how your students can meet them. If the answer is no, you need to provide corrective feedback.

Here are a few tips on providing effective corrective feedback. The examples provided focus on corrections at the beginning of the year, but these same strategies are essential for effective corrections throughout the entire year. (More detailed information on using corrective feedback is provided in chapter 5.)

- *Correct the misbehavior immediately.* When students are not meeting behavioral expectations, let them know *then*. Do not ignore it, and do not wait until the end of an activity. Ignoring can be an effective strategy for responding to chronic misbehavior that is designed to elicit attention. But when you are trying to establish your expectations at the beginning of the year, students may interpret ignoring as your not being really serious about your expectations.

- *Correct the misbehavior calmly.* Correcting misbehavior calmly shows students not only that you are serious and have high expectations, but also that you are completely in control and will not be rattled by their misbehavior. Emotional corrections are more likely to give power to the misbehavior and put you in a position of appearing controllable. Students may think that they can upset you with a certain behavior.

- *Correct misbehavior consistently.* For the first several days of instruction, correct most misbehavior with mild verbal reprimands that focus on the behavior, not the person. Simply restate what the students should be doing at the time. Always be direct. Saying something like, "Tina and Adam, you should be working quietly on your lab notebooks at this time," is much more appropriate and effective than, "Tina and Adam, you are acting very immaturely. I should not have to remind you that this is a work period, not a time to socialize."

- *Follow through.* When it becomes necessary to use a corrective consequence, it is imperative that you demonstrate that you will issue the appropriate consequence. If your students know that you will threaten consequences without actually issuing them, they will start to abuse the system. Again, this is where your consequences should be mild enough that you feel comfortable implementing them with each instance of the misbehavior.

Feedback at the end of an activity.

Early in the year, you should plan on ending each activity or transition by giving students feedback on how well they met your CHAMPS or ACHIEVE expectations as a class. When an activity or transition is finished and before the next activity begins, let the group know whether things went well and they behaved as expected, or whether they need to improve their behavior the next time that particular activity or transition occurs. When an activity goes perfectly, you have a wonderful opportunity to reinforce the class and begin establishing a sense of group pride: "Class, the way this work period went is exactly the way a lab activity of this type should go. Everyone followed safe lab procedures. Conversations at the lab stations were quiet, and all the conversations that I heard were focused on the lab activity. This is going to be a great class!"

If an activity does not go well, describe the specific behaviors that need to be different, without pointing out individuals, and set a goal for the next time you have that activity: "Class, during the teacher-directed portion of the math lesson that we just completed, there were several times that I had to remind people that if they had something to say, they need to raise their hand. Please remember that whenever anyone is presenting to the class, whether it is me or another student, there should be no side conversations. Tomorrow I want you to remember: no side conversations, and keep your attention focused entirely on whoever is speaking." If you do not provide this specific feedback and review, students will assume that their performance was acceptable. The absence of feedback generally indicates everything went smoothly, and this increases the likelihood students will do the same thing the following day.

Avoid statements such as, "Almost everyone remembered the expectation about talking only if you raise your hand and are called on." A statement of this type is *not* positive feedback; it serves only to get students wondering who did not meet the expectations.

Conclude the class period by orienting students to your end-of-class procedures (see chapter 3, task 4).

Because this is the first day of school, allow plenty of time to end class. Review the materials your students need to bring the next day. Make sure they have all important papers to take home, such as the parent or guardian orientation letter. Carefully explain the procedure for classroom dismissal and follow through with it. Don't allow students to run out at the bell. It is important to establish positive habits that follow your routines from the very first day. You also want to create a sense of closure so that students leave your classroom feeling comfortable, eager to return, and with the sense that you are interested in all of them.

The strategies presented in this task will help you get your first day of school off to the best start. Remember that the information you present and the atmosphere you establish on this day will yield valuable dividends throughout the school year.

Task 4: Gradually Decrease the Amount of Time You Spend Teaching Expectations, Procedures, and Routines

No matter how carefully you communicate your expectations on the first day, few students will know exactly how they are supposed to behave after just one day. Keep reminding yourself that your expectations are unique to you, and what is considered misbehavior in your class may be perfectly acceptable and even reinforced by another teacher your students have during the day. In addition, remember that most students' attention is scattered on the first day. Their excitement, and possibly anxiety, may get in the way of learning and retaining information presented by their teachers at the start of the school year. Therefore, continue to implement the three-step process introduced in chapter 4 until students demonstrate they consistently meet your expectations. (See figure 6.1 to review this cycle.)

Your students will internalize your expectations if you continue to use the three-step communication process for a couple of weeks. You should begin every activity with a brief lesson on the expectations, continue to monitor student performance, and provide feedback to both individual students and the whole class. Remember that your students will be hearing expectations from several other teachers, and they may get tired of hearing them. They may also get confused about details from teacher to teacher, as one may let them talk during independent work and others may not. Be sure to vary the format of your lessons so as to avoid student boredom (Fisher et al., 1980).

As the first month of school progresses, the lessons should become increasingly brief and focus mainly on any specific expectations that are not being met. When students seem to fully understand and remember expectations for an activity or transition, you can start to phase out the lessons (Meece, Blumenfield, & Hoyle, 1988). You might start introducing the activity or transition by letting students know that because they have been responsible, you will not review your expectations: "Class, we are now going to have a twenty-minute work period for you to get going on the math assignment. Because we've done so well with this kind of work before, I don't think we need to review the expectations today. Please begin work on the assignment on the board."

Another option to consider is alternating lesson plans by teaching different expectations on different days. During a math lesson on Monday, you might present expectation lessons for the teacher-directed and cooperative group portions of class, and on Tuesday you might cover independent work and cooperative groups but not teacher-directed activities. If you rotate expectations in this manner, you will cover them all regularly without having to repeat yourself every day. Whenever a particular activity or transition has not gone as smoothly as you would like, plan to use the three-step process the next day to reassert your expectations.

If the number of students who have not been meeting your expectations is more than five, plan on reteaching your expectations to the entire class from the beginning. Do *not* review them, but cover every step of your expectations again as if your class had never heard your class plans before. If only one or two students are having problems, use the three-step process with them as individuals. Figure 6.2 shows some slides from a presentation created by Stanford Lewis, a teacher at Hillcrest High School in Dallas, Texas, for his high school band class. He presents a forty-slide presentation, "Discipline: A Management Guide," to his students on the first day of school and has them write down all the information from the slides. Because the information is presented in short bites, he can easily pull out a slide to go over expectations that need to be retaught.

As students begin consistently meeting your expectations, you can start to reduce the length and frequency of your expectation lessons and spend more time instructing students in class content. Before you stop the lessons, however, verify that your students fully understand your expectations (Covington, 2000). One way of evaluating this is by determining how well your students have met your expectations across consecutive days. Before you fade lessons for any activity or transition, students should demonstrate that they can meet your expectations for three days in a row. You can also conduct some informal and formal evaluations of student understanding; some methods for doing so are set out at the end of this task.

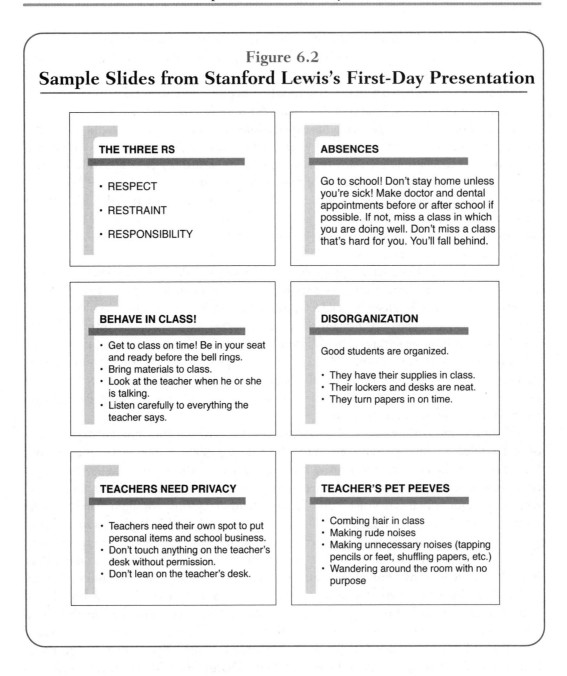

Figure 6.2
Sample Slides from Stanford Lewis's First-Day Presentation

THE THREE RS

- RESPECT
- RESTRAINT
- RESPONSIBILITY

ABSENCES

Go to school! Don't stay home unless you're sick! Make doctor and dental appointments before or after school if possible. If not, miss a class in which you are doing well. Don't miss a class that's hard for you. You'll fall behind.

BEHAVE IN CLASS!

- Get to class on time! Be in your seat and ready before the bell rings.
- Bring materials to class.
- Look at the teacher when he or she is talking.
- Listen carefully to everything the teacher says.

DISORGANIZATION

Good students are organized.

- They have their supplies in class.
- Their lockers and desks are neat.
- They turn papers in on time.

TEACHERS NEED PRIVACY

- Teachers need their own spot to put personal items and school business.
- Don't touch anything on the teacher's desk without permission.
- Don't lean on the teacher's desk.

TEACHER'S PET PEEVES

- Combing hair in class
- Making rude noises
- Making unnecessary noises (tapping pencils or feet, shuffling papers, etc.)
- Wandering around the room with no purpose

The second step in the communication cycle for expectations—monitoring student performance—must be maintained even as students demonstrate success. As stated in chapter 1, if a class requires only a low-structure management plan, you can get by with less direct monitoring, but some level of monitoring is essential for classes of every structure throughout the year.

During the first several days of instruction, plan on giving students frequent feedback on how they are meeting expectations. This is the third step in communicating your expectations and might almost be an ongoing monologue during the activity. With low-structure classes, you can begin to reduce the amount of positive feedback you give as soon as any activity has gone well for several consecutive days. The corrective feedback can be reduced to simply stating the name of a student who is not meeting your expectations. If two students are talking when they should be listening, you may be able to simply say the names of the two students, making brief eye contact, and then continue with your lesson. If you have a class with higher structure, plan to keep the frequency of positive feedback and the descriptive clarity of corrective feedback at a higher level for as long as the first month of school.

Verify that your students understand what is expected from them.

During the second or third week of school, you will need to determine whether your students really understand what you want from them (Assor & Connell, 1992). What you find will help you decide whether to continue actively teaching your expectations or begin tapering them off because students have mastered them. If you find that most of your students can accurately answer specific and detailed questions about your expectations (verbally or on paper), you can begin to phase out the process. However, if you see that a significant percentage cannot answer your questions, continue to conduct lessons on your expectations.

Making the effort to determine your students' understanding of your expectations by giving a quiz, doing a group activity, or conducting interviews will do more than provide you with information on whether they fully understand your expectations: by being willing to take the time to do one or more of these, you further communicate to students the importance you place on them and their knowledge. The easiest and most reliable way to determine whether students understand your expectations is by giving a short written quiz. Later in this task is a sample of a quiz. If this seems too structured for your class, talk to your students to determine what they have retained from your lessons. You could do a thumbs-up, thumbs-down activity or conduct an interview with each student on specific expectations. The disadvantage to this is that unless you interview all of your students or can conduct a whole-class activity to determine student understanding, you may fail to spot those who still do not know exactly what you expect. Unless you are able to interview all your students individually, consider the quiz instead.

Give a quiz.

A written quiz is a simple way to see how much information on your expectations your students are retaining. A major advantage of the quiz, as opposed to interviewing your students, is the relative speed with which you can see how well you are communicating your expectations. A disadvantage is that you are sampling knowledge of only some of your classroom procedures and routines.

Follow these directions for giving a quiz on expectations:

1. *Decide on a format for the quiz.* You can choose from true or false, multiple choice, fill in the blank, short answer, or any combination of formats you like. If you want to hear students' feelings and perceptions of your expectations, you will clearly learn more from a short-answer quiz. If you are interested only in finding out whether students recall procedures as you taught them, one of the simpler formats will work just fine.

2. *Determine the specific content you want to investigate.* Choose one or two activities and one or two transitions to be the focus of your quiz, targeting those for which you have the most complex expectations or that seem to be giving students the most difficulty. The questions on your quiz should deal with whether students can talk during an activity, what kind of movement is allowed, if any, and how students demonstrate participation in an activity. Keep the quiz short enough that your

students can complete it in ten minutes. In addition, you can quiz students on any of the policies and procedures from the syllabus you think are particularly important to review.

3. *Prepare your students to take the quiz.* Announce a few days in advance that you will be giving a quiz to help you identify whether the class understands your expectations and can explain why those expectations are important. Decide whether to grade the quiz, and then make that clear to your students. If it is to be graded, let students know that they cannot succeed academically without knowing how to function responsibly. If the quiz will not be graded, explain to your students that you still expect their best, and that if they do well on the quiz, they will likely be given more responsibility in the future. If you will be covering information from the syllabus, show students the portions they should study. Set aside some class time before the quiz for any questions your students may have. Exhibit 6.4 is a sample quiz on expectations. (See the DVD for a blank reproducible of this form.)

Exhibit 6.4
Sample Quiz on Expectations

Name *Lily Masters*   Date *9/3*

Circle the letter for the best answer to each question.

1. When you enter the classroom and begin working on the challenge problem ...

   (a) you should be completely silent from the moment you enter the room.

   b. you can talk quietly as you enter but must be silent when you take your seat.

   c. you can talk quietly about anything, but when the bell rings, you should be in your seat and then you can talk only about the challenge problem on the overhead projector.

   d. you can talk loudly about anything, but when the bell rings, you should get to your seat within two minutes and then get quiet.

2. During class, you can use the pencil sharpener ...

   a. only before and after class.

   (b) before and after class and during independent work periods.

   c. any time you need to.

   d. at no time without teacher permission.

3. When the teacher gives the attention signal and says, "Class, your attention please," you should ...

   (a) be silent and have your eyes on the teacher within five seconds.

   b. be silent and have your eyes on the teacher within ten seconds.

   c. be silent and have your eyes on the teacher within twenty seconds.

   d. loudly tell other students to be quiet and pay attention to the teacher.

4. During the time the teacher is speaking to the class, you may ...

   a. talk quietly to someone near you and get out of your seat only to sharpen your pencil.

   b. talk quietly to someone near you and not get out of your seat for any reason.

   c. talk only if you have been called on by the teacher and get out of your seat only if you need a drink of water or supplies.

   (d) talk only if you have been called on by the teacher. You may not get out of your seat without permission.

5. Active participation while the teacher is presenting lessons should look and sound a certain way. Circle the items that describe active participation. There are six correct answers.

(a) Sit up straight or lean forward.

(b) Raise your hand if you have something to say.

(c) Answer questions when called on.

d. Write notes to your friends.

(e) Write notes to keep in your binder that will help you study for tests.

f. Tell people who are talking that they need to be quiet and listen.

g. Have things on your desk that will help entertain you during the lesson.

(h) Keep your eyes on the person speaking or on the class notes you are writing.

i. Let your mind wander.

j. Talk while the teacher is talking.

k. Be respectful toward the teacher and other students in what you say and how

l. Call out answers to questions.

m. Be vocal with your opinion.

(n) Actively discuss the lesson.

6. When you return after an absence, you should …

a. ask the teacher, "Did I miss anything while I was gone?"

b. ask another student for his or her notes.

(c) go to the file by the drinking fountain and find the folder for this class period; then take the copied pages for the days you were absent.

d. go to the teacher's desk and open her plan book to the dates you missed, and copy all the important information.

7. In the parentheses after each of the following statements, put a **T** if the concept is true and an **F** if the concept is false about the weekly points you earn for behavior and effort.

a. Every student starts the week with 10 out of 20 possible points. (F)

b. Every reminder the teacher gives you about your behavior or effort in class costs 1 point. (T)

c. Every compliment the teacher gives you about your behavior or effort in class adds 1 point. (T)

d. These points are added into the grade book and are part of your academic grade. (T)

e. The teacher will take points away without informing you about each incident. (F)

f. For severe misbehavior, you can have a choice between an office referral or a loss of points. (F)

g. You can make an appointment to discuss anything you do not understand or think is unfair about this system. (T)

If you find a significant number of errors on the quiz, continue the three-step process of teaching expectations, monitoring behavior, and providing positive and corrective feedback with the whole group or individuals. If the students understand your procedures and expectations, you can begin to eliminate the teaching of expectations. Always remember to keep monitoring, however, by circulating and scanning to keep students aware that you are observing their behavior.

Teach expectations to new students.

The first two weeks of school are the most important time for teaching behavioral expectations and classroom routines. However, most teachers will experience some flux in student population over the course of the year. You are likely to have at least one student leave and at least one new student enter your class. Some schools have such high student mobility rates that fewer than half the students who are in a class at the beginning of the year are still there at the end.

When a new student enters your classroom, some form of orientation, similar to what you provide for all students during the first two weeks of school, is essential to get the student off to a successful start. You must have a plan for this. The higher you expect your student mobility rate to be, the more prepared you will need to be to teach your expectations to new students. There are three basic strategies for teaching your expectations to new students.

Teach the new student individually.   The most common method of orienting a new student to your class is to spend some time with the student one on one, teaching her your expectations. To do this, you should speak with the student for a couple of minutes at the beginning of every activity and transition for several days, up to a week. While your other students do what is expected of them, tell the new student what is happening, and explain your behavioral expectations for that activity or transition. If you used CHAMPS or ACHIEVE sheets to prepare your expectations, you might give the student a copy. At the conclusion of the activity, let the student know how she did and orient her to the next transition and activity.

The advantage of this approach is that it generates frequent contact between you and the new student during her first week in class. The disadvantage is that it requires a great deal of your time, and your focus will be drawn away from the whole class at times. If you are likely to get between one and three new students during the year, pairing this approach with the next step of reteaching the entire class is probably the most effective. However, if you are likely to have many new students during the year, it will be impractical for you to take that much time with each new student.

Reteach the entire class.   You can use the need to orient a new student as an opportunity to go over your expectations for all activities and transitions with the entire class. For one day, immediately before each activity and each major transition, ask students to volunteer some information about procedures and expected behaviors aloud for the benefit of the new student—for example, "Please raise your hand if you can describe one of the important expectations for independent work periods during math class." Call on students until all the important information has been reviewed. If students leave out something critical, review it in detail.

You should take only one day to review all expectations, but expect to spend a bit of time on this material in the next few days until your new student is as comfortable with your expectations as the rest of the class. Offer points to students who go out of their way to help the new student with notes, advice, or help during class if it is clear the new person does not know what is expected of him or her. This procedure has several advantages. The new student gets the essential information, and you review and reinforce the information for the other students.

Having students present the information communicates that the expectations are shared by the class, and not just the teacher. Finally, taking a couple of minutes to do this before each activity or transition makes a statement that you believe that student knowledge of the right way to do things is important enough to take the time to go over it.

The main disadvantage of this system is that if you have to do it more than once or twice, it will take time away from your class, and students may get weary of discussing the same expectations over and over. Therefore, if you get a new student soon after you've reviewed your expectations for another new student, use the method of teaching the student individually or follow the next procedure for student mentoring.

The student mentor system.   With this procedure, you give individual class members the responsibility of orienting new students to the routines and procedures of your class—for example, "Paul, this is Rico. Rico is a student who really gets the procedures that will help him to be successful in this class. He will teach you what a class day will be like and tell you what is expected for each activity. Throughout the class period, you two have permission to quietly talk, even during times when you usually wouldn't be allowed to. Paul, if you have a question about how we do things, you can quietly ask Rico or me. Rico, any time during the next week that something is going on that may be new to Paul, please quietly explain to him what we are doing and why."

If you plan on using this procedure and are likely to have a lot of new students during the year, take time in the second or third week of school to talk to the entire class about how you may call on them individually to help orient a new student. You will likely need to demonstrate and model how a student appropriately mentors a new student. Many students will not know how much or how little guidance to give and may not be skillful in providing constructive feedback. Be sure not to use the same student as a mentor again and again. Have your class share the responsibility of teaching new students class expectations, and as new students demonstrate they are clear on your expectations, they can begin mentoring other newer students.

The advantage of this approach is that it takes pressure off you to spend instructional time with a new student. It also communicates your faith in your students to understand and implement your expectations fully. Be aware, however, of opportunities when you can have some good contact with the new student. You do not want her to feel disconnected with you, and you also want to make sure that she views you as the authority figure. Make a point of interacting with the new student by helping her check her work, or asking if she's comfortable or has any questions.

Task 5: Mark on Your Planning Calendar Particular Times When You Will Reteach Your Expectations

At certain times of the year, student behavior may tend to deteriorate: before and after major breaks, before and after major tests or projects, and toward the end of each school year. If you reteach your expectations before these times, you may be able to reduce this predictable, but not inevitable, phenomenon (Wolf, Bixby, Glenn, & Gardner, 1990). To reteach your expectations during these times, implement the three-step process you used at the beginning of school. Implement step 1 and clarify your expectations before every activity. Then, following step 2, continue to monitor student behavior in a more obvious way than usual. Be more conspicuous with your observing, and move about the class more than you normally would. Finally, using step 3 of the process, provide feedback immediately after each activity and transition. If things go well, congratulate your students on their maturity and responsibility. If things do not go so well, let them know that you expect a higher level of independent management and cooperation from each of them. Briefly go over your expectations again, noting where your students met them and where they did not.

In addition to reteaching behavioral expectations, plan to reteach your Guidelines for Success. Pump up your students to strive to exhibit the traits outlined in the guidelines. Let students know that you will be striving to exhibit these traits yourself, and inform them that you have high expectations for them to do so as well.

For each of the times noted, put a reminder to yourself in your planning calendar to reteach expectations and include a note to yourself about why reteaching at this particular time may be important.

Thanksgiving break.

The length of Thanksgiving break may vary in your school district. In this reference, consider it as the three days before the holiday *and* the three days after it. Students often think that because the week is so short, not much will be going on in school. Remind students each day before the holiday that although the week is short, there will still be a lot of important work that needs to be done and you expect them to have the maturity to stay focused and behave in a responsible and self-disciplined manner. With any break, it is advisable to avoid too many filler or nonrelevant instructional activities because this can contribute to a breakdown in behavior and motivation. Every school day makes a difference in whether students make adequate progress and attain academic benchmarks. If things go well on Monday, you do not need to completely reteach expectations on Tuesday. Simply give a quick reminder at the beginning of class about how well the students did yesterday and how you expect the same today. On Wednesday, plan to reteach your expectations but maintain your normal classroom routine as much as possible. If it is your practice to give some extra free time on the day before a holiday, this should not stop you from doing so. The idea is simply to remind students that their time and behavior in class should not be affected by outside events.

Before winter break.

Throughout December, plan to review your expectations one day each week and remind your students that your expectations in class will not change just because of the holiday season. Emphasize that by continuing with the established procedures and routines, they can concentrate their mental energy on mastering their academic objectives.

If the routines and procedures break down, chaos will result, and nobody learns or thrives in a chaotic classroom. During the last week before the winter break, plan to reteach your expectations at least twice that week, and every day if it becomes necessary.

After winter break.

The days immediately after winter break are a time to begin again. Especially when this is the start of a new semester, inform students that you are going to treat the first day or two back from vacation almost like the first day of school. If you are teaching a semester-only class and have a brand-new group after returning from winter break, follow the procedures outlined at the beginning of this chapter for the first day of school.

Either way, plan to go over the syllabus and pass out extra copies to any students who may have lost theirs. Put special emphasis on policies or procedures that were problematic during the first semester. Use the teaching expectations cycle for the first few days, emphasizing the *positive opposite* of any misbehaviors that begin to occur or that may not have been completely eliminated before the holiday. *Positive opposite* refers to the positive behavior that a student should be engaged in instead of the misbehavior. For example, if students have been responding in disrespectful ways to comments made by other students during group discussions, you could inform students of the problem and let them know that a respectful reaction would be to say nothing, comment positively, or disagree with the content of what the previous speaker said, but not "diss" the person making the comment.

Before major tests.

Two weeks prior to any major accountability testing such as final exams or state testing, plan to reteach your expectations. Let students know that both teacher and students may feel a sense of pressure heading into any high-accountability situation. These stresses can lead to irritability, impatience, and hostility. The best way for the class to avoid such problems is for everyone to strive to do their best, treat everyone with respect, and generally make sure to follow the Guidelines for Success and the class rules. In addition, at least once or twice a week as the testing approaches, reteach your expectations. Emphasize that everyone will do well on the test if the days before the test are well organized, orderly, and efficient rather than frantic and chaotic.

After major tests.

Immediately after any major accountability testing, use the three-step cycle to review your expectations. Some students will assume that once testing is over, class is over and the rest of the year will be free time. Use the act of reteaching expectations to communicate that testing does not mark the end of anything. Emphasize that in your class, you use the entire year, and you expect them to take advantage of the opportunity this gives them.

Spring break.

Immediately before and after spring break, reteach your expectations and the Guidelines for Success in much the same way you did before and after the winter break.

End of the school year.

During the last three to four weeks of school, students will push limits and try to get you to let go of your structure. Return once more to the cycle to let your students know that your structure will stay in place until the last day of school. Let students know that when they have a job, employers do not want efficiency to go down just because a vacation is coming up. Reemphasize the Guidelines for Success and your expectations at least once each week during the last four weeks of school.

Any time multiple students are not meeting your expectations.
Return to teaching your expectations any time student behavior is deteriorating. This is far more effective and time efficient than relying solely on consequences to prompt students about appropriate behavior.

In Conclusion

Careful planning can lead to a positive first day of class, which will set the stage for a productive year. In this chapter, you were shown how to pull everything together by developing a syllabus for your students that you can use to teach your organizational routines and procedures. A template was provided to assist you in this effort. This chapter examined final details to consider before the first day and provided information on how to implement an effective and positive first day of school. Then you learned how to fade the amount of time spent teaching expectations, procedures, and routines, while also planning to reteach your expectations at key times during the year. Each of these steps will bring you closer to having a prepared, contained, and successful class.

Preparation and Launch Self-Assessment Checklist

Use this worksheet to identify which parts of the tasks described in this chapter you have completed. For any item that has not been completed, note what needs to be done to complete it. Then transfer your notes to your planning calendar in the form of specific actions you need to take (for example, "September 5, make a sign for the classroom"). A blank worksheet is on the DVD.

	Task	Notes and Implementation Ideas
☐	*TASK 1: Finalize your classroom management plan, and prepare to communicate that plan to your students.* I reviewed and completed the essential tasks from chapters 1 through 5. I have: • Developed and posted Guidelines for Success (chapter 1, task 3) • Created positive expectations for all students (chapter 1, task 4) • Reviewed the basic principles of behavior management (chapter 1, task 1) • Determined the level of structure for my class (chapter 4, task 1) • Outlined the activities students will engage in during a typical week (chapter 5, task 1) • Decided on what basis I will give grades (chapter 2, tasks 2–4) • Developed classroom procedures (chapter 3, tasks 3–5) • Developed a regular daily schedule (chapter 3, task 1) • Arranged the physical space in the classroom (chapter 3, task 2) • Identified an attention signal (chapter 3, task 3) • Developed beginning and ending routines (chapter 3, task 4) • Identified and posted classroom rules (chapter 4, task 2) • Defined and prepared lessons on behavioral expectations (chapter 4) I have decided how I will communicate my classroom plan to my students (for example, comprehensive syllabus).	*All done, except may need to adjust classroom layout. American History rosters are bigger than usual, so may not be able to use desk clusters.*

☐	*TASK 2: Complete your preparations for the first day.* I understand that having my first day planned will help me spend more time with my students and put them at ease, and help me feel confident, organized, and prepared to motivate my students toward responsible behavior. Toward this end, I have: - Developed a modified class schedule for the first day of school - Made a sign that identifies my classroom - Prepared an initial activity for students to work on when they enter the room - Prepared an orientation handout for parents and guardians	*Need to finish orientation handout by Wed. in time to print for first day.* *May need to adjust first-day schedule based on assembly schedule.*
☐	*TASK 3: Implement your plan for the first day.* I understand that effective implementation of my plan for the first day of school will make my students feel welcome and help them learn to behave responsibly from the beginning. The following strategies will help me do that: - Greeting students individually as they enter the room - Getting students' attention as soon as the bell rings - Communicating essential classroom information in the first ten minutes of the day (class) - Teaching my attention signal - Orienting students to the posted first-day schedule and using the three-step process for communicating my expectations - Concluding the class period by orienting students to my end-of-class procedures	*Currently assigned to hall duty second period. See if I can switch that to prep period (fourth period) so I can greet second-period students.*

☐ TASK 4: *Gradually decrease the amount of time you spend teaching expectations, procedures, and routines.* I understand that teaching expectations on just the first day is not sufficient. I will continue to use the three-step communication for a couple of weeks but gradually decrease the amount of time I spend communicating expectations. However, I will: • Verify that my students understand what is expected of them • Teach my expectations to new students	*Need to think about more efficient way to handle new students. One-on-one isn't going to work with the bigger classes.*
☐ TASK 5: *Mark on your planning calendar particular times when you will reteach your expectations.* I understand that student behavior may deteriorate at particular times of year; therefore, I will reteach my expectations at these times: • Before and after Thanksgiving break • Before and after winter break • Before and after major tests • Before and after spring break • Near the end of school year	*Need to finish orientation handout by Wed. in time to print for first day.* *May need to adjust first-day schedule based on assembly schedule.*

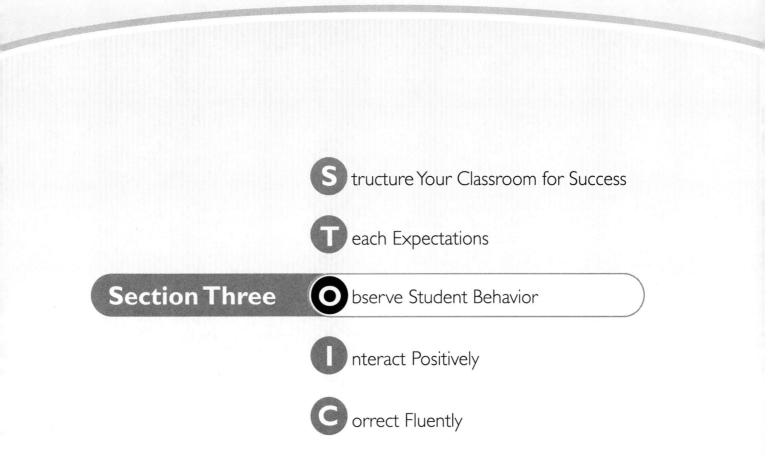

S tructure Your Classroom for Success

T each Expectations

Section Three | **O** bserve Student Behavior

I nteract Positively

C orrect Fluently

Section 3 addresses the O in STOIC: Observe student behavior. You have already structured your classroom for success and set up a plan to teach students to behave successfully. Now you will learn the importance of observing student behavior, as well as how to observe effectively. Chapter 7 provides information on circulating and scanning, as well as on making judgments about when and how to provide positive interactions and praise, and when to correct student misbehavior. The chapter then suggests a range of tools you can use for more objective observations of student behavior and to assess the effectiveness of your management plan so you can make adjustments to increase responsible behavior from your students.

Chapter 7

Monitor Student Behavior

Implement and adjust your classroom management plan

The act of observing affects the behavior of the people being observed (Kazdin, 2001; Repp, Nieminen, Olinger, & Brusca, 1988). This is more true in the classroom than almost anywhere else. You probably remember a teacher who seemed to have eyes in the back of her head. She never missed any rule violation, and there was very little misbehavior in her classroom. You also probably remember a teacher (maybe the same one with that multidirectional vision) whom you liked and admired so much that you never wanted to disappoint her. Perhaps you also remember a classroom where large numbers of students misbehaved because the teacher was so oblivious he never noticed positive *or* negative behavior—he just went through the motions of teaching as though students were not even in the room.

This chapter has two tasks:

Task 1: Circulate whenever possible, and scan all sections of the classroom continuously.

Task 2: Collect objective data about classroom behavior, and adjust your management plan accordingly.

The first task covers strategies and techniques for effectively observing your students' behavior. The second teaches you about the utility and benefits of periodic data collection to determine whether your management plan is working as well as you hope, with suggestions for modifications if it is not. This task includes a calendar plan with suggestions for times during the year to conduct these checkups. It also provides seven specific tools that can help you conduct these periodic objective observations of your classroom:

Tool A: CHAMPS and ACHIEVE versus Daily Reality Rating Scale

Tool B: Ratio of Interactions Monitoring Forms

Tool C: Misbehavior Recording Sheet

Tool D: Grade Book Analysis Worksheet

Tool E: On-Task Behavior Observation Sheet

Tool F: Opportunities to Respond Observation Sheet

Tool G: Student Satisfaction Survey

Task 1: Circulate When Possible, and Scan All Sections of the Classroom Continuously

The importance of observing students by circulating and scanning was identified in the very early research on how effective teachers manage the classroom. Kounin (1970) described effective teachers as having both "with-it-ness" and "in-touch-ness." By circulating throughout the room as much as possible and by using visual and auditory scanning (a fancy term for keeping your eyes and ears open) whether you are circulating or not, you can stay in touch with all parts of the classroom. "With-it-ness" really means that you are not just circulating, looking, and listening, but also mentally paying attention to that information.

> ## Note
> Chapter 7 does not have a self-assessment checklist at the end of the chapter because the whole chapter is about self-assessment.

For example, you are circulating around the room during a cooperative group activity. You notice (through sound and visual cues) that a group across the room—group A—is getting a bit agitated. You know the maturity level of the students, and you want to see if they can work out the problem by themselves, without your intervention. So rather than rushing over to group A, you move to group B about halfway across the room. You look as if you are listening and interacting with group B (and you are), but some of your senses and mind are actually focused on group A. If group A solves the problem, you go over and give positive feedback on their ability to disagree, stay respectful, and resolve the difference in a mature and responsible manner. But if you notice that the intensity of group A's agitation is increasing, you leave group B and go directly to group A—not to scold them, because you arrive before there is any major problem, but rather to guide them through a process for resolving the difficulty in a respectful and responsible way. A teacher who does not scan may not notice that group A is having a problem until it becomes a loud argument or fight, a situation that then requires the teacher to impose a corrective consequence.

Keep in mind that you are not just observing for problems, but also for opportunities to give the class and individuals positive feedback. When you scan early in an independent work period and notice a student working hard—someone who in the past has tended to get off task—go to that student immediately and provide a positive interaction, such as descriptive praise (more on this in chapter 8). In other words, scan for problems, but also scan for opportunities to provide meaningful positive feedback.

Circulating

Whenever possible, circulate throughout the classroom in unpredictable patterns. Do not spend the majority of your time in any one part of the room, and avoid a walking pattern that may let students know that you will not be near them for a significant amount of time. This is especially important during independent work periods and cooperative group activities. Your proximity communicates your concern for and interest in the students. It also communicates that if someone chooses to engage in misbehavior, you will likely notice.

Obviously there are times when circulating is difficult—for instance, when you are teaching a small group or presenting to the class using an overhead or digital visual presenter. However, whenever you can, try to move about the room. For example, in the middle of teaching a thirty-minute focus group, you might consider giving the students in the group a short task to perform independently while you quickly circulate among the other students. Then you can resume instruction with the small group. Or while you are teaching a math lesson to the whole class with an overhead projector, you might give students a couple of problems to work on and then circulate through the room. After looking at students' work, you can return to the overhead and continue with the teacher-directed portion of the lesson. Another benefit of this kind of circulating is that you can conduct informal checks of students' understanding. In the example, by circulating while students are attempting a few problems during the whole-class math lesson, you would be able to see how well students are understanding and following your instruction. This can help you decide whether to move on to independent work or a new subject or whether to continue with more guided practice.

Remember, as you circulate, give positive feedback to students who are meeting your expectations, answer any questions students may have, and provide gentle reprimands or consequences to students who are not meeting expectations (Colvin et al., 1997; De Pry & Sugai, 2002). And always try to avoid staying too long in any one place.

Visual Scanning

Regardless of what you and the students are doing, you should have a clear line of sight to all students and visually scan all settings in the classroom frequently (Emmer et al., 1980; Scheuermann & Hall, 2008; Shores, Gunter, & Jack, 1993). For example, when you are circulating, don't look just at the students nearest to you; visually sweep any place students are present, even a learning center across the room. When you are conducting a whole-class activity, visually scan the back rows and the front corners. When you are helping an individual student with her work, plan to stand up occasionally and look around the room. When you are teaching a small group, look up from the group periodically and observe students who are working at their seats.

As you scan, look for any misbehavior that requires correction. If a student is engaged in a misbehavior, go to the student and issue a gentle reprimand or assign an appropriate consequence. Also look for opportunities to acknowledge and encourage responsible behavior. For example, if you notice that a particular student who tends to be off task is working, go to that student at the next opportunity and give him age-appropriate positive feedback. Or if a cooperative group is handling a conflict in a responsible way, go over to the group when there is a pause in their interactions and congratulate them on the mature way they are handling the situation.

Finally, use visual scanning to identify students who may have questions or otherwise need your assistance. During independent work periods especially (when you are not engaged with a small group), look for students who have signaled that they need assistance. If you ask students to use a flag or open book as a signal for help (see chapter 2, task 6), you need to show them that the signal actually works. If students find that you don't respond when they signal, they will stop using it and instead will come to you or call out to get your attention.

Auditory Scanning

In addition to looking to all parts of the classroom, you should listen to all parts of the classroom. Within your management plan there will emerge a baseline, or normal, level of background noise in your room—though this level may be quieter or louder than the normal level of other teachers in your building. Whenever you notice a change in the baseline level of background noise, turn up your level of "with-it-ness"—that is, analyze whether the change is a problem. The noise level may increase because students are very excited and engaged about the assigned cooperative task, and they may just need a gentle reminder to keep their conversations quiet enough so that the noise does not disturb the class next door. Or the noise level may suddenly decrease because students become aware of a conflict brewing between two students in the back of the room and stop what they are doing to see what is going to happen.

Actively observe your students by circulating in unpredictable patterns whenever possible and by consistently using both visual and auditory scanning. You will use the information from this continuous observation process to make judgments about when to prompt students to solve a problem before it has escalated (see the group A example above), when to capitalize on reinforceable opportunities, and—whenever you observe rule violations—when to apply corrective consequences consistently, calmly, and immediately.

Task 2: Collect Objective Data about Classroom Behavior, and Adjust Your Management Plan Accordingly

When you objectively monitor what is going on in your classroom, you will be able to make adjustments to your classroom management plan that will increase student success. Objective data can help you determine which aspects of your management plan should be maintained, which may need to be altered, and whether your level of structure is adequate.

To help you with your decisions about these issues, this book includes a variety of tools for collecting and evaluating objective information about your classroom and a recommended schedule for when to use each tool. It is also recommended that you periodically videotape or audiotape yourself as you deliver lessons. This can make recording objective data simpler than trying to do it as you teach. Recording yourself teaching also often leads to other realizations about things that you are doing well as well as areas for improvement. Most computers have video- and audio-recording features, and there are inexpensive microphones you can purchase for your phone or mp3 player. Some districts may have restrictions about when and how you can tape students, so be sure to check with your administrator before doing any recording in your classroom.

Without accurate information, your decisions are likely to be based on hunches, guesses, or whatever feels right at the moment (Brophy, 1983; Royer, Cisero, & Carlo, 1993). One of the requirements of professionalism is making informed decisions based on objective information. To use an example from the medical profession, when you go in for a routine physical examination, your physician gathers a variety of information: pulse, respiration, blood pressure, blood sugar, cholesterol levels, and so on. Then your doctor objectively evaluates the information she has gathered, along with your subjective reports about how you feel, and makes a judgment about your overall health. She may decide that you are just fine, or she may decide that additional information needs to be collected, or she may suggest that a treatment plan be implemented. Without the objective data, your physician would be acting only off your reports and would be much less able to assess your overall health accurately or make useful recommendations regarding your health care.

You can use the tools presented in the following pages to gather objective information about the overall health of your current classroom management plan. Following is a brief description of each of these tools. Reminding yourself to use them to periodically evaluate your strengths and areas for improvement is a powerful way to grow as a professional.

Tool A: CHAMPS and ACHIEVE versus Daily Reality Rating Scales. This tool allows you to look at each major activity and transition during your class and evaluate on a five-point scale how well students are meeting your CHAMPS expectations for that activity or transition. With that information, you will then be able to decide whether you need to reteach your CHAMPS expectations or modify the level of structure you have selected as most appropriate for your students. You should monitor this particular aspect of your classroom management plan (i.e., the actual implementation of your CHAMPS expectations) several times a year. A modified version of this tool is provided for those using the ACHIEVE acronym and worksheet to define expectations.

Tool B: Ratio of Interactions Monitoring Forms. There are three versions of this tool for determining whether you have fallen into the criticism trap and are paying so much attention to misbehavior that you could be helping to perpetrate it. Putting emphasis on what students are doing right, through increasing positive ratios of interaction, has been shown to be one of the most powerful tools for behavioral change. This is discussed in detail in chapter 8. The primary Ratio of Interactions Monitoring form allows you to document your interactions with students during a particular class period. You can use the supplementary forms to document interactions with a specific student or to monitor your interactions in regard to a specific behavior. You will then be able to see how much time you spend with particular students and the amount of attention you give to particular misbehaviors or positive behaviors. This will allow you to adjust your monitoring habits to be more effective in your classroom.

Tool C: Misbehavior Recording Sheet. Keeping a systematic record of your students' misbehavior for one day with all of your classes, or for one week with one or two of your most problematic classes, can help you determine whether you need to adjust your level of structure or whether one or more of your students would benefit from a targeted behavior management plan or classwide motivation system. There are four versions of this tool; choose the one that will allow you to most easily record any misbehavior that occurs in your classroom.

Tool D: Grade Book Analysis Worksheet. An up-to-date grade book has a wealth of data. This tool shows you how to compile and analyze the data in your grade book to determine whether individual students are exhibiting chronic problems with absenteeism, tardiness, work completion, or assignment failure. You can use the information from this analysis to make judgments about whether any student, or the class as a whole, would benefit from the implementation of a behavior management plan that targets one or more of these problems.

Tool E: On-Task Behavior Observation Sheet. This simple tool can be used to determine your class's average rate of on-task behavior during independent work times. If students are on task less than 80 percent of the time, you need to reteach your CHAMPS or

ACHIEVE expectations for work periods or implement some form of classwide incentive system that will encourage students to use class work times more productively.

Tool F: Opportunities to Respond Observation Sheet. This tool can be used to examine the degree to which you actively engage students in your lesson. By making a videotape or by having a colleague observe you, you can determine how frequently students have the opportunity to respond—that is, to actually do something as opposed to being passive recipients of the lesson content. This provides one measure to help you evaluate the effectiveness of your instructional presentations and lesson design.

Tool G: Student Satisfaction Survey. Just as many businesses find it worthwhile to look at the satisfaction of their customers, you, too, can benefit from knowing how satisfied your students are with your classroom. This is a short survey that you can give to students at the end of the year or the end of each semester. The information will help you identify any aspects of your classroom management plan that you need to communicate more clearly or present differently.

You are much more likely to use these tools if you build their implementation into your schedule. Therefore, write the prompts that follow into your calendar now. Each prompt should be as close to the suggested date as possible, allowing for scheduled events like class trips or testing.

As the year progresses and you come to a particular prompt on your calendar, go to the specified part of this book and follow the directions for collecting and analyzing your data. For now, simply familiarize yourself with the schedule and look at any tools you think you will use. You will not need to be thoroughly familiar with any of them at this time. When it is time to use a tool, plan on carefully reviewing it before implementing it.

Here is a possible schedule:

Week 3	Student interviews or quiz on classroom expectations (chapter 6, task 1)
Week 4 or 5	CHAMPS versus Daily Reality Rating Scales (Tool A)
Second month (early)	Ratio of Interactions Monitoring Forms (Tool B)
Second month (late)	Opportunities to Respond Observation Sheet (Tool F)
Third month (early)	Misbehavior Recording Sheet (Tool C)
Third month (late)	Grade Book Analysis Worksheet (Tool D)
Fourth month	On-Task Behavior Observation Sheet (Tool E)
End of semester	Student Satisfaction Survey (Tool G)
January (early)	CHAMPS versus Daily Reality Rating Scales (Tool A)
January (late)	Misbehavior Recording Sheet (Tool C)
February (early)	Ratio of Interactions Monitoring Forms (Tool B)
February (late)	On-Task Behavior Observation Sheet (Tool E)
March (early)	Grade Book Analysis Worksheet (Tool D)
April (after spring break)	Opportunities to Respond Observation Sheet (Tool F)
End of semester	Student Satisfaction Survey (Tool G)

Even if you have started implementing this book during the school year, you can still use this time line. From today's date, identify the next recommended evaluation activity. Write it on your planning calendar along with all the activities suggested for the remainder of the year. Implement those activities at the appropriate times.

Tool A: CHAMPS and ACHIEVE versus Daily Reality Rating Scales

The CHAMPS (or ACHIEVE) versus Daily Reality Rating Scales will help you determine the degree to which student behavior matches your expectations during daily activities and transitions.

Why
- To help you decide whether you need to reteach expectations
- To help you decide whether your current level of structure fits the needs of your class
- To help you decide whether you need a classwide system to increase students' motivation

When
- During the fourth or fifth week of school
- Shortly after winter break

How
1. Find the appropriate forms on the DVD and print copies. Exhibit 7.1 is designed for those using CHAMPS expectations, and exhibit 7.2 is intended for those using ACHIEVE expectations.

2. Choose one or more class periods in which student behavior tends to be the most problematic.

3. Identify the major activities and transitions that occur during the class period. Write each activity and transition on the "Activity" line in one of the form's rating boxes.

   If you plan to do this for several classes, you may want to spread your analysis across more than one day. For example, one day you might evaluate your first and third periods and the next day evaluate fifth and seventh periods.

4. Before each activity or transition, briefly review your expectations with students. Immediately after completing the activity or transition, rate the degree to which students met your expectations, using the following rating scale:

   5 = All students met expectations

   4 = All but one or two students met expectations

   3 = Most students met expectations

   2 = About half the class met expectations

   1 = Most students did not meet expectations

5. Review the data you have collected, and determine which activities or transitions may require reteaching of expectations. Exhibits 7.1 and 7.2 show sample completed forms and conclusions for, respectively, CHAMPS and ACHIEVE. (See the DVD for blank templates of these two forms.) In addition, consider the following information as you interpret your data:

   - If all activities and transitions are rated 4 or 5, you should not have to change your class's level of structure. If you have one or two students whose behavior concerns you, consider using one of the individual behavior management plans in chapter 9.

- If only 70 percent of activities and transitions are rated 4 or 5, it may be a good idea over the next few days to reteach expectations for activities that did not consistently go well. See chapter 6, task 3 for ideas. Again, if you have one or two students who seem to be having trouble with the structure of the class, consult chapter 9 for some ideas.

- If fewer than 70 percent of activities and transitions are rated 4 or 5, reteach your expectations and the policies and procedures outlined in your syllabus. See chapter 6, task 3 for ideas. In addition, consider increasing the structure of your class. Review the tasks in chapter 3 to determine which organizational aspects of your current classroom management plan might benefit from higher structure.

- If fewer than 50 percent of activities and transitions are rated 4 or 5, implement one of the class-wide systems suggested in chapter 8, task 5. In addition, reteach your expectations and the policies and procedures outlined in your syllabus. See chapter 6, task 3 for ideas. Finally, consider increasing the structure of your class. Review the tasks in chapter 3 to determine which aspects of your current classroom management plan might be implemented in a more structured manner.

> **Note**
>
> Some teachers may want to involve students in the rating process. If you choose to do this, explain the purpose and procedures ahead of time. Be sure to make clear that their input should not refer to individual students who did not meet expectations. (Reproducible masters of enlarged versions of both rating forms are provided on the DVD; exhibit 7.1b is the CHAMPS form, and exhibit 7.2b is the ACHIEVE version.) You may want to display the appropriate enlargement on a document camera or from your computer if you plan to involve your class in the rating process.

Exhibit 7.1
CHAMPS versus Daily Reality Rating Scale

Teacher Name: Julie Howard

Class Period: Second   Date: Sept. 25

RATINGS

5 = All students met expectations

4 = All but one or two students met expectations

3 = Most students met expectations

2 = About half the class met expectations

1 = Most students did not meet expectations

Conversation 1 2 3 4 ⑤ **Help (Teacher Attention)** 1 2 3 4 ⑤ **Activity:** Before the bell **Movement** 1 2 3 4 ⑤ **Participation** 1 2 3 4 ⑤ **Success**	**Conversation** 1 ② 3 4 5 **Help (Teacher Attention)** 1 2 3 4 ⑤ **Activity:** Cooperative groups **Movement** 1 2 3 4 ⑤ **Participation** 1 2 3 ④ 5 **Success**
Conversation 1 2 3 4 ⑤ **Help (Teacher Attention)** 1 2 3 4 ⑤ **Activity:** Attendance/opening **Movement** 1 2 3 ④ 5 **Participation** 1 2 3 4 ⑤ **Success**	**Conversation** 1 2 3 4 ⑤ **Help (Teacher Attention)** 1 2 3 4 ⑤ **Activity:** Getting ready for independent work **Movement** 1 2 3 4 ⑤ **Participation** 1 2 3 4 5 **Success**
Conversation 1 2 3 4 ⑤ **Help (Teacher Attention)** 1 2 3 4 ⑤ **Activity:** Teacher-directed instruction — Math **Movement** 1 2 3 ④ 5 **Participation** 1 2 3 ④ 5 **Success**	**Conversation** 1 2 3 ④ 5 **Help (Teacher Attention)** 1 2 3 4 ⑤ **Activity:** Independent Work **Movement** 1 2 3 ④ 5 **Participation** 1 2 3 4 ⑤ **Success**
Conversation 1 ② 3 4 5 **Help (Teacher Attention)** 1 2 3 4 ⑤ **Activity:** Getting into cooperative group (T) **Movement** 1 2 3 4 ⑤ **Participation** 1 2 3 ④ 5 **Success**	**Conversation** 1 2 3 ④ 5 **Help (Teacher Attention)** 1 2 3 4 ⑤ **Activity:** Wrap-up/closing **Movement** 1 2 3 4 ⑤ **Participation** 1 2 3 4 ⑤ **Success**

Analysis

In this sample, only one activity (Cooperative Groups) and one transition (Getting into Cooperative Groups) have ratings that are less than 4 or 5. The ratings indicate that the main problem is that students are talking too loudly, so the noise level in the room is excessive. Therefore, the teacher decides to leave the classroom at a low level of structure. However, she plans to reteach her behavioral expectations, with a special emphasis on how students in each cooperative group can monitor and manage the voice levels within their own groups.

Exhibit 7.2
ACHIEVE versus Daily Reality Rating Scale

Teacher Name: Frank Wu

Class Period: Fourth   Date: Oct. 5

RATINGS

5 = All students met expectations

4 = All but one or two students met expectations

3 = Most students met expectations

2 = About half the class met expectations

1 = Most students did not meet expectations

Activity: Before bell					
Conversation	1	②	3	4	5
Help	1	2	3	4	⑤
Integrity	1	2	3	4	⑤
Effort	1	2	③	4	5
Value	1	2	3	④	5
Efficiency	1	2	③	4	5

Activity: Attendance/Opening					
Conversation	1	2	③	4	5
Help	1	2	3	4	⑤
Integrity	1	2	3	4	⑤
Effort	1	2	3	④	5
Value	1	2	3	4	⑤
Efficiency	1	2	3	④	5

Activity: Teacher instruction					
Conversation	1	2	3	④	5
Help	1	2	3	4	⑤
Integrity	1	2	3	4	⑤
Effort	1	2	3	④	5
Value	1	2	3	4	⑤
Efficiency	1	2	3	4	⑤

Activity: Independent work					
Conversation	1	2	3	④	5
Help	1	2	3	④	5
Integrity	1	2	3	4	⑤
Effort	1	2	3	4	⑤
Value	1	2	3	4	⑤
Efficiency	1	2	3	4	⑤

Activity: Computer time					
Conversation	1	2	3	④	5
Help	1	2	3	④	5
Integrity	1	2	3	4	⑤
Effort	1	2	3	4	⑤
Value	1	2	3	4	⑤
Efficiency	1	2	3	④	5

Activity: Partners/teams					
Conversation	1	2	3	4	⑤
Help	1	2	3	4	⑤
Integrity	1	2	3	4	⑤
Effort	1	2	3	④	5
Value	1	2	3	4	⑤
Efficiency	1	2	3	④	5

Transition 1: Arriving/Getting ready for class					
Length of transition	1	②	3	4	5
Amount/type of conversation	1	2	③	4	5
Appropriate movement	1	2	③	4	5
Appropriate participation	1	②	3	4	5

Transition 2: Breaking into partners/teams					
Length of transition	1	2	3	④	5
Amount/type of conversation	1	2	3	4	⑤
Appropriate movement	1	2	3	4	⑤
Appropriate participation	1	2	3	④	5

Transition 3: Moving to/from computer area					
Length of transition	1	2	③	4	5
Amount/type of conversation	1	2	3	④	5
Appropriate movement	1	2	③	4	5
Appropriate participation	1	2	3	④	5

Analysis

In this sample, the activities before the bell and attendance/opening have ratings lower than 4 or 5. The ratings indicate that the students are spending too much time talking with each other instead of getting ready for class and starting the assignment Mr. Wu posts on the board. The lack of focus carries over into the opening/attendance procedure. Mr. Wu decides to reteach the morning routine and also evaluate the assignments he posts to see if they need to be more engaging or challenging. Ratings also indicate that the transition to and from the computer area could be more efficient. Because students take turns using the computers (rotating by team), Mr. Wu decides to time the transitions this week to see if the problem is specific to certain teams.

Tool B: Ratio of Interactions Monitoring Forms

The Ratio of Interactions Monitoring forms will help you to determine whether you are interacting with students at least three times more when they are behaving responsibly than when they are misbehaving. Note that on the DVD, there are three separate formats for the template: monitoring during a particular time of day (exhibit 7.3a), with a particular student (exhibit 7.3b), and with a particular behavior (exhibit 7.3c). The example later in this section, exhibit 7.3, is monitoring during a particular time of day.

Why

- To help you evaluate whether you have fallen into the criticism trap: responding to misbehavior so frequently that although the misbehavior stops in the short run, it will actually increase over time

- To help you decide whether you need to increase the number of interactions you have with students when they are behaving appropriately

When

- During the second month of school
- In early to mid-February

How

1. Print a copy (or copies) of exhibit 7.3 from the DVD.

2. Make sure you thoroughly understand the difference between positive interactions with students and negative interactions with students. Review the following:

   - Student behavior, not the teacher's tone or intent, determines whether the interaction is counted as positive or negative. When you interact with a student who is engaging in appropriate or desirable behavior, the interaction would be counted as "Attention to Positive."

     Attention to Positive Examples

Praise	"Owen, you have been using this work time very efficiently and have accomplished a great deal."
Noncontingent attention	"Charlene, how are you today?"
Implementing a positive system	"Theresa and Josh each earned a marble in the jar for the class. They worked out a disagreement without needing my help."

     Note that the comment under "Implementing a positive system" would be counted as two positive interactions because the teacher gave attention to two different students.

   - When you interact with a student who is engaging in inappropriate or undesirable behavior, the interaction should be recorded as "Attention to Negative."

Attention to Negative Examples

Reminders	"Cody, you need to get back to work."
Reprimands	"Hanna, you know that you should be keeping your hands to yourself."
Corrections	"Ty, I don't think you need to tell me about that because I think you can handle it on your own."
Warnings	"Jennifer, if I have to speak to you again about talking in class, I will have to call your mother."
Consequences	"Priya, that is disruptive. You owe one minute at the end of class."

3. Determine the class periods during which you seem to have the most trouble being positive with students. Record (using audio- or videotape) those periods for one day.

4. Listen to (or watch) the recording, and mark your interactions on the Ratio of Interactions Monitoring Form. To do this, make a tally mark under "Attention to Positive" for each interaction you had with a student or the class when the behavior was responsible. Make a tally mark under "Attention to Negative" for each interaction you had with a student or the class when the behavior was irresponsible. Do not mark instructions to the group, like what page to turn to or instructions on an activity, at all. You should, however, count an instruction to an individual student, such as, "Beth, please turn out the lights," as positive or negative based on how the student was behaving at the time of the instruction.

5. If you wish to get more detailed information, consider using codes instead of simple tally marks for each interaction. For example:

    M or F: Brief attention to an individual male or female student

    C: Brief attention to the class or a group

    F/15: Attention to an individual female lasting approximately 15 seconds

    NC: Noncontingent attention to a student (for example, "Good morning")

    NV: Nonverbal attention (that is, a reassuring smile or a threatening look)

6. Calculate your ratio of positive interactions to negative interactions with students. If you coded your interactions as suggested in step 5, you can further analyze them by type of attention, gender, and so on.

7. Analyze your performance. Evaluate whether you achieved an overall three-to-one ratio of positives to negatives. Evaluate whether your ratio of positives to negatives varies by category (e.g., your ratio is lower with girls than boys). Evaluate the overall style of your interactions, noting your tone of voice, sincerity, and intensity, and determine whether you are satisfied with it. Evaluate the contingency of the positive feedback you give to individual students. Evaluate whether one or two individuals received most of the negative interactions. If so, plan to use the Ratio of Interactions with a Particular Student form. Evaluate if you had to correct a particular category of behavior (e.g., off-task talking) more frequently than other problems. If so, use the Ratio of Interactions Monitoring Form with a Particular Behavior.

8. Plan a course of action. If your overall interactions, or any subset of interactions, do not reflect a three-to-one positive-to-negative ratio, use the strategies suggested next

and make an effort to decrease attention to negative behavior and increase attention to positive behavior. After approximately two weeks, monitor your interactions again to see if you have achieved the desired three-to-one ratio. Once you have successfully done this, check for an improvement in student behavior. If students are behaving better, congratulate yourself and keep up the good work. If they are not, carefully read chapter 8 to see if there are any variables regarding student motivation that you have not implemented. In addition, read chapter 9 to determine whether a motivation system might be appropriate.

Exhibit 7.3 shows a completed sample form with a brief analysis of its results.

> **Note**
>
> If your ratios of interaction are skewed toward the negative, consider reteaching your expectations in addition to making efforts to increase your positive interactions. This will make it more likely that students are demonstrating the expected behaviors, giving you additional opportunities to praise and acknowledge with positive interactions. Continue with different methods of reteaching and reviewing your expectations until your ratios of interaction are three-to-one positive to negative.

Increasing Positive Interactions

As necessary, implement one or more of the following strategies:

1. Each time you have a negative interaction, remind yourself that you "owe" three positives.

2. Identify specific times during each day when you will give individual students, or the whole class, positive feedback on some aspect of their behavior or class performance. For example, at the beginning of the math lesson, you might compliment five or six students who are doing well or are paying attention.

3. Use individual conference times to compliment individual students on their performance.

4. Frequently scan the room for behaviors you can reinforce.

5. Identify particular events that occur during the day (e.g., a student getting a drink of water) that will serve as a prompt to observe the class and identify a behavior to reinforce.

6. Reduce the amount of attention (time and intensity) a student receives for misbehavior. Increase the amount of attention (time and intensity) a student receives when not engaged in misbehavior.

7. Mentally tell yourself that each time you attend to a negative behavior, you "owe" that student three positive interactions when she or he is not engaged in misbehavior.

8. Interact with students frequently with noncontingent positives.

Decreasing Negative Interactions

As necessary, implement one or more of the following strategies:

1. Identify whether you might modify any aspects of the physical setting, schedule, organization, or something else to reduce the probability that students will misbehave. For example, if some students push others in the rush to get out the door, excuse the students by rows or table groups.

2. Try "precorrecting" misbehavior. For example, if you anticipate that students will push each other while leaving the classroom, give a prompt like, "Remember to keep your hands and feet to yourself as you are leaving the room when I excuse the class."

3. Try praising someone for doing it the "right way" and intervene only if the misbehaving student does not change the behavior.

4. Classwide motivation systems provide gentle peer pressure on students to eliminate common misbehaviors or increase specific positive behaviors. This will reduce the likelihood that you need to intervene and have a negative interaction. Classwide systems work especially well for high-frequency, lower-level misbehaviors, like reducing minor disruptions (e.g., side talking, blurting, out of seat) or for increasing specific positive behaviors like homework completion and punctuality. For example, if the class is averaging twenty-five incidents of disruptive misbehavior that you are having to address (twenty-five negative interactions), create a class system that emphasizes reducing the number of disruptions. Or if the class is averaging 80 percent on students being on time with all needed materials, create a class system with a goal of increasing punctuality to 90 percent. See chapter 8, task 5 for more information on how to develop and implement a classwide motivation system.

Your goal here is not to eliminate all negative interactions. Some are essential. For example, if a student does not know that a particular behavior is unacceptable, a gentle correction is the most direct and efficient way to provide the information the student needs to be successful. Or if you have a preestablished corrective consequence for a particular behavior, you must intervene any time a student exhibits that behavior in order to maintain consistency. The goal is to shift the focus of your attention primarily from the negative to the positive. This will teach students they gain more attention, praise, and other positive things from appropriate behavior rather than from inappropriate.

Exhibit 7.3

Ratio of Interactions Monitoring Form during a Particular Time of Day

Teacher: Mrs. Hammond   Date: October 12

Period/Class/Time of Day: Third period

Coding System:

M = Male

F = Female

N = Nick

C = Class (as a whole)

Attention to Positive	Attention to Negative
M, M, M, F, M, F	N, N, M, N, F, F, N
F, C, F, N, F, M	N, C, M, M, N
C, M, M, N, F, M	

Analysis and Plan of Action:

My overall ratio is 1.5:1, so I need to decrease negatives and increase positives to get to 3:1 ratios. (If Nick's data are pulled out, I am almost at 3:1!!)

My interactions with Nick are 1:3 (negative), so I should work on this and monitor my interactions with Nick in a week.

Tool C: Misbehavior Recording Sheet

The Misbehavior Recording Sheet will help you determine whether you require an intervention plan to deal with specific types of student misbehavior. There are two forms of this template on the DVD: a recording sheet by student name (exhibit 7.4a) and a recording sheet by the weekly seating chart (exhibit 7.4b). The example for this section, exhibit 7.4, uses the student name form. If you are using behavior and effort grading (see chapter 2), you probably already have a very good record of the frequency and kind of misbehaviors occurring in your class. This tool will help you analyze student misbehavior with greater specificity.

Why

- To help you identify how often and why you are intervening with students regarding their inappropriate behaviors
- To help you detect any patterns in your students' misbehavior (e.g., time of day, day of the week, individual students)
- To give you specific and objective information about individual student behavior that you can share with the student and her family when necessary
- To help you decide whether you need a classwide system to increase students' motivation to behave responsibly

When

- During the early part of the third month of school
- Again in mid- to late January

How

1. Determine how you will track misbehavior in your class.

    Decide whether to monitor misbehavior in one, two, or all of your classes. Try it initially with only one class for a week. You should probably start with the class with the most misbehavior. If you find the information useful, you can then decide whether to use the form with the rest of your classes.

    Choose either exhibit 7.4a or 7.4b from the DVD, and print copies from it. If you wish to design your own form, you can certainly do so, but you should look to those in this chapter for the essentials. The example for this section, exhibit 7.4, is a weekly record of misbehavior by day, organized by student name. This form is designed for one class, so if you plan to monitor multiple classes, use a separate copy for each.

    The second form on the DVD, exhibit 7.4b, is for teachers who find it easier to use a seating chart rather than an alphabetical listing to record data. It provides weekly records of misbehavior organized by student seating, with a square representing each desk. Use the form weekly, with one form per class. Use the horizontal lines within the square to track the days of the week. If the desks in your classroom are arranged in clusters or a U shape, you will have to create your own form.

2. Put the appropriate misbehavior recording sheet on a clipboard. Plan to keep the clipboard close by for a week of the classes you have decided to monitor.

3. Explain to students that for the next five classes, you will be recording any time you have to speak to them about inappropriate behavior.

4. Whenever you speak to a student about a misbehavior, note the specific misbehavior on the form, using a coding system such as the following:

   o = Off-task

   h = Hands/feet/objects bothering others

   t = Talking

   d = Disruption

   s = Out of seat

   a = Arguing

   It is essential that your code consist of easy-to-remember letters to represent each major type of misbehavior you are likely to deal with.

5. Analyze the data and determine a plan of action. You may find that the behavior of some students improves simply because you are keeping records. If so, consider using the misbehavior recording sheet on an ongoing basis, although if you do so, you may wish to build in a positive component as well, which you can do by using a behavioral grading method (see chapter 2, task 2).

   Make a subjective decision regarding your level of concern about the amount of misbehavior in your class. If you are not particularly concerned, do not bother making any changes.

   If you *are* concerned about the amount of misbehavior in your class, analyze the data from the Misbehavior Recording Sheet. First, determine how much of the misbehavior is exhibited by just a few students. Identify the two or three students who had the most frequent incidents of misbehavior, and calculate the percentage of the total class misbehavior that can be attributed to them. To find this number, divide the total number of misbehaviors exhibited by the two or three students by the total number of misbehaviors exhibited by the entire class. For example, if the three students' total for two days was 45 and the total for the rest of the students was 16, divide 45 by the misbehavior total of 61 (45 + 16) to get a percentage of 74.

Once you have identified the percentage of misbehavior exhibited by the top two or three misbehaving students, use the following criteria to determine the most appropriate action:

- If more than 90 percent of the total classroom misbehavior can be attributed to those particular students, keep your level of structure and procedures as they are. For the individuals with the most misbehavior, consider implementing individual behavior management plans (see chapter 9 for strategies for individual students).

- If 60 to 89 percent of the total classroom misbehavior can be

Note

It may seem to you right now that you will spend all your time recording information. However, remember that you are only going to mark one letter each time you have to speak to a student about misbehavior, which takes only a second or two. The hardest part of this task is not the time but remembering to keep the form near you when you are teaching and while you are circulating throughout the room.

attributed to the two or three individuals, plan to reteach your expectations for a few days and then once per week for another month (see chapter 8, task 1). In addition, consider individual behavior management plans for the students whose behavior is the most problematic (see chapter 9).

- If less than 60 percent of the misbehavior can be attributed to the two or three individuals, your problem is classwide, and you should review and implement all the suggestions for high structure in chapter 3. Also, plan to reteach your expectations for a few days and then once a week for another month (see chapter 8, task 1). Also consider implementing one or more of the classwide systems discussed in chapter 8.

Tool D: Grade Book Analysis Worksheet

The Grade Book Analysis Worksheet will help you determine whether the rates of tardies, attendance, work completion, and work quality among your students are satisfactory.

Why
- To help you decide whether you need to implement a plan to improve:

    Student punctuality rates

    Student attendance rates

    Student work completion rates

    The quality of student work

When
- During the third month of school
- Again in early to mid-March

How
1. Make copies of the form shown in exhibit 7.5 from the DVD. (A completed example can be found later in this section in exhibit 7.5.)

2. Calculate rates of punctuality, attendance, work completion, and work quality for each student in your class and then record them on the Grade Book Analysis Worksheet.

    - To calculate the *punctuality rate* for each student, divide the actual number of days the student arrived on time to your class by the total number of days school has been in session.
    - To calculate the *attendance rate* for each student, divide the actual number of days the student has been at school by the total number of days school has been in session.
    - To calculate the *rate of work completion* for each student, divide the actual number of in-class and homework assignments the student has turned in by the total number of in-class assignments that have been due to now.
    - To calculate the *percentage of quality work*, first determine what you consider to be quality work. You can define quality as any assignment with a passing grade or above, or you may prefer to define quality as a particular grade. For each student, divide the number of assignments that meet your definition of quality by the total number of assignments given to date.

Exhibit 7.4
Misbehavior Recording Sheet, Daily by Student Name

Date 11/3   Reminders On Wed. remind about Fri. test   Class Period 2

Name	Mon.	Tues.	Wed.	Thurs.	Fri.		Total
Anderson, Chantel				J			1
Bahena, Ruben							0
Carrouza, Melinda		J		J	J		3
Cummings, Teresa							0
Demalski, Lee			J				1
Diaz, Margo							0
Fujiyama, Kim							0
Henry, Scott	D D J	D O		D J	J		8
Isaacson, Chris							0
Kaufman, Jamie				D			1
King, Mark							0
LaRouche, Janel				J			1
Morales, Maria Louisa				J			1
Narlin, Jenny							0
Neely, Jacob			O	O			2
Nguyen, Trang							0
Ogden, Todd	J J D	D	O O	J	J J		9
Pallant, Jared							0
Piercey, Dawn			J	O	J		3
Reaves, Myra							0
Thomason, Rahsaan	J J		J	J	J J		6
Vandever, Aaron							0
Wong, Charlene							0
Yamamota, James		J		O J			3

Codes: D = Disruption, O = Off task, J = Talking

Analysis and Plan of Action: Scott Henry, Todd Ogden, and Rahsaan Thomason are the students who misbehave the most. Together they had a total of 23 misbehaviors for the week. The class total including them was 39. That means the misbehaviors of these three students accounted for approximately 64% of the total class misbehavior! This suggests a medium level of structure is appropriate for the class, which is what I already have in place. I do not believe the class requires a motivation system, but I will reteach expectations until behavior improves. I will also look at the strategies in chapter 9 to see if there are individualized methods I can use to help Scott, Todd, and Rahsaan improve their behaviors.

3. Calculate the overall grade status of each student in your class, and record the information on the worksheet. To calculate the overall grade status, simply use your grade book to determine the current grade of each student.

4. For each area you are evaluating (e.g., attendance, work quality), determine a cut-off percentage that indicates a cause for concern. For example, with punctuality, attendance, and work completion, it may be 95 percent; for work not meeting your quality standards, it may be 80 percent. You may wish to highlight the percentages for any student whose scores fall below your cutoff so the results are easier to analyze.

5. Analyze your results, and decide on a plan of action for each area. If only one or two individuals fall below the cut-off percentage in any area, examine any interrelated information in the data. For example, a student may be failing because she is not attending class regularly and is therefore not completing work. Consider implementing some kind of individual intervention. For example, you might:

   - Arrange to discuss the problem with the student.
   - Arrange to discuss the problem with the student and the student's family.
   - Make sure the student is capable of doing assigned tasks independently.
   - Establish an individualized motivational plan for the student.
   - Discuss the problem with your school counselor, school psychologist, or behavior specialist.

6. If more than two or three individuals fall below the cut-off percentage in a particular area, consider implementing some kind of whole-class intervention. For example, you might:

   - Revise or reteach your expectations for independent work periods (see chapter 8).
   - Review and, if necessary, revise your procedures for managing work completion (see chapter 3).
   - Publicly post and discuss daily class percentages (see chapter 9).
   - Implement a classwide motivation system for improving the group's percentage in the particular area of concern. For example, for improving class punctuality from 80 to 90 percent of the class for a period of two weeks, the class earns a night off from homework. (See chapter 8, task 5 for how to implement whole class motivational systems.)

Exhibit 7.5

Grade Book Analysis Worksheet

Teacher: Ms. Fernandez   Date: 11/14

Student Name or Number	% Attendance	% Punctuality	% Work Completion	% Quality Work	Overall Grade Status
Abbott, K.	100	95	100	100	A
Bal, N.	100	95	100	90	A
Beltran, E.	95	100	90	90	A
Carson, P.	(60)	(90)	(50)	(30)	D
Cross, D.	100	(80)	100	90	B
Devereaux, J.	95	(75)	100	85	B
D'Orio, Q.	100	95	100	90	A
Ellis, P.	100	(80)	95	80	B
Felton, K.	90	100	100	100	A
Gordon, J.J.	95	100	98	90	B
Guttierez, M.	100	95	95	90	B
Herman, C.	100	(70)	96	60	D
Ho, B.	100	(90)	96	75	C
Iwanaga, J.	100	98	100	100	A

Analysis and Plan of Action:

P. Carson falls below expectancies on all variables. I will schedule a conference with the student and family to develop an attendance plan. I also note that five students are under 95 percent for punctuality. I will post daily percentages for punctuality and set up a whole class motivation system. Finally, I note that C. Herman has a D grade despite reasonable rates of work completion. I will have the student work with a small group on in-class assignments and will speak with the student after class about taking advantage of the school's math center during study hall or before/after school.

Tool E: On-Task Behavior Observation Sheet

The On-Task Behavior Observation Sheet can help you determine the degree to which your students are using their in-class independent work time effectively.

Why

- To help you decide whether you need to reteach your expectations for independent work periods
- To help you identify the possible cause of poor work completion rates and misbehavior during independent work periods

When

- During the fourth month of school
- Again in mid- to late February

How

1. Print copies of the form shown in exhibit 7.6 from the DVD. A filled-in example is provided in this section.

2. Identify the independent work periods you wish to monitor. Target any class or classes that have frequent misbehavior or trouble completing their work.

3. Determine whether you will be conducting your own observation or if you will ask a colleague to do it. Having a colleague collect the data for your class has several advantages. First, it frees you to do whatever you usually do during this work period, such as circulating and answering questions. In addition, a colleague is likely to be more objective. You may have an unconscious tendency to make students look better or worse than they really are. Finally, exchanging classroom observations with a colleague gives both of you an opportunity to share ideas about how to help students improve their overall rate of on-task behavior.

4. During the observation period, the person who is collecting data should use the instantaneous time sampling method of observation. For this method, the observer should be positioned away from high-traffic areas, in a place where she can easily see all students working at their seats. She should have a blank on-task behavior observation sheet and a pen or a pencil.

   The observer should choose an observation pattern that allows her to observe each student in the class a minimum of three times. For example, if students are in rows, the observer might start with the student in the front row to the left. She would then look at the next front-row student to the right, and then the next, until she has observed each student in that row. Then the observer would watch the students in the second row, moving from left to right, then the third row, and so on. After observing the last student in the back row, she repeats this pattern at least two more times. The pattern is important: it keeps the data much more accurate than simply taking a randomly viewed sample of the students.

   When observing an individual student, the observer should look at that student for only an instant. Then she looks down at the observation sheet and asks herself whether the student was on- or off-task at the time of observation. If the student was on-task, the observer marks a plus sign. If the student was off-task, she marks a minus sign.

This is repeated for every student, following the pattern established. The idea is for the observer to set up a rhythm with a quick pace, spending no more than three to five seconds on each student. The observing party should view the student, react to his or her behavior, mark it down, and move on. It should take no longer to do than it does to read or describe. The mark should reflect what the student is doing at the moment of observation. It should *not* reflect what the student was doing immediately before or after.

The observer should follow the pattern and take in the whole class at least three times. When finished, the observation sheet should look something like the example shown in this section in exhibit 7.6, taken from a class with thirty students. Notice that no effort is made to record which student was on- or off-task. That would defeat the purpose of looking for a class average.

5. Determine the percentage of on-task behavior by dividing the total number of on-task marks (pluses) by the total number of marks (pluses and minuses). In the sample shown, this would be 70 divided by 90, meaning that during the observation period, the class was on task approximately 78 percent of the time.

6. Analyze the data and, if necessary, determine a plan of action.

- *If your class had an on-task rate of 90 percent or higher,* provide positive feedback to your class, including telling them how they did, and encourage them to keep up the good work. If you feel that the percentage does not accurately reflect their typical behavior because they were behaving for the observer or some other reason, let them know that you are pleased with what they demonstrated they could do and that you want them to strive to behave the way they did for the observer every day. If you know that most or all of the off-task behavior was exhibited by one or two students, arrange a private discussion with those individuals. Use the time to set improvement goals for the students and, if necessary, develop individualized management plans to help them learn to manage work times more responsibly.

- *If the class had an on-task rate of between 80 and 90 percent,* tell them how they did and let them know that although they did fairly well, there is room for improvement. Together with the students, identify strategies that individuals might use to monitor and improve their own on-task behavior. If you feel that the percentage does not accurately reflect their typical behavior, let them know that you are pleased with what they demonstrated they could do and that you want them to strive to behave the same way every day. If you know that most or all of the off-task behavior was

> ## Note
> If the process of monitoring seemed to improve your students' behavior, take advantage of it. Consider teaching the students how to use the form, and periodically ask a student to observe the class and record their behavior. Give the class feedback at the end of the work period. Use this procedure once a week until the class is consistently 90 percent on task or better.

exhibited by one or two students, arrange a private discussion with those individuals. Use the time to set improvement goals for the students and, if necessary,
develop individualized management plans to help them learn to manage their
work time more responsibly.

- *If the class had an on-task rate of less than 80 percent,* you are losing valuable
  instructional time, and you need to intervene. Tell the class what their percentage was
  and explain that they need to improve. Review your expectations for independent
  work periods, placing special emphasis on what constitutes appropriate participation
  (see chapter 8). At a later time, examine your grade book. If, despite their high rates
  of off-task behavior, the class has high rates of work completion (above 95 percent),
  consider the possibility that you are giving your students too much class time to do
  their assignments. If both on-task behavior and work completion are low, you may
  want to establish a classwide system, such as public posting of work completion (see
  chapter 9).

Exhibit 7.6
On-Task Behavior Observation Sheet

Teacher: Mr. Abdullah   Date: 2/22

Observer: Ms. Porter

Activity: In-class writing assignment

```
+ + + — — + + + + + + + + — + + + + + + + + + + — — + — +
+ + — + + + + + + — + + + + + + + + + + + — + + + + + — — —
+ + + + + + + + — — + + — + + + — + + — — — + + + — — + + +
```

Analysis and Plan of Action: Class was on task for about 78 percent of observation
time (70/90). Students are averaging 85 percent work completion rate, so problem is
not that they have too much time for the assignment. Mr. Abdullah decides to review
independent work expectations before the next two or three independent assignments.
He will also review the whole-class motivation systems described in chapter 8 and
implement one if on-task percentage does not improve.

Tool F: Opportunities to Respond Observation Sheet

The Opportunities to Respond Observation Sheet will help you determine the degree to
which your students are engaged during the teacher-directed instruction parts of your class.

Why

- To help you decide whether you need to modify your instructional methods to create
  more active student involvement

- To help you identify possible causes of poor work completion rates and misbehavior during teacher-directed lessons

When
- During the fourth month of school
- Again in mid- to late February

How
1. Make copies of the form shown in exhibit 7.7 on the DVD. A sample is provided later in this section as exhibit 7.7.

2. Identify the teacher-directed lessons that you wish to monitor. Target any class or classes that have trouble staying focused or have frequent misbehavior during lessons.

3. Determine whether you will conduct your own observation using videotape or have a colleague observe your lesson.

   Analyzing your own lesson has several advantages. First, it will be less threatening to your students than having someone else watch you teach. In addition, you will learn a great deal about your own teaching by observing students during your lesson. The major disadvantage is that students may behave differently when you observe them than they would for a neutral party. Another disadvantage is that there may be restrictions on taping students without getting permission from parents or guardians.

   Having a colleague collect the data has several advantages:

   - A colleague is more likely to be objective.
   - You may have an unconscious tendency to make students look better or worse than they really are.
   - Exchanging classroom observations with a colleague gives the two of you an opportunity to share ideas about how to create lessons that facilitate active student engagement.

4. During the observation period, plan to focus on three or four specific students. If you are videotaping, set the camera to the side of the room toward the back. Inform students that you are taping your teaching so you can improve the quality of your lessons. Focus the camera on a group of four students, preferably four who represent different ability levels, so you can see them making written and verbal responses.

   If you are having a colleague observe, arrange for him to sit to one side of the room, toward the back. Have him observe four students of different ability levels.

   On the Opportunities to Respond Observation Sheet, you (or the observer) should record the start time of the lesson. During the lesson, mark on the observation sheet with a *V* each time any of the target students makes a verbal response. Mark a *W* each time any of the target students makes a written response. At the end of the teacher-directed portion of the lesson, record the stop time and the length of the lesson. If you have an observer who is not available for the entire class period, have him or her record the length of the observation.

5. Determine the average number of responses per minute. Determine the average response rate for the four students by adding up the total number of *V*s and *W*s and dividing by 4. Divide the average response rate by the number of minutes. This figure is the average responses per minute.

6. Analyze the data and, if necessary, determine a plan of action. Preliminary research with younger students determined that learning was maximized when students were responding with 80 percent accuracy between four and six times per minute during instruction on new material and responding with 90 percent accuracy between nine and twelve times per minute during drill and practice work (Council for Exceptional Children, 1987; Gunter, Hummel, & Venn, 1998).

There is little research on what represents optimal response rates for older students with more complex tasks and different types of activities, such as discussion and lecture. Therefore, you (and your colleague, if you had an observer) need to determine whether the number of student responses is optimal for your class. Recognize that the more students are doing something that engages them with the lesson content, the greater the chances will be that they are learning the essential content.

If students seemed overly passive during your lesson, explore with colleagues or instructional supervisors and department chairs how to get students to participate more actively. More active response methods could include whole group choral responses, whole group physical responses (e.g., "Stand up if the statement is true; stay seated if false"), copying notes, and quick ungraded quizzes.

> **Note**
>
> If data indicate a need to increase opportunities to respond, review chapter 6, "Eliciting Responses," in the book *Explicit Instruction* by Anita Archer and Charles Hughes (2010). If multiple teachers in a school identify increasing opportunities to respond as a goal, consider purchasing the secondary version of Anita Archer's Active Engagement DVD in-service series (2013; Pacific Northwest Publishing).

Exhibit 7.7

Opportunities to Respond Observation Sheet

Teacher: Mrs. Orleans   Date: 12/1

Observer: Mr. Lloyd

Activity: American History teacher-directed instruction

Lesson start time: 9:30   Lesson end time: 10:15

Duration of observation (number of minutes): 10

Student 1	Student 2	Student 3	Student 4
V, V, W, W, V, V, V, V, V	W, W, W, W, V, V, V, W, V, V, V	V, W, W, W, V, V, V, V, W, W, V, V, V, V	V, V, V, W, W, V, V, W, W, V, V, V, V, W

Mark a V for each verbal response. Mark a W for each written response.

Total number of responses: 48 ÷ 4 equals: 12 (average number of responses)

Average number of responses ÷ by number of minutes equals 1.2 (average responses per minute)

Notes on subjective perception of the degree of student engagement in the lesson: All but one student seemed attentive during presentation of new material. One student appeared to be reading a different assignment and did not respond to most group questions.

Analysis and Plan of Action: Work on adding opportunities to respond to keep students engaged when presenting new material. Try to move around the classroom more during instruction to keep students focused on the lesson.

Tool G: Student Satisfaction Survey

The Student Satisfaction Survey will help you determine how your students perceive various logistic and organizational features of your classroom.

Why

- To help you identify those aspects of your classroom program that are working well and those that may need modification
- To help you identify whether there are aspects of your classroom program that you need to communicate more clearly to students and their families

When

- Last two weeks of school
- Midyear (optional)

How

1. Check with your administrator to make sure that giving a survey of this type won't violate any policies or procedures.

2. Print copies of the two-page form shown in exhibit 7.8. A customizable reproducible is provided on the DVD. (The survey can and should be modified to reflect your classroom program and any areas of concern that you may have.)

3. Determine if you will have students complete the survey independently in class or if you will try to involve their parents. Recognize that attempting to involve the parents reduces the probability that you will get surveys back from all students. If you plan to try to get these from parents, determine how you will let families know that the survey is coming and the logistics of how they will receive and return the survey. Also consider whether you will need to have the survey translated for some of the families. For example, you could send the surveys home with students and have students return them. Or if your school can budget for postage, you could send the surveys by mail with preaddressed, postage-paid return envelopes enclosed. You might also send the surveys by e-mail, but make sure that you have addresses for all parents or an alternative delivery plan for those parents without e-mail access.

4. If you are giving the survey in class, remind students that the surveys are anonymous, but you hope they will give honest and productive answers to help you become a more effective teacher. Let them know that they can place completed surveys in a box by the door, so you will never see who made particular responses. When all surveys have been returned, analyze the results. Keep in mind that although the information is subjective opinion, it can help you identify aspects of your classroom that may require further review. For example, if 50 percent of the families respond that students do not have enough homework, carefully consider whether the amount of homework you assign is sufficient. Or if 60 percent say the amount of homework is about right, 20 percent say it's too much, and 20 percent say it's not enough, you can probably assume that the amount of homework matches the average family's perception of what is appropriate.

Giving a survey of this type can be unnerving for you. As you examine the results, remind yourself that you cannot take critical information personally. Rather, you are looking for patterns of information that will help you fine-tune your classroom program.

Exhibit 7.8
Student Satisfaction Survey

Dear Students,

    As we approach this point in the school year, I want to thank you all for your help and support. As a professional trying to meet the needs of all students, I am always looking for ways to improve. You can help by giving me feedback about the strengths and weaknesses you see in my program. Please take a few minutes to fill out the following survey.

    Note that there is no place to put your name. I will not know who wrote what unless you wish to sign your name. Once you have completed the survey, fold it in half and place in the box by the door.

    Sincerely,

Homework

    1. The amount of homework assigned has been:

        ❑ Way too much   ☒ A bit too much   ❑ About right   ❑ Not enough

    2. The difficulty of homework has been:

        ❑ Way too much   ❑ A bit too much   ❑ About right   ☒ Too easy

Assignments and Class Work

    1. The amount of in-class work assigned has been:

        ❑ Way too much   ❑ A bit too much   ☒ About right   ❑ Not enough

    2. The difficulty of in-class work has been:

        ❑ Way too much   ❑ A bit too much   ☒ About right   ❑ Too easy

    3. Most of the time I felt that the work has been:

        ❑ Stupid   ❑ Boring   ☒ OK   ❑ Interesting   ❑ Fun

    4. Describe one valuable thing you learned this year:

        I learned to write different kinds of essays. I think the argumentative essay is valuable as a way to express and support my opinions.

5. Identify one type of activity there should be more of:

   ❑ Lecture   ❑ Discussion   ☒ Cooperative groups   ❑ Independent work   ❑ Simulations

6. Identify one type of activity there should be less of:

   ❑ Lecture   ❑ Discussion   ❑ Cooperative groups   ☒ Independent work   ❑ Simulations

Classroom Atmosphere

1. Most of the time, I have …

   ❑ hated coming to this class   ☒ felt that this class is OK   ❑ looked forward to this class

   Please explain your answer:

   I don't really like to write so I can't say I looked forward to it. But the reading was interesting, and I really liked working with my group to refine our essay ideas.

2. I think the teacher has treated me with respect …

   ❑ not often   ❑ most of the time   ☒ all of the time

   Please explain your answer:

   Ms. Zercher was awesome. She really listened to our ideas and worked with us to express them. We had some excellent discussions in class.

3. What might I have done differently to make this year a more pleasant and productive experience for you?

   Maybe leave more time between assignments. Sometimes I didn't think I had enough time to revise my draft before it was due because I also had work in other classes.

In Conclusion

Even the most carefully thought-out classroom management plan needs to be monitored and adjusted based on the needs of any particular class. How fast or slow to fade the teaching of expectations should be based on how well the class demonstrates knowledge and mastery of the classroom expectations, procedures, and routines. Problematic times of the year may require more structure and reteaching. By using a variety of methods to collect data on student behavior at different times of the year, you can metaphorically take the temperature and pulse of the class and make decisions about the "health" of your management plan. If you find the plan is working well, carry on; after all, if it isn't broken, don't fix it. However, if you find areas that need improvement, you can tweak any number of variables to facilitate more responsible student behavior.

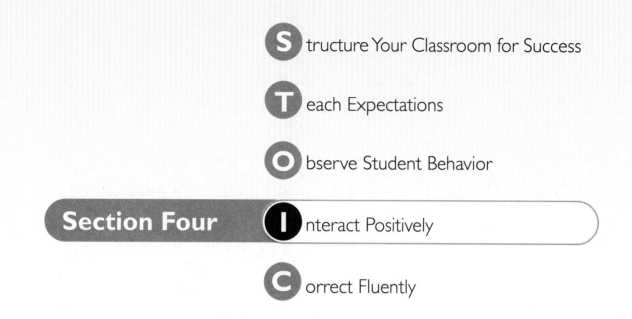

Structure Your Classroom for Success

Teach Expectations

Observe Student Behavior

Section Four   **I**nteract Positively

Correct Fluently

Chapter 8 provides information on increasing student motivation. While observing student behavior, you are looking for opportunities to increase your students' motivation to continue behaving responsibly and to try to behave even better in the future. In this chapter, you will learn how to use attention and praise as tools to increase motivation and how to avoid unintentionally reinforcing negative behavior with your attention. Finally, the chapter addresses when and how to use classwide motivation systems effectively.

Chapter 8

Motivation

Enhance students' desire to succeed

As you review the tasks in this chapter and consider student motivation (or lack of it), keep in mind the following concepts from chapter 1. First, the students' behavior will let you know what they are motivated to do and what they are not motivated to do. As necessary, you will have to work on increasing their motivation to engage in appropriate or desired behaviors or decrease their motivation to engage in inappropriate or undesired behaviors. Second, when trying to increase student motivation to behave appropriately, use procedures that address both intrinsic and extrinsic motivation. Third, remember that students' motivation to engage in any behavior will be related to the degree to which they value the rewards of that behavior, as well as their expectation of succeeding at the behavior (Cameron, Banko, & Pierce, 2001; Laraway, Snycerski, Michael, & Poling, 2003).

Five tasks are presented and explained in this chapter:

Task 1: Understand the importance of building personal relationships with students.

Task 2: Use every possible opportunity to provide each student with noncontingent attention.

Task 3: Give students positive feedback on their successes in a variety of ways.

Task 4: Plan to interact at least three times more often with students when they are behaving appropriately than when they are misbehaving.

Task 5: Effectively employ a classwide system or systems if needed to increase motivation and responsible behavior.

The Menu of Classwide Systems following task 5 describes reward- and nonreward-based systems commonly used in classrooms.

Immediately after the Menu of Classwide Systems is the Self-Assessment Checklist designed to help you determine which tasks or parts of tasks you have done and which you still need to do. There is also a Peer Study Worksheet on the DVD in the appendix B folder. This worksheet presents a series of discussion questions and activities that can be used by two or more teachers who want to share information and collegial support as they work to improve their classroom management practices.

Task 1: Understand the Importance of Building Personal Relationships with Students

You will dramatically increase the probability of having cooperative and motivated students if they perceive that you both like and respect them (Hamre & Pianta, 2001; Reddy, Rhodes, & Mulhall, 2003). Think back to your own experience in school, to a particular teacher who made you feel valued and important and how strong an impact that teacher had on you. Many people remember the name of their favorite teacher throughout their lives. Although you don't have to be every student's favorite teacher, by making an effort to build relationships with students, you are demonstrating to students that you, as a teacher, hope to have a positive influence on their lives. Robert W. Blum, lead researcher of the National Longitudinal Study of Adolescent Health, concluded that making connections with students is more important than organizational variables such as classroom size, rules, and other structural considerations. Blum was at the helm of a study that tracked ninety thousand students in grades 7 to 12 to examine their health choices. He and his colleagues identified that students who had an emotional connection with their school were far less likely to use illegal substances, engage in violence, or initiate sexual activity at an early age than students without an emotional investment in their school. The study determined that one major factor that affected the emotional connection a student had with the school was positive classroom management (McNeely, Nonnemaker, & Blum, 2002).

The goal of this task is to ensure you build positive relationships with each of your students. This can be difficult because you have time limitations and may see up to two hundred students a day. Later tasks in this chapter provide tips on how you can build relationships with your students, but for now, just think about that special teacher who had such an effect on you. Think about the power of simply using a student's name when you greet him or her. When you address a student by name—"Good morning, Tamisha"—those three words let her know you notice her and therefore value her. You are interested in her as a person, not just as a mark in your grade book.

This does not mean you have to be every student's friend. They do not need you to use their slang or follow their trends. They only need you to be their teacher—a teacher with clear expectations, who is fair and consistent, and who cares about them. They need to know you care about them, you are helping them succeed not only as a student but as a person, and you accept them for who they are (even if you don't accept negative behavioral choices!). Just as maintaining a positive attitude toward your students is essential for their success, so is maintaining a personal connection with them. If they feel you don't really care whether they succeed, they may not work at succeeding. If they feel you want them to succeed but don't feel as if you care about them, they may not work to succeed, no matter how positive you are. As the one in authority, you want to communicate that you value and are interested in every one of your students as individual people (Hamre & Pianta, 2001).

Positive attitude and personal connection work as two of the foundation stones of your classroom management plan. If either is lacking, the entire structure will be lacking (Patrick, Turner, Meyer, & Midgley, 2003).

Task 2: Use Every Possible Opportunity to Provide Each Student with Noncontingent Attention

It is imperative that you make an effort to provide every student with attention that is not contingent on any specific accomplishment (Alberto & Troutman, 2003; Chance, 1998). Contingent positive attention (described in tasks 4 and 5) means interacting with and giving feedback to students when they have accomplished or demonstrated improvement on important behavioral or academic goals. Noncontingent attention means giving students time and attention not because of anything they've done but just because you notice and value them as people. Ways of giving noncontingent attention include greeting your students when they enter your room, calling on students during class, and showing an interest in their thoughts, feelings, and activities.

The benefits of noncontingent attention for students should be obvious. Like all of us, they need to be noticed and valued, and when they feel noticed and valued, they are more likely to be motivated to engage in appropriate behaviors. The benefits to you include (1) feeling more connected to your students, (2) providing students with a model of pleasant, supportive social interactions, (3) improving student behavior, and (4) making each day much more pleasant by improving classroom climate.

Noncontingent attention is especially important for your students who struggle the most with behavior and effort. These students often need the most attention, and if you don't find a positive way to give it to them, they may demonstrate misbehavior simply to get the negative interaction. However, you might find it difficult to provide positive attention to the student because of frequent misbehaviors in your class. Noncontingent attention may be your main way in which you can work to build a positive relationship and rapport with the student, which will allow you to begin working with the student on changing his or her behavior. In addition, increasing noncontingent attention often begins to change student behavior for the positive, even without other major efforts.

You may wonder how simply saying hello and making an effort to talk to students can improve their behavior. Vern Jones (Jones & Jones, 2004), a leading expert on student discipline and motivation, explains it as being akin to putting something in the bank. Each time you interact with a student and show an interest in him or her as a person, you make a deposit. When you have invested enough (i.e., interacted enough so the student feels valued by you), the student is more likely to want to follow your rules and strive to achieve your Guidelines for Success. In addition, if you make enough deposits, there will be reserve capital for those times that you may have to make a "withdrawal" when a student misbehaves. Whether the withdrawal consists of a gentle reprimand, a discussion, or a consequence designed to help improve the student's behavior, the more you have invested in the student, the more likely he or she is to understand *that you are trying to help him or her and may think, Mrs. Jacobsen cares so much about me that she is taking the time to help me learn to be responsible. I want to do what she is asking me to do.* When nothing has been invested, the student may feel that you are simply trying to control his or her behavior—for example: *Mrs. Jacobsen wants me to sit down and be quiet because she doesn't like me. Well, screw that! I'll do whatever I want, whenever I want! She can't make me sit down.* Noncontingent attention helps build a spirit of cooperation between you and your students.

Consider noncontingent attention in another way. Imagine a boss who rarely interacts with employees other than to explain an assignment or periodically compliment them on something well done. When she walks through the office, she doesn't say hello to employees or ask how they are doing. She doesn't know anything about them outside of their work efforts. While employees appreciate the recognition of their efforts, they do not feel especially connected to their boss. Now imagine a different boss who frequently makes efforts to interact with employees about positive work efforts but who also makes an effort to give noncontingent attention. When she goes through the office, she frequently greets employees by name, and she sometimes makes efforts to stop and ask them how their kids are doing or find out how an employee's recent vacation went. For which boss would you feel compelled to put in your best ideas and effort? Which boss would make you more excited to come to work each day? For whom would you be more willing to step outside your comfort zone and try new things?

The following are more detailed explanations of some ways to give your students noncontingent attention.

Greet your students.

This is the simplest but perhaps most important way to provide noncontingent attention. As students enter your room at the beginning of class, you can say such things as, "Hello, Jonathan. Good morning, Wachera. Francine, how are you today? You know, I'm tired this morning too. You and I may have to nudge each other to stay awake in class. Maria, Jacob, Tyrone: good to see you today." You may not be able to greet every student each day, but you should try to greet enough students each day that over the course of a week, every student will have been greeted.

You can also make a point of greeting your students when you see them in the hall. They may barely respond (some students will be self-conscious if they are with friends), but they will notice if you *don't* take the time to acknowledge them.

Show an interest in students' work.

During independent work periods, when no one needs immediate assistance, go to individual students (or cooperative learning groups) and look at the student's work. Taking a moment to look at what a student is doing demonstrates that you are interested in the student and her work. Sometimes you may offer praise in this context; other times you can simply say something like, "I'm looking forward to reading this when you're finished, Tamai."

Invite students to ask for assistance.

Occasionally ask individual students how they are doing in class. If anyone indicates that he or she is having trouble, arrange a time for that student to get some additional help from you. For those who say they are doing fine, let them know that if they ever have trouble, they should not hesitate to come see you. If you make an offer of assistance to every student in the first couple of months of school, you communicate that you are aware of them as individuals and that you are available to them.

Whenever time permits, have a conversation with a student or a group of students.

Having a conversation demonstrates even more than just a greeting that you are interested in your students and their experiences and ideas. Brief social interactions create an emotional connection between you and your students, and they are not hard to do. For example, as three students enter your classroom at the beginning of the passing period, you can casually chat with them as you stand at the door and greet other entering students. You might talk quietly with a couple of students as you go down the hall. Find out about their individual interests and ask about them (e.g., ask a student about her soccer game the previous evening). Periodically share something about yourself—for example, "My son played goalie for his team in college. What position do you play?"

Make a special effort to greet or talk to any student with whom you've had a recent interaction regarding a misbehavior.

This kind of gesture on your part communicates that what happened before is now past and that you do not hold a grudge. It also lets the student know you are prepared for a fresh start.

For example, if you had to talk to a student about being disruptive, that student should be one of the students you greet the next day: "Aaron, good to see you. How are you doing?" A greeting in these circumstances decreases the probability that the student will misbehave in the next instructional activity.

Task 3: Give Students Positive Feedback on Their Successes in a Variety of Ways

Among the most important practices an effective teacher engages in is letting students know about their behavioral and academic progress and success. Giving positive feedback is a powerful way to encourage responsible behavior (Martens, Lochner, & Kelly, 1992). When done well, it confirms for students that they are on the right track and increases the probability that they will demonstrate the same behaviors in the future.

This task discusses five hallmarks of effective positive feedback. If you incorporate these suggestions into the positive feedback you give your students, you can significantly increase the probability that your feedback will encourage and motivate them to behave more responsibly in the future (Lalli et al., 1999; Silva, Yuille, & Peters, 2000).

Feedback should be accurate.

Effective positive feedback should be related to a behavior (or set of behaviors) that did in fact occur. When an individual receives positive feedback about something he or she did not actually do, the feedback is basically meaningless. If you comment to a student that his accuracy in completing math assignments is improving, you need to be sure that the student's accuracy is really improving. Before you note that a student demonstrated improved self-control by staying in her seat during an entire instructional period, be sure that the student did stay in her seat.

Feedback should be specific and descriptive.

When giving positive feedback, be sure to tell students exactly what they did. Feedback should be information laden, confirming for a student what it was she did that was important or useful. If you want to let a cooperative group know they have done well, describe the specific behaviors that they exhibited. When writing a note regarding a student's paper, identify what specifically he did that contributed to the quality of the paper.

Specific descriptive feedback lets the student know which aspects of his or her behavior you are commenting on. Simply writing "Excellent work" at the top of a paper, with no other comments, does not give the student any information about what aspects of the paper led to your positive comment. Was it the effective use of figurative language? The organization? The use of vocabulary? The creative use of the overall ideas? The use of topic sentences? The clarity of the descriptive language? The more detail you are able to give students, the more they will understand about your criteria the next time. In addition, when you provide specific verbal feedback to one student, it reinforces your expectations to students who are nearby, sometimes prompting more positive behavior and efforts from others.

Following are some common mistakes teachers make when providing positive feedback. All of them can be avoided by providing specific descriptions of student behavior:

- *The Good Job syndrome.* It's easy for teachers to fall into a simple repetitive phrase that they use over and over and over to give positive feedback. There are two problems with this. First, most simple phrases such as, "Good job," "Nice work," or "Fantastic," provide no specific information about what exactly the student did that was useful or important. Second, an overused phrase becomes background noise, and students will cease to notice it.

•   *Making judgments or drawing conclusions about the student.* Be cautious about stating or implying that a student is "good" or "smart" or "brilliant." When a student answers a difficult question, it can be tempting to say something like, "Allison, you are so smart." The problem is that a statement like this not only doesn't provide specific information about what the student did, but it may imply to the student that if she had not come up with that particular answer, you might not think of her as smart. It's far more effective to say, "Allison, you applied the formula, performed a series of computations, and came up with the correct answer."

•   *Calling attention to yourself.* Some teachers praise by saying, "I like the way you …" Even when what follows this statement specifically describes the student's behavior, that initial phrase may inadvertently be taken by the student to mean that he or she should behave to please you. In fact, what you are working toward is for students to behave in particular ways because it will help them be successful learners. Another problem with an "I like the way you …" type of phrase is that some students might get the idea that you like them when they are good and infer that you *don't* like them when they are not good. Keep the focus of your feedback on the student and what he or she did, not on your own likes and dislikes. The one exception is when a student does something particularly helpful to you. In that circumstance, feel free to let the student know that you appreciate his or her help. For example, if you drop some papers and a student helps you pick them up, it is reasonable and logical to say something like, "Thank you for helping me pick those up. I appreciate having such a thoughtful student."

Feedback should be contingent.

The student behavior you provide feedback on should have some level of importance. That is, it should not be an overly simple behavior for the individual who demonstrated it. To understand why, imagine that someone you know and respect (e.g., a favorite college professor, your minister, your boss) sees you drive into the parking lot, and as you step out of your car comes over to you and says, "Excellent left turn into this parking lot! You used your turn signals, you checked your blind spot, and you controlled your speed as you pulled into the parking space to ensure that you did not scratch the car on either side of you."

This feedback may be accurate, but it is also at best meaningless and at worst insulting. It implies that these driving behaviors are something special, when making a left turn into a parking lot and a successful turn into a parking space is what's expected of all drivers. You'd probably wonder why the person was being so gushy and excited about something that you had done successfully many times before. There's a good chance this meaningless feedback would reduce your respect for that person.

Three major circumstances contribute to positive feedback being contingent. The first is when the feedback occurs while someone is learning a new skill or behavior. When you were learning to drive, your driving instructor may have given you positive feedback similar to the statements in the previous example. The difference is that because you may have driven only once or twice before, your instructor's praise was probably not at all insulting or meaningless; it provided specific and descriptive confirmation of what you did correctly (Alberto & Troutman, 2003).

Feedback is also contingent when it refers to a behavior that requires effort—whether or not it is a new behavior. For example, imagine that you have been making a concerted effort to increase your helpfulness around the house (because your partner has been carrying more than his or her fair share). If your partner expresses gratitude for the extra help or shares appreciation that the household chores are more equally divided, that positive feedback is not likely to be meaningless or insulting to you. The behavior isn't new or particularly complex, but it does take effort to change a habit. Feedback that acknowledges one's efforts is likely to be valued and can lead to maintaining or increasing the frequency of the behavior in the future.

The third circumstance in which positive feedback will be contingent is when it concerns a behavior about which the individual is proud. For example, think about a time when you handed in a paper on which you felt that you had done an especially good job. Chances are that when you got the paper back, you looked at the grade and then went through the paper page by page to see if the instructor had written any comments. Far from being seen as meaningless or insulting, positive comments in these circumstances are welcome, particularly if the instructor described which parts were well thought out or well written.

With contingent feedback, remember that what is new, is difficult (requires additional effort), or will make a student proud will vary considerably by student. A student who is used to getting straight A's may be disappointed by a B. Praising him or her for this effort would likely make the student upset. However, for a student who consistently gets Ds and Fs, a B is a huge accomplishment and should be acknowledged. If a student has struggled with a particular behavior in the past, make a special effort to recognize positive efforts and growth. Also consider the student's general capabilities and need for praise and recognition: students who are used to being successful, have strong academic abilities, and consistently demonstrate mature and responsible behavior are those who generally need the least amount of praise and contingent feedback. Make a special effort to acknowledge the efforts of average students: their accomplishments may not stand out, and they may not draw negative attention to themselves. Don't let these students fade into the woodwork. Your students who have the most behavioral challenges and lowest academic skills often need the most frequent contingent feedback to reinforce positive efforts and demonstrate that they receive more attention when they are behaving than misbehaving. One of the reasons these "tough" students need the most is they have the greatest number of prosocial behaviors that are either new or difficult for them.

Feedback should be age appropriate.

For obvious reasons, the way you give feedback to a kindergartner will be different from the way you provide it to a high school student. For example, you can use more sophisticated vocabulary to describe behavior with older students. And in terms of being contingent, it is more appropriate to focus on advanced behaviors with older students. At the same time, be careful not to embarrass older students when providing positive feedback. High school students may feel a great deal of peer pressure to fit in or not stick out. Think about the thousands of messages they get that suggest that being good in school makes them a geek or a nerd. If you provide feedback in a way that embarrasses a student, it may actually discourage the student from behaving responsibly in the future. For example, many students avoid behaving responsibly if they are praised in a way that results in their being accused of being the teacher's pet. If a student seems to be embarrassed when you give positive feedback, consider experimenting with one or more of the following suggestions:

- *Use a quiet voice when providing feedback to individuals.* If students feel you are making a public display of them, it may increase the possibility that they will feel embarrassed in front of their friends.

- *Be brief.* If you go on too long, accepting the praise graciously may be difficult for the student.

- *Be somewhat businesslike.* Simply state the positive behavior the student engaged in. If you sound too excited or pleased when you praise, it can make a student feel like a Goody Two-Shoes: "I pleased the teacher—yay."

- *Avoid pausing and looking at the student after you praise.* A pause can seem to imply that you expect the student to respond, and this puts a student in a difficult position. Are you waiting for a smile or a thank you? Smiling or saying thank you in front of peers can be socially embarrassing, especially to a student who has an image of being tough. Such a student will often make a smart-aleck comment or engage in misbehavior to reassert to peers how tough and bad she is.

Remember that it is important to make a special effort to give contingent feedback when a skill is new or difficult for a student. However, this can also be embarrassing if other students previously mastered the skill. For example, all of the students in a math class have been using an algebraic formula with ease, but one student continues to struggle. For weeks, the teacher works with this student individually on the concept while other students build more advanced skills. When the student demonstrates he can consistently use the formula, the teacher praises him publicly, recognizing his persistence and the fact that he *finally* got the concept. This public recognition would be highly embarrassing for the student and might result in resentment of the teacher and a refusal to make similar efforts in the future. In these cases, it is important to acknowledge the student's growth and perseverance, but private recognition may be much more effective.

Feedback should be given in a manner that fits your own style.

There is no single good way to give positive feedback. There is plenty of room for individual style, even when you incorporate recommended techniques. A teacher who has a more buttoned-down personality can and should employ a more businesslike style of providing positive feedback. A teacher who tends to be excited and energetic may be somewhat more like a cheerleader when giving feedback. And a soft-spoken teacher's feedback will naturally be more soft-spoken than that of a more boisterous teacher. In most cases, if you are comfortable with your style of giving feedback, your students will be too. In fact, you probably only have to consider the preceding tips on age-appropriate and nonembarrassing feedback if your students are responding to your style with obvious embarrassment or reduced positive behavior after feedback is given.

Level of structure and positive feedback.

The greater the number of risk factors your class has, the greater your need is to manage student behavior by positive as opposed to punitive means. With a low-structure class, you may be able to get away with relatively low rates of positive feedback and still have students behave responsibly. This is certainly not recommended, but it is plausible. If your students come from relatively stable situations and families in which they receive encouragement, they may work hard and behave well without getting much positive feedback from you—although they will probably not feel much joy about your class.

However, when students need higher structure (in classes with many risk factors), frequent positive feedback is essential. Without it, some students will not know exactly what you want from them. Furthermore, if students are trying to meet your academic and behavioral expectations and they do not receive any feedback that you notice what they have done, some of them will cease striving to meet the expectations, perhaps wondering, *I try to do what she wants and she never even notices. Why should I bother?* The greater the number of high-needs students you have, the greater the need for you to provide frequent, positive feedback in a skillful manner.

Students who respond negatively to positive feedback.

Some students may respond negatively to a teacher's efforts to provide positive feedback. For example, shortly after being told that he is behaving responsibly, a student may exhibit the worst behavior he ever has in class. The temptation here might be to withhold all future positive feedback or acknowledgment. Actually, this is relatively common; there are several possible explanations. One reason a student may misbehave immediately after receiving positive feedback is that it embarrasses him. If you suspect this is the case, try modifying your feedback. See whether making the feedback more private, stating it in a more succinct and businesslike way, or eliminating pauses after you provide positive feedback results in a more positive reaction.

The other reasons a student might behave this way tend to be more complex and hence harder to remedy. Perhaps the student is trying to maintain a tough image, or feels peer pressure to remain aloof, or does not know how to handle success appropriately. When you provide feedback to a student who has one or more of these issues, the feedback won't fit the student's self-image and can make her feel uncomfortable (even terrified by her own success). Exhibiting misbehavior helps a student like this get back to feeling like a troublemaker or a loser again. It may even be that the student does not believe she really is capable of being successful and feels a need to show you that the success was an aberration of some kind. In addition, the misbehavior takes some pressure off by communicating that you can't expect the student to be successful all the time. Regardless of the reason for a student's misbehavior after receiving positive recognition, you can try experimenting with one or more of the following suggestions:

- *Treat the misbehavior as a momentary interruption in the student's success.* The key is to refrain from communicating anger or disappointment. This can be tough. When a student falls apart after you acknowledge his success, it is natural to feel angry or disappointed. You may want to say something like, "Jamie, you were doing so well, and now you go and do this sort of thing. I just don't understand, and I am very disappointed." A reaction like that may feed a student's negative attitude and reinforce him in the wrong direction. Worse, it takes the pressure off the student to continue to succeed: the teacher has once again seen the worst the student has to offer.

- *At a neutral and reasonably private time, talk to the student about his tendency to misbehave after getting positive feedback.* See if the student can give you any insights into why this occurs. Ask him if he has any suggestions about ways you can give him positive feedback that will reduce the chance that he will feel a need to misbehave afterward. Try experimenting with any reasonable suggestions the student makes. If the student cannot come up with any strategies for you to try, ask him what he thinks about some of the suggestions included here. If the student simply does not know how to respond in an appropriate way to positive feedback, work with the student to develop a response that he or she can use. Have the student practice a head nod or other subtle form of acknowledgment that feels comfortable to the student.

• *Be more private with (or otherwise modify the form of) the positive feedback you provide to the student.* The student may prefer to get a note rather than public praise. He may prefer to have you give the feedback at the end of the period rather than during it. He may prefer that you use a signal that only he knows (e.g., scratching your forehead) to let him know he is behaving responsibly.

• *Switch from giving specific descriptive feedback to simply interacting with the student when she is behaving responsibly.* Say hello to the student as she enters class. If she is on task during independent work, don't specifically praise her, but do go over and ask if she has any questions or needs any help. If she has behaved responsibly in your class for the past several days, don't praise, but ask her if she would be willing to pass out some papers that need to be distributed to the class. At the end of the class, tell her to have a good day. This attention, given when she is behaving responsibly, may reinforce the appropriate behavior, even though you are not providing specific descriptive positive feedback.

If eliminating the positive feedback is successful (the student handles the attention as long as no praise is included), continue to withhold praise for at least four weeks. If the student's behavior is improving, gradually introduce subtle praise. Once a week or so, make a matter-of-fact statement about something the student has done. Don't gush or in any other way make a big deal of it; just make a comment—for example, "Thank you for getting that assignment in on time," or, "That was a creative contribution you made to the cooperative group you were working with." If you see a downturn, back off and return to attention without praise. However, if the student is handling it, gradually increase the frequency of specific descriptive feedback you give the student.

Task 4: Plan to Interact at Least Three Times More Often with Students When They Are Behaving Appropriately Than When They Are Misbehaving

One of the most essential behavior management strategies is also perhaps one of the most difficult: making the effort to interact with every student more frequently (at least three times more frequently) when the student is behaving appropriately than when he or she is behaving inappropriately (H. S. Henderson, Jenson, & Erken, 1986; Martens et al., 1992). To understand why this strategy is so essential, consider the following:

• Some students are starved for attention. Most teachers have direct experience with how demanding of attention some students can be, and most have seen the desperate lengths some students go to for attention.

• For the student who is truly starved for attention, the form of attention may not matter. A reprimand for misbehaving may be just as satisfying of this student's need for attention as praise for behaving responsibly. In fact, it might be even more satisfying because the scolding will probably last longer and involve greater emotional intensity. Furthermore, the student may not even realize this attention is negative because it is the only form of interaction he or she has with adults—especially if his or her family interactions are especially volatile.

• With students who are starved for attention, the behavior you pay the most attention to is the behavior you will get more of in the future. That is, if you have more interactions with students when they are behaving appropriately, you will see an increase in positive behavior over time. If you have more interactions with students when they are behaving inappropriately, you will see an increase in negative behavior over time.

Your interactions with students are considered positive or negative based on the behavior the student is engaged in at the time you attend to him or her. If a student is off-task and you say, "Wanda, you need to get back to work or you won't complete your assignment," that would be considered a negative interaction—even if you made the request pleasantly and your intention was to help the student. It is a negative interaction because the student was engaged in a negative behavior (being off-task) when you initiated the interaction. Some teachers mistakenly believe that if they are being nice to a student, the interaction is positive interaction, and if they are acting in a hostile way or sound angry, the interaction is negative.

It's also important to realize that just because an interaction is considered negative, it does not mean it is wrong. It may in fact be the most useful way to get the student back on task at the time. However, it is important to understand that unless you make an effort to interact with this same student more frequently when she is on task, the student may learn that it is easier to get your attention (which may be what she wants) for being off task than it is for behaving well. Remember that each time you give attention to a student, you may be reinforcing the behavior you are paying attention to—whether the behavior is positive or negative. This is the reason for the recommendation that you make it your goal to pay three times more attention to students when they are exhibiting positive behavior than when they are exhibiting negative behavior.

This is not always easy. In fact, observational studies regularly show that most teachers pay significantly more attention to students' misbehavior than they do to students' positive behavior. In 1971, Wes Becker and Siegfried Engelmann wrote about studies Becker had done with elementary-level teachers who had been reprimanding and reminding students about out-of-seat behavior during work periods. He encouraged the teachers to reprimand students more immediately and more consistently: "Don't miss a single student who gets out of their seat at the wrong time." The teachers assumed this would decrease the out-of-seat behavior. In fact, the number of students getting out of seat at the wrong times actually increased.

Becker called this phenomenon the *criticism trap*: although the teachers thought they were doing something effective (reprimanding or issuing a consequence for an inappropriate behavior), the students who were starved for attention were getting out of their seats, at least in part, to get their teachers to look at and talk to them. The students' need for attention was satisfied when their teachers told them to get back in their seats—which they typically did, at least initially. This tended to reinforce the nagging on the part of the teacher because the students usually sat down when asked to do so. But before long, the students would realize, consciously or unconsciously, that they were not getting attention when they were doing what the teachers wanted, so they would get out of their seats again. The teachers would reprimand again, giving the desired attention, and the students were again reinforced for getting out of their seats. Although these studies were done at the elementary school level, the phenomenon can frequently continue to the secondary level.

This quickly becomes a destructive pattern in which everyone gets what he or she wants in the short run: the student gets attention when he violates the teacher's expectations, and the teacher gets momentary compliance each time he reprimands. However, when this cycle continues, no one gets what they want in the long run. Over time, students behave less and less responsibly and the teacher gets more frustrated and more negative. The only real way out of the criticism trap is to have more interactions with students when they are behaving responsibly than when they are misbehaving.

If you think you have fallen into the criticism trap or believe that your ratio of positive to negative interactions with students is fewer than three to one, consider implementing one or more of the following suggestions for increasing positive interactions:

- Go back to your brainstormed list of common misbehaviors (exhibit 4.3 in chapter 4). For each listed misbehavior, consider one or two statements that praise the positive opposite of the misbehavior. Plan to use these statements frequently throughout class when students are behaving responsibly. For example, if students frequently blurt out responses instead of silently raising their hands to comment, do not acknowledge the comments of the students who blurt out and instead call on the students with raised hands. Each time you call on these students, acknowledge that they followed expectations with the statement, "Thank you for raising your hand appropriately."

- Each time you have a negative interaction with a student, tell yourself that you owe that student three positive interactions.

- Identify specific times each day that you will give students positive feedback on some aspect of their individual behavior or class performance. For example, you might decide that at the beginning of each math period, you will compliment five or six students.

- Schedule individual conference times with students to compliment them on their performance.

- Make a point of periodically scanning your classroom, seeking out specific reinforceable behaviors for which you can acknowledge students.

- Identify particular events that occur during the day (e.g., a student getting a drink of water) that will prompt you to observe the class and identify a reinforceable behavior.

- Make a point to reduce the amount of attention (time and intensity) a student receives for misbehavior and increase the amount of attention (time and intensity) the student receives when not engaged in misbehavior.

- Engage in frequent noncontingent positive interactions with the students.

- After you give a correction to a student, acknowledge the student as soon as he or she begins demonstrating the appropriate behavior. Even a simple nod or smile can go a long way to demonstrate that you see a student's positive efforts.

You may also want to periodically monitor your ratios of interactions to determine if you have fallen into the criticism trap. Use the Ratio of Interactions Monitoring Form (exhibit 7.3 in chapter 7).

Level of structure and ratio of positive to negative interactions.

The higher the level of structure you have determined to be necessary for your students, the greater the probability is that at least some of the students will be starved for attention. This means that you are likely to have some students who will try to get their attention needs met through misbehavior, which can lead to a pattern of frequent nagging and reprimanding and the classic spiral into the criticism trap. Therefore, the greater your class's need for structure is, the more you need to make an effort to maintain positive interactions at a very high level. This task is absolutely essential for classes needing high structure. Maintaining a three-to-one ratio of positive to negative interactions is also important with low-structure classes, but it is generally easier to do because there isn't as much misbehavior to which you need to respond.

Task 5: Effectively Employ a Classwide System or Systems If Needed to Increase Motivation and Responsible Behavior

The previous tasks in this chapter suggested basic strategies for promoting student motivation—using effective instructional practices and giving students meaningful and relevant positive feedback on their behavioral and academic progress. This task expands those suggestions by explaining when and how to implement an effective classwide system or systems to increase student motivation to behave responsibly and strive to achieve goals such as your Guidelines for Success (see chapter 1, task 4). A classwide system is an organized and systematic set of procedures designed to have a positive impact on all of the students in your class (Fairbanks, Sugai, Guardino, & Lathrop, 2007; Farmer et al., 2006; Lohrmann & Talerico, 2004; Shores, Gunter, & Jack, 1993).

Many teachers report that classwide systems are highly effective in many freshman classes as a way to provide an additional boost to students as they learn to cope with the increased demands of high school, especially students who lack some of the requisite maturity or understanding of high school expectations and procedures. And while some people may believe that classwide systems are effective or necessary only with immature or unmotivated students, they can also be used to boost the motivation of even the most responsible eleventh- and twelfth-grade classes. With these students, a classwide system could be used to promote individual student goals, more advanced scholarly effort from the whole class, or increases in citizenship—getting students to go above and beyond expectations.

Using a classwide system to boost motivation can be appropriate in many circumstances, for example:

- The behavior of many students in your class is challenging in many different ways—for example, not following directions, wasting class time, and showing disrespect.

- Students are for the most part responsible, but quite a few students have a problem with one specific behavior, such as work completion, turning in homework, or talking during work periods.

- Your class behaves responsibly enough, but students have grown somewhat apathetic.

This task provides information on how to decide which kind of system (nonreward or reward based) to use. It also discusses how to implement, maintain, and fade a reward-based system. Finally, it provides a menu of easy-to-implement classwide systems: you can choose one or more that are most appropriate for your situation.

To help you accomplish this task, information is presented based on the three steps presented in exhibit 8.1:

Step 1. Identify problems, goals, level of structure needed, and the type of system you will use.

Step 2. If needed or useful, select a system (one or more) and prepare to implement it—effectively choosing, designing, and implementing a classwide system.

Step 3. For reward-based systems, identify how you will effectively maintain, modify, and fade the system.

Step 1: Identify Problems, Goals, Level of Structure Needed, and the Type of System You Will Use

The following material covers the issues and decisions you will need to consider to complete step 1 of exhibit 8.1 (see the DVD for a blank reproducible of this form). Use each section below to guide you as you complete the corresponding questions on the reproducible form. Two sample versions of exhibit 8.1 are shown. Exhibit 8.1a reflects a freshman classroom where the teacher is concerned about many student behaviors, responsibility, and motivation (high structure). Exhibit 8.1b is an example of an AP Physics class in which the teacher has no major concerns but would like to promote even more advanced effort from her students. Note that these examples include issues and strategies that will be discussed later in this task.

Exhibit 8.1a
Develop or Revise Your Classwide Motivation System: Example for a High-Structure Class

Teacher _Mr. Ramirez_   Grade _Freshman_   Class _Biology_   School Year _____

Step 1: Preparation

1. What problem(s) are you trying to solve?

   Callouts, interruptions during instruction (jokes, off-topic comments, side talking), disrespectful comments, horseplay, poor-quality work, missing assignments, foul language

2. Describe the goal(s) of your system. Limit your objective to one major category of behavior (e.g., reduce disruptions and name-calling, increase work completion, or decrease apathy/increase motivation).

   Decrease disruptions: callouts, interruptions during instruction, disrespectful comments, horseplay, foul language

3. At the present time, the level of structure I need is: ☒ High ☐ Medium ☐ Low

4. Decide whether you need a nonreward-based or a reward-based system.
   ☐ Nonreward-based ☒ Reward-based

Step 2: Select a System (One or More) and Prepare to Implement It

1. Read through the different systems to find one appropriate for the level of structure your class currently needs. The system I will implement (one from DSC or something else) is:

   Whole-class points (time interval)

2. Describe the system.

   I will set the timer to go off every 20 minutes. When the timer goes off, I will award the class 0 to 3 points.

   > _3 = No disruptions/everyone worked hard_
   >
   > _2 = No disruptions_
   >
   > _1 = Only a few disruptions_
   >
   > _0 = Too many disruptions_

3. Identify materials needed to monitor behavior and record progress (e.g., visual charts, monitoring forms, tickets).

   I will block off a space on the board for period 4 points. I will record points earned in this space and also keep a record on my clipboard. I will also write the reward goal, where I will record the number of points students need to earn in order to get their next reward. I will need a timer to remind me about the 20-minute intervals.

4. Identify the rewards to be used. If you will involve the students in generating the list of rewards, describe how.

   I will conduct a brainstorming session with students to get ideas for rewards and activities to work toward. I will decide which rewards are feasible. Then I will write all of the rewards on note cards and place the cards in a box. When students earn a reward, we will draw a card to see which reward they earned. There will be low-value and high-value rewards. Some ideas: a night off from homework, 10 minutes of socializing time, showing a movie in class, pizza, redo an assignment/test pass, letter home to families about the growth and maturity of their student and the class.

5. Identify when and how you will explain the system to the students and the date for implementation.

During Friday's time for discussing class business (upcoming due dates, class progress), I will explain the point chart on the board, the timer, the 0—3 points per interval, and the way they will earn a reward. We will brainstorm possible rewards. Anything goes in the brainstorm, but I will have final say on what goes in the box. We will do some review of expectations and an activity to determine what behaviors will earn points and what behaviors are not acceptable to earn points. We will do practice runs during class from 10:00—10:20 and 10:25—10:45. If they do well, I will put points on the chart to give them a jumpstart. On Monday, I will tell them which rewards are in the box, and we will start the full system.

Step 3: For Reward-Based Systems, Identify How You Will Maintain, Modify, or Fade the System

1. How will you use the system to provide meaningful feedback about student behavior?

After each interval in which they do well (2 or 3 points), I will explain the things they were doing right and how that advances our class objectives. If they do poorly (0 or 1 point), I will keep the focus on what they can do during the next interval to get a 3, possibly providing some targeted reteaching or practice of the positive opposite of the disruptive behaviors that lost them points.

2. How will you make the system more challenging as the class reaches a high level of consistent success?

I will start at a 20-point goal: when students earn 20 points, we draw a reward from the reward box. We will continue at this until the class is getting 2 or 3 points at each interval consistently for 3 days. I will let the class know that their goal will eventually bump up to 25 points, then 30 points, as they begin to demonstrate the mature and responsible behaviors of upperclassmen. Then I will change the time interval to 30 minutes, but go back to the 20-point goal. Then I will make the interval 60 minutes but with a 15-point goal, eventually getting to full period ratings and a 30-point goal.

3. Once the system is fairly lean, how will you move to increasingly intermittent rewards?

While still using the system, I will intermittently give other rewards and activities on days when they demonstrate a lot of success and effort, or when they have a stretch of several days without disruptive behavior. After noting their growth, I will encourage the class to realize they do not need the time interval system any longer and will switch to intermittent rewards.

4. When appropriate, fade the system by having a discussion with the students about abandoning the system and/or switching to goal-setting systems.

After using the intermittent system for at least several weeks, and if positive behavior continues and students seem proud of their success, I will implement individual goal contracts. We will then discuss whether the class still needs the reinforcement system.

Exhibit 8.1b

Develop or Revise Your Classwide Motivation System:
Example for a Low-Structure Class

Teacher *Mrs. Walters* Grade *Juniors/Seniors* Class *AP Physics* School Year

Step 1: Preparation

1. What problem(s) are you trying to solve?

   No problems, but I would like to push more students to do more than the minimum to get a good grade — both with their behavior in class and also the amount/quality of work. Basically, I want them to sometimes choose something other than the easy way out.

2. Describe the goal(s) of your system. Limit your objective to one major category of behavior (e.g., reduce disruptions and name-calling, increase work completion, or decrease apathy/increase motivation).

   For all students to identify a place where they are just doing what they need to in order to get by in this class and have them strive for more in that area

3. At the present time, the level of structure I need is: ❑ High ☒ Medium ❑ Low

4. Decide whether you need a nonreward-based or a reward-based system.)
   ☒ Nonreward-based ❑ Reward-based

Step 2: Select a System (One or More) and Prepare to Implement It

1. Read through the different systems to find one appropriate for the level of structure your class currently needs. The system I will implement (one from DSC or something else) is:

   Guide students in selecting goals: Goal contract

2. Describe the system.

   I will use the Goal-Setting Form (exhibit 8.2) to record a goal for each student in the class. Then we will conduct a class activity for students to identify their own goals; I will provide examples of how to do this. After I review student goals, we will have individual conferences to discuss my goal and their goal and develop a goal contract using the one we prioritize. During the first two weeks, I will check in with each student at least twice a week so we can mark down how they are progressing toward their goal and provide suggestions and help. I will also provide lots of positive feedback when a student shows he or she is making efforts toward the goal. For the rest of the month, this will be more sporadic unless a student is struggling, in which case we will problem-solve together. When students have demonstrated consistent success, we will work on setting new goals.

3. Identify materials needed to monitor behavior and record progress (e.g., visual charts, monitoring forms, tickets)

   Goal-Setting Form (exhibit 8.2) for the class, Goal Contract (exhibit 8.3) for each student — including progress monitoring portion of form

4. Identify the rewards to be used. If you will involve the students in generating the list of rewards, describe how.

   Positive feedback, calls home about progress, maybe a class reward if everyone is making efforts or reaches his/her goal

5. Identify when and how you will explain the system to the students and the date for implementation.

   I will get the Goal-Setting Form completed by Wednesday of this week. I will introduce the goal-setting process Friday and have students brainstorm possible goals. Next Monday during independent work time, I will have a brief conference with each student to decide on a goal and write the Goal Contract.

Step 3: For Reward-Based Systems, Identify How You Will Maintain, Modify, or Fade the System

1. How will you use the system to provide meaningful feedback about student behavior?

2. How will you make the system more challenging as the class reaches a high level of consistent success?

3. Once the system is fairly lean, how will you move to increasingly intermittent rewards?

4. When appropriate, fade the system by having a discussion with the students about abandoning the system and/or switching to goal-setting systems.

The following information and suggestions should help you with the issues and decisions in step 1.

What problems are you trying to solve?

Begin by thinking about behavioral and motivation concerns. Use the list of common misbehaviors you developed in chapter 4, task 2, or brainstorm a list now. Does it seem that a significant number of students do just enough to get by? What misbehaviors occur fairly frequently? These are the types of concerns to list. If you are addressing this question before the year begins but have taught in this school in the past, use the past couple of years as a guide to the problems you may encounter. If you have not taught in this school before, talk to your new colleagues who have taught these students. The issues you list will guide you toward the objectives of your system.

Goals of your system.

Based on your brainstormed list of concerns, decide what you want to achieve by implementing a classwide system. If you listed many problems, you may need to limit the focus of your system. For example, you may prioritize and say that initially the system will focus on reducing disruptions (callouts, disrespect, name-calling) and later, after disruptions are under control, you will modify the system or build a new system that focuses on increasing work completion and quality of written work.

Level of structure.

Think about your class's current need for structure. If you are thinking about class structure before the year begins, base this decision on the Classroom Management and Discipline Planning Questionnaire (exhibit 4.1 in chapter 4). If you are thinking about your structure needs during the year, base this decision on your subjective perception of the behavior and motivation of the class—the worse the behavior and motivation, the greater the need for high structure. Also consider any objective data you have, such as results from one or more of the tools in chapter 7, in particular tools A, C, E, and G. If there are rare or very few problems, low structure is probably fine. If many students misbehave on a frequent basis, you probably need high structure.

Nonreward- and reward-based systems.

Classwide motivation systems generally fall into one of two categories:

- Nonreward-based systems potentially improve students' desire to behave responsibly and achieve goals by enhancing their intrinsic motivation.
- Reward-based systems use extrinsic reinforcers to increase student motivation to behave responsibly and strive for goals.

If your students are for the most part behaving responsibly, completing most of their work, and exhibiting cooperation, they do not need extrinsic rewards to be motivated. In a class that is functioning this well, students demonstrate daily that they are intrinsically motivated to meet classroom expectations. A nonreward-based system such as goal setting is perfectly reasonable for this class. In fact, goal setting can be an effective strategy for not only maintaining but also enhancing already acceptable levels of motivation (Copeland &

Hughes, 2002; Fuchs, Fuchs, & Deno, 1985; Johnson, Graham, & Harris, 1997; Troia & Graham, 2002). Goal-setting procedures are designed to give students something to strive for so they do not fall into patterns of going through the motions in the classroom. If you do not need a reward-based system for your students because the class is already behaving responsibly, skip the information about rewards on the following pages and go directly to step 2 and the descriptions of various goal-setting systems in the "Menu of Classwide Systems" section later in this chapter. Select one that seems appropriate for you and your class.

If you are frustrated by the amount of misbehavior or the lack of student productivity in your class, your students are demonstrating that they are not intrinsically motivated to behave responsibly. Implementing a system in which they can earn extrinsic rewards for responsible behavior may be just what is needed to encourage them (Cameron et al., 2001; Scheuermann & Hall, 2008). A reward-based system may provide the incentive needed to light a fire under students and get them moving in a more positive and productive direction.

Even if the descriptions indicate that your class would benefit from a reward-based motivation system, you may find yourself reluctant to implement a system that depends on extrinsic rewards. Some people have concerns about the use of rewards and reward-based systems to improve student behavior. Following are answers to some of the most commonly raised questions about using rewards. The information provided should help you understand how a reward-based system (or systems) can be usefully and effectively incorporated into your classroom management and discipline plan. After looking over the following questions and answers, read the sections on effectively choosing a reward-based system (step 2) and maintaining, modifying, and fading a reward-based system (step 3). Then review the menu and choose the system or systems that you want to use or modify.

Shouldn't students work without needing rewards? Yes, they should, but some don't. When you can motivate students by making your expectations clear and your instruction effective, that's what you should do. If all of your students seem to be working up to their fullest potential, you do not need and probably should not implement a reward-based system. However, if you have some (or many) students who are not working as hard or as well as you think they should and you have done what you can to make expectations clear and instruction compelling, your choices are limited. You can let the students fail, continue to try to increase their intrinsic motivation to behave, or experiment with rewards.

Keep in mind that using rewards effectively does not mean that you use them forever. A reward-based system is meant to be gradually modified until students are intrinsically or naturally reinforced by the task. This concept is called *behavioral momentum*: once students start experiencing success, they are increasingly motivated to be successful and thus work harder, experiencing even greater levels of success. In other words, success breeds success.

Isn't rewarding behavior the same as bribery? Emphatically not! A bribe is an offer of payment, usually monetary, to do something illegal, unethical, or immoral. For example, when a building contractor offers to pay a building inspector under the table to ignore inadequate or unsafe aspects of a construction project, that is a bribe. Establishing a system in which students are rewarded for improving their rates of schoolwork completion is not bribery. It is more analogous to someone getting credits for successfully completing classes and eventually earning a diploma or someone getting a paycheck for doing a job.

Won't students get hooked on the rewards? Possibly. If you can sufficiently motivate your students without using rewards, you should do so. However, recent research reviews have found that concerns about students becoming dependent on extrinsic rewards are unwarranted (Akin-Little, Eckert, & Lovett, 2004) and that positive reinforcement may actually increase intrinsic motivation (Cameron et al., 2001). If you find that you need some form of reward system, always keep your focus and enthusiasm on what students are doing, not on what they are earning. Initially students may work mainly for the reward, but if you make a point of emphasizing their accomplishments, eventually most of them will begin to work for the enjoyment of the task and a sense of satisfaction with a job well done—whether they earn rewards or not (Skinner, 1982).

Isn't intrinsic motivation better? Maybe. Nobody really knows. However, as noted in chapter 1, most behaviors are the result of a complex mix of both intrinsic and extrinsic motivation. Think about your own experience as a student. Would you have done all of the assignments for all of your college classes if it weren't for the extrinsic reinforcement of credits (points) toward the degree? Put another way, would most people show up at work every day and put in their best effort and attitude if they were not working for a paycheck and possibly toward a promotion or raise?

The basic rule for teachers is this: if you can't motivate students intrinsically, use extrinsic rewards to get the desired behavior established. Once the desired behavior is established, you can fade the extrinsic rewards because students will readily access the natural rewards, such as praise for or the joy of mastering a new academic skill, associated with meeting expectations (O'Leary & Becker, 1967; Scheuermann & Hall, 2008; Skinner, 1982; Walker & Holland, 1979).

Will giving students rewards reduce their intrinsic motivation? Possibly. While there is evidence that positive reinforcement may increase intrinsic motivation (Cameron et al., 2001), it is likely that when students are already exhibiting desired behaviors, using high-powered rewards may slightly reduce their willingness to work without rewards. Therefore, if students are intrinsically motivated to meet your expectations, do not use structured rewards; instead use goal-setting procedures and age-appropriate positive feedback. However, if less-structured methods have failed or seem likely to fail to motivate students to behave responsibly, consider the use of structured rewards (Cameron et al., 2001; Scheuermann & Hall, 2008).

Step 2: Select a System and Prepare to Implement It

The issues and decisions to consider in step 2 of the Develop or Revise Your Classwide Motivation System form (exhibit 8.1) relate to selecting and implementing a classwide system.

To select a system, read through all of the systems described for the level of structure your class needs in the Menu of Classwide Systems at the end of this task. If you are planning to use a reward-based system, also read the information and suggestions below before selecting your system.

Pick the system that you think will accomplish your goals, best fit your style, and meet the needs of your students. Describe a few of the essential components of the system on exhibit 8.1 as a quick reminder to yourself so that you do not have to keep referring back to the book.

> ## Note
>
> If your class if made up of predominantly highly responsible students who sometimes seem slightly apathetic and one or two students who exhibit behavioral or motivational challenges, consider using goal-setting procedures as your whole-class approach to improving motivation while also setting up individualized extrinsic systems with those challenging students. Individualized approaches to behavior management are discussed in Chapter 9. One suggestion is to set up individual reward contracts. However, if you have three or more students with behavioral challenges, set up a reward-based classwide system. Managing too many individualized systems is much more work than managing one classwide system. The classwide system may improve the behavior of all but one student, and then you could work on an individualized intervention with that student.

Using a reward-based system.

If you decide that a reward-based system will be appropriate and helpful for improving your students' motivation, be aware that it is important to carefully choose, implement, maintain, and eventually fade the system or systems you use. In fact, the effectiveness of a reward-based system, like all other aspects of your management plan, depends on how well you facilitate it (Shores et al., 1993). Read through the following information to guide you in choosing or designing a reward-based system that best fits the needs of your class.

As you choose your system, keep in mind that some systems are regular and highly systematic in terms of how students earn rewards ("If you do X, then you earn Y") while others give students intermittent and unpredictable rewards. Intermittent systems are not so regular ("Sometimes when you do X, you might earn Y"). Regular systems tend to be more appropriate when you are trying to motivate a class that needs high structure, but they can also be harder to maintain and fade than intermittent and unpredictable systems. Intermittent reward systems are often sufficient for medium-structure classes.

From a technical standpoint, intermittent systems are actually the more powerful (Alberto & Troutman, 2006; Cooper et al., 2007; Scheuermann & Hall, 2008; Skinner, 1953). All gambling, for example, is based on intermittent reward schedules. We are motivated to keep putting money in the slot machine because we never know when we are going to win. However, in the initial stages of teaching and motivating a high-structure class, you may need a systematic and regular system (Alberto & Troutman, 2006). The regular system is important for teaching and getting students to buy in because it encourages them to practice the skill regularly and provides a high rate of reinforcement (rewards, positive feedback). Once students are consistently successful with a regular system, one step on the way to fading to intrinsic rewards is to switch to an intermittent system.

Try to select the simplest system that seems likely to grab the interest of your students and get them to exert gentle peer pressure to succeed—for example, telling each other things like, "Allan, please quit talking so we can earn a point." Gentle peer pressure is one of the most powerful reasons that group systems are successful, especially in high school when students may be more open to influence by peers than by adults. In addition, if peers take on some of the responsibility for gently correcting minor misbehaviors, this reduces the amount of misbehavior you need to directly address, which can further improve your ratios of interaction.

All reward-based systems, regular and intermittent, require maintenance after they are up and running (Conroy, Sutherland, Snyder, & Marsh, 2008; Kazdin, 2001; Kerr & Nelson, 2002). It's like having a car. No matter how well engineered it is, you still have to put fuel in it and make sure it gets the occasional oil change, brake job, and tune-up. In fact, you wouldn't expect your car to run without gas and periodic mechanical work. Unfortunately, some teachers think that once a motivation system is in place, it should pretty much run by itself. It won't. Furthermore, in most cases, a reward-based system should be a temporary measure that you employ to get the class into a pattern of successful behavior. Your eventual goal should be to fade it so that your students' intrinsic motivation maintains their responsible and enthusiastic behavior.

Following are tips on how you can effectively choose and implement a reward-based system, keep it running well, and eventually fade it altogether.

Make sure the rewards students will be working toward are highly motivating If students don't care about or don't want to earn the reward they are working toward, your system is not likely to be effective. You should use high-powered rewards—ones that students want so badly that they are motivated to try to meet your expectations in order to earn it. Therefore, you need to identify a range of rewards that the whole class will want to earn. If a few students in the class have no interest in the rewards, especially if those students frequently exhibit misbehavior, they may purposefully sabotage the system or simply continue to exhibit misbehaviors without regard to the system.

Some examples of rewards that may be motivating to high school students are free time in class, getting out of class a few minutes early, choice of seating for a day or week, reduction in the number of problems or questions assigned for homework, or some kind of food reward. You should be prepared to vary the rewards so that students don't become bored or satiated with one reward (Hall & Hall, 1980).

Sometimes it can be useful to have students help you decide on the rewards for the class (Lerman et al., 1997; Northup, 2000; Thompson, Fisher, & Contrucci, 1998; Wheeler & Richey, 2005). For example, you might conduct a brainstorming session and ask students to identify rewards that they as a class can get or do when all students demonstrate responsible behavior. During a brainstorming session, write down any suggestion that any student makes unless it is obscene or disrespectful. Continue the activity for at least five to ten minutes so that a number of ideas are generated.

When the brainstorming session is complete, go back and eliminate any items that are too expensive or otherwise unrealistic—it is important that you select rewards that you can and will use (Hall & Hall, 1980). Some of the items on your final list will probably have more value than others. For example, some may cost money while others do not, some may cut into more class time than others, and some may require more time from school personnel than others. When you implement your system, do not hesitate to start with rewards that have a fairly high value. The value of the reward should correlate with the effort required to receive it (Hall & Hall, 1980; Walker & Holland, 1979). Bigger rewards should be used for behaviors that students are least motivated (possibly because of difficulty) to display. The system should be exciting enough that most of the students feel it is in their best interest to improve their behavior.

Another way to increase student interest in the system while keeping a balance of low- and high-value rewards is to list each reward on an individual note card and place the cards in a box. When students earn a reward using whatever system you choose, draw from the box to determine the reward. Students might earn a high-value reward—something that is more time-consuming or costs money—or they might earn a lower value reward. Initially it is advisable to have more high-value rewards in the box so that students know they are likely to gain something of value. As students demonstrate success with the system, you can tell them you will be adding additional low-value rewards to make things a little more challenging.

Set up the system so that student success is likely   Students must believe that they have a high probability of succeeding. If students think their chances of earning a reward are low, they are not likely to change their behavior—even if they really want the reward. (Think about the concept of "Expectancy × Value = Motivation" discussed in chapter 1, task 2.)

One way to increase the probability of student success is to ensure that any time limits are short enough that students can meet your criteria (Alberto & Troutman, 2006; Walker, Severson, Feil, Stiller, & Golly, 1998) or that the behavioral change that you are requiring is incremental. For example, a freshman teacher implements a system in which the class earns one point for each sixty-minute class period in which the entire class behaves responsibly. However, students have exhibited frequent misbehavior consistently throughout each class for over a month, sometimes as many as fifty misbehaviors per period. Students may reasonably believe that they will never earn any points because the chances are slim that they will make it through a full period without someone messing up. This system is likely to fail because the students will never feel motivated enough to make it work. If expectancy of success is zero, it does not matter how valuable the reward is: motivation will be zero. The system would be stronger and probably more effective if it was set up so that the class earns a point for no more than five misbehaviors in each twenty-minute period. If students achieve this goal, they reduce their misbehaviors from fifty per sixty-minute period to no more than fifteen. Over time, the teacher can reduce the number of misbehaviors allowed to earn a point and can extend the time period, gradually working toward responsible behavior throughout an entire class period.

Another way to make students believe that success is possible is to make the cost of earning the rewards relatively inexpensive. In other words, students initially need to see that they will get a reward relatively quickly when they meet your expectations (Alberto & Troutman, 2006; Scheuermann & Hall, 2008). Say you establish a system where your students can earn a five-minute class break by accumulating twenty-five points, but the most points they can earn in a day is five. At best, the students will have to work for a whole week before they get the break time—too long for these students to wait for any payoff. As a result, their attitude may be, "Why bother?" In this example, the break is more likely to motivate students if it costs ten points instead of twenty points: they could potentially earn the break in just two days. The less mature your students are, the more immediately obtainable the rewards need to be for the system to be effective.

Once students are consistently behaving responsibly, you can and should make the time intervals longer or the rewards more expensive (or both) as part of the process of gradually fading the system. See step 3 in this chapter for tips on effectively maintaining and fading a reward-based system.

Avoid systems with arbitrary time limits   A weakness of many reward-based systems is that they include an unnecessary and arbitrary time limit: the points must be earned within a certain time period in order for students to receive the reward. For example, consider a system in which a class can earn five points a day if everything goes extremely well. If the class earns fifteen points by Friday, the students get the last fifteen minutes of class to do a group activity of their choice.

The arbitrary time limit in this system creates several potential problems. First of all, if students have trouble behaving well early in the week, they may know by the end of class Tuesday that they cannot possibly earn the reward that week and thus have no incentive to behave well on Wednesday, Thursday, and Friday. Or they might do so well that they have fifteen points by the end of class Wednesday. At least some of them will realize that they can misbehave all they want on Thursday and Friday because the reward has already been earned. Still another potential problem with a time limit is the difficult decision you face if the class has fourteen points by Friday. If you give them the reward because they came so close, they learn that you do not follow through on what you say (they cannot really trust you). However, if you do not give them the reward, meaning they start back at zero points on Monday, they may feel so discouraged they won't even try.

All of these potential problems can be eliminated by simply removing the time limit. The system in the above example would be much stronger if, as soon as the class earns fifteen points, students get the last fifteen minutes of the next class period for the group activity. They may earn the points in three days, or it may take a couple of weeks, depending on how well students manage their own behavior.

Carefully organize the entire system before you begin implementation   Many teachers rush to implement a motivation system when faced with behavior problems. To implement an effective system, however, you need to think carefully about your goals for the class's behavior and then develop a preliminary implementation plan in your mind. Once you create your mental plan, write it down. The act of writing out the procedures can help you identify possible weaknesses with the system and issues that need to be addressed (Scheuermann & Hall, 2008). As you identify those problems or issues, resolve them and make decisions.

What will you do if one student repeatedly behaves in a way that prevents you from giving the point or reward to the entire group? You will give that student a warning and tell him that his continued misbehavior will not prevent the group from earning points. At the same time, when the class earns the reward, he will not get to participate in the reward activities. If necessary, you will set up an individualized behavior management contract.

After you have a written plan that addresses all questions and issues you can think of, discuss the plan with a colleague. Speak to someone who is teaching or has taught the grade level you teach. Ask him or her to listen to your proposed plan with a critical ear. Encourage this person to identify any weaknesses and unanswered questions in your plan.

Make sure your expectations for student behavior are clear and that you have adequate procedures for observing student behavior   Even a well-designed reward system can fail when the expectations for student behavior within the system are unclear (Conroy et al., 2008; Scheuermann & Hall, 2008). Without clearly defined behavioral expectations, you may be inconsistent in determining whether students have met the criteria for earning their reward (Anderson, Evertson, & Emmer, 1980; Evertson & Emmer, 1982). That is, you may award points on a day when you are in a good mood, but the next day, when you are feeling more frustrated, you don't award any points, even though the students behaved the same way. This sort of inconsistency is destructive to motivation because earning the reward is not contingent on the behavior students actually display. Students are likely to stop trying to meet expectations that are unclear and inconsistent (O'Leary & O'Leary, 1977).

In addition to clear expectations, you must have adequate procedures for observing and recording student behavior (Conroy et al., 2008; Scheuermann & Hall, 2008). In fact, the only way you can reasonably implement a reward-based motivation system is if you can adequately monitor student behavior. For example, if you have a system to increase the percentage of students who are on time to class but you do not have a clear system for recording if students are tardy, your system will rely on your memory of who was on time and prepared. Work to design clear and efficient record-keeping procedures for the system you put in place.

Teach the students how the entire system works. Include a strong emphasis on the rationale behind the system Before you implement any system, prepare one or more lessons to teach the students how the system works. When students don't understand all aspects of a system, there is very little chance it will motivate them, particularly the least mature students. If, when preparing the lessons, you find that the system seems too complicated for students to grasp, you should revise it. If you can't make it clear, concise, and easy to understand, you probably need a different system.

After you teach students how the reward system will work, verify that they understand. Make sure that any English Language Learners in your classroom understand the system. Ask questions to determine their level of understanding. If specific aspects of the system are confusing, reteach those aspects. In addition, you may want to give students an opportunity to suggest refinements or modifications. If students make suggestions that would strengthen the system—for example, rewards that would increase their interest in the system—try to incorporate those suggestions.

You will also want to spend some additional time clarifying the expectations for any behaviors that will be monitored within the system. Make certain that students understand exactly which behaviors will be monitored, how they demonstrate the specific appropriate behaviors that will earn rewards, and what constitutes crossing the line into inappropriate behavior.

Because the goal is to eventually fade students from extrinsic rewards by developing the intrinsic motivation to perform the same behaviors, make the rationale for the positive behaviors as clear as possible. Keep the focus of the system on the long-term outcome of how these behaviors will help students be successful in school, getting and keeping a job and any other broader positive outcomes, rather than just the rewards they will earn.

Make sure you believe the system will help improve student behavior Start with the assumption that your students will meet your expectations regarding the system. If you believe the system will work, the students will pick up on your optimism. And if you believe the system will probably fail, the students will sense that you do not expect them to be successful. It's in your best interest to be optimistic. Even if the system does not work initially, an optimistic attitude will lead you to try to identify refinements and modifications that will make the system work. With a pessimistic attitude, you are likely to give up if the system does not produce immediate and drastic improvement in student behavior. Remember: Optimists are wrong just as often as pessimists; the big difference is optimists have a lot more fun.

Step 3: Identify How You Will Maintain, Modify, and Fade a Reward-Based System

The following information should help you maintain your system as long as necessary at one level as well as help you decide when and how to modify the system. If the system is not working, you should either modify it or select a new system. If the system is working well, you can make it incrementally more challenging for students and eventually fade it out altogether.

Present activities and tasks in a manner that induces student motivation.
The energy and excitement you invest in the system and in acknowledging student successes should be concentrated on what students do to earn the reward, not the reward itself (Horcones, 1992). That is, say to students, "Look at what you did!" rather than, "Look at what you get." By keeping your focus on the students' improved growth, maturity, and progress, you increase the chances that they will begin working less for the reward and more for their sense of satisfaction in meeting expectations successfully (Kazdin & Bootzin, 1972; O'Leary & Becker, 1967; Scheuermann & Hall, 2008; Skinner, 1982; Walker & Holland, 1979).

Continue to use other motivational strategies at a high level. Chapter 1 and the first four tasks in this chapter covered a number of basic strategies for establishing and maintaining student motivation. All the classwide systems for boosting motivation discussed in this task require you to maintain your use of these basic strategies:

- Use effective instructional practices and present tasks in interesting ways.
- Provide frequent noncontingent attention.
- Provide frequent positive feedback that is contingent, specific, descriptive, and age appropriate.
- Pay more attention to every student when he or she is engaged in responsible behavior than when he or she is engaged in misbehavior (minimally, a ratio of three-to-one).

To increase the likelihood that students will continue to be successful, be prepared to increase your use of these strategies as you begin to fade back the use of the external reward system (Kazdin, 2001; O'Leary & Becker, 1967; Walker & Holland, 1979).

When a system has been successful for a period of time, start making it more challenging.
Once student behavior improves to the point where your class is successfully meeting your expectations most of the time, modify the system to make it more challenging so students don't get bored with it and so student behavior continues to improve. As students become more successful at meeting expectations, also increase the standards for success so that you continue to move closer to fading the system and having students rely on intrinsic motivation. Following are suggestions for making a system more challenging:

- Increase the time interval in which students need to demonstrate the appropriate behavior to earn a point (say, from fifteen minutes to twenty minutes).
- Increase the number of points students need to earn a reward.
- Increase the number of behaviors being monitored; for example, make the target behavior "reduced disruptions" rather than "reduced blurt-outs" so that more behaviors are included within the definition.

This example shows how a teacher might alter a classwide system over a period of months as students demonstrate success:

Expectation Being Monitored

- "Respectful comments only to staff." Students may earn 1 point per interval if all students follow the expectation:

- 15-minute intervals: 10 points required for reward
- 15-minute intervals: 13 points required for reward
- 20-minute intervals: 13 points required for reward
- 20-minute intervals: 18 points required for reward

- "Treating everyone with respect" added to expectation:

  - 30-minute intervals: 18 points required for reward
  - 30-minute intervals: 25 points required for reward
  - 45-minute intervals: 25 points required for reward
  - 45-minute intervals: 35 points required for reward
  - 60-minute intervals: 35 points required for reward

Don't increase a system's difficulty until students have been consistently successful. If you make things too difficult before students feel somewhat in control of their own success, they may be inclined to give up and stop trying to meet the expectations.

It's also important to give students plenty of advance notice before making this kind of modification. Emphasize to students that you are making the change because they have been successful. Be careful not to sound apologetic about this change. If students complain, let them know that the system, like many other things in life, is challenging and may increase in difficulty, but emphasize that they have the skills to be successful.

By making changes like these gradually, the system becomes increasingly lean: students demonstrate highly responsible behavior for relatively small extrinsic rewards (Freeland & Noell, 1999). Notice that in the preceding example, students started out working in 15-minute intervals and needing 10 points for a reward, so 150 minutes of responsible behavior earned students a reward. A few months later, the same class works in 60-minute intervals and needs 35 points for a reward, meaning that 2,100 minutes of responsible behavior earns a reward.

Once a system is fairly lean, modify it to be based on intermittent rewards.
Some of the systems in the menu that are identified as appropriate for medium-structure classrooms involve the use of intermittent rewards—rewards that are given only on some occasions rather than every time performance criteria are met. Even if your classroom is highly structured, you should eventually shift to intermittent rewards once the students have learned and are consistently displaying the skill or skills that are the focus of your classwide system. Moving to intermittent rewards is important for two reasons:

- It is not practical for you to deliver rewards at a high rate over a long period of time (Freeland & Noell, 1999).
- Intermittent schedules of reinforcement have been shown to be most effective in maintaining student behavior over time (Alberto & Troutman, 2006; Cooper et al., 2007; Scheuermann & Hall, 2008).

Moving to intermittent rewards is another step in making your motivation system more challenging.

Once a class is working successfully for intermittent rewards, consider adding or switching to one of the goal-setting systems described in the Menu of Classwide Systems.
Goal setting is one of the last steps in fading students from the support of extrinsic rewards to reliance on their own intrinsic motivation. While you are still using a system of intermittent

rewards, begin setting individual goals for each student (or have the students set their own goals) and help the class set a classwide goal. Then, make a point of providing frequent positive feedback to students for meeting the goals. Once you have motivated students to strive toward their individualized goals and you are maintaining high rates of positive feedback to individuals and the whole class, you will be very close to being able to abandon reward-based systems altogether (O'Leary & Becker, 1967; Skinner, 1982).

When appropriate, have a class discussion about abandoning the use of the reward-based system.

When the class seems ready—most students seem to take pride in behaving responsibly—arrange to conduct a whole-class discussion about whether students feel they can continue to behave responsibly without getting rewards. If the tone of the discussion suggests that most students think they can maintain their responsible behavior without a reward system, set a classwide goal such as:

> We, the students in Room 14, can behave responsibly and we will strive to meet our Guidelines for Success without needing a reward system.

When students can agree to this kind of classwide goal, you can stop using a reward-based system. However, you do need to continue providing positive feedback and occasional special recognition (which might be a reward) when the class exhibits ongoing responsible behavior.

Menu of Classwide Systems

The rest of this chapter describes a variety of classwide systems for increasing student motivation—a menu of procedures. Those appropriate for high-structure classes are presented first, followed by those for medium- and then low-structure classes. Read through the systems that fit the level of structure your class needs (you will probably want to read others as well to gain some perspective); then choose the system or systems that you think will be practical to implement and will improve the motivation of your students. You can also use the ideas presented here as a basis for creating your own system, if you wish. Table 8.1 lists the systems described in the menu in the order they appear.

Reward-Based Systems for High-Structure Classes

Whole-class points (time interval).

In this system you provide feedback, both positive and corrective, to the entire class at regular intervals. For each interval during which the behavior of the class meets your expectations, the group earns a point, or if you prefer, a range of points (for example, zero to three points). Once the group earns a predetermined number of points, the entire class gets a reward. This is an excellent system to use when you have quite a few immature students in the class. However, it is not a good choice when most of your class behaves well and one or two students are responsible for most of the misbehavior.

When using this system, first determine the duration of the interval—each hour, each half-hour, or each quarter-hour, for example. The less mature your class is, regardless of

Table 8.1.
Classwide Motivational Systems

Reward-Based Systems Appropriate for High Structure	Reward-Based Systems Appropriate for Medium Structure	Nonreward-Based Systems Appropriate for Low Structure
Whole-class points (time interval)	Group response cost	Teacher sets goals for students
Reinforcement based on reducing misbehavior	Lottery tickets	Teacher guides students in setting goals
Team competition	Target and reward a specific behavior	Teacher guides students in setting classwide goal (public posting)
Behavioral grading	Whole-class points (intermittent)	

grade level, the shorter the intervals should be. Keep track of the duration using an alarm on your watch, a timer, a preprogrammed classroom computer, or some other regular method.

Next, have a class brainstorming session to identify possible rewards. Use the suggestions in step 1 of task 5 for working with students to choose meaningful and highly motivating rewards.

The last consideration is how you will keep track of the points. With most classes, this could be as simple as marking points in a small designated box on the board for that class period. Or you could make a simple chart with the goal at the top and color in the total number of points earned at the end of each period.

Once these decisions are made, implementation is fairly simple. At the conclusion of each interval (when the timer goes off after the designated time), review the behavior of the entire class during that interval. If students met your expectations, tell them the number of points they earned and praise their efforts. If the group earns anything less than full points, describe the inappropriate behaviors that led to your assessment, but do not name the students who misbehaved. Then clarify what students can do to earn full points during the next interval: "Because I had to give several of you reminders about talking during independent work, the group does not get any points for this time period. However, I am resetting the timer, and I am sure that in the next thirty minutes you will be able to earn two points. Remember, the expectation is that there is zero talking during independent work time. If you need to ask a question, place your textbook upright on your desk, keep working, and I will get to you as soon as I can."

If student behavior does not improve, increase the amount of positive feedback you give to individual students and to the class during each interval. If improvement is still insufficient, consider using shorter intervals (fifteen minutes rather than thirty). When the class earns a reward, begin the system again with increased difficulty if students are demonstrating consistent levels of success.

Reinforcement based on reducing misbehavior.

This system is designed to reward an entire class for significant reductions in the total number of misbehaviors that occur on any given day. It is particularly effective when many different students in the class exhibit a wide variety of misbehavior.

To implement the system, use either a daily or weekly Misbehavior Recording Sheet (see chapter 7, tool C) and keep data on class misbehavior for at least five days. Design a chart with spaces to record the data from those five days along with at least another twenty to thirty days. Then determine the average number of misbehaviors per day that occurred during your five-day baseline period (add up the total number of misbehaviors you recorded and divide by five).

From the average number of incidents per day, build a sliding scale for awarding points. Create the scale so that if the average number of incidents (or more) occurs, students earn no points, but as progressively fewer incidents occur, they earn an increasing number of points that can be applied toward a reward. For example, if the average number of incidents for the five days was thirty-three (obviously this hypothetical class has a lot of misbehavior), your point scale might look like this:

More than 32 incidents	0 points
22–32 incidents	1 point
15–21 incidents	2 points
7–14 incidents	3 points
3–6 incidents	4 points
1–2 incidents	5 points
0 incidents	6 points

Post the chart and point out to students the number of incidents that occurred over the preceding five days. Explain your concern and inform students that you are willing to provide the class with some rewards if they work on reducing the amount of misbehavior that occurs each day. Then show students your scale of number of incidents and corresponding points.

Next, have students brainstorm a list of class reward ideas. Once you have a reasonable list, set prices for each of the possible rewards in terms of how many points will be required to get it. The prices need to be set by you, and you should base them on the instructional, personnel, or monetary costs of the items. Follow the suggestions toward the beginning of task 5 for generating a list of highly motivating rewards and choosing which rewards will be used.

Each day keep a careful count of the number of incidents of misbehavior. At the end of the day, record the total number of misbehavior incidents and tell the class how many points they earned that day. Also let students know each day the total number of points they have accumulated to date. When the class has enough points, they get the designated reward. Then the system starts again, and they have zero points. Remind the class of the expected behavior, the number of points they need to earn for the reward, and the reward (if specified).

Team competition.

A system that involves team competition (groups of students competing against each other) can be useful for reducing minor but frequent annoying behaviors such as students calling out or other disruptions. Of course, whenever you do anything with teams—especially when the competition involves academic or behavioral performance—it's important to ensure that the teams are as comparable as possible. Thus, you should assign students to teams rather than letting them self-select. Make sure that no team is overloaded with "problem" or "extremely responsible" students.

Divide students into two or more teams. These teams could be based on room arrangement, such as rows or table groups. Every time students misbehave by not following the expectations for the specific behavior you are targeting, you will place a mark next to their team name on the board. The team with the fewest marks at the end of the day, or both teams if they stay under five marks, receives a small reward, such as being excused first from class.

An alternative is that the winning team each day earns a point toward a larger reward. Whenever a team reaches the number of points for the reward, they earn that reward. For example, whenever either team reaches eight points, all members of that team earn a reward. Note that this procedure works only for rewards that do not require your time and supervision, as only half the class will earn a reward at a given time. For example, you would not want half of your class earning a period of free time while the remaining half is expected to work with you, especially in high-structure classes where the whole class likely requires your supervision and attention. Therefore, this procedure would work with a small food reward. Whenever the first group earns their points, you bring them the food item. This group then begins working on a new reward. The other group can earn the first item whenever they reach the required number of points.

Another alternative within this system is that the winning team for the day gets the name of their team entered into a drawing. At the end of a two-week period, a team is drawn from all the entries and each member of the winning team gets a "Full Credit for One Daily Homework Assignment" certificate.

Behavioral grading.

If you have already implemented behavioral grading (as described in chapter 2, task 4), consider whether the grading criteria can be altered slightly to target the specific misbehaviors you wish to eliminate or the positive behaviors you wish to increase. If you have not already implemented a behavioral grading component, this is an effective classwide system to consider. Follow the procedures outlined in chapter 2, task 4 to develop or refine your system.

You may also wish to combine the individual behavioral grades into a broader classwide system. Calculate the average percentage the class earns for behavioral grades each week. Add up the total number of points earned by all students in the behavioral grade category. Find the total number of points possible by multiplying the number of students in the class times the number of points each student can earn per week. Then divide the total points earned by total points possible to get the percentage.

Set a goal for the class to improve this percentage. For example, if the class is averaging 70 percent on their behavioral grade each week, set a goal that students will collectively earn 80 or 85 percent. If students achieve this goal the following week, they will earn a designated reward. Follow the other procedures in this task for determining rewards, increasing the difficulty of the system as students demonstrate success, and fading the classwide system.

Reward-Based Systems for Medium-Structure Classes

Group response cost.

Group response cost is a simple system that can be used very effectively to reduce one specific misbehavior that several different students in the class tend to exhibit. It is also effective in improving a group's behavior in terms of following directions and being efficient during transitions.

To use this system to reduce a common group misbehavior (e.g., reducing profanity), first set up a time at the end of the week for a reward activity, say, ten minutes of socializing time at the end of the period on Friday. On a chart with one vertical bar, write times in thirty-second intervals from ten minutes to zero—in the bottom box, write "10 minutes," on the next, "9 minutes, 30 seconds," on the next "9 minutes," and so on until you reach 0 at the top. Tell students that each week, the class will start out with ten minutes of socializing time for the end of the week, but any time you hear profanity, they will lose thirty seconds of that socializing time. Fill in the bottom box and demonstrate how when you hear profanity, you will mark the chart, moving the bar to the "9 minutes, 30 seconds" mark. The time that is marked on the chart will show how much time the class gets at the end of the week.

When using this system to improve behaviors such as following directions and being efficient during transitions, make a chart for a specific amount of time. Let students know that when you give a directive for a transition ("Everyone get out your math books and a blank piece of paper"), they have a specific amount of time—say, one minute—to complete the transition. Tell students that if it takes them more than one minute, the additional time will come off the ten minutes of socializing time. Then after you give your first directive in a day, wait for one minute. If the class is ready, thank students for their efficiency. If students are not ready, hold up the chart, and for every thirty seconds that the transition is not complete, fill in another box on the chart. Continue this process, without saying a word, until all students are ready. After you give the next directive for a transition, follow the same procedure. Over the course of a day, each block of thirty seconds that students waste will cost them thirty seconds off the socializing time at the end of the week.

Because group response cost is predominantly punitive (taking time away from the socializing time), you need to make a concerted effort to provide students with frequent positive attention, positive feedback, and even intermittent rewards when they behave appropriately. Too much focus on a negative behavior without frequent positive interactions can backfire on you: students may try to lose the ten minutes quickly just to frustrate you and see what you will do next. In addition, if students have lost the socializing time early in the week, you will need to build contingencies into the system so that they continue to exhibit effort through the remainder of the week. For example, if students have lost their ten minutes by Wednesday, they might have the opportunity to earn back fifteen seconds for each transition that goes faster than the one-minute expectation.

This system is most likely to work when more than three or four students exhibit one specific misbehavior. If only one, two, or three students are causing the problem, you are better off setting up individualized plans (both positive and corrective) with those students. The system is also unlikely to be powerful enough to be effective if your class frequently exhibits many different misbehaviors.

Lottery tickets.

A relatively simple but highly effective way to encourage appropriate behavior or a specific positive behavior is to use an intermittent weekly lottery reward system.

Each week, on an unpredictable basis, present individual students who are following the rules or demonstrating responsible behavior with lottery tickets for a weekly drawing. The simplest way to do this is to purchase a roll of raffle tickets such as those sold at most office supply stores.

When you give a ticket, have the student write her name and the date on it. Be sure to tell the student exactly why she is getting the ticket so she can write a brief description (such as "completed all homework"). Have the student put the completed ticket in a container for a drawing that will occur at the end of the week. Each Friday before the drawing, identify two rewards you think students would like—perhaps a free homework pass or a candy bar of the student's choice. At the time of the drawing, announce the first reward and draw a lottery ticket from the container. The student whose name is on that ticket receives the reward. Repeat the process for the second reward. Throw away or recycle the tickets that remain in the container. The next Monday, start giving out tickets for that week's drawing.

With this system, it is important to watch that you are not being discriminatory. For example, it would be easy to inadvertently harbor a grudge toward individual students who have been especially troublesome during the current week or in the past, and so not notice their positive behavior. It can also be easy to fall into the trap of noticing the small improvements of your more difficult students and the great leaps of your high achievers but not recognizing or acknowledging the ongoing, sustained effort of your average students.

Target and reward a specific behavior.

This simple classwide behavior management system is useful when quite a few different students exhibit one specific behavioral problem, such as name-calling or put-downs. For a couple of days, count the number of times the targeted behavior occurs. Don't bother to count how many incidents any individual student has, just the total number of incidents during the class period.

After two days, share the information you have collected with students and tell them they need to reduce the frequency of this misbehavior. Guide the class in the process of setting a realistic improvement goal—reducing the number of daily incidents from 40 to 32, for example. Students may be tempted to set an unrealistic goal such as reducing the number of incidents from 40 per day to zero. Explain that if they set an unreasonable goal, it will be very difficult to achieve the goal. Explain that a realistic goal—say, no more than 32 incidents—increases their chances of success. Also tell them that once they achieve their initial (reasonable) goal, they can start setting more challenging goals for themselves.

Have the class generate a list of classwide rewards. Create a Grab Bag—write each reward on a small card and put all the cards in a container. On any day that the class meets the goal, one of the students gets to draw a card from the container. The class receives the reward written on the card. When you are ready to start fading the system, let students know that you have put some cards into the container that say "Congratulations! Today you have the satisfaction of having attained your goal." Explain that when one of these cards is drawn, students will not get an actual reward that day. Instead, it will give them the opportunity to learn that people do many things in life not for any reward but simply for the satisfaction of doing something well. The more of these cards you add, the closer you move students toward eliminating the system completely.

Whole-class points (intermittent).

An alternative to using whole-class points based on time intervals (see the high-structure examples) is to intermittently catch the class when everyone is behaving well and award one or more points. Use the time interval concept, and have the class brainstorm various reward items and activities. You set the prices. Then at times when you notice that everyone in the class is meeting expectations, you can announce that you are awarding one (or any number you wish) points.

The advantage to this variation is that the system is entirely under your control: you decide when to award points. You can make it a high-structure system if you award points frequently. The disadvantage is that without a specific interval (as marked by the timer going off or by the end of a work period), it is easy to forget about the system. Ironically, this is especially true if the students are behaving really well. So if you are going to use this system intermittently, keep reminding yourself to catch the class and award points. If you do this well and student behavior responds quickly, an easy way to begin fading this system is to use longer intervals (on average, because this is an intermittent system) between the times you award points. For example, during the early days of using the system, you might catch the class ten or fifteen times a day. Later in the year, you catch the class only once or twice per day.

Nonreward-Based Systems for Low-Structure Classes

Goal setting involves helping students learn to strive for positive goals they can achieve (Rader, 2005). This is an important strategy for even the most responsible and mature high school students to learn and master because it is one of the most common qualities of successful adults. Goals can be academic, behavioral, or a mix of both.

Because the focus tends to be on increasing desired behaviors as opposed to reducing negative ones, goal-setting systems are generally most appropriate for students who need only a low-structure management plan. If a class exhibits frequent misbehavior, there may not be sufficient intrinsic motivation among the students for goal-setting procedures to have much of an impact. But if a class is behaving responsibly for the most part, by definition a significant amount of intrinsic motivation is being demonstrated. When this is the case, goal-setting procedures can often extend and channel that intrinsic motivation in productive directions.

A goal-setting system such as setting goals for each student and sharing them with the individual students represents a first level of implementation. Once students understand the concept of striving to achieve a goal and are motivated to do so, you can teach them to set their own goals and goals for the class as a whole.

You should work with a class for at least a month before implementing any goal-setting system. Following are descriptions of three effective goal-setting procedures.

Teacher sets goals for students.
To use this procedure, go through your class list student by student and think about each one: what attitude, behavior, or trait would help each individual student be more successful? Examples of goals you might identify for different students include these:

- Complete more work.
- Write more neatly.
- Follow directions without arguing.
- Get along better with other students (be more patient).
- Be willing to take more risks and accept more challenges.
- Have a more positive attitude; complain less.
- Accept and learn from mistakes.
- Stay focused on work during class.
- Talk only at appropriate times.

- Demonstrate more self-control (anger management).
- Master specific academic skills the student has struggled with.
- Become more independent and self-reliant.
- Interact more with other students (be less shy).
- Be more creative.
- Be willing to try new things.

You can use exhibit 8.2 to record goals for each student in your class. (See the DVD for a blank reproducible of this form.) Write the name of each student on the form. Then take fifteen to thirty seconds per student and think about what that student most needs to learn. Consider the lasting legacy you want to leave with this student: "If I could help her learn only one thing, it would be ..." Leave the Priority column blank for now. If you can't think of a goal for a particular student, skip that student and come back to her later. When you go back to that student, try to identify why you could not come up with a goal. Perhaps the student is already hard working and responsible; if this is the case, you could set the goal that the student continue to be highly motivated ("Continue to do your best and continue to persevere with difficult tasks"). If you do not know a student well enough to identify a goal, do not set a goal for the student, but set one for yourself to get to know that student better. This task of identifying a goal for each student (and going back to the students who require more thought) should take between fifteen and thirty minutes for each class.

Exhibit 8.2
Goal-Setting Form

Student	Goal	Priority (1+, 1, 2, 3)
Allison, Keith	Keep up good work!	3
Bhatt, Vang	Participate more	1
Cedeno, Rosa	Manage temper better	1+
Draper, Melissa	Neatness	2
Erlandsen, Joe	No more late work	2
Foley, Trent	Stop rude comments	1+
Green, Jamaya	Keep up good work!	3
Houzedah, Ashraf	Stay focused in groups.	2
Jackson, Rainbow	Finishing work	1
Katayan, Jazmin	Neatness	2
Lachowicz, Peter	No talking during class	2
Moreno, Nando	Keep up good work!	3
Newhouse, Yolanda	Participate more	2
Norbert, Tory	Lower voice in groups	2
Pacheco, Felipe	Raise hand to speak	2

Once you identify a goal for each student, set priorities. You need to determine which goals have an element of urgency to them and which represent goals that are merely desirable. Plan on committing greater time and attention to helping the students who may not be successful in school and life if they do not achieve their goal or learn the skill or trait. If a goal is less urgent (the student will probably do fine whether or not he improves in this particular skill or trait), it will not require as much time or attention from you. This step of prioritizing students' goals is essential because even the best teacher cannot do everything at once.

The Priority column on exhibit 8.2 calls for rating each student's goal with a priority of 1+, 1, 2, or 3. Table 8.2 is a guide for determining which rating is most appropriate and identifying the corresponding action you should take to help the student achieve the goal.

Be careful about identifying too many goals as priority 1+. If you identify eight or more students with priority 1+ goals, the class probably needs a reward-based motivation system.

Once you identify a goal for each student and specify priorities for all the goals, determine how to make students aware of the goals you hope they will achieve (Fuchs et al., 1985; Johnson et al., 1997). One way is to have a conference with each student to discuss the goal and provide the student with a written description of the goal. Many readers are probably now thinking (or shouting!), "I don't have time to meet with every student! I have thirty students in every class!" Prioritizing will help potentially overwhelmed teachers through this procedure. You should plan to meet with the students who have the highest-priority goals, those with a 1+. In fact, for students with these goals, you should try to meet with the individual student and his or her family. For students who have priority 1 goals, you should

Table 8.2.
Guide to Rating Goals

Priority Level	Urgency for the Student	Action by the Teacher
1+	This student must immediately learn to meet this goal in order to succeed in my classroom and in the future.	I will meet with the student and family, fill out a goal contract, provide frequent positive feedback, and may set up an individualized contract.
1	This student would benefit greatly from learning to meet this goal.	I will meet with the student and family, fill out a goal contract, and provide frequent positive feedback when the student strives to meet the goal.
2	This student might benefit from learning to meet this goal.	I will provide frequent positive feedback when the student strives to meet the goal.
3	This student is going to be fine whether she/he learns to meet the goal or not.	I will provide occasional positive feedback when the student strives to meet the goal.

also meet with the student, but you do not need to involve the family. You can hold off scheduling meetings for the students who have priority 2 and 3 goals. In fact, it's fine if you meet with these students only if you can find the time.

When you meet with a student or the student and his or her family, complete a Goal Contract (see exhibit 8.3). To fill out this contract, first identify the overall goal: it will probably be what you wrote for the student on the Goal-Setting Form. However, if your goal for the student is framed in terms of something the student should not do, transform the goal into a positive statement of what the student should do (e.g., "stop being disruptive" becomes "participate responsibly in lessons and study times"). Then list three specific ways the student can demonstrate that he or she is striving to achieve the goal. It is very important to tell the student that he can exhibit tangible, objective behaviors to show you he is working toward his goal. You should also have a rationale in mind that you can present to the student about how striving to achieve this goal will help him. Communicate all of this information to the student during your conference. Also, plan for regular times in subsequent weeks to fill in the Progress Monitoring section of the Goal Contract.

Another way you can share your goals with students is by having brief conferences: take time during independent work periods to briefly inform individual students of the goals you hope to see them strive to achieve. You might use these conferences with students who have priority 2 and 3 goals.

Finally, you can communicate your goals for students somewhat indirectly by looking for and capitalizing on opportunities to give each one positive feedback related to the behavior or trait that you hope to help him or her achieve. This method of communication works even if you have not yet had a goal conference or a brief conference with the student. When a student exhibits behavior that reflects the identified goal, comment on it.

For example, your goal for a student is for him to "talk only at appropriate times," and he participates appropriately while a guest speaker is in the room. You might say, "Jamal, while our guest speaker was here this morning, I noticed that you gave him your full attention. You talked only during the times that he wanted you to discuss things at your table and when you raised your hand to be recognized. That demonstrated a great deal of respect for the speaker."

Whether or not you've had a goal discussion or completed a Goal Contract with a student, feedback of this nature will help the student realize that this is a behavior that you are monitoring and that you feel is important for him to learn. Providing this type of contingent, descriptive, and immediate positive feedback is also extremely valuable after you have conducted a goal conference with a student.

Wait to use goal setting as a classwide motivation system until you have worked with your students for at least a month, but plan to do it with your classes several times throughout the year. As you repeat the goal-setting process, your goal for a particular student may vary. If a student has not made progress on the goal or has made some progress but still has more to go, maintain the same goal. If the student has met your goal, consider setting a new goal. Each time you go through the process, you should restate the priorities and conduct conferences with students who have priority 1+ and 1 goals and brief conferences with students who have priority 2 and 3 goals. For all students, give positive feedback when you see them taking steps toward their goals.

Exhibit 8.3
Goal Contract

Name: *Rosa*   Date: *3/2*

A goal for you to work toward is: *to finish all your in-class assignments and hand them in on time*

You can show you are working toward this goal by:

A. *Focusing on the assignment during independent work*

B. *If you have a question about something, ask one of your neighbors or ask me*

C. *Keeping any distractions (phone, books) off your desk while working*

Progress Monitoring

Date (within a week of starting date): *3/9*

How will you know if you are being successful in taking steps toward the goal? *Use Assignment and Grade Tracking Log (exhibit 2.4) to keep track of when you hand in your in-class assignments. I will also monitor how often I have to remind you to stay focused on work.*

What progress has been made toward the goal? *Tracking Log shows only one late assignment for the week. I had to give you three reminders to put your phone away on Thursday, but no reminders on the other days.*

What needs to continue or change to reach the goal? *You are off to a great start!*

What help is needed to make the goal more attainable? *I will remind you as needed to focus.*

Student Signature_____   Teacher Signature _____

Progress Monitoring

Date (Two weeks from start):

How will you know if you are being successful in taking steps toward the goal?

What progress has been made toward the goal?

What needs to continue or change to reach the goal?

What help is needed to make the goal more attainable?

Student Signature_____   Teacher Signature _____

Progress Monitoring

Date (One month from start)

How will you know if you are being successful in taking steps toward the goal?

What progress has been made toward the goal?

What needs to continue or change to reach the goal?

What help is needed to make the goal more attainable?

Student Signature_____   Teacher Signature _____

Teacher guides students in setting goals.

Once students understand the concept of striving to achieve a goal, you can conduct one or more lessons to teach them how to set their own goals. If they are involved in their own goal setting as opposed to the teacher setting goals for them, they may be more likely to work harder (Fuchs, Bahr, & Rieth, 1989). Begin by discussing the importance of goal setting. Remind students that they have been working hard to achieve the goals that you set for them. Then explain that learning to set goals and striving to meet them is a beneficial skill that can help them succeed in school, work situations, and life in general.

Have students identify and discuss some short-term goals they want to achieve for themselves. Encourage them to focus on school-based goals; however, let them know that setting goals in areas outside school, such as sports, hobbies, and personal relationships, can also be very useful. You may want to put some sample goals on the board to provide ideas for students who have trouble coming up with goals of their own. Pass out copies of the Goal Contract (exhibit 8.3). Have each student write an overall goal and three ways to demonstrate that he or she is trying to achieve the goal. If you complete a contract for yourself as students do the activity, you validate the students for their efforts. Once students complete their contracts, tell them to keep a copy of their goal on their desk or on the front cover of a notebook so they will be reminded frequently of the goals they are striving to achieve.

For a couple of days after this session, try to meet with each student to discuss his or her Goal Contract. If a student has set an unreachable goal, help her to make the goal more realistic. Record each student's goal on a blank version of the Goal-Setting Form so that you have a summary of all the students' goals on one or two pages. Once you sign all the contracts and summarize all of the students' goals, watch for any opportunity to give students positive feedback on their efforts to achieve their goals (as you did when you set the goals for students). Plan to have students fill in the Progress Monitoring sections of their Goal Contracts in subsequent weeks and check in with how they are doing at attaining their goals. Provide feedback and advice if students are struggling to make improvements.

If this process proves useful—behavior is improving, motivation is increasing—repeat the activity once each month.

Teacher guides students in setting a classwide goal.

Consider guiding your students in the process of setting a classwide goal. The goal might involve reducing a classwide problem (eliminate teasing), increasing a positive behavior (improve classroom climate through increased positive interactions), or participating in a service project (make regular visits to a retirement home). Put a reasonable time limit on achieving the goal so that you and the class will have a specific date to evaluate their success.

Establishing and working toward a common goal as a group is a powerful way to increase students' sense of purpose and belonging (Rader, 2005). It can build classroom pride and create a powerful sense of community.

A simple way of working toward a class goal is to use public posting. When there is one specific behavior you want to increase (e.g., homework completion) or decrease (e.g., use of student-to-student put-downs during class), you can chart that behavior in a place and in a way that all students can see it. This is especially useful when quite a few students in the class exhibit a specific problem as opposed to a problem that only a couple of students exhibit. Public posting makes everyone aware of how pervasive a problem is and gives the entire group positive feedback when the situation improves.

For example, if a remedial class has trouble with frequent name-calling, laughing at other students' mistakes, and other forms of student-to-student disrespect, you could start by keeping a simple tally of the total number of disrespectful actions that occur each day for three days. Then post a chart with the data from those three days. Posting the chart serves as the impetus for holding a class discussion about the problem, the benefits of reducing the negative behavior, and strategies that individual students might employ to help reduce the problem. In this example, one strategy that you could share is that individuals should avoid laughing when someone calls someone else a name or otherwise puts somebody down. Each day, keep a simple count of the number of disrespectful incidents. At the end of the day, record those data on the chart. At least twice a week when you post the data, initiate a short discussion about whether the problem is getting better, getting worse, or staying about the same. If the situation is staying the same or getting worse, have students discuss other actions they can take to help reduce the problem.

Public posting can also be effective in helping you increase a positive behavior—daily work completion, for example. To use the system for this purpose, start by determining the class's daily percentage of completed work turned in on time for a period of one week. You can do this by counting the number of assignments turned in each day and dividing that number by the total number of assignments that should have been turned in that day. This figure is the class's percentage of work completion for that day. Record a week's worth of daily work completion percentages on a chart placed prominently in the room.

Use the initial record to prompt a discussion of the importance of work completion, the benefits to each individual of completing his or her work, and strategies students can use to help increase their own work completion. Then compute the class's daily percentage of work completion and plan to record it on the chart the next day. At least twice a week, preferably daily, discuss the data on the chart and whether the percentage of work completion is increasing, decreasing, or staying about the same.

If you wish to use this procedure with a medium-structure class, you can add rewards for when the class reaches prespecified levels on the chart—for example, for improving their percentage of work completion by 10 and 20 percent.

In Conclusion

Motivating your students will often be challenging, but the rewards will be worthwhile. When you have a highly motivated class, you will see higher rates of on-task behavior; experience decreased disciplinary problems, fewer referrals, and less absenteeism; and you will find that you have more lesson time to devote to the "good stuff." Different students must be reached on different levels, but if you are diligent, you will find a way to inspire each of your students. Make sure each student is aware that you are expecting his or her success because you know he or she *can* succeed. Make the same effort to reach each student on more than one level, motivating them externally and intrinsically. Inspire them, and you may just find that they return the favor.

Motivation Self-Assessment Checklist

Use this worksheet to identify which parts of the tasks described in this chapter you have completed. For any item that has not been completed, note what needs to be done to complete it. Then transfer your notes to your planning calendar in the form of specific actions you need to take (for example, "November 2: take time to reflect on how I am connecting with students and maintaining a positive attitude toward them"). A blank worksheet is on the DVD.

	Task	Notes and Implementation Ideas
☑	TASK 1: *Understand the importance of building personal relationships with students.* I understand that I will dramatically increase the probability of having cooperative and motivated students if they perceive that I both like and respect them. Therefore, I will take a personal interest in my students and their success. I will value my students. I will make a concerted effort to maintain a personal connection with my students, and to maintain a positive attitude toward them.	
☐	TASK 2: *Use every possible opportunity to provide each student with noncontingent attention.* I understand that there are many benefits to giving students noncontingent attention. I have considered how I will provide each of my students with noncontingent attention by: • Greeting students • Showing an interest in students' work • Inviting students to ask for assistance • Conversing with a student or group of students when time permits • Making a special effort to greet or talk to any student with whom I've had a recent interaction regarding a misbehavior	*Think about different ways to do this and set a goal for each week. In the past, I haven't paid enough attention to this after the first week or so. I will make a special effort to make contact with the students who tend to be very quiet and do not have many peer interactions.*

☑	TASK 3: *Give students positive feedback on their successes in a variety of ways.* I have made a plan to ensure that I am incorporating the following characteristics into the positive feedback I give students regarding their academic and behavioral performance: • Accurate feedback • Specific and descriptive feedback • Contingent feedback • Age-appropriate feedback • Feedback given in a way that fits my personal style I have considered the structure level of my class in determining how much positive feedback I need to give, realizing that high-structure classes need more positive feedback. I also realize that even low-structure classes have students who cease to try to meet expectations if they do not receive positive feedback. If any student seems to be responding to my positive feedback with an increase in inappropriate behavior, I am prepared to make modifications to the feedback I am giving.	
☐	TASK 4: *Plan to interact at least three times more often with students when they are behaving appropriately than when they are misbehaving.* I understand how important it is for me to interact with each of my students at least three times more often when they are behaving responsibly than when they are misbehaving. I will watch for any tendency on my part to fall into the criticism trap. I realize that the higher the level of structure of my class, the more I need to make an effort to maintain positive interactions at a very high level.	*I will monitor my ratio of positive to negative attention in at least one class each month — probably the class in which I am nagging the most.*

☐ *TASK 5: Effectively employ a classwide system or systems if needed to increase motivation and responsible behavior.* I understand that a classwide system may be helpful to increase student motivation to behave responsibly and achieve goals. I realize that what system I choose will depend on the level of structure needed for my students and the types of problems I am trying to address. I have evaluated, subjectively and/or with systematic monitoring tools, the behavior and motivation level of my students. I have carefully considered whether my students would benefit from a nonreward- or a reward-based motivation system. If a nonreward-based system is appropriate, I am prepared to use some form of goal setting with my students. If a reward-based system is needed, I have reviewed the information on how to use a reward-based system and am prepared to do the following: • Choose or design a system that is appropriate to the needs of my students. • Implement the system in a way that enhances its effectiveness with my students. • Maintain the system so that it continues to have a positive effect on my students' motivation. • Fade the system eventually so that students' improved behavior and/or increased motivation stems primarily from their own intrinsic motivation.	*Plan to use the Misbehavior Recording Sheet (exhibit 7.4) for all classes in second month to see if classwide systems are needed. May try goal setting in the senior elective regardless to keep them focused.*

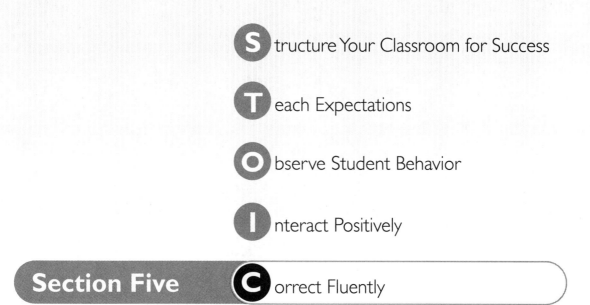

S tructure Your Classroom for Success

T each Expectations

O bserve Student Behavior

I nteract Positively

Section Five **C** orrect Fluently

As a teacher, you will observe misbehavior: one student makes disruptive noises during a lesson, another is chronically disrespectful and insubordinate directly to you, and two students are caught cheating on a test. Chapter 9 discusses how to correct student misbehavior in a way that reduces the probability that it will occur in the future. This skill may sound simple, but in fact it's one of the most difficult teaching techniques to master. When you "Correct Fluently"—the title of this part—you respond to misbehavior in a manner that does not disrupt other students or the flow of instructional activities. You enforce routines and rules in a way that reduces the chance that the misbehaving student, or any other student, exhibits that misbehavior in the future. You also correct in a way that does not have side effects: you don't harm the relationship you have established with the misbehaving student or reduce that student's motivation to do her best in your classroom. This chapter also includes information for addressing chronic misbehavior: when an individual student's behavior is resistant to the efforts described above, you will analyze why the behavior is occurring and develop a plan to intervene.

Chapter 9

Proactive Planning for Chronic Misbehavior

No matter how well organized your classroom may be and no matter how effectively you have communicated your behavioral expectations to your students, a certain amount of misbehavior is bound to occur. Although the rates of misbehavior will be much less if you have applied the techniques from this book, some misbehavior is inevitable. If an occasional misbehavior occurs but does not become repetitive, then there is no need for a systematic plan. However, once a misbehavior becomes chronic, intervention is necessary to break the pattern. Unfortunately, many teachers have a tendency to react to chronic student misbehavior in ways that actually lead to more, rather than less, inappropriate behavior (Chance, 1998; Lalli et al., 1999). This chapter is designed to help you view misbehavior as an opportunity to continue to educate your students about appropriate versus inappropriate behavior. It will prepare you to respond appropriately and effectively to student misbehavior, both with the majority of students and with students whose misbehaviors are chronic and more resistant to general management practices and intervention.

Use Effective Correction Techniques

Before you begin implementing an individualized or specific group intervention plan as described in the remainder of this chapter, check to see that you are effectively responding to student misbehavior, especially in regard to the student or group of students who are exhibiting chronic misbehavior. What correction strategies are effective is a debatable topic. A fundamental question to consider is: What is the purpose behind a correction, and what do you hope to accomplish by giving a corrective consequence? Is it to make you feel better because you made it clear that the student's behavior made you angry? Is it to remove the student from the classroom so that you no longer have to deal with the misbehavior? In the Discipline in the Secondary Classroom (DSC) approach, an effective correction is one that:

- *Changes the future occurrence of the behavior.* The correction reduces the chance that the student will exhibit that behavior in that situation in the future.

- *Does not disrupt other students.* In other words, the correction is fluent. The teacher's response does not stop the flow of instruction and does not distract other students from the work they are doing at the time the student misbehaved.

- *Treats the student who misbehaved with dignity and respect.* Corrections should never humiliate, ridicule, or belittle the student. Therefore, avoid sarcasm or biting remarks.

- *Does not reduce the student's motivation to exhibit positive behaviors.* Imagine a high school coach who corrects athletes in a manner that makes students want to quit the team, as opposed to a coach whose corrections inspire all players to want to work even harder in the future.

- *Does not jeopardize the positive relationship you have worked to establish with the student.* The student should still perceive that you like her and have high expectations for her—both academically and behaviorally.

Correcting student misbehavior is surprisingly difficult to do well for a variety of reasons. As a teacher, you need to be prepared to deal with the full range of behaviors, and your corrective strategies need to match the severity of the infraction (Barbetta, Norona, & Bicard, 2005; Conroy, Sutherland, Snyder, & Mars, 2008; Lewis & Sugai, 1999; Simonsen, Fairbanks, Briesch, Myers, & Sugai, 2008). The difficulty in effectively correcting misbehavior is compounded by the myriad things the teacher is required to do at any given moment. When teaching lessons, the teacher has to be thinking about making them interesting, differentiating instruction for different ability levels, keeping the students safe, staying on schedule, and so on. When a student misbehaves, the teacher must enforce the rules, but in what manner? Does she take on the role of umpire, cop, judge, boss, or …? It depends on the type and severity of the misbehavior. But the teacher cannot stop teaching for an hour, or even for three minutes, to decide how to respond.

It is difficult to correct effectively, but it is absolutely essential. The following attributes of effective corrections and consequences are described in detail in chapter 4, task 3, but the main points are summarized below:

- Make sure that students understand and can perform the expected behaviors. When in doubt, always go back to teaching and reteaching expected behaviors in new and novel ways. This can be done with a group of students who are exhibiting specific misbehaviors or with an individual student who is struggling to meet your expectations.

- Implement corrective consequences consistently. Plan to give the same consequence every time the misbehavior occurs and with every student who exhibits the misbehavior.

- Make sure the corrective consequence fits the severity and frequency of the misbehavior. Design consequences that are mild enough that you feel comfortable assigning them every time the misbehavior occurs rather than implementing based on an accumulation of misbehavior.

- Implement consequences unemotionally, giving the appearance that you are calm and unflappable.

- Interactions should be brief. Avoid arguing or justifying. Simply state the rule and the consequence, and continue with instruction. Inform students that they can make an appointment to speak to you any time they feel a longer discussion or rationale is needed.

- Continue to make efforts to increase your positive ratios of interaction with the student who is struggling, paying particular attention to times when the student is exhibiting the positive opposite of behaviors of concern.

Implementing the previous suggestions effectively should minimize the number of students who demonstrate chronic misbehavior. This will allow you to apply the in-depth strategies and plans presented in the remainder of this chapter with a manageable number of students. If you have several large classes every day, you will realistically be able to design individualized behavior plans for only one or two situations at a time. As you read this chapter, keep in mind a situation that involves a specific chronic misbehavior that you would like to improve. This could be a problem with an individual student or a group. If the problem is the behavior of the entire class, go through the other chapters of this book again to identify variables you can manipulate to have a positive impact on the entire class. In particular, pay attention to chapters 3 through 6 and chapter 8.

Addressing Chronic Misbehavior

The tasks in the chapter are designed to help you correct in a manner that helps the student whose behavior is chronically problematic, reduces the degree to which that student's behavior interferes with the learning of others, and makes it easier for you to have a sense of efficacy about your role as a teacher.

This chapter addresses several severities of misbehavior using four levels of intervention. Before reviewing them, it is useful to understand two basic concepts about correcting misbehavior that will help you respond to it in an intellectual and planned manner, not in an emotional way.

First, it is vital to have a plan for how you will deal with student misbehavior. When teachers know in advance how they will respond to misbehavior, they are less likely to get frustrated and more likely to be effective (see chapter 4; Lovitt, 1978; McLeod, Fisher, & Hoover, 2003). By preplanning consequences for rule infractions, you will know exactly what to do whenever a rule is violated. This chapter will help you learn how to deal with those misbehaviors that persist in spite of rules and consequences.

Second, correction procedures can be considered effective only when they reduce the occurrence of the misbehavior they address in the long term (O'Neill, Horner, Albin, Storey, Sprague, & Newton, 1997). This is a key point because it is not uncommon for a teacher to deal with an inappropriate behavior in a way that may resolve the problem at the moment but make the situation worse in the long run. Chapter 8 introduced the notion of the criticism trap—that students who are starved for attention may be encouraged to misbehave as a result of the repeated attention they get when the teacher corrects them. Although the student may stop a particular behavior for the moment, he will know that if he ever feels the need for attention, he can demonstrate the behavior and get it immediately.

The concept of evaluating the effectiveness of correctional procedures based on their impact on students' long-term behavior applies to situations other than those involving attention-seeking misbehaviors. For example, a teacher who sends an extremely disruptive student out of class may feel that he has solved the problem. However, if the student continues to misbehave, the student clearly does not feel that being sent out of class is a negative consequence. This is why observation and gathering information is such a vital part of this process. Analyzing and understanding the way your students view the consequences you assign them is key to gauging their effectiveness (Horner, Vaughn, Day, & Ard, 1996).

Finally, because most chronic misbehavior serves a purpose for the individual who demonstrates it and because there are many reasons for misbehavior, correction efforts for specific misbehaviors will be more effective if they address the underlying causes of those behaviors (O'Neill et al., 1997). Students may misbehave for any number of reasons, including not knowing what the teacher expects, being unaware that they are demonstrating a behavior, not knowing the appropriate behavior, being starved for attention, or feeling a sense of power through exerting control over events around them. Some students even misbehave because being sent out of class or given a corrective assignment means they don't have to do course work they don't understand.

This chapter has three major tasks designed to help you effectively address chronic misbehavior. Task 1 is the easiest suggestion: try implementing the ideas in this task first. If problems remain, move on to the suggestions in task 2, and then, if necessary, task 3.

Task 1: Analyze and, if needed, adjust the implementation of your basic management plan.

Task 2: Analyze and, if needed, adjust the strategies you are using to build a positive relationship with the student.

Task 3: Analyze the misbehavior and develop a function-based intervention.

Plan A. Develop an intervention for awareness-type misbehaviors.

Plan B. Develop an intervention for ability-type misbehaviors.

Plan C. Develop an intervention for attention-seeking misbehaviors.

Plan D. Develop an intervention for habitual and purposeful types of misbehaviors.

Task 1 provides a form you can use to evaluate whether the basics of your management plan are fully in place, along with suggestions for minor adjustments you can make to your plan to help the student improve his behavior. Task 2 provides a form you can use to evaluate whether there are minor adjustments you can make in your interactions with the student that may increase the student's motivation to engage in positive behaviors and thus reduce the frequency and severity of the chronic misbehavior. Task 3 is longer and more complex than any other in this book. It will help you analyze the nature of any chronic problem that has been resistant to prevention and less intensive intervention. This task presents ways to collect data on the misbehavior, helps you analyze which of the four types of misbehavior the situation might involve, and suggests different types of intervention strategies for each of the four types of misbehavior.

At the end of this chapter is the Self-Assessment Checklist. You may also wish to review the Peer Study Worksheet for Chapter 9 (provided on the DVD) with a colleague, and, if possible, arrange to observe each other's classrooms. This will allow you to help one another fine-tune and implement your plan to intervene with a particular chronic misbehavior.

Task 1: Analyze and, If Needed, Adjust the Implementation of Your Basic Management Plan

In some cases, making some minor adjustments to your classroom management plan for the individual student who exhibits chronic misbehavior may be enough to help the student improve her behavior (Lewis & Sugai, 1999; Scheuermann & Hall, 2008). For example, moving the student's desk to a different location or being even more explicit with the student about your expectations may help improve the situation.

To work through this task, carefully consider the questions and suggestions on the Classroom Management Plan: Reflection and Implementation form, presented as a completed example (exhibit 9.1). (See the DVD for a blank reproducible of this form.) The DVD includes a fillable version of this form. It is followed by a version (exhibit 9.2) with bullet points for you to consider as you fill out your own form. (See the DVD for a blank reproducible of this form.) Note that the ideas and suggestions in this task have been covered earlier in the book, but you are now exploring how you might adjust the suggestions to help an individual student.

Try the easy thing first. Make some minor tweaks to your management plan or how you implement your management plan. If you are successful, you can turn a chronic problem into no problem. Be sure to keep your positive feedback at a very high level with this student and tell the student's family that improvement is taking place. If these adjustments in your plan prove ineffective after a couple of weeks, try implementing the procedures in task 2.

Exhibit 9.1
Classroom Management Plan:
Reflection and Implementation

Student Eleana   Teacher Mr. Torres   Date 10/16

As you reflect on these questions, make notes about adjustments you can make in how you implement your plan with this student.

1. Do classroom variables such as physical setting, schedule, and beginning/ending routines affect the student's inappropriate behavior?

   I will try moving her desk location from the middle of the class to the front center where she will be closer to me. I can observe and give feedback more easily. I will require that she get permission to leave her seat during class because she bothers other students when she has the freedom to get up without permission.

2. Does this student fully understand your behavioral expectations and your concerns about the misbehavior? If not, or if you are unsure, plan a discussion with the student to further clarify your expectations.

   I think she understands what is expected, but I will make an appointment to sit down with her and go over my concerns and the positive behaviors she should exhibit. I will ask her to come in tomorrow after school for this conference. If the behavior continues, I will contact her family.

3. Are your classroom rules clear? Does this student fully understand the rules? If not, or if you are unsure, schedule a planned discussion and lesson to clarify your rules and consequences.

   During the discussion with Eleana, I will clarify the rules and let her know that, at least for a while, she has an extra rule that does not apply to the other students — "Ask permission from Mr. Torres before leaving your seat." I will explain that when she can successfully follow this rule and show that she no longer bothers other students while they are working or I am presenting lessons, she will earn the privilege of leaving her seat without permission to hand in work, pick up supplies, and so on.

4. Is your enforcement of these rules:

   a. Consistent? (e.g., day to day or hour to hour, relative to your mood)

      No, I need to work on this. When I am feeling good, I probably do not correct her. When I am stressed, I probably do correct her. I will work on correcting her for bothering others even if it does not concern me at that moment.

   b. Fair? (Are other students who violate these rules corrected?)

      Yes, I try to correct any student who is bothering others. However, while Eleana's new rule is in place, I will correct her for getting out of her seat without permission even though other students have the right to leave their seats. In explaining this concept to her, I will use the example of a driver who gets his license suspended for six months because he has too many speeding tickets.

   c. Brief? (Does the student receive five seconds or less of attention at the time of the misbehavior?)

      I probably talk too much. I will try to correct by giving a quick reminder. If Eleana does not immediately stop bothering others and go back to her seat, I will calmly let her know that she is owing time until she does get back to her seat. Time owed will be paid after class. After three instances of time owed in one period, I will assign detention.

d. Calm? (Are you emotionally neutral when correcting this student's behavior?)

For the most part, yes. I never act really angry, but I may show exasperation or frustration. I will work a bit more to be completely neutral when I correct her.

e. Respectful? (Are you correcting objectively, not judgmentally, and as privately as possible?)

Yes.

5. Is this student misbehaving to cover some learning problem and/or an inability to understand or complete the work?

No — her work is very high quality, and she gets it all done. However, maybe I should have some fun enrichment assignments or cushion assignments that she can do when she completes the basic classwork. Maybe I should talk to the special ed teachers about whether she is eligible for the Talented/Gifted program.

6. Does this student have an "expectancy of success"?

Yes — at least academically. Maybe I should put more emphasis on how I know she can be responsible and helpful in the classroom so I build up her expectancy of behavioral success.

Exhibit 9.2
Classroom Management Plan: Reflection and Implementation—Bulleted Plan

Student   Teacher   Date

As you reflect on these questions, make notes about adjustments you can make in how you implement your plan with this student.

1. Do classroom variables such as physical setting, schedule, and beginning/ending routines affect the student's inappropriate behavior?

   - Consider whether the student would be less distracted or disruptive in a different part of the room.
   - Consider whether you can observe more frequently and easily if the student is in a different part of the room.
   - Giving stand-up and stretch breaks during long work periods may help this and other students stay focused.
   - Giving the student a job assisting with some part of your beginning and ending routines may help the student stay focused and cooperative.
   - Skim chapters 1, 2, and 3 to see if other variables of this type may help this student.

2. Does this student fully understand your behavioral expectations and your concerns about the misbehavior? If not, or if you are unsure, implement a planned discussion to further clarify your expectations.

   - Consider whether the student is unaware that the misbehavior of concern is an example of not meeting the expectations.
   - Schedule a neutral time to discuss the misbehavior with the student—a time when there will not be an audience of other students.
   - Keep the focus on the positive expectation, then refer specifically to the problem, and then reemphasize the positive expectation. End with high expectations: say that you know the student will make an effort to meet your expectations and be successful in the classroom.
   - Consider inviting the family to participate in this planned discussion, especially with a severe problem or a minor problem where you have seen no improvement after discussing it with the student only.
   - Examine your CHAMPS or ACHIEVE expectation sheets (or reread chapter 5).

3. Are your classroom rules clear? Does this student fully understand the rules? If not, or if you are unsure, schedule a planned discussion and lesson to clarify your rules and consequences.

   - Schedule a time to meet with the student to discuss your rules and consequences. This can be added to the discussion above when rule violations are part of the problem.
   - Clarify that enforcing the rules is part of your job as the teacher and that this enforcement has nothing to do with liking or disliking the student.
   - Clarify that the student is not bad. When he or she breaks a rule, it is the behavior at that moment that is a problem, not the student.

4. Is your enforcement of these rules:

   a. Consistent? (e.g., day to day or hour to hour, relative to your mood)

- Do not let the student get away with misbehavior when you are in a good mood if you would correct that same misbehavior when you are in a bad mood. Using a sports metaphor, offside in football should be called whether the referee is in a good mood or a bad mood.

b. Fair? (Are other students who violate these rules corrected?)

- Be cautious about any bias — even unconscious — wherein you hold one group of students (e.g., based on gender, race, academic ability) to one standard of rule following and another group to a different standard.
- Note that on some occasions you may adapt an expectation or rule (as shown in the sample in exhibit 9.1). This is analogous to a driver getting her license suspended for a period of time. Be very careful about doing this so you don't have to keep track of too many exceptions to your management plan.

c. Brief? (Does the student receive five seconds or less of attention at the time of the misbehavior?)

- Don't talk too much. Instead, take action.
- In the early stages of correcting a misbehavior, you may use that opportunity as a teachable moment, which will take longer than five seconds. However, once a problem is chronic, your reprimand or consequence should take five seconds or less so you can immediately return to the flow of instruction and give positive feedback to students who are following the rules.
- If you think the student needs a "lesson," schedule a planned discussion. Do not have that discussion at the time of the misbehavior.
- If the student tries to argue, say, "You can make an appointment to speak to me later about this, but right now I must go on with the lesson." Then ignore any further attempts by the student to suck you into a power struggle.

d. Calm? (Are you emotionally neutral when correcting this student's behavior?)

- Some students love having the power to upset a teacher.
- When you stay calm as you are correcting misbehavior, you do not give these students any power.
- Staying calm also reduces the chance that in the heat of the moment, you may say something insensitive, embarrassing, or hurtful.
- Remember that you do not necessarily have to be calm; you just have to act calm.
- There is a great quote about staying calm that middle school teachers will appreciate: "Arguing with an adolescent is like mud-wrestling a pig: you both get dirty and the pig loves it."

e. Respectful? (Are you correcting objectively, not judgmentally, and as privately as possible?)

- Remember that the only absolute rule in the CHAMPS or ACHIEVE approach is that students must be treated with dignity and respect.
- It is easy to get frustrated with a student and then put the student in his place. Try to avoid this.
- Correct as privately as the immediate situation allows.

- Comment on the behavior, not the person.
- Provide an objective description about the behavior, not a label. Don't resort to name-calling.
- Avoid sarcasm in your words, tone of voice, and even body language (e.g., rolling eyes).
- Try to treat students as you would like to be treated. If your principal was concerned about some aspects of your job performance, how would you like her to provide corrective feedback or enforce district rules? (e.g., reasonably private, objective descriptions of the problem).

5. Is this student misbehaving to cover some learning problem and/or an inability to understand or complete the work?

- Can the student read the assigned work fluently and accurately?
- Does the student comprehend when reading?
- Can the student do handwriting easily, or does she hold the pencil in a death grip?
- Can the student complete independent assignments independently, or does she need lots of assistance?

If the answer to any of these questions is no, make academic adaptations (differentiation). If you are unfamiliar with how to differentiate, talk to colleagues in special education for ideas.

6. Does this student have an "expectancy of success"?

- Reexamine the Expectancy × Value theory of motivation in chapter 1.
- Sometimes a student can do the work, but does not see himself as capable. You may need to pump up the student so he believes he can succeed.

Task 2: Analyze and, If Needed, Adjust the Strategies You Are Using to Build a Positive Relationship with This Student

Research suggests that students are more likely to behave well and work hard to meet a teacher's expectations when the student-teacher relationship is positive and respectful (Borich, 2004; Brophy, 1983; Cameron & Pierce, 1994; Gettinger & Stoiber, 1998; Hall, Lund, & Jackson, 1968; Marzano, 2003; Niebuhr, 1999; Pianta, Hamre, & Stuhlman, 2003). Negative interactions are associated with poorer academic and social behavior outcomes (Murray & Greenberg, 2006; Murray & Murray, 2004).

Any adult is also more likely to be highly motivated when he works for a great boss than when he feels used, abused, and disrespected by his boss. Most people who have an abusive boss do only the minimum amount of work required to stay out of trouble, and some may even take great delight in subtly sabotaging or embarrassing that boss (yes, even adults sometimes engage in misbehavior). In this task, you will explore how to build a plan to try to improve your connection with an individual student and increase the student's motivation to behave appropriately and succeed academically.

To work through task 2, carefully consider the questions and suggestions on exhibit 9.3, a completed sample of the Connect/Motivation Plan form. (See the DVD for a blank reproducible of this form.) Exhibit 9.4 is a version with bullet points for you to consider as you fill out your own form. (See the DVD for a blank reproducible of this form.)

If you implement a connect/motivate plan for at least two weeks and it is not effective, you have learned at least one important thing: this is a chronic problem. How do you know? Because the problem has been resistant to your basic management plan that works for most students, this student did not respond successfully to some individualized adjustments to that plan (task 1), and she did not respond to your organized plan to enhance your relationship with the student (task 2). So it's time to move on to the hard work of task 3.

> **Note**
>
> Special thanks to Mike Booher for developing the connect/motivation plan concept and form.

Exhibit 9.3
Connect/Motivation Plan: Reflection and Implementation—Questions to Ask When an Individual Student Is Not Motivated to Succeed in Your Class

Student _Sally_   Teacher _Mrs. Bradford_   Date _11/13_

Targeted Activities (activities in which the student is unmotivated or unsuccessful)	The Student's Strengths
• Coming to class regularly • Completing assignments in class • Completing homework	• Gets along well with others • Easily redirected • Enjoys nonacademic activities

1. List three strategies you will use to provide noncontingent attention to the student every day.

   A. I will give her a smile or a compliment (e.g., "You look sharp this morning" or "My daughter has a pair of shoes like yours"), or both, every day as she enters the classroom.

   B. When I see her exhibiting appropriate social behaviors when interacting with other students, I will establish eye contact and discreetly wink, smile, give a thumbs up, or some other signal.

   C. Every time she is absent, I will say to her on the day of her return something like, "I'm so glad you're back. It's just not the same without you here."

2. For which targeted activities will you provide positive verbal feedback to the student?

   A. Beginning an assignment on time

   B. Following a direction or responding to a redirection

   C. Turning in her homework

3. What will you do if he or she doesn't respond well to positive feedback?

   Try a different method of providing the feedback, such as writing her a private note.

4. Identify two strategies for increasing your ratio of interactions with the student and describe how and when you will use them.

   A. I will make a point to greet her every day when she enters the room and will tell her at dismissal that I'm looking forward to seeing her the next day.

   B. I will provide both positive feedback and noncontingent attention when she is appropriately interacting with other students. I will find discreet ways to provide the attention to avoid embarrassing Sally.

Exhibit 9.4

Connect/Motivation Plan: Reflection and Implementation—Questions to Ask When an Individual Student Is Not Motivated to Succeed in Your Class, Bulleted Plan

Student   Teacher   Date

Targeted Activities (activities in which the student is unmotivated and/or unsuccessful)	The Student's Strengths
• Give specific examples; do not say "everything" • Identify each academic area • Consider study skills and work habits	Consider: • Academic strengths • Behavioral strengths • Social strengths • Interests

1. List three strategies you will use to provide *noncontingent attention* to the student every day.

   These strategies should be specific (e.g., verbal greetings, hand gestures like thumbs up or handshake, facial expressions like smile, head nod, or wink) that are delivered at specific times of the day (e.g., entering or leaving the classroom, during small group work, *and* whenever appropriate (e.g., seeing student in the hallway).

2. For which targeted activities will you provide *positive verbal feedback* to the student?

   • Look at the student's strengths, and consider using some of them as opportunities for providing positive feedback.
   • Positive feedback should also be given for behaviors that are new, difficult, or a source of pride for the student.
   • Remember to deliver verbal positive feedback calmly and quietly, and within three to four feet of the student. Be brief, specific, and descriptive.
   • Be cautious of giving too much feedback in front of other students. You might embarrass the student.
   • Provide age-appropriate feedback; for example, it is inappropriate to praise a tenth grader for tying his shoe correctly.

3. What will you do if he or she doesn't respond well to positive feedback?

   • Does the student feel embarrassed by the public display of positive feedback or not know how to accept positive feedback?
   • Ask yourself if you are being too public or too dramatic with the feedback.
   • Are you pausing expectantly after giving feedback so that the student feels compelled to respond verbally?
   • Adjust feedback delivery accordingly, and revert to giving only noncontingent attention for several weeks if the student continues to reject positive feedback.

4. Identify two strategies for increasing your ratio of interactions with the student, and describe how and when you will use them.

The goal is to provide a ratio of at least three positive interactions when the student is behaving appropriately to one negative interaction when the student is engaged in inappropriate behavior. Here are some ways to increase the rate:

- Schedule individual conference times.
- Scan the room to identify reinforceable behaviors.
- Give the student plenty of noncontingent attention when she enters the room, when you see her in the hallway, and so on.
- Use gestures (e.g., thumbs up, head nod, "okay" sign) to acknowledge appropriate behavior.
- Post visual reminders to praise students on your plan book, wall, desk, or overhead.
- Give students more opportunities to respond.
- Publicly post examples of positive work by students.
- After praising one student, find and praise another student who is displaying the same behavior.
- Provide precorrection (quick reminders of how to behave appropriately when you anticipate students might have problems behaving appropriately).
- Emphasize attending to positive behaviors after responding to misbehavior.

Task 3: Analyze the Misbehavior and Develop a Function-Based Intervention

The good news is that you have ruled out certain interventions: you tried them and they did not work, so you know you have a fairly complex problem. The bad news is that a complex problem is not likely to be solved by a simple solution. This task introduces some basic concepts about these more complex chronic misbehaviors, explains why you need data and how to use them to make decisions, and describes how you might build an intervention plan for major categories of chronic misbehavior.

Because most chronic misbehavior serves a function, or purpose, for the student (the behavior is happening for a reason) and because there are many different reasons that students misbehave, correction efforts for specific misbehaviors are more effective when they address the underlying reasons for those behaviors (Crone & Horner, 2003; Lewis & Sugai, 1996a, 1996b; Martella et al., 2003; O'Neill et al., 1997). In addition, we can often reliably identify specific activities or contexts that increase the likelihood that one or more students may misbehave. Some of these contexts may be internal to the student (being hungry, sleepy, or sick) or external (working on independent seatwork tasks, participating in large group instruction). Following is a list of common reasons that students misbehave, including situations that may be resistant to simpler interventions:

> **Note**
>
> If you have never done a function-based analysis of a chronic misbehavior, you may wish to consider working through the remainder of this chapter with a school psychologist or behavior specialist who assists teachers in constructing implementation plans for students with chronic misbehavior.

Students are not aware of their behavior They do not know precisely what the teacher expects (Brophy & Good, 1986; Emmer, Evertson, & Anderson, 1980). For example, the teacher views a student as disruptive because she gets up to sharpen her pencil while the teacher is speaking, but the student's previous teachers did not mind if students did this.

They are unaware of when or how much they exhibit an inappropriate behavior. A student doesn't realize that he complains every time the teacher asks him to do something, for example.

Students are unable to, or do not know how to, exhibit the desired behavior They may not be physically able to perform a task or don't have the knowledge to exhibit the appropriate behavior (Carr & Durand, 1985; Gresham, 1998). For example, a student's parents consistently model screaming, yelling, and swearing when they are upset. The student has had no models for solving conflict reasonably and has never learned any strategies for dealing with anger or frustration.

Students are seeking attention They are starved for attention and find it easier or more effective to get attention through reprimands than through praise (Gunter & Jack, 1993; Sutherland, Wehby, & Copeland, 2000). An example is a student who frequently gets out of her seat and wanders around, so the teacher is continuously giving corrections such as, "Allison, how many times do I have to tell you to get back to your seat?"

The behavior serves some other purpose for the student Some students generally feel powerless and have discovered they get a sense of power by making adults frustrated and angry (Cole & Kupersmidt, 1983; Walker, Ramsey, & Gresham, 2004). A student who talks back and argues with adults, for example, finds that some peers look up to him as bad or tough.

Other students want the teacher to send them out of class in order to avoid the task or looking stupid at attempting a task (Carr, Newsom, & Binkoff, 1980; Chandler & Dahlquist, 2002). A student who is disrespectful to the teacher gets sent out of class and suspended for a week, and so escapes school work.

Correcting chronic misbehavior requires more time and effort than correcting most other classroom misbehavior. In fact, with chronic misbehavior you should be prepared to analyze the nature—the reason and purpose—for the behavior and develop and implement a comprehensive intervention plan that is directly linked to your assessment (Crone & Horner, 2002; O'Neill et al., 1997). These following six steps represent the overall approach recommended for addressing any misbehavior that you identify as chronic.

Step 1: Identify the target (problem) behavior and collect objective data. Use those data as you proceed to step 2.

Step 2: Develop a hypothesis (educated guess) about the function of the misbehavior.

Step 3: Identify any specific contexts and conditions (time, locations, tasks) when the target behavior typically occurs or does not occur.

Step 4: Identify a preliminary behavior change (intervention) plan based on your hypothesis about the function of the misbehavior and your understanding of when (under what conditions) the behavior typically occurs.

Step 5: Discuss your preliminary intervention plan with the student and, if appropriate, the student's family.

Step 6: Implement the intervention plan for at least two weeks. Continue to collect data on the target behavior to evaluate the plan's effectiveness.

The form in exhibit 9.5 will guide you through designing a function-based intervention plan. (Consider printing this form from the DVD and using it to take notes as you read the following directions and suggestions for each step of the planning process.)

Exhibit 9.5
Function-Based Intervention Plan

Student _Courtney Driver_   Teacher _Ms. Fang_   Date _10/19_

Step 1
The target behavior is: complaining

I collect data on this behavior by: frequency count. I will mark a tracking sheet each time Courtney complains about an assignment or direction.

Step 2
My hypothesis about the function of this target behavior is:

- ❏ Lack of awareness
- ❏ Lack of ability or skill
- ☑ Attention seeking
- ❏ Habitual/purposeful

Step 3
Identify any specific contexts or conditions (times, locations, tasks) when the target behavior typically occurs (or does not occur).

Courtney usually complains when I assign independent work and homework. She will complain during independent work about how hard it is or how there's too much to finish in the time allotted. She doesn't complain when I am presenting or when working in small groups.

Step 4
Develop a preliminary behavior change (intervention) plan based on your hypothesis about the function of the misbehavior.

I will announce to the class that I am going to ignore all complaints about their assignments. I will answer any questions about the work. Then I will ignore Courtney's (and any other students') complaints and praise her when she works without complaining.

Step 5
Discuss your preliminary intervention plan with the student and, if appropriate, the student's family.

I will talk with Courtney after class on Friday.

Step 6
Implement the intervention plan for at least two weeks. Continue to collect data on the target behavior so that you can evaluate the plan's effectiveness.

Intervention Planning Steps

Step 1: Identify the target (problem) behavior and collect objective data; Use those data as you proceed to step 2

It's important to collect information about a behavior that concerns you before you develop an intervention plan (Alberto & Troutman, 2006). Understanding the cause will help you understand the best way to deal with it. Identify a specific behavior or category of behavior that is the target of your concerns and will be the target of your intervention plan. The student may have multiple problems, but pick one behavior (disrespectful comments) or one category of behavior (classroom disruptions such as callouts, noise making, use of obscenity, bothering other students by not keeping hands to self).

If the target problem is unclear—you are not sure exactly why the behavior bothers you or how to collect data on it—keep anecdotal notes for a few days. Anecdotal notes are brief descriptions of specific situations that trouble you. With notes from several incidents over a few days, you can usually clarify the nature of the problem behavior. Then you can collect more objective data on its frequency or duration.

If you have identified the target behavior or category of behavior, plan to immediately start collecting data on the frequency, duration, and intensity of the behavior. The objective data you collect will help you define the problem more precisely and give you a baseline from which you will be able to make judgments about the effectiveness of any intervention plan you implement.

Then instead of relying on your instincts, you will have objective data available to help you make decisions about what to do next (Hintze, Volpe, & Shapiro, 2002; Sugai & Tindal, 1993). Data can be systematic, clear, and concise—but it can also be unsystematic, unclear, and of little use. To make sure you collect relevant, useful data, use the following common methods of data collection. This information about frequency data, duration data, latency data, and rating magnitude or quality is adapted from Beck (1997).

Frequency data   Frequency data record the number of occurrences of a given behavior within a specific time period. For example, use of obscenity can be recorded as the number of times profanity is used during a class period. Frequency data can be recorded using any one of the following techniques:

- *Tally sheet kept on a clipboard or an index card.* Make a mark each time the target behavior occurs. If you are tracking several different behaviors, you can easily divide the card into sections. For example, you could have a card with the name Joshua and two headings below the name—one for disruptive noises and one for negative comments.

- *Wrist or golf counter.* Each time the target behavior occurs, advance the counter. You can easily keep the counter in a pocket if you want to be unobtrusive.

- *Paper clips in a pocket.* Keep a supply of small objects (beads, beans, paper clips, buttons) in one pocket. Each time the target behavior occurs, move one of the objects to another pocket or a container. The number of objects collected at the end of the time period is the number to record. This technique lets you track only one behavior at a time, but is very effective and simple to use.

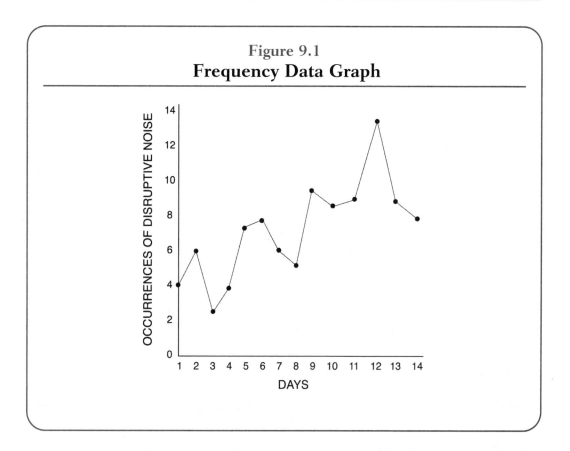

Figure 9.1
Frequency Data Graph

- *Pages in a book.* Keep a book on your desk open to page 1. Each time the target behavior occurs, turn a page. Note that you can count the pages turned or look at the page number at the end of the day and divide by two.

Frequency data can be displayed on a simple graph like the one shown in figure 9.1.

Duration data Duration data express the total amount of time a student engages in a given behavior. For example, off-task behavior can be expressed as the number of minutes a student is off task during a fifty-minute class period.

This information can be useful when a student engages in a behavior for extended periods of time. A student may technically be off task only one time during the class, but it may be for the entire length of the class. In such a case, tracking the total number of incidents would not be useful. Use a stopwatch to record the duration. Start the watch when the target behavior begins and stop it when the target behavior stops. Start it again if necessary. The total minutes on the watch when class is over tell you how much time the student spent misbehaving. The time can then be recorded on a graph like the one shown in figure 9.2.

Latency data Latency data express how much time passes between a directive and the student's response. Latency data is almost always used in the context of tracking compliance and following directions. To track this information for a student who is frequently noncompliant, you need a stopwatch. Each time you give a direction, start the timer. Stop it when your instructions are carried out. If you do this during the entire class,

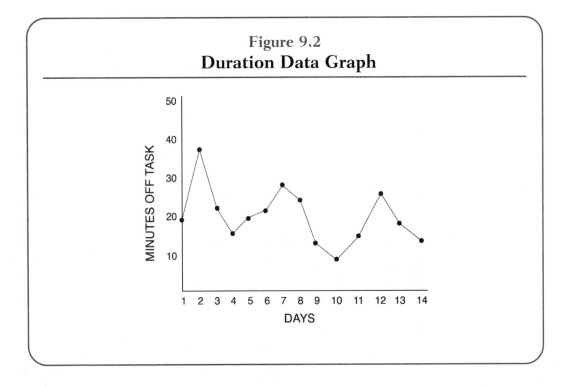

Figure 9.2
Duration Data Graph

you will have a latency total by the end of the class. Figure 9.3 shows an example of a latency graph.

Magnitude or quality   Rating magnitude or quality is a way to record data by rating a student's behavior during a specified time period using a scale—for example, from 1 to 5. At the end of each class period, you and the target student rate the degree of cooperation and respect the student demonstrated toward you. A rating of 1 means that the student was disrespectful and uncooperative the entire time, while a rating of 5 indicates that the student was respectful and cooperative during the entire class period.

Although this method is subjective, discussing and determining the rating standards with your student before you implement it can make this method an accurate and helpful way to record data. Because each rating is a numerical value, the information can be graphed easily for quick reference. You can also track information on more than one student at a time. See figure 9.4 for an example.

Data collection process.

Meet with the student or students you plan to track before you begin collecting data. Inform them of your plan and emphasize that you are collecting this information to determine if there is a problem. Then meet with the student for a few minutes each week to discuss the data on your graph.

The act of collecting data in a systematic way sometimes serves to improve a problem situation (Scheuermann & Hall, 2008; Sprick, Booher, & Garrison, 2009). Perhaps this is because the student becomes aware of how serious you are about the problem or because the student receives increased attention from you. It may be that by collecting data, you are communicating that you value the student enough to have expectations that the situation will improve. It may simply be the placebo effect—a sugar pill sometimes helps a person's health improve just because he thinks he is receiving helpful treatment. Regardless of the

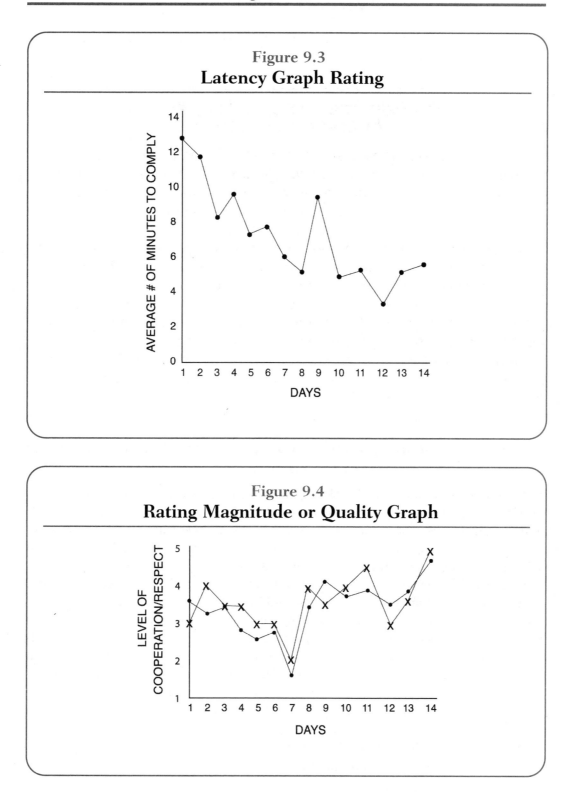

Figure 9.3
Latency Graph Rating

Figure 9.4
Rating Magnitude or Quality Graph

reason, the phenomenon is frequent enough that regular data collection and debriefing with the student is a reasonable strategy when a simple intervention, like those described in tasks 2 and 3, was not sufficient.

In addition, the data help you decide whether the situation is improving, staying the same, or getting worse. Without data, you will have subjective perceptions about progress or lack of progress. A busy teacher focusing on many different students may form inaccurate subjective perceptions.

For Example: Using Data to Assess Intervention Success

Let's say that you have collected data on the frequency of a student's sarcastic and disrespectful comments toward you. The data show that the frequency has decreased from an average of ten comments per week to six per week over a period of three weeks. The six comments per week may be so aggravating that you think the situation is not improving. However, the data indicate a 40 percent reduction—from ten per week to six—in the frequency of the problem, so you know you actually implemented a very successful intervention and should continue it without modification.

Conversely, let's say that over four weeks, you find that the comments continue to average about ten per week. With data in hand, you know with confidence that the current intervention plan is not sufficient and a more carefully planned intervention is warranted—and that it is probably time to ask for assistance from a school psychologist or behavior specialist.

Step 2: Develop a hypothesis (educated guess) about the function of the misbehavior

With the target behavior in mind, look at the data you have collected and reflect on why the problem might be occurring. Knowing the function (reason and purpose) of a misbehavior is important because correction procedures that are effective with behaviors that serve one particular purpose for the student may not be effective with other behaviors that serve a different purpose (Iwata, Dorsey, Slifer, Bauman, & Richman, 1994). For example, if a student is misbehaving because she wants attention, giving that student corrective consequences each time she misbehaves is not likely to work because she is getting what she wants—attention. Using planned ignoring will be far more effective in this case. On the other hand, if a student continually gets out of her seat because she does not realize that it is inappropriate or because she does not know how to stay in her seat, ignoring her out-of-seat behavior is not likely to change that behavior. This student needs information—she needs to be taught what the appropriate behavior is and how she can exhibit it.

As stated previously, the four subcategories of chronic misbehavior are:

- Misbehaviors due to lack of awareness
- Misbehaviors due to lack of ability or skill
- Attention-seeking misbehavior
- Purposeful/habitual misbehavior

Think about the function of your student's target behavior—it probably falls into one of these subcategories. To help you decide, read the following descriptions of the four subcategories. Specific suggestions for how to effectively intervene with misbehavior in each of these subcategories are presented in step 4.

Misbehaviors due to lack of awareness.

Sometimes a student who seems to be willfully misbehaving is actually unaware of the behavior he is exhibiting. An example of a misbehavior caused by a lack of awareness is a tenth grader who always responds argumentatively to corrective feedback—at school for behavioral and academic performance and, according to his family, at home as well. The teacher tries the early-stage correction strategy of discussing the problem with the student but sees no improvement in his behavior. Because this student responds negatively every time he is given corrective feedback and because initial efforts to correct the behavior with information have been ineffective, it is reasonable to assume that the student may not be aware of how negatively he reacts when he is given corrective feedback.

When a student engages in ongoing misbehavior because of a lack of awareness, the intervention plan needs to include the following:

- Make expectations clear.

- Help the student become aware of his or her behavior.

- If necessary, provide incentives to encourage the student to change his or her behavior.

Plan A in task 4 has information on developing an intervention plan for this type of misbehavior.

Misbehaviors due to lack of ability or skill.

Sometimes a student misbehaves because he or she is unable to or does not know how to exhibit the desired behavior (Carr & Durand, 1985; Gresham, 1998; McGinnis & Goldstein, 1994; Ostrosky, Drasgow, & Halle, 1999).

When students misbehave due to issues of ability, you must first ascertain whether the student is physiologically capable of exhibiting the desired behavior by reviewing the student's records. If he or she is capable, the intervention plan needs to include teaching the student the necessary skills and knowledge. If the student is not physiologically capable of exhibiting the behavior, modifications need to be made to the student's environment or adjustments made to the expectations (or both).

Plan B in task 4 addresses how to intervene effectively with these types of misbehaviors.

Attention-seeking misbehavior.

Attention-seeking misbehaviors are behaviors that a student engages in to satisfy his or her (often unconscious) need for attention. Chronic blurting out, excessive helplessness, bragging, and minor disruptions are examples of behaviors that may be attention seeking in nature. When a student is seeking attention through misbehavior, any intervention effort that involves giving the student attention when he is misbehaving is likely to actually reinforce the inappropriate behavior (Gunter & Jack, 1993; Sutherland, Wehby, & Copeland, 2000).

Planned ignoring is designed to reduce or eliminate the attention the student receives for engaging in misbehavior (while at the same time giving the student frequent attention when he is not engaged in misbehavior) and should be part of any intervention plan for this category of misbehavior. Planned ignoring has been shown to increase appropriate behaviors when used in conjunction with other strategies such as reteaching rules and praising appropriate behavior (Hall, Lund, & Jackson, 1968; Madsen, Becker, & Thomas, 1968; Yawkey, 1971).

Information on developing an intervention plan for attention-seeking misbehaviors is presented in plan C in task 4.

Purposeful/habitual misbehavior.

When chronic misbehavior does not stem from a student's lack of awareness or ability and is not being exhibited because the student wants attention, you need to assume that it is serving some other purpose for the student. Some students misbehave to escape something aversive—for example, they would rather get sent to the office for misbehaving than take a test they believe they will fail. Other students use misbehavior to demonstrate and achieve a sense of power and control—talking back and arguing with adults to look tough in front of friends.

Still other students may engage in misbehaviors that provide competing reinforcement, such as reading during instructional lessons, because they find it more enjoyable than participating in the lesson. For some students, misbehavior has become so habitual that the original purpose of the misbehavior is unclear or no longer relevant. For example, a student who has successfully engaged in attention-seeking behaviors for years may initially continue to misbehave even when planned ignoring is implemented because the inappropriate behaviors are firmly established in her behavioral repertoire.

With truly purposeful or habitual misbehavior, you will probably need to include corrective consequences for the misbehavior as part of your intervention plan.

Plan D in task 4 provides information on developing an effective intervention for this type of misbehavior, including guidelines for using corrective consequences and a menu of specific consequences that you can use.

Step 3: Identify Any Specific Contexts or Conditions (Time, Locations, Tasks) When the Target Behavior Typically Occurs (or Does Not Occur)

In what context or under what conditions does the target behavior occur? Are there times when it does not occur? Understanding what typically happens before and after the target behavior occurs may give you a better idea about the purpose of the misbehavior for the student. In addition, this information is useful for building your intervention plan. If the student typically has difficulty during independent work times, for example, your support plan probably won't need to include large group instruction.

Step 4: Develop a Preliminary Behavior Change (Intervention) Plan Based on Your Hypothesis about the Function of the Misbehavior and Your Understanding of When (Under What Conditions) the Behavior Typically Occurs

Once you develop a hypothesis about why the target behavior may be occurring, review the decision-making chart shown in figure 9.5. Think about the target misbehavior as you examine the chart. Information about each category of misbehavior and suggested interventions is presented in the following pages. Figure 9.5 is designed to guide you to the appropriate procedures that will fit the nature of the target problem.

Use the suggestions in the following pages or modify them as necessary to develop a preliminary plan for improving the target behavior. Although the specific procedures for intervening within each subcategory of chronic misbehavior (awareness, ability, attention seeking, and purposeful/habitual) are different from each other, there are several critical

Figure 9.5
Analysis of Chronic Misbehavior and Suggested Interventions

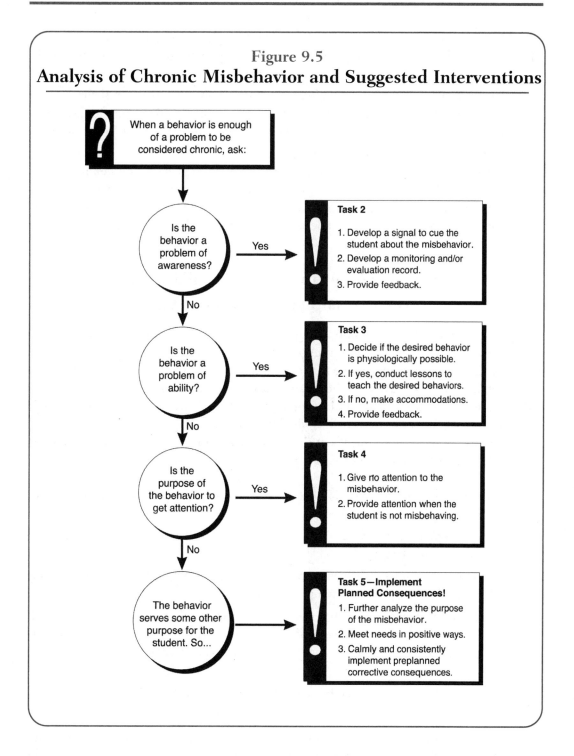

When a behavior is enough of a problem to be considered chronic, ask:

Is the behavior a problem of awareness?

Yes →

Task 2
1. Develop a signal to cue the student about the misbehavior.
2. Develop a monitoring and/or evaluation record.
3. Provide feedback.

No ↓

Is the behavior a problem of ability?

Yes →

Task 3
1. Decide if the desired behavior is physiologically possible.
2. If yes, conduct lessons to teach the desired behaviors.
3. If no, make accommodations.
4. Provide feedback.

No ↓

Is the purpose of the behavior to get attention?

Yes →

Task 4
1. Give no attention to the misbehavior.
2. Provide attention when the student is not misbehaving.

No ↓

The behavior serves some other purpose for the student. So...

→

Task 5—Implement Planned Consequences!
1. Further analyze the purpose of the misbehavior.
2. Meet needs in positive ways.
3. Calmly and consistently implement preplanned corrective consequences.

features to include in any plan (Crone & Horner, 2002; O'Neill et al., 1997; Scheuermann & Hall, 2008; Sugai, Horner et al., 2000):

1. Think about strategies you can put into place to prevent the problem behavior from occurring in the first place.

2. Plan for possible skill-building or teaching strategies. Even if there is no skill deficit, it is likely that you will have to teach some components of the support plan to the student.

3. Include procedures for encouraging the positive opposite of the misbehavior. For example, if the target misbehavior is disrespect, the intervention plan should identify how you will encourage and increase demonstrations of respectful behavior by the student.

4. Plan needs to specify exactly how you will respond to instances of the misbehavior in ways that allow you to be calm, consistent, and brief. Once you develop a preliminary plan using the information about each of these subcategories presented in this chapter, you can continue with the remaining planning steps.

Plan A: Develop an Intervention for Awareness-Type Misbehaviors

When a student misbehaves because she isn't aware of when or how often she is engaging in an irresponsible behavior, your intervention plan should focus on increasing her awareness of her behavior. It is not appropriate to use traditional corrective consequences in the form of punishment in this situation. When a student lacks awareness of her misbehavior, you first need to make sure that the student understands how she is supposed to behave; only then can you help her learn to recognize when she is misbehaving.

If you determine that a student's misbehavior stems from a lack of awareness, develop and implement this four-step intervention plan:

1. Make sure the student knows what behavior you expect her to exhibit (the target or goal behavior).

2. Respond to instances of the misbehavior in a manner that lets the student know she is not meeting the goal.

3. Monitor the student's behavior so that you, the student, and the student's family have an objective basis for discussing progress.

4. Provide positive feedback when the student is successful or makes improvements. If positive feedback doesn't seem sufficient to motivate the student to stop exhibiting the behavior, consider using some kind of incentive (reward).

Step 1: Make Sure the Student Knows What Behavior You Expect Her to Exhibit (the Target or Goal Behavior)

When you meet with your student to discuss the situation, be sure to explain the behavior you want her to demonstrate. It may be helpful to demonstrate examples and nonexamples of both the expected and the problem behaviors to make sure the student clearly understands the difference and is able to discriminate between them (Kame'enui & Simmons, 1990). (See chapter 5 for more details on teaching expected behaviors.) Emphasize the benefit to the student of demonstrating this new behavior. Be prepared to identify actions you will take to help her learn this new behavior. Consider writing the behavioral goal into an informal contract, following the suggested goal contract form shown in exhibit 9.6 (see the DVD for a blank reproducible of this form).

Exhibit 9.6
Goal Contract

Student Annika

Class English

Description of problem
Homework turned in late or not at all

Goal
Turn in all homework assignments when due

Student responsibilities for achieving the goal
Before leaving class, Annika will make sure assignments are in her homework folder. She will bring folder home each night and work on the assignment between 7—8 pm. If she forgets the folder, she will check the class website for the assignment, or contact Trevyn or Gail for the information. Annika will put completed assignments in the basket. If she forgets, she will bring the assignment to Mr. Romero before the next class.

Teacher support responsibilities
Mr. Romero will periodically ask Annika if she has her folder as she is leaving class. He will also periodically remind her to turn in her assignments. Mr. Romero will make sure all assignments are posted on the class website.

Evaluation procedure
Each Friday, Mr. Romero will let Annika know how many assignments she completed and didn't complete that week. He will base the numbers on his grade book.

Date of goal evaluation 11/2

Student's signature _____

Teacher's signature _____

Time-prediction self-monitoring.

An example of a way to help students become aware of your expectations is a time-prediction self-monitoring strategy. This simple strategy can be effective with students who have a difficult time completing assignments or staying on task. It is also appropriate for students who lose focus when given open-ended time for individual work. Essentially you give the student an opportunity to predict how long it will take him to complete an assignment. When the student has a personal target in mind, the framework becomes based on the student's intrinsic motivation rather than an extrinsic factor.

Write the following at the top of the student's paper:

> Time Started: Time Predicted: Time Completed:

Say to the student, "It is now [8:15]."

Ask, "What time do you think you will complete the assignment?" If possible, have the student write his or her response.

Say, "When you are finished with your task, please come up and show me so we can see if you reached your goal!"

You may have the student write down the time of completion to reinforce his ownership of the goal.

If the student simply rushes through assignments to reach the goal, have him predict his percentage of correct answers as a second goal.

If the assignment is to be completed in a specific amount of time, the following variation is useful. Write on the board:

> Time Available: Predicted Number of Completed Questions:
> Completed questions:

Say to the student, "You have ten minutes to complete this assignment."

Ask, "How many questions do you think you can complete in ten minutes?" Have the student write his prediction.

Say, "When you're done with your work, please let me know."

The time-prediction self-monitoring strategy allows students to set small personal goals and monitor their own progress. It reinforces the importance of staying on task. Students may even enjoy the "beat the clock" aspect or the notion of competing against themselves to see their work potential. (Submitted by and used with permission from school counselor Anthony Pearson, EdS, author of *Guidance with Good Measure* from YouthLight Books.)

Step 2: Respond to Instances of the Misbehavior in a Manner That Lets the Student Know That She Is Not Meeting the Goal

Do not forget that students should not be punished for behavioral mistakes that are related to a lack of awareness or ability. Instead, each time an error occurs, give the student information about the inappropriate behavior and what she should be doing instead. Following are descriptions of several information-based correction strategies. Choose one or more that you can use to provide the student with information that will help her be more successful in the future. Remember, just like a student learning to correct errors in math, a student who is learning a new behavior may make frequent errors and need to be corrected each time.

Gentle verbal reprimands. Effective reprimands are brief, proximate (close), respectful, clear, and reasonably private. Provide a verbal description of what the student is expected to be doing (Abramowitz, O'Leary, & Futtersak, 1988; Acker & O'Leary, 1988; McAllister et al., 1969; O'Leary & Becker, 1967; Winett & Vachon, 1974). When students make errors in math, one of the most effective correction procedures is to tell them what they should have done: "You need to remember to convert before moving on to the next step." Use a similar businesslike tone when giving a correction. (Reprimands were discussed in detail in chapter 4.)

Redirection. Redirection involves turning a student's attention back to what she should be doing instead of misbehaving. Instead of verbally reminding the student, you will literally direct the student to the desired activity. For example, if a student is looking at someone else's paper, guide the student's focus back to his own work by pointing at his paper while complimenting other students for keeping their eyes on their own work. This can and should be done without giving the student much attention.

Signal. If a student seems truly unaware of when she is misbehaving, it can be helpful to use a verbal or nonverbal cue to signal the student. For example, if you have a student who hums while doing seatwork, the signal might be to say her name to get her attention and give your head a small shake. As long as you have discussed this with the student in advance, she will know the meaning of this signal and should stop humming every time she receives this signal. It may be effective to consult with the student beforehand to determine the most appropriate or effective signal.

Precorrection. When you can determine, based on prior history, that a student is likely to exhibit misbehavior in a particular situation, consider using a precorrection to help the student be successful. Before the student has a chance to exhibit the misbehavior in the typically problematic situation, give her information that increases the likelihood she will exhibit responsible behavior (De Pry & Sugai, 2002; Lampi, Fenty, & Beaunae, 2005; Walker, Ramsey, & Gresham, 2004). This will preempt the misbehavior and thus help break habitual misbehavior. If a student has trouble accepting corrective feedback, you could use something like the following precorrection just before you return papers: "Sheila, I have some graded papers here for you. You solved most of the problems correctly, but you did make a couple of errors. Give some thought to the neutral or positive ways of reacting that we discussed. I'm sure you will be able to manage your reaction in a responsible way."

Step 3: Monitor the Student's Behavior So That You and the Student Will Have an Objective Basis for Discussing Progress

When a student is unaware that he is engaging in a misbehavior, an important part of increasing this awareness is objectively discussing his progress or lack of progress. He may not be able to identify when and if gains have been made; therefore, keep a continuous record of the number of incidents that occur each day. Records of positive and negative behavior are an excellent way to demonstrate his progress.

You can chart each day's positive and negative behavior totals and arrange to review the chart periodically with the student. In some cases, it can be beneficial to give the student a recording sheet and have him record the incidents himself (Alberto & Troutman, 2003). However, if the student is unlikely to keep an accurate record or would be embarrassed to record his behavior in front of peers, you should do the recording. Arrange to meet with the student periodically (even every day if the issue occurs frequently) to chart the incidents and discuss progress.

For more ideas on this type of recording and for a sample recording sheet, see chapter 2, task 3. Sometimes it can be useful to track a positive and negative behavior concurrently. Exhibit 9.7 is a monitoring sheet you can use to record both appropriate and inappropriate reactions to a situation—for example, corrective feedback. (See the DVD for a blank reproducible of this form.)

Exhibit 9.7
Monitoring Appropriate and Inappropriate Behavior Form

Name Devyn Kirkland   Class Period Third   Week of: 3/15

Behaviors to be Counted:

(Appropriate) Raising hand and waiting to be called on

(Inappropriate) Shouting out answer

Monday
Appropriate Behavior
| ① | ② | ③ | ④ | ⑤ | 6 | 7 | 8 | 9 | 10 |
| 11 | 12 | 13 | 14 | 15 | 16 | 17 | 18 | 19 | 20 |

Inappropriate Behavior
| ① | ② | ③ | 4 | 5 | 6 | 7 | 8 | 9 | 10 |
| 11 | 12 | 13 | 14 | 15 | 16 | 17 | 18 | 19 | 20 |

Tuesday
Appropriate Behavior
| ① | ② | ③ | ④ | ⑤ | ⑥ | ⑦ | 8 | 9 | 10 |
| 11 | 12 | 13 | 14 | 15 | 16 | 17 | 18 | 19 | 20 |

Inappropriate Behavior
| ① | ② | 3 | 4 | 5 | 6 | 7 | 8 | 9 | 10 |
| 11 | 12 | 13 | 14 | 15 | 16 | 17 | 18 | 19 | 20 |

Wednesday
Appropriate Behavior
| 1 | 2 | 3 | 4 | 5 | 6 | 7 | 8 | 9 | 10 |
| 11 | 12 | 13 | 14 | 15 | 16 | 17 | 18 | 19 | 20 |

Inappropriate Behavior
| 1 | 2 | 3 | 4 | 5 | 6 | 7 | 8 | 9 | 10 |
| 11 | 12 | 13 | 14 | 15 | 16 | 17 | 18 | 19 | 20 |

Thursday
Appropriate Behavior
| 1 | 2 | 3 | 4 | 5 | 6 | 7 | 8 | 9 | 10 |
| 11 | 12 | 13 | 14 | 15 | 16 | 17 | 18 | 19 | 20 |

Inappropriate Behavior
| 1 | 2 | 3 | 4 | 5 | 6 | 7 | 8 | 9 | 10 |
| 11 | 12 | 13 | 14 | 15 | 16 | 17 | 18 | 19 | 20 |

Friday
Appropriate Behavior
| 1 | 2 | 3 | 4 | 5 | 6 | 7 | 8 | 9 | 10 |
| 11 | 12 | 13 | 14 | 15 | 16 | 17 | 18 | 19 | 20 |

Inappropriate Behavior
| 1 | 2 | 3 | 4 | 5 | 6 | 7 | 8 | 9 | 10 |
| 11 | 12 | 13 | 14 | 15 | 16 | 17 | 18 | 19 | 20 |

When a student's behavior problems involve more qualitative than quantitative issues (how well rather than how much), it can be useful to have the student use a self-evaluation monitoring form. The student rates the quality of a given behavior at particular times during the period or just at the end of the period. Exhibit 9.8 is a self-evaluation sheet appropriate for a student to rate behaviors like "responding appropriately to feedback," "using respectful language," and "following directions within a reasonable amount of time." (See the DVD for a blank reproducible of this form.)

If you decide to incorporate student self-evaluation into your intervention plan, set the system up so that the student has a good chance of earning a high rating most of the time. For example, if a student in a two-hour blocked period rating himself on how well he uses in-class work times gets to evaluate himself only once for the entire period, he may have to give himself a poor rating. However, if it is set up so that he evaluates his behavior for each twenty-minute work period throughout the block, he is likely to experience more success overall. Although there may be some time periods when he has to rate himself low, there should also be several work times during the period when he can give himself a high rating. These smaller blocks of time will also allow him to keep his focus on "making it through" each twenty-minute chunk of time, which may increase his likelihood of success.

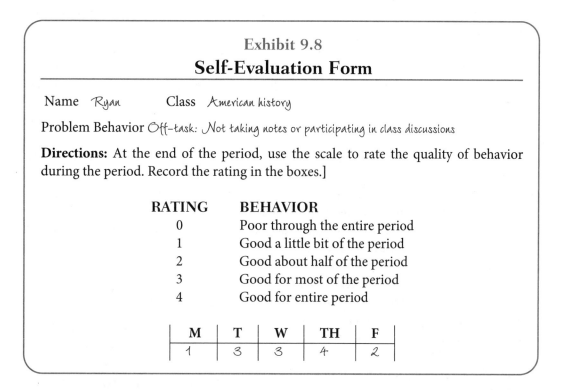

Exhibit 9.8
Self-Evaluation Form

Name *Ryan*   Class *American history*

Problem Behavior *Off-task: Not taking notes or participating in class discussions*

Directions: At the end of the period, use the scale to rate the quality of behavior during the period. Record the rating in the boxes.]

RATING	BEHAVIOR
0	Poor through the entire period
1	Good a little bit of the period
2	Good about half of the period
3	Good for most of the period
4	Good for entire period

M	T	W	TH	F
1	3	3	4	2

Step 4: Provide Positive Feedback When the Student Improves

Throughout the class period, as the student demonstrates success or takes steps toward success, provide positive verbal feedback (Hall et al., 1968; Madsen et al., 1968; O'Leary & Becker, 1967; Stormont, Smith, & Lewis, 2007). This reinforces the student's understanding of when she is exhibiting the appropriate behavior. Without positive feedback, the student may get discouraged by the corrective feedback you provide when she makes an error (Sponder, 1993).

If you do not see a decrease in the misbehavior within a couple of weeks, consider establishing a simple system of reward-type incentives. A student who is learning to reduce the frequency of disruptive fidgeting (e.g., pencil tapping or drumming on desk) could earn a point for each day of the week when the number of times you needed to signal a reminder to stop the noise was below an agreed-on level. When the student accumulates eight points, he could earn a "get out of one homework assignment" ticket to be used for a short nightly task of his choosing (not a term paper!).

Plan B: Develop an Intervention for Ability-Type Misbehaviors

For ongoing misbehaviors that stem from a student's lack of ability or skill, be prepared to develop and implement an intervention plan that includes modifying the expectations or environment for physiological inability or providing instruction in the goal behavior for lack of skill.

Sometimes a student misbehaves because he is physiologically unable to exhibit the appropriate behavior or does not know how to do so. The most effective intervention plans in these situations address the underlying cause of the situation. If a student is physically or neurologically unable to exhibit the desired behavior, your intervention must involve making modifications to the student's environment, adjusting your expectations, or both. If the student is capable of the behavior but does not know how to exhibit it, your intervention must teach the student how to exhibit the desired behavior. This is frequently called *teaching a replacement behavior*. If the student is physiologically unable to exhibit the desired behavior or does not know how, implementing corrective consequences is inappropriate at best and inhumane at worst. Consequences will not help the student learn the new behavior and will only make the student feel at fault for something he has no control over.

Let's say that a student in your class has Tourette syndrome. When reviewing this student's records, you see the notation that teachers are supposed to ignore "outbursts such as barking, snorting, or swearing" from this student in class. Your first thought might be that such a recommendation is ridiculous. However, the only way a student with Tourette syndrome can control these kinds of behaviors or tics is through medication, and this works only for some. In such a situation you will have to adjust your expectation that these kinds of interruptions will not occur in your class. You may have to work with other students in your class to adjust their expectations as well. If you are unsure whether a desired behavior is within a student's physiological capability, you will need to check with your special education staff, school psychologist, or the student's physician.

Students who are incapable of doing assigned work because of skill deficits often behave in a manner that makes the teacher think the student is misbehaving simply because he does not want to do his work. In reality, he cannot do the work no matter how hard he tries. In this case, the intervention plan would involve academic remediation

> ## Note
> Unlike individuals with Tourette syndrome, children who have been identified as having attention-deficit disorder—with or without hyperactivity—can learn to control their behavior. Although a student with this diagnosis may have some ability-type problems, those problems can be treated using some of the strategies outlined here.

and possibly adaptation of work in the interim. It would also need to include some behavioral intervention to get the student to demonstrate appropriate behaviors while working on addressing the skill deficit that led to those behaviors.

This task presents a four-step process for helping students who exhibit misbehavior that is related to a lack of ability but who can demonstrate the desired behavior.

Step 1: At a Neutral Time, Have a Discussion and Provide Information That Teaches the Replacement Behavior

At least three days a week, conduct private lessons with the student. Use these lessons to describe the desired behavior and have the student practice it. Keep in mind that when a student lacks the ability to demonstrate a particular behavior, just talking about it may not be enough for the student to grasp it (Marzano, 2003). Coaches know this. The basketball coach who would have her team excel in free-throw shooting not only provides step-by-step instructions and demonstration, but has the players practice the skill by taking free throws—lots of them. She provides repetition and daily practice across a period of weeks.

If it does not seem possible to provide the instruction yourself, talk to your administrator. Ask if an instructional aide could cover your class for ten minutes a day a few days a week while the intervention is starting. Perhaps a school counselor could conduct the lessons with the student. In fact, if several students in your school have similar ability-type problems, the counselor might be able to run a small-group session.

Step 2: Correct Errors in a Manner That Provides Instruction

Punishing students for exhibiting inappropriate behavior when they have not yet learned to exhibit the behavior is potentially cruel. On top of that, it's not likely to work. It is far more likely that the misbehavior will improve if you respond with a corrective strategy such as proximity, gentle reprimands, a signal, or redirection (all of which were described in chapter 4, task 3). For example, if you have a student labeled with attention-deficit disorder who tends to drum on his desk, you might arrange to give him a signal each time he starts to drum. Teach him that when he sees you give the signal, he needs to stop drumming. This would be far more effective and appropriate than imposing a consequence.

Step 3: Make Accommodations to Increase the Student's Chance of Success

Determine whether you can make modifications in terms of daily schedule, class structure, behavioral expectations, your classroom's physical arrangement, or your classroom interactions that would make it easier for the student to be successful (Alberto & Troutman, 2003; Babkie, 2006; Barbetta et al., 2005; Scheuermann & Hall, 2008; Trussel, 2008). For example, if the student struggles with appropriate peer interactions during transitions with a lot of movement, consider how you can alter the structure of your transitions. You might minimize movement when turning in papers by asking students to pass papers to the end of the row rather than having all students out of their seats to put papers in the basket. Though this may seem like a major change to accommodate the needs of one student, imagine how altering this procedure would benefit all of your students. By increasing the likelihood that the student with chronic misbehavior is successful, you reduce the likelihood for conflicts in class. Other students may appreciate that they do not get into negative interactions with this student during transitions. They will benefit from increased instructional time because transitions will be more efficient and you will not be spending time responding to student altercations. In addition, the overall tone and climate of the classroom may feel more calm and under control.

Step 4: Provide Positive Feedback When the Student Is Successful or Improves

It is essential that you give frequent positive feedback any time the student demonstrates success or growth with the target behaviors. As the student demonstrates success or takes steps toward success, give her positive verbal feedback. Students who exhibit ability-type misbehaviors need to know when and what they are doing well. Without this positive feedback, these students may feel overwhelmed or discouraged by the corrective feedback they receive when they make errors (Hamre & Pianta, 2001).

If the student fails to make progress within a week or two, consider establishing a simple incentive system. For example, if you have a student who has difficulty sitting still, give her points toward a reward for every specific period of time she is able to sit still.

Plan C: Develop an Intervention for Attention-Seeking Misbehaviors

For ongoing minor to moderate attention-seeking misbehaviors, be prepared to develop and implement an intervention plan that includes maximal attention for appropriate behaviors and planned ignoring of problem behavior.

An attention-seeking misbehavior is a behavior that a student knows is unacceptable but engages in anyway to get teacher or peer attention. When a student is seeking attention through misbehavior, responding with a corrective strategy or consequence will give the student the attention he is looking for and reinforce the misbehavior (Horner et al., 1996). The strategy that is most likely to correct this kind of misbehavior is planned ignoring. However, this strategy is not appropriate for early-stage attention-seeking misbehavior because ignoring the misbehavior in the early stages may lead the target student, and perhaps other students who observe the situation, to assume that the behavior is acceptable because you are not addressing the problem. In the early stages, provide verbal reprimands or other gentle corrective actions to communicate that you are serious about your expectations.

Should you determine that the problem is more chronic, beyond early stages, ignoring is appropriate. By implementing planned ignoring, you reduce or eliminate the attention a student receives for engaging in misbehavior while concurrently giving the student frequent attention when he or she is behaving appropriately. The goal is for the student to learn that using misbehavior to get attention is ineffective and that behaving responsibly results in frequent and satisfying attention. Planned ignoring is not the same as tolerating a student's misbehavior. Tolerating misbehavior implies that one has given up expecting a change and has decided to live with the misbehavior. Planned ignoring is a conscious strategy applied in an effort to change the misbehavior.

Following are suggested steps for implementing planned ignoring as part of an intervention plan designed to help a student learn to get his or her attention needs met without engaging in misbehavior:

1. Determine whether ignoring is an appropriate response.
2. Discuss the proposed plan with the student.

3. When the misbehavior occurs, continue what you are doing and provide positive feedback to other students.

4. When the attention-seeking misbehavior ceases, give the student attention.

5. Maintain frequent interactions with the student when he is not misbehaving.

6. Monitor the student's behavior to determine whether progress is being made.

Step 1: Determine Whether Ignoring Is an Appropriate Response

To determine if ignoring is the best strategy for the problem behavior, ask yourself the following questions.

Is this misbehavior really attention seeking in nature?

If the student's misbehavior is a function of lack of ability or awareness, ignoring will not work and will encourage the behavior to continue. It can also be somewhat cruel. Not paying attention to a misbehavior caused by lack of awareness or ability is as inappropriate as ignoring math mistakes that students make. Without correction, students will assume they are doing things correctly. If a student thinks he is being helpful to you by coming and telling you about the misbehavior of others he has observed (tattling), he needs lessons and feedback about the difference between tattling and social responsibility. But if the student fully understands that a behavior is not acceptable yet uses the misbehavior as a way to seek or demand attention from teacher or peers, planned ignoring is likely to be effective.

Is the actual problem the frequency of the behavior, not the behavior itself?

Sometimes the issue with attention-seeking behavior is not that the behavior itself is inappropriate, but rather that the frequency or duration with which the student engages in the behavior is problematic. Say you have a student who asks lots of questions and is always seeking teacher assistance. Although you do not want to discourage the student from asking questions or seeking assistance when necessary, if he asks for help more often than he really needs to, he has learned that displaying helplessness will get him attention (often called *learned helplessness*).

You cannot ignore a student's questions or requests for assistance. You would not be able to justify such an action to the student, his family, or your principal. However, with a problem of excess, you can specify what a reasonable amount of the behavior would be. As with other examples in this chapter, your role is part detective as you collect and use data. You should first determine how much this student asks for help compared with other students of similar intellectual ability. For a couple of days, keep a record of how many times the student asks for help and how many times one or two similar students ask for help. At the end of the second day, you might have a record that looks something like this:

Mark [attention-seeking student]: Monday, 12 times; Tuesday, 11 times

Olivia [student of similar ability]: Monday, 2 times; Tuesday, 3 times

Rose [student of similar ability]: Monday, 3 times; Tuesday, 2 times

This objective information shows that your concern is warranted. It also lets you know that your goal should be to get Mark to the point where he asks for help no more than two or three times during a class period. One technique to help him is to set up a system where each day you give him a small card that is numbered from 1 to 10. Every time he asks for help, he crosses off a number (or you do). When all of the numbers are crossed off, you cannot help him—you ignore his requests for assistance once he has gone beyond his ticket limit. Conversely, each number that is left over at the end of the day is worth one minute of time to visit with you before or after class (a reward he has identified he would be willing to work toward). Once he is consistently staying below ten requests in a period, you can modify the system so that he will get only the numbers 1 through 8 on his card. Continue the system until he has only three numbers each day.

Is the misbehavior so severe that ignoring it is inappropriate?

Sometimes a behavior that is attention seeking in nature is so severe that you cannot responsibly ignore it. For example, if a student is hitting other students, you must intervene. Or if a student's disruptive behavior is so severe that lessons cannot continue, you must intervene. When an attention-getting misbehavior is that severe, you need to treat it as purposeful and habitual misbehavior and include the use of corrective consequences (see task 5). Remember, though, that the student wants attention, so when you assign a consequence, make every effort to do so in a manner that gives the student as little attention as possible. In addition, continue to make a concerted effort to give him frequent attention when he is not engaged in misbehavior. The goal is for the student to learn that although he will get attention for misbehavior, it is less satisfying than what he can easily get for behaving responsibly.

Will you ignore such behavior from all students or just from the target student?

If the behavior is exhibited chronically by one or two students and intermittently by several others, you should ignore any student who exhibits it. If blurting out an answer without raising a hand is a problem for quite a few students, make a classwide announcement that you are going to ignore blurting out and call on only students who remember to raise their hands. If the behavior is exhibited primarily by one student, plan to ignore that student when she engages in the misbehavior, and give verbal reprimands to any other student who exhibits the misbehavior.

Once you determine that a behavior is attention seeking and that ignoring is an appropriate correction strategy, the next step is to develop an intervention that includes using planned ignoring. To develop an effective plan, you need to give careful thought to exactly which behaviors you will ignore. Determine which behaviors you will assign corrective consequences for and which you will encourage. For example, you might end up with a list like the following:

Behaviors to Ignore	Behaviors to Assign Consequences For	Behaviors to Encourage
Blurting out	Bothering other students	Raising hand
Noises	Hitting	Hands/feet to self
Tapping pencil		Working quietly
		On task
		Getting immediately to work
		Following directions

Step 2: Discuss the Proposed Plan with the Student

When the problem involves only one student, arrange to meet with that student and, when appropriate, his family. During the meeting, describe the problem behavior and your proposed solution to ignore it. Be sure to make clear that your intent is not to ignore the student as a person, but only the behavior the student is using to draw attention to himself. Explain that because you have such high expectations for the student's ability to manage this behavior, you are not going to give reminders or assign consequences. Inform the student that if he engages in more severe misbehaviors that cannot be ignored, like violent behavior in class, you *will* assign corrective consequences. Finally, let the student know that you will be looking for opportunities to give him your time and attention when he is behaving responsibly.

Decide whether you will need to discuss the plan with the entire class—for example, if other students will wonder why they are getting a minor consequence and this student is not. If you believe a class discussion is necessary, inform the student during your initial meeting. Make sure the student knows that you will present the plan in a way that communicates to the class that everyone has behaviors to work on, and ignoring is a strategy used to help a student learn to manage his or her behavior.

If the situation involves a behavior that many students exhibit, inform the entire class that you will use ignoring as a strategy. Emphasize that ignoring does not mean the behavior is acceptable. Rather, explain that you are using ignoring because this particular behavior is so clearly unacceptable that you should not have to take valuable time to tell students not to do something they already know they should not be doing. Keep the tone of this discussion positive, not accusatory, and remember to communicate your high expectations.

Step 3: When the Misbehavior Occurs, Continue What You Are Doing and Provide Positive Feedback to Other Students

Once you have informed the student of your plan to ignore, give no attention to the misbehavior. Some teachers feel a need to tell the student each time, "I am ignoring you now." This is not ignoring and will undermine your strategy. Pay *no* attention at the time of the misbehavior. Do not shrug, sigh, or act exasperated. Simply continue to teach. Give your attention to students who are behaving responsibly at that moment. If other students pay attention to the student engaged in misbehavior, give a gentle verbal reprimand: "Chloe, please finish your math problems." If another student laughs at the student, simply remind him to focus on his own work.

Be aware that during the first several days of using planned ignoring, the behavior may get worse before it begins to get better (Alberto & Troutman, 2003; Chance, 1998). In fact, that a behavior is getting worse is a sign your strategy is working. Remember that the student has received attention for exhibiting this behavior in the past and that attention has been satisfying. Now when she exhibits the behavior, she does not get attention. The student's logical response, then, is to try harder to get your attention using the behavior that has been so successful for her in the past. If you continue to ignore her, eventually she will learn that if she really wants attention, she needs to behave responsibly.

Be consistent. Ignoring intermittently is worse than not ignoring at all. For example, if you have decided to ignore blurting out, ignore *all* blurting out. If you ignore it the first five times it happens and then get frustrated and assign a consequence the sixth time, you simply teach the student to be more persistent—"The teacher will eventually give me attention if I misbehave long enough or if I just get more and more obnoxious."

A common question is, "What if I am ignoring a student's noises and blurting out, and he exhibits a severe misbehavior like hitting someone?" The answer is that you follow through on school policy for a behavior of this severity, which in all probability will be writing a disciplinary referral. The reason you should develop a list of behaviors to ignore, behaviors that require consequences, and behaviors to encourage is in anticipation of these kinds of situations. You need to be prepared to consistently ignore the behaviors that will benefit from ignoring. However, if the student then ups the ante by exhibiting a behavior that you previously decided would require consequences, you need to stop ignoring and implement the consequence.

Step 4: When the Attention-Seeking Misbehavior Ceases, Give the Student Attention

Demonstrate to the student that responsible behavior results in attention. Shortly after the student begins behaving responsibly, give her attention. Make an effort to give this attention within five minutes or less so that the student doesn't begin to think her efforts have gone unnoticed. Either praise the student for the responsible behavior or just go over and talk to the student for a few moments: "Suenn, you are working so quietly, I thought I would come over and see if you had any questions or needed any help. You're doing a great job."

Step 5: Maintain Frequent Interactions with the Student When He Is Not Misbehaving

Chapter 8 explained the importance of providing at least three times more attention to positive behavior than to negative behavior. This is essential whenever you are using planned ignoring. If the student does not experience lots of attention when behaving responsibly, he will simply increase his misbehavior until you are forced to acknowledge him. You must praise this student frequently and give him lots of noncontingent attention.

Step 6: Monitor the Student's Behavior to Determine Whether Progress Is Being Made

At least once per week, count the frequency or record the duration of the behavior. After two weeks of using planned ignoring with the target behavior, evaluate whether the situation is improving. If it is not, continue ignoring the misbehavior and increase the amount and intensity of attention you provide when the student is not misbehaving. If there is still no improvement after another two weeks, abandon planned ignoring as a strategy and treat the misbehavior as purposeful or habitual (see Task 3).

Plan D: Develop an Intervention for Habitual and Purposeful Types of Misbehaviors

For ongoing misbehaviors that are habitual or serve a purpose other than getting attention, be prepared to develop and implement an intervention plan that includes the use of corrective consequences.

Chronic misbehavior may occur for reasons other than a lack of awareness or ability or a need for attention. It may help a student avoid something aversive or achieve a sense of power and control. Sometimes the original goal of a student's misbehavior has been long lost, and the student misbehaves just because the inappropriate behaviors have become firmly established in her behavioral repertoire (Sterling-Turner, Robinson, & Wilczynski, 2001).

When ongoing misbehavior is truly purposeful or habitual, it will probably be necessary to use corrective consequences to help the student learn that the misbehavior has negative costs. Because the student is not responding to your classwide management plan, the use of corrective consequences alone, however, is not likely to be sufficient to change the student's behavior (Mayer, 1995). Therefore, in addition to corrective consequences, an intervention plan for purposeful or habitual misbehaviors also needs to include efforts to remove any reinforcing or satisfying aspects of engaging in the misbehavior, as well as efforts to continuously demonstrate that positive behavior leads to positive results (O'Neill et al., 1997; Sugai, Horner et al., 2000).

The remainder of this task describes guidelines for planning an intervention for purposeful and habitual misbehavior. This task addresses the three important components of an intervention plan for this type of misbehavior:

1. Remove any positive or satisfying aspects of demonstrating the misbehavior.
2. Demonstrate to the student that positive behavior leads to positive results.
3. Respond to the misbehavior by assigning appropriate corrective consequences.

Step 1: Remove Any Positive or Satisfying Aspects of Demonstrating the Misbehavior

Remember that the misbehavior you want to change has served a purpose for the student at some point. A student may misbehave in order to escape doing the academic work or not participate in class because he enjoys reading a book or listening to music more than paying attention to the lesson. As you develop your intervention plan, you need to ensure that the student will no longer get whatever it is that he has been getting from the misbehavior. If a student has gotten power by engaging in arguments with you, your plan will need to address how you will avoid engaging in arguments with this student. If a student has been using misbehavior to escape doing his work, you will need to ensure that the corrective consequence you use does not let the student get out of his work. If a student enjoys hurting other people's feelings with mean comments, you will need to train yourself and the other students not to take his critical comments personally.

Step 2: Demonstrate to the Student That Positive Behavior Leads to Positive Results

In addition to making sure that the student will not benefit from the misbehavior, your intervention plan should specifically address how you can continually demonstrate to your students that responsible behavior is worthwhile (Hamre & Pianta, 2001). This can include efforts to meet the student's needs in positive ways and efforts to increase the student's motivation to behave responsibly. It is important to consider ways to make the appropriate behavior more efficient than the problem behavior in gaining positive results for the student.

Meet the student's needs in a positive way.

Once you identify what purpose the misbehavior is serving, you need to find a positive way of satisfying that purpose. For example, if a student talks back as a means of gaining power, you might ask the student if he would be willing to be a positive help around the school. You could give the student a choice among several different jobs, such as tutoring a younger student or helping in the computer lab by learning to be a technical assistant to the computer teacher. Using appropriate corrective consequences along with giving the student a positive position of power can solve this kind of problem behavior much sooner than consequences alone.

If a student is seeking to escape academic work, you need to determine whether the student is capable of doing the work successfully. If not, modify his assignments or your expectations while you are working to get some kind of help for the student so he will begin to experience success.

When a misbehavior involves competing reinforcement (e.g., another activity the student enjoys), you can arrange for the student to have access to the desired reinforcement when he has met your expectations. If a student would rather read a novel than do his work, you might set it up so that he can read when his other work is completed. In addition, when the student has been doing well, you might occasionally give the student an alternative assignment that involves reading a novel and giving a report to the class.

Increase the student's motivation to behave responsibly.

For some students, a change in the type or frequency of positive feedback may be sufficient to increase their motivation to behave responsibly (see chapter 8). In other cases, it may be necessary to establish some form of positive feedback system, like one in which the student earns rewards for exhibiting positive behavior. (For ideas on individual contracts and systems, see chapter 8, task 5 on classwide systems.) An example of an individual system for increasing homework completion is shown in exhibit 9.9.

Exhibit 9.9
Individual Motivation System for Becoming Less Disruptive

When a student is not concerned about the designated consequences of failing to turn in completed homework or does not value the sense of satisfaction that comes with completing and turning in required work, you may need to implement a system of external incentives (rewards and consequences) to motivate him to turn in completed homework on time. If possible, involve the student's parent or guardian in developing this plan. If the family is supportive, it is likely that the rewards and consequences will be more powerful than those you could provide at school.

1. Establish a structured system for reinforcing the appropriate behavior and providing a consequence for the inappropriate behavior.

   a. With the student, create a list of rewards he would like to earn. The rewards may need to be relatively high in perceived value in order to create a powerful incentive to motivate the student to get his homework completed on a regular basis. To get some ideas for the list, watch what the student does during a less structured time in class when he has choices. You can ask the student his preferences; if the parents are involved, ask for their ideas on activities, privileges, or other rewards that the student might like to earn.

   b. Assign "prices" (in points) for each of the rewards on the list, and have the student select the reward he would like to earn first. The prices should be based on the instructional, personnel, or monetary cost of the items. Monetary cost is clear: the more expensive the item, the more points are required to earn it. Instructional cost refers to the amount of instructional time lost or interfered with by a particular reward. An activity that causes the student to miss part of academic instruction should require more points than one the student can do on his own free time. Personnel cost involves the time required by you or other staff to fulfill the reinforcer. Lunch with the principal, therefore, would cost more points than spending five minutes of free time with a friend. The prices should be low enough that the student will think, for example, "You mean all I have to do is X, and I can earn Y!" If the desired reinforcers are priced too high and will take too long to earn (from the student's perspective), he may not be any more motivated to complete his homework than he was without the system.

c. Develop a homework completion self-monitoring form, and establish a system to translate each successfully filled-in space into points. For example, the student might earn one point each for accurately recording the assignment, the due date, and the necessary materials (three points total). When the assignment is completed and turned in, the student might earn another five points, making each homework assignment worth eight points. Larger assignments or projects, such as writing a report, could be broken down into steps, each with its own line and due date on the monitoring form. For example, the outline, the note cards, the rough draft, and the final draft could be treated as separate assignments, each worth eight points—making the whole report worth a possible thirty-two reinforcement points.

d. When the student has accumulated enough points to earn the reward he has chosen, he "spends" the points necessary, and the system begins again. He selects another reward to earn and begins with zero points.

2. Respond consistently to the inappropriate behavior.

a. Gently correct the student when he fails to turn in his homework.

b. Establish consequences (in addition to any predetermined classwide consequences) for not being responsible for his homework. The most obvious consequence would be that if the student does not turn in the work, he fails that assignment. However, that consequence alone may be too abstract and delayed to affect the student's behavior in the short run. A more immediate consequence will probably be necessary (for example, the student is assigned after-school detention until the work is caught up).

c. When neither home-based nor school-based consequences are possible for whatever reason, there is more pressure on the positive aspects of the intervention to ensure that the plan is powerful enough to motivate the student to complete his homework, despite the lack of consequences for not turning it in.

3. Use reinforcement to encourage appropriate behavior.

Give the student extra praise and attention for turning in completed homework on time. In addition, show interest and enthusiasm about how the student is doing on the system: "Salvador, every day this week you have earned all eight points for every assignment. Congratulations! You should be very proud of your organizational skill."

Step 3: Respond to the Misbehavior by Assigning Appropriate Corrective Consequences

When misbehavior is purposeful or habitual, you need to carefully plan how you will respond to specific instances of that behavior. If you do not preplan what your response will be, there is a high probability that you may inadvertently reinforce the misbehavior. The following suggestions can help you choose and implement an effective corrective consequence, one that will help the student learn that engaging in misbehavior has a logical cost associated with it. (See chapter 4, task 4 for a descriptive menu of corrective consequences you may implement in your classroom.)

Implement the corrective consequence consistently.

If corrective consequences are going to reduce or eliminate purposeful or habitual misbehavior, they must be implemented consistently (O'Neill et al., 1997). When you implement a corrective consequence only some of the time, the consequence (no matter how severe) is not likely to change the behavior. In fact, it may even make things worse than having no consequence at all. When a student is able to engage in misbehavior and not receive the designated consequence, he is likely to feel a great sense of satisfaction. Getting away with it can be so reinforcing—"How many times can I get away with it?"—that it offsets many corrections.

Teachers tend to implement corrective consequences based on an accumulation of misbehavior. Thus, teacher emotion ends up controlling the use of consequences. The student gets away with a misbehavior the first five times because the teacher doesn't implement a consequence. On the sixth time, the teacher is finally fed up with the misbehavior and implements a consequence. Though this is understandable, it leads to grossly inconsistent responses. To change purposeful or habitual misbehavior, you need to define specific behaviors that are unacceptable and then implement corrective consequences for those behaviors each time regardless of how you feel about the behavior at the time.

Your goal should be to develop clear expectations of what behaviors are unacceptable so that you can be consistent. If you are concerned about disruptions, specify the precise behaviors you consider disruptive and identify examples of behaviors that are not disruptive. If your concern is a student who is disrespectful, describe specific ways the student has been disrespectful and ways in which she could have behaved in the same situation that would have been respectful. Creating a T-chart that specifies responsible and irresponsible examples of behavior can help. Use the chart when discussing your expectations and consequences with the student. Exhibit 9.10 is a sample T-chart for a student who makes disruptive noises. You may need to give concrete examples of behaviors that have small differences (e.g., making noise by wadding up paper as opposed to the minimal noise created by quietly placing a sheet of paper in the trash can).

Exhibit 9.10
T-Chart Sample for Disruptive Behavior

Responsible Noise	Irresponsible Noise
• Putting paper in the trash	• Only one voice at a time can be heard
• Getting paper out	
• Quietly opening and closing notebook rings	• Tearing up paper
	• Snapping open and closed notebook rings or slamming notebook on desk
• Writing, sharpening pencil at breaks	
• Raising hand, waiting to be called on, using an appropriate volume level	• Tapping pencil
	• Blurting out without raising hand or waiting to be called on
• Working quietly	• Humming, making clicking noises with tongue
• Once or twice a work period, asking a neighbor a work-related question	• Talking about anything other than work during work periods

Once you have developed a T-chart and discussed with the student what constitutes responsible and irresponsible behavior, be sure to implement the designated corrective consequence every time the student exhibits one of the irresponsible behaviors on the list. Be aware that your greatest tendency to be inconsistent will not occur on a bad day when you are tired or feeling unwell, but rather on a good day when you are feeling relaxed and refreshed. On good days, disruptive behavior may not bother you and so you may be inclined to be lenient and ignore it. **Do not do this.** The student needs to know that each time he engages in the misbehavior, the consequence will be implemented regardless of whether the behavior bothers you at the particular moment.

Make sure the corrective consequence fits the severity and frequency of the misbehavior.

When deciding on the corrective consequence that you will implement, choose one that matches the severity of the problem (Mendler & Curwin, 1999). Start by examining the irresponsible behaviors listed on your T-chart. Choose a consequence that fits even the mildest example of the unacceptable behavior. All too often, teachers pick a consequence that is so harsh they are unwilling to implement it when the occasion arises, such as detention for a small infraction. This leads to inconsistency. The consequence should be mild enough that you will be comfortable implementing it every time the student exhibits one of the irresponsible behaviors. As you think about your choice of a consequence, look at each example of a misbehavior listed on your T-chart. Consider how often you might need to assign a consequence for each misbehavior during a class period. How many times is the misbehavior likely to occur? If the consequence seems too harsh for any of the examples of that behavior, you may need to select a milder consequence. When determining the severity of consequences, always err on the side of making consequences too mild because you may not follow through when consequences are overly harsh.

Whatever corrective consequences you choose, plan to implement the consequence in the same way for all of the misbehaviors. In other words, if you have decided to use demerits, all disruptive acts should result in one demerit. Do not create a situation in which some disruptive acts get more demerits than others. If you decide to use time owed as a consequence for a student who tends to be disrespectful, have each infraction equal the same amount of time owed—one minute, for example. Do not set it up so that some instances of disrespect cost one minute while others cost five minutes. Otherwise, you will have to explain why you are assigning one minute some times and five minutes other times.

In addition to matching the corrective consequence to the severity of the infraction, consider the frequency of the infraction. For example, at first glance, it might seem reasonable to say that every time a student is disruptive, the student will be assigned an after-school detention. However, if the student is likely to be disruptive three to four times during a class period, he will end up not paying for most of his infractions. Once you have assigned a detention for the first infraction, what can you then do in response to the second infraction and the third? If you did assign a detention for every infraction, the student might justifiably decide by the middle of the week that there is no reason to even bother to behave; she already has detentions stacked up for the next week and a half.

Furthermore, when consequence severity does not match misbehavior frequency, you might be more inclined to be inconsistent with implementation. For example, by the second infraction, you might start thinking that you'll let some of the behaviors go by because you don't want the student to build up too many detentions too quickly. Overly harsh consequences make consistency difficult for most teachers. The basic consequence should be only fifteen seconds owed immediately after class for each infraction. By taking into account the frequency and establishing a consequence that can realistically be implemented for every infraction, you ensure that you can implement your consequence for every instance of the misbehavior. When it comes to correcting chronic misbehavior, what you use as a consequence is less important than doing something consistently.

Plan to implement the consequence unemotionally.

With purposeful or habitual misbehavior, there is a high probability that the student has learned that she can make adults frustrated, hurt, or angry. If you get angry when correcting the student, that response may reinforce the misbehavior. When a student feels hostility toward adults, seeing an adult get angry can be highly satisfying. For a student who feels powerless, getting an adult upset on a regular basis can provide a huge sense of power and control. Strive to implement corrective consequences unemotionally so your reactions do not give the student the idea that misbehavior is a way to achieve power over you.

Plan to interact with the student briefly at the time of the misbehavior.

When a student misbehaves, your interaction with that student should last less than five seconds. Simply state the misbehavior and then the consequence. A common mistake is to explain and justify. Resist this impulse. All explanations should be done in your initial discussion with the student or in a regularly scheduled follow-up meeting.

If the student has a tendency to argue or deny that he exhibited the misbehavior, tell the student during your initial discussion that at the time of an incident, you will not argue or negotiate and that you will ignore any attempts on his part to do so. At the same time, let the student know that if he ever wants to speak to you about something he thinks is unfair, he can make an appointment to see you before or after school. Once you have made this clear, simply remind the student that he can make an appointment to see you if he tries to argue. Then resume teaching.

Although keeping interactions brief may be a difficult habit to get into, it allows you to keep your focus where it belongs: on teaching and providing positive feedback to all students when they are meeting your expectations. Think about the consequence you are planning to use for the targeted misbehavior. If you cannot imagine implementing that consequence without lengthy explanations or negotiations at the time of the misbehavior, you should select a different consequence.

Step 4: Implement the Intervention Plan for Purposeful/Habitual Misbehavior

The preceding pages addressed the three important components of an intervention plan for purposeful and/or habitual misbehavior:

1. Remove any positive or satisfying aspects of demonstrating the misbehavior.

2. Demonstrate to the student that positive behavior leads to positive results.

3. Respond to the misbehavior by assigning appropriate corrective consequences.

Once you define the behaviors (positive and negative) and consequences, ask yourself some "what-if" questions:

- What if the student objects?

- What if the parents object?

- Will my administrator support me if there are objections?

- What if the behavior increases for a few days?

- Can I still follow through with this consequence?

- Do I need to explain this consequence to the entire class?

- Will I apply the consequence to anyone who exhibits this behavior or just to the target student?

The more issues you can identify and address, the greater the likelihood is that your intervention plan will be effective in reducing, and eventually eliminating, the misbehavior. Discuss any what-if questions you cannot answer yourself with a school administrator or counselor. Do not implement any intervention plan until you know you can follow through on all aspects of it. Remember that your plan needs to address these two questions:

- How will you eliminate or reduce the probability that the student will get positive benefits from engaging in the misbehavior?
- How will you see that the student experiences positive benefits from exhibiting responsible behavior?

Once all aspects of your plan have been developed and all potential difficulties have been resolved, meet with the student to explain what will happen each time she engages in the misbehavior. Make sure the student knows the cost of choosing to exhibit the misbehavior in the future, but keep the tone of this discussion positive.

Step 5: Discuss Your Preliminary Intervention Plan with the Student and, If Appropriate, the Student's Family

Before implementing an intervention plan for any chronic misbehavior, schedule a time to discuss your concerns about the target behavior and your proposed plan with the student or the entire class if many students are exhibiting the behavior. Decide whether to include the student's family in the discussion. If the behavior involved is quite serious (e.g., the student is hitting other students or is verbally abusive), the family should be asked to participate. But if the behavior is a relatively minor one (perhaps the student is restless and overuses the pencil sharpener and the drinking fountain), it may not be necessary to include the family. If you are not sure whether to involve the family, you should probably include them (Dishion & Stormshak, 2007; Gortmaker, Warnes, & Sheridan, 2004; A. Henderson & Mapp, 2002; Miller & Kraft, 2008; Ysseldyke et al., 2006).

During the discussion, define the target behavior for the student as clearly as you can. Whenever possible, describe the behavior in observable terms and share any objective data about the behavior that you have collected: "Troy, you have called other students hurtful names fourteen times in two days." Avoid making statements that imply judgments: "Tamika, you are so out-of-control most of the time that something has to be done."

After you explain the nature of the problem, present your proposed plan. Ensure that the student and the family, if present, understand all aspects of it. You should invite ideas from the student and family for improving the plan. Incorporating reasonable suggestions will give the student and family a sense of ownership in the plan and demonstrate that you want them to be active partners in efforts to improve the student's behavior (Esler et al., 2008; Freer & Watson, 1999; Gortmaker et al., 2004; Keith et al., 1998; Rones & Hoagwood, 2000; Sheridan, Kratochwill, & Bergan, 1996).

Exhibit 9.11 is a template for structuring a phone conversation with a student's family about joining you and the student for a discussion. (See the DVD for a blank reproducible of this form.)

Exhibit 9.11
Request for a Family Conference to Address Chronic Problems

1. Introduce yourself and provide an appropriate greeting:
   Hello, Mr. Horton? This is Ms. Garcia, Toby's biology teacher. May I take a few moments of your time?

2. Inform the family that you are calling about a problem:
   I am calling about something that happened at school today during class.

3. Describe the problem (avoid labeling or passing judgment on the student):
   Toby was working on a lab assignment with a small group of other students. They got into a disagreement that led to Toby's getting quite angry with one of the female students in the group, a student named Akiko. Now, there is nothing wrong with disagreeing with and even getting angry at another student. But Toby called Akiko some very inappropriate names that cannot be tolerated at school. Although this incident was the worst, Toby has gotten angry with fellow students a couple of other times and treated them disrespectfully.

4. Describe why the behavior is a problem (keep the focus on the student, not yourself or the other students):
   To succeed in my class, other classes, and later in life, Toby will have to learn that when he is angry, calling people names is not acceptable behavior. I have noticed that some of the students in the class try to avoid being in Toby's group because of how he reacts when angry.

5. Explain why you think a conference would be useful and specify whether the student should attend the conference:
   I would like to meet with Toby and you to discuss how we can help him learn to disagree with others without becoming angry and how to respond in a more appropriate way when he does become angry.

6. Inform the family if other school personnel (or other agency personnel) will be in attendance:
   I would also like to invite Mr. Freen, our school counselor, to the meeting. He can tell us about resources that are available at the school.

Date of this contact:
Time and place for the conference:

Step 6: Implement the Intervention Plan for at Least Two Weeks; Continue to Collect Data on the Target Behavior to Evaluate the Plan's Effectiveness

Once you have analyzed the behavior, developed a preliminary plan, and discussed the plan with the student and family, you are ready to implement the plan. Keep your plan in effect for at least two weeks: you should collect daily data for about two weeks before you can make a reliable decision about the student's progress (Farlow & Snell, 1994). Objective data about the frequency or duration of the behavior allow you to determine whether the problem is improving. Do not be alarmed if the behavior gets worse during the first week, a phenomenon known as an *extinction burst*. This sometimes happens even with a plan that eventually will be successful (Lerman et al., 1999; Watson, 1967).

For example, when you begin ignoring an attention-getting behavior, the student is likely to try even harder to get attention by misbehaving more frequently. If you persist in ignoring the behavior, the student eventually learns that responsible behavior leads to more attention than misbehavior does. However, if you eventually give in to the student's increased attempts to get your attention, you may reinforce the misbehavior at the new intensity and the misbehavior may remain at the elevated level (Alberto & Troutman, 2006).

After two weeks, reevaluate the situation. If the behavior is getting better, continue to implement your plan. Remember that most successful behavior changes occur gradually, improving a little each week. Eventually, when the student is demonstrating success, you will want to explore ways to fade the plan, especially if it uses structured reinforcement and rewards. For more information on fading a structured reinforcement system, see chapter 8, task 5. The suggestions in that chapter for fading group-based reward systems can be easily adapted to reward systems for individual students.

However, if you see no behavioral improvement after two weeks, try modifying one or more aspects of your plan. Ask the student for ideas on what would make the plan more effective. Whenever you make a change in your intervention plan, implement the new plan for a minimum of two weeks and continue to evaluate effectiveness.

In Conclusion

Chronic misbehavior presents one of the greatest frustrations and challenges to classroom teachers. In designing an intervention plan, always try the easy thing first. Try to use the strategy that is likely to have the biggest impact on the student's behavior. If more than one or two students are chronically misbehaving, work on the implementation of your overall management plan because trying to implement multiple individualized interventions while teaching a class with twenty to thirty other students is too challenging for even the most skilled teacher. If one or two students are chronically misbehaving, first try an intervention plan that makes minor adjustments to your management plan, tailored for that student or small group of students.

If that is ineffective, design an intervention that specifically focuses on building a positive relationship with the target student. If that is ineffective, begin collecting data and design a function-based intervention plan. An intervention will be fundamentally different depending on whether the problem is one of awareness, ability, attention seeking, or habitual or purposeful. Although this kind of plan is a great deal of work, a well-designed and well-implemented individualized intervention has the potential to bring about life-altering behavior change for an at-risk student.

Use the Self-Assessment Checklist to keep track of tasks you've completed and those that require further work. The appendix B folder on the DVD contains the Peer Study Worksheet that you can use to review with a colleague, and, if possible, arrange to observe each other's classrooms. This will allow you to help one another fine-tune and implement your plan to intervene with any particular chronic misbehavior.

Proactive Planning for Chronic Misbehavior Self-Assessment Checklist

Use this worksheet to identify which parts of the tasks described in this chapter you have completed. For any item that has not been completed, note what needs to be done to complete it. Then transfer your notes to your planning calendar in the form of specific actions you need to take (for example, "October 3, meet with Jonathan to discuss why I will begin keeping a frequency count of his disrespectful behavior"). A blank worksheet is on the DVD.

	Task	Notes and Implementation Ideas
☐	*TASK 1: Analyze and, if needed, adjust the implementation of your basic management plan.* I have evaluated my classroom management plan and have worked through the reflection/implementation form (exhibit 9.1). I have considered the questions and suggestions and will make some minor adjustments to my management plan or its implementation that may help my student improve his behavior. If no improvement is noted after two weeks, I will proceed to task 2.	*Will do this for intro to woodshop class if misbehavior continues into next week.*
☑	*TASK 2: Analyze and, if needed, adjust the strategies you are using to build a positive relationship with this student.* I have evaluated my relationship with the student and have worked through the connect/motivation plan—reflection/implementation form (exhibit 9.2). I have considered the questions and suggestions and will make some minor adjustments in my interactions with the student that may increase the student's motivation to engage in positive behaviors and decrease the frequency and severity of the chronic misbehavior. If no improvement is noted after two weeks, I will proceed to task 3.	

TASK 3: Analyze the misbehavior and develop a function-based intervention.

Plan A: Develop an intervention for awareness-type misbehaviors.

I understand that with misbehaviors that stem from a student's lack of awareness of when (or how much) he or she is engaging in a misbehavior, I should use the following steps:

- Make sure the student knows the behavior I expect (the goal behavior).

- Respond to instances of the misbehavior in a way that lets the student know that he or she is not meeting the goal.

- Monitor the student's misbehavior so that I will have an objective basis for discussing progress with the student (and family).

- Give the student positive feedback when he or she is successful, and consider some type of incentive system, if necessary.

Plan B: Develop an intervention for ability-type misbehaviors.

I understand that with ability-type misbehaviors, the first thing I need to do is ascertain whether the student is physiologically capable of exhibiting the goal behavior. If the student is not capable, then I must modify the environment or adjust my expectations, or both. I understand that if a student misbehaves due to a lack of knowledge, I should use the following steps:

- At a neutral time, have a discussion or provide lessons about the goal behavior.

- Respond to instances of misbehavior in a way that provides instruction to the student.

- Make accommodations to increase the student's chance of success.

- Provide positive feedback when the student is successful and set up an incentive system if necessary.

Plan C: Develop an intervention for attention-seeking misbehaviors.

If a student exhibits a mild, ongoing misbehavior that seems to stem from a need for attention, I will first ask myself the following questions to ascertain whether ignoring is the best strategy:

- Is the misbehavior really attention seeking in nature?
- Is the actual problem the frequency of the behavior, not the behavior itself?
- Is the misbehavior so severe that ignoring it is inappropriate?
- Will I ignore such behavior from all students or just from the target student?

After determining whether ignoring is an appropriate response, I will implement the following steps:

1. Discuss the proposed plan with my student.
2. Continue what I'm doing when the student misbehaves and provide positive feedback to other students.
3. Give the student attention when the student stops the attention-seeking behavior.
4. Maintain frequent interactions with the student when he is not misbehaving.
5. Monitor the student's behavior to determine whether progress is being made.

Plan D: Develop an intervention for habitual or purposeful-type misbehaviors.

For chronic misbehavior that does not stem from a lack of awareness or ability or a need for attention, I will develop and implement a comprehensive intervention that:

1. Removes any positive or satisfying aspects of demonstrating the misbehavior

2. Continually demonstrates to the student that positive behavior leads to positive results by:
   - Meeting the student's needs in a positive way
   - Working to increase the student's motivation to behave responsibly

I will ensure that corrective consequences are appropriate for the problem behavior by:

- Implementing the corrective consequences consistently
- Making sure the consequence fits the severity and frequency of the misbehavior
- Implementing the consequence unemotionally
- Interacting with the student only briefly at the time of the misbehavior (I never argue)

The Evidence Base behind Discipline in the Secondary Classroom

Billie Jo Rodriguez, PhD

Based on the most recent recommendations set forth by researchers and the US Department of Education, Discipline in the Secondary Classroom (DSC) is an evidence-based approach to classroom behavior management. It is not a curriculum or program but a collection of recommendations that are based on more than thirty years of research in the fields of education and psychology. Also see exhibit A.1 at the end of this appendix. Safe & Civil Schools has many examples of district-based studies where DSC and CHAMPS, the elementary approach that parallels DSC, have been implemented with remarkable results. Improvements include reductions in classroom disruptions, office referrals, and in-school and out-of-school suspensions, along with corresponding increases in teachers' perceptions of efficacy and student motivation and behavior. (For information on efficacy data, contact Safe & Civil Schools [800/323–8819] or visit www.safeandcivilschools.com.)

The field of education has been particularly vulnerable to adopting unproven interventions based on current fads, whims, or material attractiveness (Scheuermann & Evans, 1997). However, the political and societal expectations that schools face have dramatically shifted over the past twenty years. For example, today's entry-level jobs require reading skills that are more advanced than the reading level of approximately half of current high school students (Fielding, Kerr, & Rosier, 2007). To meet these heightened expectations and combat fad-based educational approaches, federal mandates such as No Child Left Behind (NCLB, 2001) and the Individuals with Disabilities Education Act (IDEA, 2004) have shifted from suggesting that most children be successful to mandating that every child be successful. Both NCLB and IDEA legislation focus on the use of evidence-based practices (US Department of Education, 2002c) and documenting the progress of each child's learning. This age of educational accountability comes at a time when the resources to support students are declining

(Walker & Sprague, 2007) and the composition of the student population is expanding in its diversity of needs, skills, and expectations (Merrell, Ervin, & Gimple, 2005; Ortiz & Flanagan, 2002).

Though the field of education has not come to complete agreement on the definition of evidence-based practice, we have received some guidance. The US Department of Education (2002c) defined scientifically based evidence as "research that involves the application of rigorous, systematic, and objective procedures to obtain reliable and valid knowledge relevant to education activities and programs" (p. 2). More recently, Lembke and Stormont (2005, p. 271) defined research-based practices as those that "are supported by rigorous substantiation of effectiveness." They clarify that research-based (proven or promising) practices are those that "have been demonstrated to be effective for a group of students as compared to a group of students that did not get the intervention" and have generalized results when "examined in a variety of settings, replicated over time, utilized with a variety of learners."

The research should document whether the independent variables of interest produce changes in the dependent variables through the use of a group or single-subject design. Single-subject designs have been recommended for use in research focusing on special populations (*Scientifically Based Evaluation Methods*, 2005). Horner, Carr, et al. (2005) offer further guidance for determining the rigor of single-subject designs. Schools receiving federal funds to implement the Reading First Program (US Department of Education, 2002a) have also received guidance on the types of research that constitute evidence-based practice. Recommended research are:

- Systematic, empirical methods that draw on observation or experiment
- Rigorous data analyses that are adequate to test the stated hypotheses and justify the conclusions drawn
- The use of measurements or observational methods that provide reliable and valid data across multiple evaluators or observers, across multiple measurements and observations, and across studies by the same or different investigators
- Evaluation using experimental or quasi-experimental designs with control groups to evaluate the effectiveness of the conditions, with a preference for random assignment designs or other designs that contain within-condition or across-condition controls
- Acceptance in a peer-reviewed journal or approved by a panel of independent experts through a comparably rigorous, objective, and scientific review
- Experimental studies that are presented in sufficient detail and clarity to allow replication or systematic expansion of the findings

The reason for this shift from access to outcomes may lie in the compelling and compounding evidence documenting the long-term stability and poor outcome trajectories for students who demonstrate early academic and social behavior difficulties (Kazdin, 1987; Walker, Horner et al., 1996; Walker & Severson, 1992).

It is often the case that students who need the most support receive the least. The interaction between learning and social behavior is reciprocal. Typically high-achieving students experience greater social and academic success, while low-achieving students experience increased social and academic failure (Caprara, Barbaranelli, Pastorelli, Bandura, & Zimbardo, 2000; Catalano, Loeber, & McKinney, 1999).

Academically successful students often assume responsibility for learning (e.g., use self-regulation and goal orientation, exhibit positive social behaviors) and are intrinsically motivated (Caprara et al., 2000; Ellis, 1992; Ellis & Worthington, 1994; Grimes, 1981; Swift & Swift, 1968, 1969a, 1969b, 1973), while students with high needs often engage in behaviors that interfere with learning (McKinney, Mason, Clifford, & Perkeson, 1975; Shinn, Ramsey, Walker, Stieber, & O'Neill, 1987; Walker & McConnell, 1988; Walker et al., 2004).

Some school factors have been correlated with increased risk of failure for at-risk students. These factors include inconsistent management of behavior, inappropriate use of reinforcement contingencies, and ineffective instruction (Kauffman, 2005; Keogh, 2003; Walker et al., 2004). Research has shown that teachers may provide less instruction to students who exhibit high levels of problem behaviors (Carr, Taylor, & Robinson, 1991; Wehby, Symons, Canale, & Go, 1998) and that teachers of students with high rates of behavioral difficulties rarely use praise (Sutherland, Wehby, & Copeland, 2000; Van Acker, Grant, & Henry, 1996) and often use more disapproval than approval (Jack et al., 1996). Teacher praise has been shown to result in many benefits, including:

- Decreased problem behavior (Madsen, Becker, & Thomas, 1968; O'Leary & Becker, 1967; Ward & Baker, 1968)
- Increased appropriate behavior and instructional time (Broden, Bruce, Mitchell, Carter, & Hall, 1970; Ferguson & Houghton, 1992; Hall, Lund, & Jackson, 1968)
- Increased student intrinsic motivation (Cameron & Pierce, 1994)
- Competence development for the student (Brophy, 1981; Gottfried, 1983; Swann & Pittman, 1977)

Negative interactions are associated with poorer academic and social behavior outcomes (Murray & Greenberg, 2006; Murray & Murray, 2004). Research also suggests that students are more likely to behave well and work hard to meet a teacher's expectations when the student-teacher relationship is positive and respectful (Borich, 2004; Brophy, 1981; Cameron & Pierce, 1994; Hall et al., 1968; Marzano, 2003; Niebuhr, 1999; Pianta et al., 2003; Reinke et al., 2007; Sutherland et al., 2000).

Students achieve more when teachers have high expectations for them (Brophy & Good, 1986; Fuchs, Fuchs, & Deno, 1985). When teachers implement effective behavior management techniques, they can simultaneously increase student engagement and improve academic achievement (Brophy, 1981, 1996; Brophy & Good, 1986; Christenson et al., 2008; Gettinger & Ball, 2008; Luiselli, Putnam, Handler, & Feinberg, 2005; Scheuermann & Hall, 2008; Smith, 2000). With the increase in diverse student needs and the strong research that links classroom structure, positive feedback, and student-teacher relationships with improved outcomes, it is especially important that teachers of at-risk students work to provide a structured classroom with high rates of positive feedback for appropriate behavior (Stormont, Smith, & Lewis, 2007).

Discipline in the Secondary Classroom is not a program but rather a compilation of how-to strategies that support teachers in the very skills that have been associated with student success. It is a systematic, prevention-oriented approach that guides teachers in providing universal classroom supports likely to promote appropriate behavior and reduce disruptive behavior in the classroom. Once the teacher has implemented the core supports, there is guidance for how to structure supports that target smaller groups or individual students who need additional supports. Systemic models like the one used in DSC were initially implemented in public health and now span the fields of medicine, welfare, and education (Walker et al., 1996). Educational research has shown that when these levels of support are in place and incorporate the meaningful involvement of relevant parties (e.g., teachers, parents, peers), positive student outcomes can be achieved (Horner et al., 2005; J. R. Nelson, Martella, & Marchand-Martella, 2002; Walker et al., 1996; Walker & Shinn, 2002).

The foundational principle of DSC—the idea that behavior occurs for a reason and can be taught and changed—is also well supported in the literature (Alberto & Troutman, 2006; D. M. Baer, Wolf, & Risley, 1968; Carr, 1993; Cooper, Heron, & Heward, 2007; Gresham, Watson, & Skinner, 2001; Johnston & Pennypacker, 1993; Langland, Lewis-Palmer, & Sugai, 1998; Skinner, 1953). In addition, the core features of DSC are organized around the STOIC acronym:

S	Structure your classroom
T	Teach expectations
O	Observe and supervise
I	Interact positively
C	Correct fluently

Each core recommendation is directly linked to studies that document its effectiveness.

Structure your classroom for success. The way the classroom is organized (physical setting, schedule, routines and procedures, quality of instruction, and so on) has a huge impact on student behavior; therefore, effective teachers carefully structure their classrooms in ways that prompt responsible student behavior (G. Baer, 1998; Evans & Lowell, 1979; Gettinger & Ball, 2008; Good & Brophy, 2000; Scheuermann & Hall, 2008; Udvari-Solner, 1996; Walker & Bullis, 1990; Weinstein, 1977). Well-designed physical space prevents a wide array of potential behavioral problems (Evans & Lowell, 1979; Simonsen, Fairbanks, Briesch, Myers, & Sugai, 2008; Weinstein, 1977). Research suggests the physical arrangement should allow the teacher to visually scan all parts of the room from any other part of the room (Pedota, 2007; Shores, Gunter, & Jack, 1993) and allow movement that minimizes distractions for students who are working at their seats (Evertson, Emmer, & Worsham, 2003; Jenson, Rhode, & Reavis, 2009).

Teach behavioral expectations to students. Effective teachers overtly teach students how to behave responsibly and respectfully in every classroom situation and during all major transitions (Brophy & Good, 1986; Emmer, Evertson, & Anderson, 1980; Evertson, Emmer, & Worsham, 2003; Lewis & Sugai, 1999). The research supports the effectiveness of teaching rules (Brophy & Good, 1986; Mendler & Curwin, 1999, 2008) using positive and negative examples (Gresham, 1998; Kame'enui & Simmons, 1990; Sugai & Lewis, 1996) with a focus on what teachers expect students to do. This ensures that students know the expected behavior and sets the stage for student success (Barbetta, Norona, & Bicard, 2005; Colvin, Sugai, & Patching, 1993; Darch & Kame'enui, 2004; Emmer et al., 1980; Greenwood, Hops, Delquadri, & Guild, 1974; Lewis & Sugai, 1999; Marshall, 2001; Mayer, 1995; Simonsen, Fairbanks, Briesch, Myers, & Sugai, 2008; Walker et al., 1996).

Observe and supervise. Effective teachers monitor student behavior by physically circulating whenever possible and visually scanning all parts of the classroom frequently. One of the most effective behavior management strategies a teacher can implement is to circulate throughout the room as much and as unpredictably as possible (Colvin, Sugai,

Good, & Lee, 1997; De Pry & Sugai, 2002; Gettinger & Ball, 2008; Schuldheisz & van der Mars, 2001). In addition, effective teachers use meaningful data to observe student behavior (particularly chronic misbehavior) in objective ways and monitor trends across time (Alberto & Troutman, 2006; Evertson et al., 2003; Scheuermann & Hall, 2008; Shores et al., 1993).

Interact positively with students. Teachers should focus more time, attention, and energy on promoting and acknowledging responsible behavior than on responding to misbehavior (Beaman & Wheldall, 2000; Brophy & Good, 1986; Martella et al., 2003; Rosenshine, 1971; Sprick, 2006; Thomas, Becker, & Armstrong, 1968; Walker et al., 2004). Increased positive interactions between teachers and students have been shown to decrease misbehavior and lead to increases in on-task behavior (Beaman & Wheldall, 2000; Brophy & Good, 1986; Thomas et al., 1968; Walker, Ramsey, & Gresham, 2004).

Correct fluently. Teachers are encouraged to preplan their responses to misbehavior to increase the likelihood they will respond in a brief, calm, and consistent manner. This practice helps ensure that the flow of instruction is maintained (Brophy & Good, 1986; Lewis & Sugai, 1999). Research has consistently shown that students learn more efficiently when they receive immediate feedback about their behavior (Gettinger & Ball, 2008; Good & Brophy, 2000; Hudson & Miller, 2006; Kame'enui & Simmons, 1990). The research supports correcting misbehavior by providing instruction about the rule and how to follow the rule (Darch & Kame'enui, 2004; Emmer et al., 1980, 2003; Evertson et al., 2003) in a direct, brief, and explicit manner (Abramowitz, O'Leary, & Futtersak, 1988; McAllister, Stachowiak, Baer, & Conderman, 1969). There is a focus on implementing corrective consequences consistently (Acker & O'Leary, 1988; Alberto & Troutman, 2006; Scheuermann & Hall, 2008) and matching consequences to the severity of the problem (Simonsen et al., 2008; Wolfgang & Glickman, 1986). In addition, with chronic and severe misbehavior, the teacher is prompted to consider the function of the misbehavior and build a corresponding plan to help the student learn and exhibit the appropriate behavior (Alberto & Troutman, 2006; Crone & Horner, 2003; O'Neill et al., 1997).

Simonsen and colleagues (2008) conducted a systematic review of the behavior support literature. They identified twenty practices that in general are supported by the research and have sufficient evidence to recommend their adoption to support classroom behavior. The practices were then grouped into five evidence-based critical features of classroom management:

1. Maximize structure and predictability (including using a physical arrangement that minimizes distraction).

2. Post, teach, review, monitor, and reinforce expectations (and provide active supervision).

3. Actively engage students in observable ways.

4. Use a continuum of strategies to respond to appropriate behaviors (including specific and/or contingent praise, classwide group contingencies, behavioral contracting, and token economy strategies).

5. Use a continuum of strategies to respond to inappropriate behaviors (including error corrections, performance feedback, differential reinforcement, planned ignoring plus praise and/or instruction of classroom rules, response cost, and timeout from reinforcement strategies).

These recommendations directly align with the practices incorporated into the STOIC model, providing additional evidence for the use of DSC to guide classroom behavior support.

Exhibit A.1
NREPP Recognition

In November 2011, the Safe & Civil Schools Positive Behavioral Interventions and Supports Model was reviewed by the Substance Abuse and Mental Health Services Administration (SAMHSA) and added to the National Registry of Evidence-based Programs and Practices (NREPP). NREPP is an online registry that the public can search to identify scientifically based interventions that have been reviewed and rated.

Inclusion in NREPP means that independent reviewers found that the philosophy and procedures behind *Discipline in the Secondary Classroom*, *CHAMPS*, and other *Safe & Civil School* books and DVDs have been proven through research to demonstrate:

- Higher levels of academic achievement
- Reductions in school suspensions
- Fewer classroom disruptions
- Increases in teacher professional self-efficacy
- Improvement in school discipline procedures

For more information, visit www.nrepp.samhsa.gov.
— R.S.

Billie Jo Rodriguez, PhD, is an assistant professor in the Department of Educational Psychology at the University of Texas at San Antonio.

Schoolwide Implementation of Discipline in the Secondary Classroom

Discipline in the Secondary Classroom (DSC) is an approach. It's a way of thinking, not a fixed program, so the process of implementing it schoolwide is difficult to describe in precise terms. If DSC were a canned program, it would be easy to describe implementation: "All staff should follow steps A, B, and C ..." In fact, no set of simple steps can help manage and motivate all, or even most, students. As the introduction to this book states, DSC is designed to help classroom teachers develop (or fine-tune) an effective classroom management plan that is proactive, positive, and instructional. It guides teachers in how to be effective in making decisions about managing behavior—everything from how the physical setting is organized, to the teaching of expectations, to when and how to provide positive feedback. The DSC approach guides teachers in making research and data-based decisions about classroom management, with the final decisions about managing the behavior of their students left up to the teacher. This approach allows each teacher to reap the benefits of research-based strategies and provides the teacher the opportunity to feel comfortable including his or her individual personality and style choices when designing a classroom management plan.

Making those initial decisions and then implementing a unique classroom management plan is the beginning of a year-long process. Any time a student, a group of students, or a whole class is misbehaving or is not fully motivated, the DSC approach dictates that the teacher modify some aspect or aspects of his management plan to try to solve that behavioral or motivational problem. If his management plan works, he can target another behavioral or motivational concern and tweak his plan to have a positive effect on that problem. If those tweaks are ineffective, he should experiment with different variables of his plan to seek a positive effect on the target concern. Those trained in behavior analysis will notice that DSC is simply a user-friendly how-to manual for implementing behavior analysis in the classroom. When the DSC approach is used effectively, the result is the implementation of a proactive, positive, and instructional classroom management plan.

One implication of this uncanned approach to student behavior and motivation is that you can never say, "I tried DSC and it didn't work." You can legitimately say, "The things I have implemented to date have not worked"—and within the DSC approach, the logical response to that statement would be, "So the next things that I am going to focus on are . . ."

A second implication of the uncanned nature of DSC is that when implementing the approach schoolwide, school administrators need to be very careful to avoid inadvertently implying to staff that they must follow steps A, B, and C. For example, some schools and districts have told teachers that they must post DSC expectations in the classroom. Though there may be a compelling reason to consider doing this (discussed later in this appendix), some teachers may consequently think that all there is to DSC is putting up some posters. Using a visual display of the CHAMPS or ACHIEVE acronym has many benefits; however, the careful reader of this book will recognize that whether to use visual displays of classroom expectations is only one of many decisions the teacher needs to make when defining her classroom management plan.

Truly implementing DSC schoolwide requires that the entire school staff (both professional and noncertified employees) engage in proactive thinking about how to manage behavior and also in active problem solving—including analyzing data and designing and implementing positive strategies to solve behavior and motivational problems. Staff will work together to manipulate the STOIC variables (Structure, Teach, Observe, Interact, Correct) to continuously refine and improve the strategies used to help students—both individuals and whole classes—learn to behave responsibly and be academically successful.

Schoolwide Consideration 1: Administrators Must Create Clear Expectations regarding the Outcome of Teachers' Implementation of DSC in the Classroom

When DSC is implemented on a schoolwide basis, agreements between administrators and teachers must be developed regarding the expected outcomes of effective implementation. To do this, faculty and staff must believe that any change in student behavior starts with the adults in the school changing their approach to behavior management. Everyone must understand: "If we want good student behavior, we must teach it!"

The outcomes of an effective management plan are threefold:

- *High rates of academic engagement.* When a teacher's management plan is working well, students should be on task and academically focused at least 90 percent of the time or more. If engagement is less than 90 percent, the teacher should work to solve the problem.

- *Consistently respectful interactions.* When a teacher's management plan is working, students should be treating each other and the teacher with respect, and the teacher should be treating the students with respect. If interactions are not consistently respectful, the teacher should work to solve the problem.

- *The teacher's posted expectations and observed student behavior should match.* The classroom teacher or a visitor to the classroom should be able to observe students behaving in a manner that demonstrates compliance with the teacher's expectations—that is, students should be doing what the teacher expects of them. If there is not a match, the teacher needs to work to solve this problem. Note that this is a great reason for teachers to post expectations when DSC is implemented schoolwide: if the rules and behavioral expectations are clearly displayed for all to see, teachers will find it easier to teach and enforce the expectations and students will find it hard to argue that they are not breaking the rules or violating an expectation.

This focus on the outcomes of effective management has several implications. *First and foremost, if it isn't broken, don't try to fix it!* If student behavior is engaged and respectful and meets the teacher's expectations, no one should tell that teacher he needs to do something different. Second, no administrator should be visiting teacher's rooms with a "21-Point DSC Checklist" to determine whether teachers are implementing the DSC approach. Rather, use the decision-making strategies to tweak what the teacher believes she needs to improve based on the data collection tools included in chapter 7. Third, if any problems exist—low levels of engagement, disrespectful interactions, or students not following the teacher's expectations—the teacher needs to do something different. In other words, if it is broken, you have to try to fix it. This third concept means that a teacher cannot say, "I implemented DSC and it did not work." If student behavior is unacceptable, the teacher needs to experiment with the STOIC variables until he finds a strategy that solves the problem.

Schoolwide Consideration 2: Develop Staff Agreements about Which Procedures Will Be Schoolwide and Which Will Be Unique to Each Classroom

If your school or district is considering implementing DSC on a systemwide basis, a leadership team should be organized that includes the building administrator and representative classroom teachers and support staff. The team should work together to determine what standard procedures, routines, and expectations will be implemented throughout the school and what will be left to each teacher to decide for her own classroom.

As the author of the program, I strongly urge administrators to leave most decisions about expectations for classroom behavior to each classroom teacher. For example, each teacher should be able to decide expectations such as whether students can talk to each other during independent work, whether students are to raise their hand to speak during discussion activities, and when students can sharpen their pencils. Teachers need to make these decisions based on their professional judgment about what works best given their personal style, the needs of the students, and the nature of the subject being taught. Do not, in the name of consistency or clarity, take away teachers' ability to create their own unique classroom.

Nevertheless, the leadership team may want to discuss and make some decisions regarding schoolwide implementation of the DSC approach. Some suggested topics for discussion are:

- *Organization for communicating expectations to students.* Chapter 5 introduces the CHAMPS and ACHIEVE acronyms. In addition, that chapter suggests ways to communicate expectations to students — for example, T-charts, table display boards, and icons. Consider developing agreements about whether T-charts or an acronym will be used, and if an acronym, which one.

- *Required posting of visual displays.* Some schools have required that all teachers post expectations for teacher-directed instruction, independent seatwork, cooperative groups, and tests. There are at least three potential advantages to this. First, because in most high schools, students have several different teachers during the day, the visual displays (using icons or words) make it easy for students to learn the unique expectations of each teacher. If they forget, they can easily look at the display and determine, for example, "Is it okay for me to ask my neighbor a question now, or do I need to ask permission?" A second advantage to posted displays of basic expectations throughout all classrooms is that administrators or other observers can easily see that student behavior matches the teacher's expectations — that is, the student was not rude or disrespectful by asking another student a question because in this teacher's room, that is the teacher's expectation during this activity. Third, posted expectations can make a substitute teacher's job much easier and can decrease the degree to which students play games with substitutes by saying, "Our teacher doesn't do it that way." (More information about DSC for substitute teachers is provided in the following section.).

- *Behavior in common areas.* Teachers should have great flexibility to design their own expectations for classroom behaviors. However, schoolwide consistency is essential in common areas such as hallways, restrooms, and cafeterias. Although this strategy is not specifically addressed in this book, some schools have used the CHAMPS or ACHIEVE acronym to clarify expectations for behavior in these areas. Though clear and consistent expectations are important, they are only part of the picture. Safe & Civil Schools has designed specific programs to address behavior management related to common areas. These comprehensive programs suggest ways to examine structural considerations in common areas, offer detailed lessons on expectations, examine patterns of adult supervision, and provide training for supervisors. Consider using *Foundations: Establishing Positive Discipline Policies* (Sprick, Garrison, & Howard, 2002) to guide a comprehensive process for improving your common areas. The process also includes designing schoolwide Guidelines for Success that can be used as an acronym to teach common area expectations to all students. Also note that Safe & Civil Schools offers the following specific programs for managing bus behavior and hallway, restroom, and tardiness issues:

    In the Driver's Seat: A Roadmap to Managing Student Behavior on the Bus (CD-ROM and DVD program) by R. S. Sprick, L. Swartz, and A. Glang (2007). Eugene, OR: Pacific Northwest Publishing and Oregon Center for Applied Sciences. For grades K–12.

    START on Time! Safe Transitions and Reduced Tardies (CD-ROM) by R. S. Sprick (2003). Eugene, OR: Pacific Northwest Publishing. For grades 6–12.

Student expectations with substitute teachers.

By creating an environment where expectations are consistent schoolwide, you can make life much easier for substitutes. Include expectations for student behavior with substitute teachers in your schoolwide plan. Student behavior will be more consistent when a substitute is present, and teachers will return from their days away from the class to more peaceful classrooms. When students clearly understand that the behavior expectations are the same whether you are the teacher that day or not, everyone benefits. If substitutes know what the general expectations are, they will be more confident in their interactions with students and will be able to teach and maintain the expectations. They can spend more time teaching and less time dealing with misbehaving students. On average, the cumulative time students will spend with substitutes equals more than a full year of their K–12 school experience (Sykes, 2002). That year should and could be a productive and rewarding time for both students and substitutes.

For more information on organizing a school to provide effective support for substitute teachers and on training your cadre of substitutes in the DSC approach, see:

Stepping In: A Substitute's Guide to Managing Classroom Behavior by R. S. Sprick (2009). Eugene, OR: Pacific Northwest Publishing

Structuring Success for Substitutes: A Guide for Administrators and Teachers by R. S. Sprick (2009). Eugene, OR: Pacific Northwest Publishing.

Policies enforced by multiple adults.

Another component of schoolwide discipline to consider is ensuring that all adults are consistent in implementing your school's policies for dress code, truancy, tardiness, and other code-of-conduct violations. DSC does not specifically address these issues, but whether or not you are implementing DSC schoolwide, all staff must strive to be consistent in implementing these kinds of schoolwide policies and procedures. In addition, schoolwide consistency is essential for routines and procedures such as assemblies, arrival, dismissal, and transitions (passing between classes or changing schoolwide activities).

Attention signal.

Chapter 3 discussed the importance of an attention signal in the classroom. If DSC is being implemented schoolwide, consider addressing this with your leadership team and faculty, and having all faculty and staff agree to use the same signal. If everyone uses the same signal, it can be used consistently in the cafeteria, auditorium, and any other school locations, and it increases the likelihood students will respond appropriately to the signal than when they encounter different signals throughout the day.

Schoolwide Consideration 3: Create a Continuous Improvement Cycle for DSC Implementation

Because DSC is an approach, not a program, and because a good management plan is fluid (e.g., more highly structured in the last month of school than in the second-to-last month of school), teachers should develop a mind-set that emphasizes continuous improvement. Any professional, such as the physician you trust with your health, should be a lifelong learner of her craft. No matter how skilled the teacher, every classroom has some students who can learn to behave more responsibly or increase their motivation, so every teacher should periodically reflect on his or her classroom management plan and the needs of individual students. Here are some suggestions for creating an ongoing dialogue with faculty and staff about DSC implementation. These different suggestions can be combined in creative ways to keep staff thinking and talking about using DSC as a vehicle for developing a continuous improvement model:

• *Create initial in-service training opportunities at the building or district level.* The schoolwide implementation of DSC can be enhanced if all teachers receive engaging, practical, and entertaining in-service (see exhibit B.1). Initial training is best when conducted during the summer months, with additional refresher sessions conducted at least quarterly so people can discuss what is and is not working. If training begins during the school year, ideally plan to devote a three-hour class to each of the nine chapters in this book. Most class time should be spent discussing each chapter using the Peer Discussion Worksheets provided on the DVD. Note that there is no Peer Discussion Worksheet for chapter 7 because most of that chapter is about specific data collection tools. Discussion on this chapter should be about the tools and when and how to use them.

Exhibit B.1
In-Service Opportunities

If your school or district is interested in providing in-service training on DSC, you may wish to explore the professional development offered through Safe & Civil Schools. This company, headed by Randy Sprick, the author of DSC, has been partnering with schools around the country for more than thirty years to dramatically improve school climates. By providing high-quality, customized professional development, Safe & Civil Schools training empowers school staff to develop a culture of safety, civility, and academic productivity. Districts implementing these services have raised academic achievement and reduced bullying, disruptions, suspensions, and expulsions, while also improving climate and safety.

Safe & Civil Schools offers a full range of consulting, training, and coaching services in research-based behavior management practices. These services are offered at all K–12 levels and are available to address schoolwide, classroom, and individual student concerns. Training in classroom management (CHAMPS/DSC) is designed to help classroom teachers develop or fine-tune effective classroom management plans that are proactive, positive, and instructional. Teachers learn how to construct plans that not only teach students how to behave responsibly, but also instill in students the desire to be productive and positive contributors in their classrooms.

All Safe & Civil Schools trainers are educators with extensive experience as teachers and trainers (and in some cases, as building and central office administrators) who work to make discipline and behavior support training usable and entertaining for participants. Professional development focuses on delivering practical, data-driven strategies that staff members can use right away and that will dramatically improve the classroom climate and effectiveness of instruction.

Training ranges from concentrated one-day in-service to "training of trainer" to multiyear districtwide projects. Safe & Civil Schools will work with you to develop a professional development program that is tailored to the targeted needs of your school or district. Visit www.safeandcivilschools.com to learn more about training services and options, or call 1-800-323-8819 to speak directly with a Safe & Civil Schools staff development coordinator about your specific training needs.

- *In-service provided by groups within the school.* Some schools that have implemented DSC schoolwide have a system wherein different groups—departments, teams, or professional learning communities within the school—are assigned to review and lead a discussion about each chapter for the entire staff. For example, each month one department is responsible for reviewing the content and facilitating a staff discussion about a particular chapter. Note that the Peer Study worksheets provided on the DVD in the appendix B folder can be used to create these professional exchanges of ideas.

- *New staff trained by experienced teachers.* One problem with a schoolwide approach is how to train new teachers and staff who join the school two or three years after the initial training and follow-up sessions. Some schools appoint individuals or teams of experienced DSC teachers to be in charge of particular chapters. Not only does this allow the trainers to develop a level of expertise with their chapters, it also prepares the training team for when a member of the team leaves the school. The team member can then be replaced the following year by a new trainer who will benefit from assisting the remaining trainer. This process helps to ensure the sustainability of schoolwide DSC implementation. With this training model, each person is responsible for meeting with new teachers and experienced teachers new to the school sometime during the first half of the school year to introduce the content, assign the reading, and then facilitate the peer discussion questions.

- *Data collection assignments.* Chapter 7 includes a variety of data collection tools. Below is the suggested calendar plan for using these tools. The building administrator can assign staff to conduct these data collection tasks and schedule opportunities to discuss what teachers learned about their classes from the experience. Depending on other priorities, the principal may decide to implement the entire plan or only one or a few of these data collection tasks.

Suggested Data Collection Calendar

Week 3	Student Interviews or Quiz on Classroom Expectations (chapter 6, task 4)
Week 4 or 5	CHAMPS or ACHIEVE versus Daily Reality Rating (chapter 7, tool A)
Month 2	Ratio of Interactions Monitoring (chapter 7, tool B)
Month 3 (early)	Misbehavior Recording (chapter 7, tool C)
Month 3 (late)	Grade Book Analysis (chapter 7, tool D)
Month	On-Task Behavior Observation (chapter 7, tool E)
January (early)	CHAMPS and ACHIEVE versus Daily Reality Rating (chapter 7, tool A)
January (late)	Opportunities to Respond Observation Sheet (chapter 7, tool F)
February (early)	Ratio of Interactions Monitoring (chapter 7, tool B)
February (late)	On-Task Behavior Observation (chapter 7, tool E)
March (early)	Grade Book Analysis (chapter 7, tool D)
April (after spring break)	CHAMPS and ACHIEVE versus Daily Reality Rating (chapter 7, tool A)
Last two weeks	Student Satisfaction Survey (chapter 7, tool G)

Additional Training Tips

- Administrative support for schoolwide DSC training should be visible, positive, and documented.
- Establish a site coordinator and DSC training team.
- Identify willing and able trainers.
- Define your schoolwide vision.
- Identify who will facilitate training.
- Identify who will be trained first.
- Identify where training takes place.
- Identify when training will begin.
- Define expectations for participants after training.
- Establish a budget for substitutes, materials, and snacks.
- Continually reflect on your training. Is it meeting the needs of your staff?
- Use data to support continuous training and identify focus.
- Improve sustainability by training new trainers each year and provide refresher trainings for staff.

Peer Study Worksheets

See the appendix B folder on the DVD to access the Peer Study Worksheets. These worksheets provide suggested topics for discussion that correspond to each of the tasks within each chapter. *Note:* There is no worksheet for chapter 7. Discussion on chapter 7 should focus on the data collection tools and how and when to implement them. These worksheets can be used for the following:

- College credit class
- Full faculty study
- Small study group of interested professionals
- Pair of interested professionals
- Within a mentor-mentee relationship
- Homework assignments for a staff development opportunity offered within a school district

Cultural Competence

Keba Baldwin and Amalio Nieves

*I*magine that your family, including your thirteen-year-old daughter and fifteen-year-old son, has moved to a new country. You have a basic knowledge of the language, but people talk quickly and use unfamiliar words, so even simple conversations are difficult to follow.

Your family looks different from most other people. Everywhere you go, you are noticed.

The dress, food, and customs in this country are unfamiliar. Even the way people walk and greet one another is different.

The school your children will attend doesn't look like your old school. In this new place, the classes are huge, and the teaching methods are different from your experiences. What do your children need to fit in? What do your children need to thrive in this new environment?

To help your children adjust, you might hope the teachers learn a little about your culture and what your children need to learn to be successful in theirs. You may hope the teachers ask, "What can we help these children learn so they can be successful?"

When cultures are different, what must we do to help all children be successful? Culture encompasses the beliefs, customs, practices, and social behavior of a particular nation or people. As educators, it is important to recognize that these differences extend beyond obvious ones, such as those seen when students come from different countries or speak different languages. These differences may be based on race, income, disability, education level, and many other factors. If we wish schools to welcome all students, staff members need to develop cultural competence—an awareness of and respect for different cultures. With cultural competence, teachers can help students successfully bridge two worlds.

Teaching students to transition from their home culture to their school culture requires the same skillful classroom management we need to afford to all students:

Structure your classroom for success.

Teach students how to be successful in your classroom.

Observe student behavior.

Interact positively.

Correct fluently.

By following the acronym STOIC, you can educate students about the behaviors and attitudes needed for the classroom—even those that may be different from behaviors and attitudes at home. Skillfully and respectfully guiding students toward successful classroom behavior does not devalue other beliefs, customs, practices, and social behavior. If classroom behaviors are new or different for the student, it is simply "the way we do it at school."

Know the differences

Know where your students are coming from—literally, economically, and culturally. Values, beliefs, and behaviors may not be the same as yours. Consider a few examples of differences and culturally competent responses:

- *Value placed on education.* You may work with students whose family members have dropped out of school for generations and been "all right." For these students, the long-term goal and benefits of graduation need to be taught across time. In the interim, these students may need immediate and tangible goals.

- *Dual rules.* Students grow up with a set of rules that allows them to function in their homes and communities, and sometimes these rules may be very different from the school's rules of conduct. Be aware of and respect this duality. Let students know that you understand that there are different rules outside school. Nonetheless, when in school, students need to follow school rules. For example, a family may encourage their children to hit anyone who hits or wrongs them. So even though a no-hitting rule seems obvious to you, you will need to specifically teach some students that hitting is against school rules and teach them alternative ways of solving conflict.

- *Voice.* Some children may expect adults to yell at them before they will do anything because that is what they are used to at home. In some cultures, the only way to be heard and respected is to talk loudly and above everyone else. If some students equate yelling with adult authority, you may need to teach them that a soft voice deserves respect as well. In other cultures, a loud voice may convey anger. If you have a loud voice, you may need to teach some students that your loud voice does not mean anger.

- *Eye contact.* In some cultures, children are considered disrespectful when they make eye contact with an adult. Yet in mainstream American culture, children may be chastised for not making direct eye contact. If students' use of eye contact is different from what you are used to, accept this. Across time and once students are thriving, you may wish to teach students that some teachers and employers may expect eye contact when they talk with their students or employees.

- *Competition.* In some cultures, it is inappropriate to try to be better than others—to want a better grade, to want to be the best, to win a race. If students are more motivated by the progress of the group than by competition, use more whole-class praise and consider whole-class reward ideas.

- *Family involvement.* Child-rearing practices vary from culture to culture. How families feel about needing and accepting help from others may be different from the school's expectations. In some cultures, families take an active role in their child's school life by assisting with homework, attending meetings, and volunteering. In other cultures, families believe it is not their place to interfere or intervene in the educational process. The educator is the expert. Concurrently, some families may also appear to distance themselves from school because of past negative experiences with their own schooling, fear or misunderstanding of the educational system, job schedules, or limited proficiency in English. If families stay away from your school, it does not mean they are not interested or involved in their child's schooling. If there is little contact between the school and home, provide information to the home regarding the student's progress and continue to be welcoming.

Conclusion

Whether cultural differences are subtle or obvious, it isn't easy to spend the school day in one world and the rest of the day in another. English Language Learner students have the challenge of learning a new language and must sometimes face the added difficulty of relocating from a different part of the world for complex reasons. What added stresses do these families face?

Be aware of differences. Be respectful of the differences. Then teach your students how to behave successfully in your classroom, and you will demonstrate cultural competence.

Suggestions for Additional Reading

A Framework for Understanding Poverty by Ruby Payne (1995). Available from aha! Process, Inc. (www.ahaprocess.com).

Never Work Harder Than Your Students and Other Principles of Great Teaching by Robyn R. Jackson (2009). Available from ASCD (www.ascd.org).

Other People's Children: Cultural Conflict in the Classroom (2nd ed.) by Lisa Delpit (2006). Available from New Press (www.thenewpress.com).

Keba Baldwin is student service director at Currituck County Schools, North Carolina.

Amalio Nieves, MS, is a coordinator for Broward (Florida) Schools' Office of Prevention, dedicated to empowering youth through substance abuse and violence prevention strategies.

Professionalism for the First-Year Teacher

This appendix provides suggestions for how to look, think, and behave like a professional. A professional can be defined as one who works in a position that requires specialized knowledge and often long academic preparation, and exhibits a courteous, conscientious, and generally businesslike manner in the workplace.

Congratulations on embarking on an exciting adventure! Your first year of teaching will hold many rewarding and memorable experiences. This book and its many suggestions, activities, and reflective tools will assist you in proactively planning your classroom management and organizational strategies. Of course, your first year as a teacher can also include many intimidating moments. You'll encounter some of the most challenging situations of your career because many situations will be new to you. There is much to learn and much to do: learning your district's expectations about curricular expectations, insurance, and paperwork; understanding and fitting into your teaching team and school campus; and trying to meet the needs of all your students.

> ### Note
> Special thanks to Maureen Gale, district behavior coach for Orange County Public Schools in Florida, for her contributions to this appendix.

You are beginning your career as a professional. Effective teachers understand that it's important to behave in a manner that communicates professionalism. Imagine you go to see a professional—a physician, architect, or attorney—and find he is sloppily dressed and acts hesitant and unsure, or arrogant and condescending. During your discussion, he does not actively listen to you or make eye contact. He appears distracted by other matters. Later you discover he talked about your personal issues with members of your community. How would you feel about engaging this person's services? What opinion would you form about his level of expertise? Would you trust him? Would you feel a rapport with him? It is doubtful that you would have much confidence in him. Consequently, he probably wouldn't be very effective in helping you, nor would you willingly seek his advice when you needed it.

An effective teacher is a professional who works to assist all staff, students, and students' families in a manner that leaves them informed, reassured, and hopeful. An effective teacher goes the extra mile in building rapport with students and everyone who has a vested interest in the students.

This appendix provides suggestions for how to look, think, and behave like a professional. A professional can be defined as one who works in a position that requires specialized knowledge and often long academic preparation and who exhibits a courteous, conscientious, and generally businesslike manner in the workplace. Teachers who fail to demonstrate characteristics of professionalism tend to have more difficulty managing the behavior of their students, so it is appropriate to include tips on professionalism in a book about classroom management. Of course, professionalism alone will not ensure that your students don't misbehave—it's not that simple—so you will want to consider the other tasks in this book as well. However, there is no doubt that if you lack professionalism, behavioral situations with your students will tend to be worse. You, your students, their families, and your colleagues will benefit if you maintain a vision of yourself as a professional and demonstrate professionalism at all times. For additional information on how to manage your classroom in your first year of teaching, see *The Tough Kid New Teacher Book* (Rhode, Jenson, & Morgan, 2009).

Read the suggestions below, discuss them with your mentors, and reflect on whether you are exhibiting professional qualities. Keep this information in mind as you work through the tasks in this book.

Build a professional relationship with each of your students.

Students need to believe that you have their best interests at heart and that you will do everything in your power to help them succeed in your class and throughout the rest of the school. Building positive relationships with your students is an important component of any successful classroom management plan. There are many strategies you can use to achieve this goal. The first step in building this relationship is to learn students' names and use their names to greet them each day. Greeting each student by name demonstrates that you are aware of and interested in each student as an individual.

Beyond this first easy step of using students' names, the concept of building relationships gets a little less clear-cut. Building a relationship with your students is like being a great tour guide. Imagine that you arrange to take a tour in another country where you cannot speak or read the language and the culture is very different from your own. Your ideal tour guide will have enough leadership ability and organizational skill to keep the group together and safe and to take you where you want to go, ensuring that everyone has a good time in the process. This tour guide's main responsibility is to be a leader, not a friend. She will make sure you feel that she is interested in you, enjoys your company, and has your best interests at heart. So be a good tour guide—be a leader. Organize your classroom, orchestrate student behavior, and let every student know that he or she is important to you. Avoid any effort to be a friend or peer, to be cool or trendy. The students need you to be their professional guide on this journey you take together.

Building positive relationships with students does not mean that you should cut them a break by being lenient with your rules and consequences. Always enforce the rules in a consistent, calm, pleasant, professional, and nonnegotiable manner. Students need the structure and safety of your organized and consistent classroom management plan. (See chapter 4 for details on creating this plan.)

To build and maintain a positive relationship with students, avoid shutting down on a student who has misbehaved or been disrespectful to you—no matter how badly or how often. Don't take student behavior personally! Some students may even actively strive to push you away. Remember that you are the adult in this daily adventure. Even the student who seriously misbehaved on Tuesday needs a friendly greeting and a fresh start on Wednesday morning.

Keep in mind that you are modeling how to build positive relationships for your students. As an educator, you are not only building and maintaining your relationships with students, but you are also showing your students how to build relationships with their peers and the adults on campus. If you find you are struggling to either build or maintain a positive relationship with one student or perhaps several students, try these suggestions:

- Sponsor after-school activities.
- Take a walk and have a conversation with the student or a group of students.
- Implement class meetings.
- Find out more about your students through the use of interest inventories or reinforcement menus (students check their top choices from a list of items such as computer time, ticket to a school sports event, coupon to a nearby restaurant, or pizza party).
- Celebrate the good times.
- Ask a colleague to join you for a home visit with a student's family.
- Invite a small group of students to have lunch with you.
- Read a book your students have recommended, and then share your opinion of it with them.
- Greet students verbally, with handshakes, or with high fives.
- At dismissal, use specific praise with students' names for a job well done!
- Attend school functions or other activities in which you know your students are involved (e.g., sports games, concerts, plays, competitions).

Remember the "I" in STOIC—positive interactions build positive relationships! See chapter 1, task 4 for more tips on how to keep your relationships positive. Also see appendix C for suggestions on cultural competence—that is, how to work effectively with students and families from backgrounds that are different from yours.

Build professional relationships with your students' families.

Be prepared to build a professional relationship with your students' families. If you will be dealing with a large number of students, you probably won't be able to get to know every family, but you will undoubtedly have the opportunity to communicate with many of them. (This is discussed in more detail in chapter 1, task 5.) Families do not want you to be their friend or their child's friend. They want you to guide their child on her journey, to use the earlier metaphor, to successfully learn the essential skills and competencies of your subject. They expect you to keep the child's best interests at heart. Keep families informed about their child's progress on this journey.

Building relationships and connecting with families supports not only them but also your students, classes, and school community. To collaborate with and support the families of your students, keep these strategies in mind:

- Establish a rapport and positive communication.
- Respect the confidentiality of the information you have regarding their children.
- Provide reassurance.
- Be open to family input.
- Be compassionate and communicate with families whenever possible.
- The more you need to interact with a family about their child's negative behaviors or performance on school work, the more efforts you will need to make to build a positive rapport with the family. Make special efforts to report positive things whenever they occur.

If you have to talk to the family about a misbehavior their child has exhibited, keep the focus of the discussion on how the behavior is interfering with his or her academic and behavioral progress. When you focus on the child, the family will be far more responsive to supporting you than if you talk about how the child's behavior affects you or the other students in the class. Similarly, keep the focus and language of the discussion on specific behaviors the student is exhibiting rather than attributes or characteristics. For example, instead of saying something like, "Julian is a disrespectful and defiant student," it will be more effective to use a specific example of his behavior. "When Julian says things like, 'Make me,' he is exhibiting defiant behavior. I am concerned that these kinds of statements are getting in the way of his education." Avoid getting defensive if the family is critical of you. Ask a colleague or mentor to join you for a family conference if you are unsure how to proceed. Remember that you are the professional: keep the focus on what can be done to help the child be successful.

Build professional and collaborative relationships with your colleagues.

As a first-year teacher, you are entering a preexisting social structure. Treat everyone with dignity and respect: teachers, administrators, and clerical, custodial, and food service staff. Also recognize that there are formal relationships such as grade-level or departmental colleagues, as well as informal structures of friends and other alliances. In some schools, you may find cliques or groups who do not like or respect other groups. Until you have been on staff for a period of time, be careful not to get caught up in these alliances. Watch to see which relationships and groups will be productive and boost your teaching skills and love of the job, as compared to those that are destructive. Avoid gossip, and don't get pulled into negative, unproductive groups. Administrative teams and principals also have their own styles and strategies to get the job done. It's vitally important that you are aware of their preferred methods and the tone of their professional relationships with colleagues. You are the new kid on the block and need to act with humility while you learn the systems and structures of the school.

Ask questions and be flexible, cooperative, prompt, and optimistic—all professional qualities. Avoid criticizing institutional traditions that you don't understand or that existed before you began teaching. Keep in mind that if you actively work toward building positive relationships with colleagues, they will be more open to planning with you and you will learn more from each other. Volunteering to assist with committees and initiatives can help you build relationships with colleagues, but be careful not to overcommit yourself. If you don't follow through because you are overloaded or are so stressed you are unpleasant to be around, these activities can damage your collegial relationships rather than strengthen them.

As you get to know the staff, seek out mentors—people you feel comfortable going to for advice and assistance. Look for mentors who have a positive and proactive approach rather than those who are highly punitive or negative in their outlook. Seeking collegial assistance is a sign of professional strength, not weakness. This may be most clearly demonstrated by professionals in the field of medicine. When faced with a puzzling situation, most physicians discuss the case with other physicians. Teachers can and should exhibit this same level of collegial problem solving. For example, if you have a student who consistently misbehaves and your attempts to help her improve her behavior have been ineffective, you should not hesitate to ask a fellow teacher for additional ideas, especially if that teacher has had success with the student.

Be an active problem solver. When you face a problem—for example, a student is not behaving responsibly or is not making adequate academic progress—the teacher who is demonstrating professionalism analyzes the problem and takes responsibility for seeking and implementing a solution. A teacher who is not acting professionally tends to blame the problem on someone else or feels that someone else should solve the problem (or both). The teacher who is demonstrating professionalism continues to try various strategies until a solution is found—he or she never gives up. Keep Eleanor Roosevelt's words in mind: "We have never failed unless we have ceased to try."

Your professional and collaborative relationships will also benefit if you respect the confidentiality of both students and colleagues. You should not discuss your students outside school, especially if you live in the community where you teach. In addition, unless you are participating in a school-sponsored problem-solving procedure, avoid talking about school business or the concerns of your coworkers.

For example, imagine that another teacher is not giving you the help and support you need regarding a student both of you teach. The most professional response is to go directly to this person, discuss your concerns, and ask for assistance. It would be highly unprofessional to discuss the problem with other teachers or talk about the problem during a family-teacher conference. Again, look at the medical profession as an example. A physician can and should discuss cases confidentially with colleagues at work. However, it is inappropriate and unprofessional for her to talk about a patient or colleagues at a dinner party. As a teaching professional, you owe your students and fellow staff members the same level of professionalism that they expect and deserve from their doctors. Be aware that in some schools, discussions in the faculty room may border on being unprofessional—you may hear teachers discussing students in a hostile, rude, or sarcastic manner. If this happens in your school, be sure that you are not a contributor. Regardless of the behavior of others, maintain your high level of professional behavior.

Act in a professional manner.

The definition of how to act in a professional manner is somewhat subjective, but a good model for professional behavior is a physician or an attorney. Think about the demeanor you want and expect from your doctor or lawyer. Most of us probably prefer someone who seems knowledgeable, confident, and comfortable but not haughty and arrogant. We are generally uncomfortable with someone who seems hesitant or insecure, doesn't seem to like her job, or complains about her working conditions. We may not trust someone who doesn't make eye contact, and we may find it hard to interact with someone who mumbles when he talks to us.

A teacher should try to project a relaxed and confident manner. You do not need to be relaxed and confident at all times (very few of us are capable of this!), but you should *act* relaxed and confident. In fact, there will probably be times when you are unsure of yourself or unsure of how to handle a situation. While it's not necessary to give the impression that you know what to do when you really don't, do keep in mind that you are a professional. You provide a valuable service to your students and the community, and you can solve any problem—eventually. If you don't know how to handle a situation, avoid appearing panicked or out of control, and don't try to bluff your way through. Ask yourself whether you would rather go to a physician who bluffs and blusters when he is unsure or one who confidently says, "I am unsure about the best course of action, but I will find out." Calmly admit that you don't know the answer or approach, but that you will find out and address it. For example, if a student exhibits a misbehavior that you are unsure how to handle, you could say something like, "Jonathan, that was inappropriate. Take a time-out, and then get back to work. I am going to write down what just happened and I need some time to think about it. I will get back to you in the next twenty minutes so we can talk about what needs to happen next."

Professionalism also includes dependability. As a professional, you need to arrive at work on time, fulfill your various duties (e.g., supervising a bus loading area for two weeks) without needing reminders, attend staff meetings and give your full attention to the proceedings, and complete attendance and grade reports on time.

Present a professional appearance.

Your appearance affects the impression others have of you—perhaps even more than you realize. In addition to making sure that you dress neatly and cleanly, consider the degree of formality most appropriate for your work attire. Although wearing high-powered business suits is not necessary for most teachers, a teacher dressed in baggy sweatpants and a coffee-stained sweater definitely gives the wrong impression—to students, students' families, other teachers, and administrators.

Susan Isaacs, a Safe & Civil Schools trainer, shared a tip she received from a principal: "If you don't change your clothes when you get home from work, you weren't dressed for work."

Carefully select an appropriate level of formality for your school attire. For a physical education teacher who frequently provides demonstrations to students, wearing nice workout clothing is probably perfectly reasonable. However, workout clothes are probably not appropriate for classroom teachers. Specific questions like "Should men always wear a tie?" and "Are casual pants acceptable?" should be answered within the context of your particular school and the community's standards. Be aware that the level of formality can vary significantly by geographic region and district. As a general rule, dress with a level of formality that is typical of the most professional staff in your district, and it is better to be slightly overdressed than too casual. If you are unsure about what attire is considered appropriate, ask your administrator.

Engage in ongoing professional development, including reflecting on your own teaching practices.

Professionals are expected to continually learn and grow in their fields. For example, most physicians do some things differently today than when they started practicing. Professional development requires both keeping up to date on new information in your field and being willing to look at your own behavior with a critical eye. "What am I doing that is working effectively? What is not working effectively?" After identifying strategies and techniques that are not working effectively, the true professional is always looking for a better way—from peers, staff development, professional books, and the research literature. (See exhibit D.1 for more tips.)

The information in this book, along with the self-assessment checklists shown at the end of chapters and provided on the DVD, will help you examine and, as necessary, modify your behavior management practices. In addition, you should work with and learn from colleagues. The Peer Study Worksheets in the appendix B folder on the DVD help facilitate a collaborative approach to professional development. The questions from these worksheets can guide a whole staff, a small study group, or even just you and a partner in discussing the skills and procedures suggested in this book. In these discussions, recognize that there are no dumb questions. Ask—be a lifelong learner and enjoy the adventure you're about to begin!

Exhibit D.1
Tips for the First-Year Teacher

Shelley Jones, reading specialist and coauthor of the Read Well curriculum, offers these tips on collaboration for first-year teachers.

Most of the young or first-year teachers that I've worked with as a mentor or as a supervising teacher expressed great appreciation for my support, help, and collaboration with both the details of running a classroom and big issues such as discipline and lesson plans. Some of the questions these young teachers asked were:

- How and where do I get posters, maps, and other materials to put on my walls?
- How do I use the district computer system for reporting grades?
- What do I do at staff meetings? (Is it okay to grade papers at the meeting?)
- Do I have a budget for printing?
- How do I get copies of assignments for my students?
- What do I do when my students have no materials?
- What do I do when my students need counseling?
- What do I do if I think a student is being abused?

As a result of my experience, I would say the following five things are really important for a first-year teacher:

Request (or find your own) mentor. A mentor is another teacher or someone else in the educational field who can help you plan for your classes, offer tips and advice, answer questions, and provide you with supplemental materials.

Trading observations and evaluations with your mentor can be valuable training. Your mentor can observe you teach and write an evaluation, and you should be asked to do the same for your mentor. Observe, evaluate, and talk with each other as often as possible—perhaps weekly to begin with, and then monthly.

A small number of new teachers seem to think they know it all. I've found they can be the most difficult to help, and yet they often need the most assistance. More than anything else, they need a strong mentor presence.

Attend a Discipline in the Secondary Classroom training. Attend a DSC training prior to the start of the school year. If it's not offered in your district, actively seek out a training opportunity. Take your mentor along with you. If you are unable to attend a training, create your own—ask your mentor to guide you through DSC and encourage less experienced teachers (or other first-year teachers) in your building to form a DSC work group. Use the Peer Study Worksheets available on the DVD as a guide to working through the tasks for each chapter.

Invite your principal into your classroom on a regular basis. Tell your principal that you welcome his or her informal and formal observations. Most inexperienced teachers think I'm crazy when I make this suggestion. However, frequent visits to your classroom allow your principal to become familiar with your teaching style and to know what kinds of training she or he can offer privately or during staff meetings to meet your needs. It's a wonderful feeling to know that your principal is invested in your future and wants you to succeed as a teacher! Also, your comfort level with being observed will increase with every visit.

Get out of your classroom and observe. Whenever possible, take the time (yes, even your prep time) to get out of your own classroom and observe other teachers. There is nothing more powerful than seeing a master teacher at work! Once again, involve your mentor and principal. They should be able to identify master teachers in both your building and your district.

Ask questions. Ask for help. ASK, ASK, ASK! No one knows you need help unless you ask. No question is too silly or dumb. Every question is an opportunity to learn. You will undoubtedly make mistakes in your first year of teaching—turn every one of those mistakes into a learning opportunity. Ask your mentor how you can improve and constantly strive for success.

For More Information

Survival Guide for the First-Year Special Education Teacher by Mary Kemper Cohen, Maureen Gale, and Joyce M. Meyer (1994). This is a great resource for all teachers—special educators, general education teachers, and paraprofessionals—working in traditional or inclusive school settings. It provides easy-to-use suggestions for organizing classrooms, planning and record keeping, getting lessons ready for substitute teachers, building collaborative partnerships, managing stress, and working with parents, administrators, and fellow teachers. Published by Council for Exceptional Children, http://www.cec.sped.org.

A Survival Guide for New Special Educators by Bonnie Billingsley, Mary Brownell, Maya Israel, and Margaret Kamman (2013). This practical book covers the most pressing topics for beginning special educators, based on wide-ranging surveys of new special education teachers across the United States. Includes downloadable forms, templates, and checklists. Available from Jossey-Bass, www.josseybass.com.

Survive and Thrive! A Laminated Reference Card for Special Education Teachers by Maureen Gale, M.Ed. This two-sided card covers topics such as organizing your classroom, ways to improve your delivery of instruction, collaborating with colleagues and parents, and tips on data collection. Published by DayOne Publishing, http://dayonepublishing.com/Educational/S_and_T/index.html.

The Tough Kid New Teacher Book, by Ginger Rhode, William R. Jenson, and Daniel P. Morgan (2009). This easy-to-use manual is full of tips, suggestions, and proven tactics to help first-year teachers thrive. Available from Pacific Northwest Publishing, www.pacificnwpublish.com.

Mapping Discipline in the Secondary Classroom to a Framework for Teaching

The framework for teaching presented by Charlotte Danielson in *Enhancing Professional Practice: A Framework for Teaching* (2007) captures the key concepts shared by members of the profession and thereby provides a way to communicate about excellence in the field. The framework reflects practices that research has shown to be effective. Danielson outlines a number of ways in which this framework can be applied, from preparing new teachers to focusing staff improvement efforts to evaluating the quality of teaching to communicating to the larger community what teachers do. The framework identifies twenty-two components of effective teaching in four domains: Planning and Preparation, Classroom Environment, Instruction, and Professional Responsibilities. Many districts are developing observation systems or even formalized teacher evaluation systems based on this framework. The following table maps the tasks in Discipline in the Secondary Classroom that correspond to distinguished levels of performance for the components in Domain 2: The Classroom Environment. This table can be used within staff development sessions or by individual readers to identify aspects of this book that might prove helpful in achieving professional excellence within Domain 2 of the framework.

Domain 2: The Classroom Environment

Component 2a: Creating an Environment of Respect and Rapport		
Element	Distinguished Level of Performance	Covered in *Discipline in the Secondary Classroom*
Teacher interaction with students	Teacher interactions with students reflect genuine respect and caring for individuals as well as groups of students. Students appear to trust the teacher with sensitive information.	Chapter 8, task 1: Understand the Importance of Building Personal Relationships With Students Chapter 8, task 2: Use Every Possible Opportunity to Provide Each Student With Noncontingent Attention
Student interactions with other students	Students demonstrate genuine caring for one another and monitor one another's treatment of peers, correcting classmates respectfully when needed.	Chapter 5, task 1: Define Clear and Consistent Behavioral Expectations for All Regularly Scheduled Classroom Activities Chapter 5, task 2: Define Clear and Consistent Behavioral Expectations for the Common Transitions, Both Within and Between Activities, That Occur During a Typical School Day Chapter 5, task 3: Develop a Preliminary Plan, and Prepare Lessons for Teaching Your Expectations to Students

Component 2b: Establishing a Culture for Learning		
Element	**Distinguished Level of Performance**	**Covered in** *Discipline in the Secondary Classroom*
Importance of the content	Students demonstrate through their active participation, curiosity, and taking initiative that they value the importance of the content.	Chapter 2, task 2: Design Instruction and Evaluation Procedures That Create a Clear Relationship Between Student Effort and Success Chapter 2, task 3: Establish a System to Provide Students Feedback on Behavior and Effort; Incorporate This Into Your Grading System Chapter 2, task 4: Design Procedures for Students to Receive Feedback on Each Aspect of Their Behavioral and Academic Performance and to Know Their Current Grades
Expectations for learning and achievement	Instructional outcomes, activities and assignments, and classroom interactions convey high expectations for all students. Students appear to have internalized these expectations.	Chapter 2, task 5: Implement Effective Instructional Practices Chapter 2, task 6: Present Desired Tasks to Your Students in a Manner That Will Generate Their Enthusiasm Chapter 1, task 3: Develop and Implement Guidelines for Success

Component 2b (*continued*)

Component 2b: Establishing a Culture for Learning (*continued*)		
Element	**Distinguished Level of Performance**	**Covered in** *Discipline in the Secondary Classroom*
		Chapter 1, task 4: Maintain High Expectations for Students' Academic and Behavioral Performance Chapter 3, task 5: Design Effective, Efficient Procedures for Assigning, Monitoring, and Collecting Student Work
Student pride in work	Students demonstrate attention to detail and take obvious pride in their work, initiating improvements in it by, for example, revising drafts on their own or helping peers.	Chapter 2, task 2: Design Instruction and Evaluation Procedures That Create a Clear Relationship Between Student Effort and Success Chapter 2, task 3: Establish a System to Provide Students Feedback on Behavior and Effort; Incorporate This into Your Grading System Chapter 2, task 4: Design Procedures for Students to Receive Feedback on Each Aspect of Their Behavioral and Academic Performance and to Know Their Current Grades

Component 2c: Managing Classroom Procedures		
Element	**Distinguished Level of Performance**	**Covered in *Discipline in the Secondary Classroom***
Management of instructional groups	Small-group work is well organized, and students are productively engaged at all times, with students assuming responsibility for productivity.	Chapter 3, task 1: Arrange the Schedule of Activities for Each Class Period to Maximize Instructional Time and Responsible Behavior Chapter 3, task 2: Arrange the Physical Space in Your Classroom to Promote Positive Student-Teacher Interactions and Reduce Disruption Chapter 3, task 3: Decide on a Signal You Can Use to Immediately Quiet Your Students and Gain Their Full Attention Chapter 3, task 4: Design Efficient, Effective Procedures for Beginning and Ending the Class Period Chapter 3, task 5: Design Effective, Efficient Procedures for Assigning, Monitoring, and Collecting Student Work Chapter 3, task 6: Manage Independent Work Periods Chapter 7, task 1: Circulate When Possible, and Scan All Sections of the Classroom Continuously

Component 2c (*continued*)

Component 2c: Managing Classroom Procedures (*continued*)		
Element	**Distinguished Level of Performance**	**Covered in *Discipline in the Secondary Classroom***
Management of transitions	Transitions are seamless, with students assuming responsibility in ensuring their efficient operation.	Chapter 5, task 2: Define Clear and Consistent Behavioral Expectations for the Common Transitions, Both Within and Between Activities, That Occur During a Typical School Day
Management of materials and supplies	Routines for handling materials and supplies are seamless, with students assuming some responsibility for smooth operation.	Chapter 3, task 4: Design Efficient, Effective Procedures for Beginning and Ending the Class Period
Performance of noninstructional duties	Systems for performing noninstructional duties are well established, with students assuming considerable responsibility for efficient operation.	Chapter 3, task 4: Design Efficient, Effective Procedures for Beginning and Ending the Class Period
Supervision of volunteers and paraprofessionals	Volunteers and paraprofessionals make a substantive contribution to the classroom environment.	Note: This is not specifically addressed within this book; however, the following tasks could easily be expanded to include supervision of other adults in the classroom: Chapter 5 task 1: Define Clear and Consistent Behavioral Expectations for all Regularly Scheduled Activities. Chapter 7, task 1: Circulate and Scan all Sections of the Classroom Continuously

Component 2d: Managing Student Behavior		
Element	**Distinguished Level of Performance**	**Covered in *Discipline in the Secondary Classroom***
Expectations	Standards of conduct are clear to all students and appear to have been developed with student participation.	Chapter 3, task 4: Design Efficient, Effective Procedures for Beginning and Ending the Class Period Chapter 5, task 1: Define Clear and Consistent Behavioral Expectations for All Regularly Scheduled Classroom Activities Chapter 5, task 2: Define Clear and Consistent Behavioral Expectations for the Common Transitions, Both Within and Between Activities, That Occur During a Typical School Day Chapter 5, task 3: Develop a Preliminary Plan, and Prepare Lessons for Teaching Your Expectations to Students Chapter 6, task 3: Implement Your Plan for the First Day Chapter 6, task 4: Gradually Decrease the Amount of Time You Spend Teaching Expectations Chapter 6, task 5: Mark on Your Planning Calendar Particular Times When You Will Reteach Your Expectations

Component 2d (*continued*)

Component 2d: Managing Student Behavior (*continued*)		
Element	**Distinguished Level of Performance**	**Covered in *Discipline in the Secondary Classroom***
Monitoring of student behavior	Monitoring by teacher is subtle and preventive. Students monitor their own and their peers' behavior, correcting one another respectfully.	Chapter 7, task 1: Circulate When Possible, and Scan All Sections of the Classroom Continuously Chapter 7, task 2: Collect Objective Data about Classroom Behavior, and Adjust Your Management Plan Accordingly
Response to student misbehavior	Teacher response to misbehavior is highly effective and sensitive to students' individual needs, or student behavior is entirely appropriate.	Chapter 4, task 3: Develop a Plan for Correcting Early-Stage Misbehaviors Chapter 4, task 4: Develop Consequences for Committing Rule Violations Chapter 4, task 5: Know When and When Not to Use Disciplinary Referral Chapter 9, task 2: Analyze and, If Needed, Adjust the Strategies You Are Using to Build a Positive Relationship with This Student Chapter 9, task 3: Analyze the Misbehavior and Develop a Function-Based Intervention

Component 2e: Organizing Physical Space		
Element	**Distinguished Level of Performance**	**Covered in *Discipline in the Secondary Classroom***
Safety and accessibility	The classroom is safe, and students themselves ensure that all learning is equally accessible to all students.	Chapter 3, task 2: Arrange the Physical Space in Your Classroom to Promote Positive Student-Teacher Interactions and Reduce Disruption Chapter 5, task 1: Define Clear and Consistent Behavioral Expectations for All Regularly Scheduled Classroom Activities Chapter 5, task 2: Define Clear and Consistent Behavioral Expectations for the Common Transitions, Both Within and Between Activities, That Occur During a Typical School Day
Arrangement of furniture and use of physical resources	Both teacher and students use physical resources easily and skillfully, and students adjust the furniture to advance their learning.	Chapter 3, task 2: Arrange the Physical Space in Your Classroom So That It Promotes Positive Student-Teacher Interactions and Reduce Disruption

Adapted with permission from Danielson, C. (2007). *Enhancing professional practice: A framework for teaching* (2nd ed.). Alexandria, VA: ASCD.

CHAMPS Icons

This third edition of *Discipline in the Secondary Classroom* comes with three sets of icons you can use to display and teach your classroom expectations. The icons were developed to illustrate the CHAMPS expectations, but you can easily adapt them for use with the ACHIEVE acronym as well. The sets are:

Version 1: Graphic. Black-and-white graphic symbols depict expectations (illustrations by Tom Zilis)

Version 2: Sentence Strip. Text-only icons

Version 3: Road Sign. Text-based street signs in different shapes and colors

Thumbnail views of each icon appear on the following pages to help you determine which ones are most appropriate for your classroom. See chapter 4 for ideas on how to use the icons. Note that the downloadable versions of the Road Sign icons are in color, which is not reflected in the thumbnail versions.

Each set of icons is stored in a separate folder, with each numbered to match the CHAMPS expectations listed in the section that follows.

CHAMPS ICON Sets

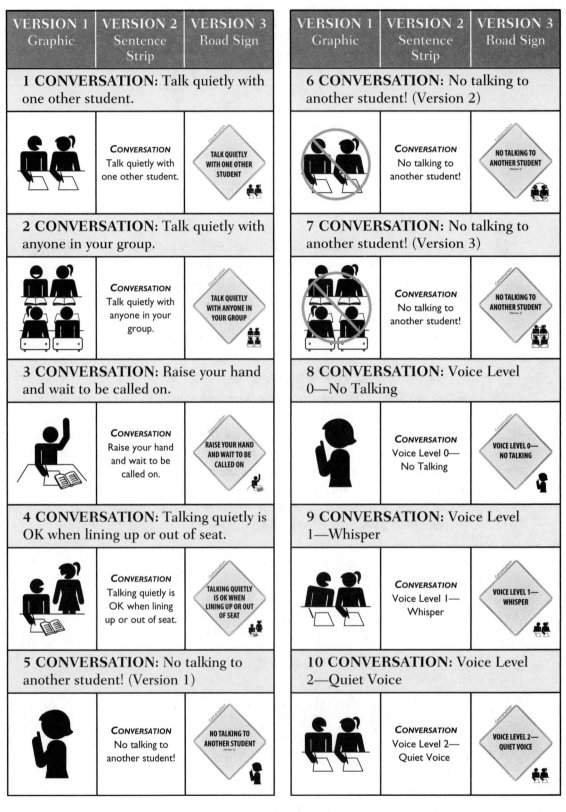

VERSION 1 Graphic	VERSION 2 Sentence Strip	VERSION 3 Road Sign	VERSION 1 Graphic	VERSION 2 Sentence Strip	VERSION 3 Road Sign

1 CONVERSATION: Talk quietly with one other student.

CONVERSATION Talk quietly with one other student. — TALK QUIETLY WITH ONE OTHER STUDENT

6 CONVERSATION: No talking to another student! (Version 2)

CONVERSATION No talking to another student! — NO TALKING TO ANOTHER STUDENT

2 CONVERSATION: Talk quietly with anyone in your group.

CONVERSATION Talk quietly with anyone in your group. — TALK QUIETLY WITH ANYONE IN YOUR GROUP

7 CONVERSATION: No talking to another student! (Version 3)

CONVERSATION No talking to another student! — NO TALKING TO ANOTHER STUDENT

3 CONVERSATION: Raise your hand and wait to be called on.

CONVERSATION Raise your hand and wait to be called on. — RAISE YOUR HAND AND WAIT TO BE CALLED ON

8 CONVERSATION: Voice Level 0—No Talking

CONVERSATION Voice Level 0—No Talking — VOICE LEVEL 0—NO TALKING

4 CONVERSATION: Talking quietly is OK when lining up or out of seat.

CONVERSATION Talking quietly is OK when lining up or out of seat. — TALKING QUIETLY IS OK WHEN LINING UP OR OUT OF SEAT

9 CONVERSATION: Voice Level 1—Whisper

CONVERSATION Voice Level 1—Whisper — VOICE LEVEL 1—WHISPER

5 CONVERSATION: No talking to another student! (Version 1)

CONVERSATION No talking to another student! — NO TALKING TO ANOTHER STUDENT

10 CONVERSATION: Voice Level 2—Quiet Voice

CONVERSATION Voice Level 2—Quiet Voice — VOICE LEVEL 2—QUIET VOICE

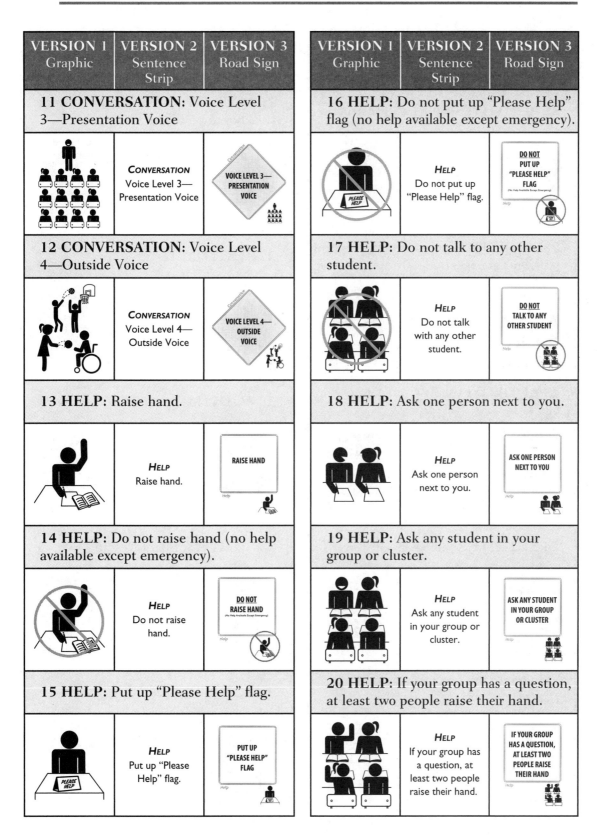

VERSION 1 Graphic	VERSION 2 Sentence Strip	VERSION 3 Road Sign	VERSION 1 Graphic	VERSION 2 Sentence Strip	VERSION 3 Road Sign
11 CONVERSATION: Voice Level 3—Presentation Voice			**16 HELP:** Do not put up "Please Help" flag (no help available except emergency).		
	CONVERSATION Voice Level 3—Presentation Voice	VOICE LEVEL 3—PRESENTATION VOICE		**HELP** Do not put up "Please Help" flag.	DO NOT PUT UP "PLEASE HELP" FLAG (No Help Available Except Emergency)
12 CONVERSATION: Voice Level 4—Outside Voice			**17 HELP:** Do not talk to any other student.		
	CONVERSATION Voice Level 4—Outside Voice	VOICE LEVEL 4—OUTSIDE VOICE		**HELP** Do not talk with any other student.	DO NOT TALK TO ANY OTHER STUDENT
13 HELP: Raise hand.			**18 HELP:** Ask one person next to you.		
	HELP Raise hand.	RAISE HAND		**HELP** Ask one person next to you.	ASK ONE PERSON NEXT TO YOU
14 HELP: Do not raise hand (no help available except emergency).			**19 HELP:** Ask any student in your group or cluster.		
	HELP Do not raise hand.	DO NOT RAISE HAND (No Help Available Except Emergency)		**HELP** Ask any student in your group or cluster.	ASK ANY STUDENT IN YOUR GROUP OR CLUSTER
15 HELP: Put up "Please Help" flag.			**20 HELP:** If your group has a question, at least two people raise their hand.		
	HELP Put up "Please Help" flag.	PUT UP "PLEASE HELP" FLAG		**HELP** If your group has a question, at least two people raise their hand.	IF YOUR GROUP HAS A QUESTION, AT LEAST TWO PEOPLE RAISE THEIR HAND

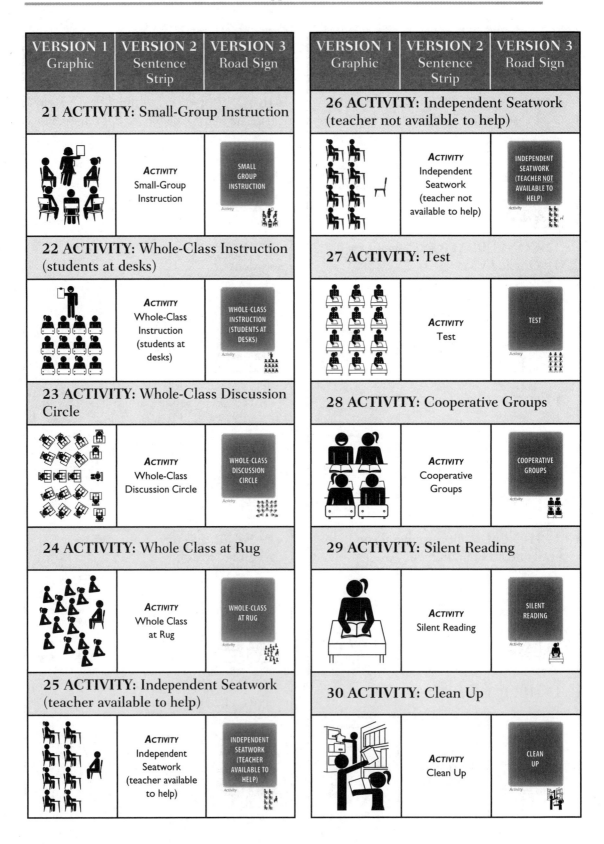

VERSION 1 Graphic	VERSION 2 Sentence Strip	VERSION 3 Road Sign
21 ACTIVITY: Small-Group Instruction		
	ACTIVITY Small-Group Instruction	SMALL GROUP INSTRUCTION
22 ACTIVITY: Whole-Class Instruction (students at desks)		
	ACTIVITY Whole-Class Instruction (students at desks)	WHOLE-CLASS INSTRUCTION (STUDENTS AT DESKS)
23 ACTIVITY: Whole-Class Discussion Circle		
	ACTIVITY Whole-Class Discussion Circle	WHOLE-CLASS DISCUSSION CIRCLE
24 ACTIVITY: Whole Class at Rug		
	ACTIVITY Whole Class at Rug	WHOLE-CLASS AT RUG
25 ACTIVITY: Independent Seatwork (teacher available to help)		
	ACTIVITY Independent Seatwork (teacher available to help)	INDEPENDENT SEATWORK (TEACHER AVAILABLE TO HELP)

VERSION 1 Graphic	VERSION 2 Sentence Strip	VERSION 3 Road Sign
26 ACTIVITY: Independent Seatwork (teacher not available to help)		
	ACTIVITY Independent Seatwork (teacher not available to help)	INDEPENDENT SEATWORK (TEACHER NOT AVAILABLE TO HELP)
27 ACTIVITY: Test		
	ACTIVITY Test	TEST
28 ACTIVITY: Cooperative Groups		
	ACTIVITY Cooperative Groups	COOPERATIVE GROUPS
29 ACTIVITY: Silent Reading		
	ACTIVITY Silent Reading	SILENT READING
30 ACTIVITY: Clean Up		
	ACTIVITY Clean Up	CLEAN UP

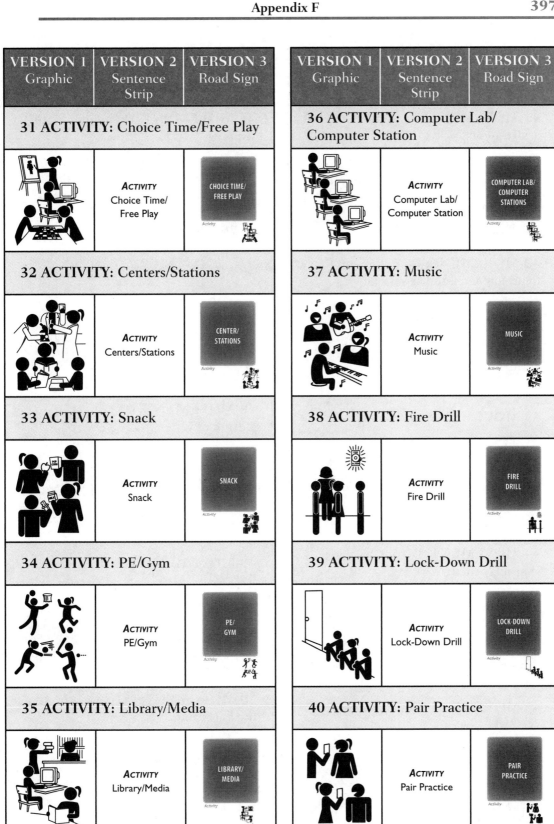

VERSION 1 Graphic	VERSION 2 Sentence Strip	VERSION 3 Road Sign	VERSION 1 Graphic	VERSION 2 Sentence Strip	VERSION 3 Road Sign
31 ACTIVITY: Choice Time/Free Play			**36 ACTIVITY: Computer Lab/ Computer Station**		
	ACTIVITY Choice Time/ Free Play	CHOICE TIME/ FREE PLAY		*ACTIVITY* Computer Lab/ Computer Station	COMPUTER LAB/ COMPUTER STATIONS
32 ACTIVITY: Centers/Stations			**37 ACTIVITY: Music**		
	ACTIVITY Centers/Stations	CENTER/ STATIONS		*ACTIVITY* Music	MUSIC
33 ACTIVITY: Snack			**38 ACTIVITY: Fire Drill**		
	ACTIVITY Snack	SNACK		*ACTIVITY* Fire Drill	FIRE DRILL
34 ACTIVITY: PE/Gym			**39 ACTIVITY: Lock-Down Drill**		
	ACTIVITY PE/Gym	PE/ GYM		*ACTIVITY* Lock-Down Drill	LOCK-DOWN DRILL
35 ACTIVITY: Library/Media			**40 ACTIVITY: Pair Practice**		
	ACTIVITY Library/Media	LIBRARY/ MEDIA		*ACTIVITY* Pair Practice	PAIR PRACTICE

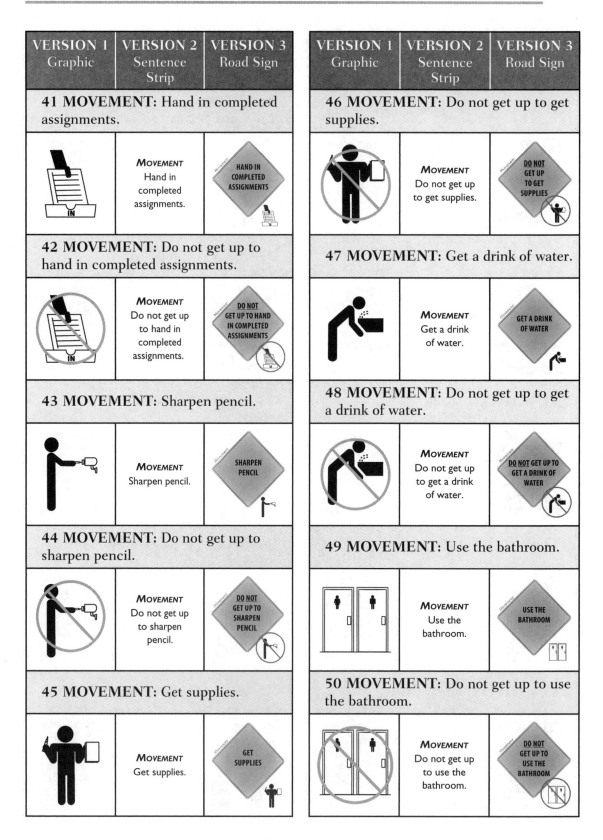

VERSION 1 Graphic	VERSION 2 Sentence Strip	VERSION 3 Road Sign

41 MOVEMENT: Hand in completed assignments.

MOVEMENT Hand in completed assignments. — HAND IN COMPLETED ASSIGNMENTS

42 MOVEMENT: Do not get up to hand in completed assignments.

MOVEMENT Do not get up to hand in completed assignments. — DO NOT GET UP TO HAND IN COMPLETED ASSIGNMENTS

43 MOVEMENT: Sharpen pencil.

MOVEMENT Sharpen pencil. — SHARPEN PENCIL

44 MOVEMENT: Do not get up to sharpen pencil.

MOVEMENT Do not get up to sharpen pencil. — DO NOT GET UP TO SHARPEN PENCIL

45 MOVEMENT: Get supplies.

MOVEMENT Get supplies. — GET SUPPLIES

VERSION 1 Graphic	VERSION 2 Sentence Strip	VERSION 3 Road Sign

46 MOVEMENT: Do not get up to get supplies.

MOVEMENT Do not get up to get supplies. — DO NOT GET UP TO GET SUPPLIES

47 MOVEMENT: Get a drink of water.

MOVEMENT Get a drink of water. — GET A DRINK OF WATER

48 MOVEMENT: Do not get up to get a drink of water.

MOVEMENT Do not get up to get a drink of water. — DO NOT GET UP TO GET A DRINK OF WATER

49 MOVEMENT: Use the bathroom.

MOVEMENT Use the bathroom. — USE THE BATHROOM

50 MOVEMENT: Do not get up to use the bathroom.

MOVEMENT Do not get up to use the bathroom. — DO NOT GET UP TO USE THE BATHROOM

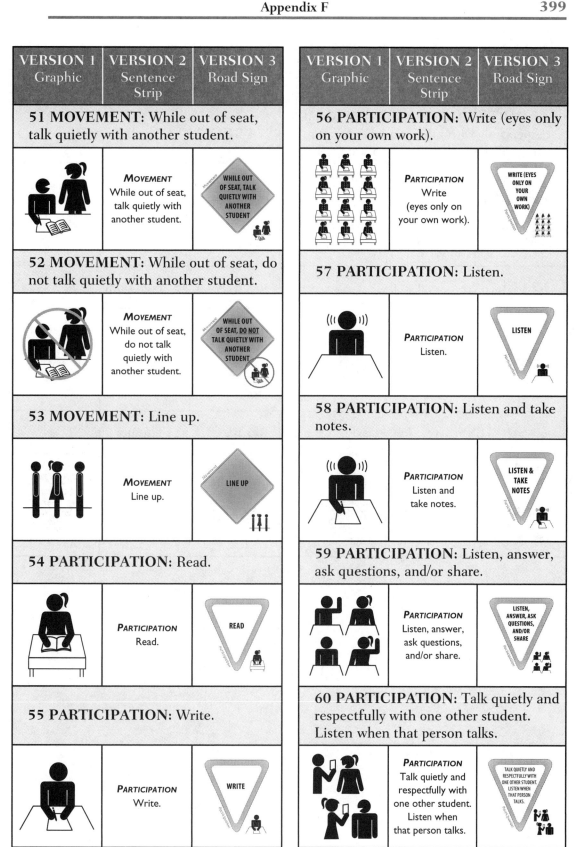

VERSION 1 Graphic	**VERSION 2** Sentence Strip	**VERSION 3** Road Sign

51 MOVEMENT: While out of seat, talk quietly with another student.

MOVEMENT While out of seat, talk quietly with another student.

WHILE OUT OF SEAT, TALK QUIETLY WITH ANOTHER STUDENT

52 MOVEMENT: While out of seat, do not talk quietly with another student.

MOVEMENT While out of seat, do not talk quietly with another student.

WHILE OUT OF SEAT, DO NOT TALK QUIETLY WITH ANOTHER STUDENT

53 MOVEMENT: Line up.

MOVEMENT Line up.

LINE UP

54 PARTICIPATION: Read.

PARTICIPATION Read.

READ

55 PARTICIPATION: Write.

PARTICIPATION Write.

WRITE

56 PARTICIPATION: Write (eyes only on your own work).

PARTICIPATION Write (eyes only on your own work).

WRITE (EYES ONLY ON YOUR OWN WORK)

57 PARTICIPATION: Listen.

PARTICIPATION Listen.

LISTEN

58 PARTICIPATION: Listen and take notes.

PARTICIPATION Listen and take notes.

LISTEN & TAKE NOTES

59 PARTICIPATION: Listen, answer, ask questions, and/or share.

PARTICIPATION Listen, answer, ask questions, and/or share.

LISTEN, ANSWER, ASK QUESTIONS, AND/OR SHARE

60 PARTICIPATION: Talk quietly and respectfully with one other student. Listen when that person talks.

PARTICIPATION Talk quietly and respectfully with one other student. Listen when that person talks.

TALK QUIETLY AND RESPECTFULLY WITH ONE OTHER STUDENT. LISTEN WHEN THAT PERSON TALKS.

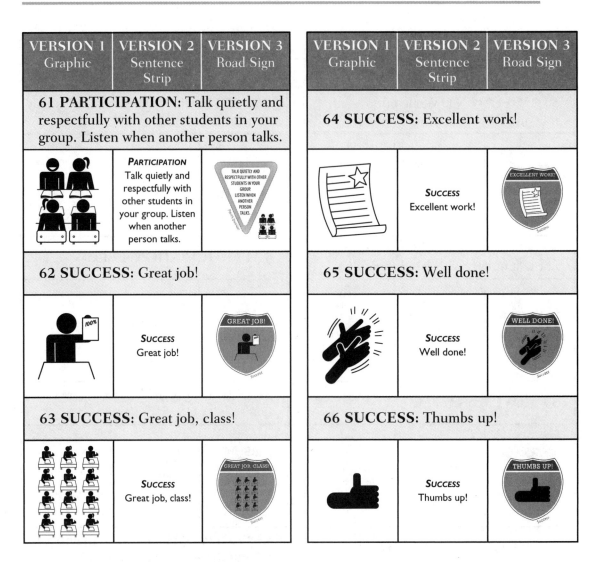

VERSION 1 Graphic	VERSION 2 Sentence Strip	VERSION 3 Road Sign
61 PARTICIPATION: Talk quietly and respectfully with other students in your group. Listen when another person talks.		
	PARTICIPATION Talk quietly and respectfully with other students in your group. Listen when another person talks.	TALK QUIETLY AND RESPECTFULLY WITH OTHER STUDENTS IN YOUR GROUP LISTEN WHEN ANOTHER PERSON TALKS.
62 SUCCESS: Great job!		
	SUCCESS Great job!	GREAT JOB!
63 SUCCESS: Great job, class!		
	SUCCESS Great job, class!	GREAT JOB, CLASS!

VERSION 1 Graphic	VERSION 2 Sentence Strip	VERSION 3 Road Sign
64 SUCCESS: Excellent work!		
	SUCCESS Excellent work!	EXCELLENT WORK!
65 SUCCESS: Well done!		
	SUCCESS Well done!	WELL DONE!
66 SUCCESS: Thumbs up!		
	SUCCESS Thumbs up!	THUMBS UP!

Icons are provided in PDF format. You can print them out on 8.5″ × 11″ sheets of paper. You can also use the free Adobe Reader to resize them and print on 11″ × 17″ paper if your printer accommodates that size sheet. To do this, open the icon file in Adobe Reader. From the File menu, select Page Setup. Select your desired paper size from the pull-down list in the Paper Size window. Then start the Print command. Set Page Scaling to Fit to Printable window. This will enlarge or reduce the icon sheet to fit your selected paper size.

If you do not have access to a graphics program such as Paint Shop Pro, Publisher, or Photoshop, you can use Adobe Reader to copy the icons to insert into a Word or PowerPoint file. To determine what version of Reader you are using, select About Adobe Reader from the Adobe Reader menu bar or download the most recent version at http://get.adobe.com/reader/. Then follow the instructions below for your version.

Adobe Reader 8 and earlier

Select the Snapshot tool from the Select & Zoom menu in the Tools menu. The Snapshot tool lets you draw a window with your cursor around the part of the PDF file you want to copy and paste. As soon as you complete the window, Adobe Reader automatically copies its contents. You can then paste into your Word or PowerPoint file and resize as needed.

Adobe Reader 9

Select the Snapshot tool from the Select & Zoom menu in the Tools menu, as in Reader 8. Draw a window with your cursor around the part of the PDF file you want to copy and paste. As soon as you complete the window, Adobe Reader automatically copies its contents. You can now paste directly into a Word or PowerPoint file. To paste into another PDF, select Paste Clipboard Image as Stamp Tool from the Tools/Comments & Markup menu.

Adobe Reader 10

Select Take a Snapshot in the Edit menu. The Snapshot tool lets you draw a window with your cursor around the part of the PDF file you want to copy and paste. As soon as you complete the window, Adobe Reader automatically copies its contents and displays a message: the selected area has been copied. Click OK on the message box. You can now paste directly into a Word or PowerPoint file.

To paste into another PDF, go to the View menu and select Drawing Markups in the Comment fly-out menu. This will display a panel at the right side of the Reader window. Select Comment at the top of the box. Then select the arrow next to Annotations to display the Annotations tools. Select the down arrow next to the rubber stamp icon. At the bottom of the menu that appears, select Paste Clipboard Image as Stamp Tool. That will insert the image you copied from the first PDF. Once you paste the icon, you can use grips to resize and reposition it.

Icons that you paste into a PDF are inserted as markups. When you print, be sure to select Print Document and Markups in the Print dialog box so that the icons print. Be careful when pasting icons into a PDF template that contains fillable fields. If the icon is entirely covered by a fillable field, you won't be able to select it to resize it.

References

Abramowitz, A. J., O'Leary, S. G., & Futtersak, M. W. (1988). The relative impact of long and short reprimands on children's off-task behavior in the classroom. *Behavior Therapy, 29*(2), 243–247.

Acker, M. M., & O'Leary, S. G. (1988). Effects of consistent and inconsistent feedback on inappropriate child behavior. *Behavior Therapy, 19*(4), 619–624.

Akin-Little, K., Eckert, T., & Lovett, B. (2004). Extrinsic reinforcement in the classroom: Bribery or best practice. *School Psychology Review, 33*, 344–362.

Alberto, P. A., & Troutman, A. C. (2006). *Applied behavior analysis for teachers* (7th ed.). Upper Saddle River, NJ: Merrill/Prentice Hall.

Anderson, L., Evertson, C., & Emmer, E. (1980). Dimensions in classroom management derived from recent research. *Journal of Curriculum Studies, 12*, 343–356.

Archer, A., & Gleason, M. (2003). *Advanced skills for school success: Modules 1 through 4*. North Billerica, MA: Curriculum Associates.

Archer, A., Gleason, M., & Vachon, V. (2005a). *REWARDS (Reading excellence: Word attack and rate development strategies)*. Longmont, CO: Sopris West.

Archer, A., Gleason, M., & Vachon, V. (2005b). *REWARDS PLUS*. Longmont, CO: Sopris West.

Archer, A., & Hughes, C. (2010). *Explicit instruction*. New York: Guilford Press.

Assor, A., & Connell, J. P. (1992). The validity of students' self-reports as measures of performance-affecting self-appraisals. In D. H. Schunk & J. Meece (Eds.), *Student perceptions in the classroom* (pp. 25–46). Mahwah, NJ: Erlbaum.

Babkie, A. (2006). 20 ways to be proactive in managing classroom behavior. *Intervention in School and Clinic, 41*, 184–187.

Baer, D. M. (1999). *How to plan for generalization*. Austin, TX: Pro-Ed.

Baer, D. M., Wolf, M. M., & Risley, T. R. (1968). Some current dimensions of applied behavior analysis. *Journal of Applied Behavior Analysis, 1*(1), 91–97.

Baer, G. (1998). School discipline in the United States: Prevention, correction, and long-term social development. *School Psychology Review, 27*, 14–32.

Barbetta, P., Norona, K., & Bicard, D. (2005). Classroom behavior management: A dozen common mistakes and what to do instead. *Preventing School Failure, 49*, 11–19.

Baron, E. B. (1992). *Discipline strategies for teachers*. Bloomington, IN: Phi Delta Kappa.

Beaman, R., & Wheldall, K. (2000). Teachers' use of approval and disapproval in the classroom. *Educational Psychology, 20*, 431–446.

Beck, R. (1997). *Project RIDE: Responding to individual differences in education*. Longmont, CO: Sopris West.

Becker, W. C., & Engelmann, S. (1971). *Teaching: A course in applied psychology*. Columbus, OH: Science Research Associates.

Bell, K. (1998). In the beginning: Teacher created a positive learning environment. *Teaching Elementary Physical Education, 9*, 12–14.

Biglan, A. (1995). Translating what we know about the context of antisocial behavior into a lower prevalence of such behavior. *Journal of Applied Behavior Analysis, 28*, 479–492.

Borich, G. (2004). *Effective teaching methods* (5th ed.). Upper Saddle River, NJ: Pearson/Merrill/Prentice Hall.

Broden, M., Bruce, C., Mitchell, M., Carter, V., & Hall, R. (1970). Effects of teacher attention on attending behavior of two boys at adjacent desks. *Journal of Applied Behavior Analysis, 3*, 199–203.

Brophy, J. (1981). Teacher praise: A functional analysis. *Review of Educational Research, 51*, 5–32.

Brophy, J. (1983). Conceptualizing student motivation. *Educational Psychologist, 18*, 200–215.

Brophy, J. (1996). *Teaching problem students*. New York: Guilford Press.

Brophy, J. (1998). *Failure syndrome students*. Champaign, IL: University of Illinois. (ERIC Document Reproduction Service No. ED419625)

Brophy, J. E., & Good, T. L. (1986). Teacher behavior and student achievement. In M. C. Whitrock (Ed.), *Handbook of research on teaching* (3rd ed., pp. 328–375). New York, NY: Macmillan.

Brown, T. (1998). Effective school research and student behavior. *Southeast/South Central Education Cooperative Fourth Retreat: Making a difference in student behavior*. Lexington, KY.

Burnette, J. (1999). *Critical behaviors and strategies for teaching culturally diverse students*. Reston, VA: ERIC Clearinghouse on Disabilities and Gifted Education. (ERIC Document Reproduction Service No. ED435147)

Cameron, J., Banko, K. M., & Pierce, W. D. (2001). Pervasive negative effects of rewards on intrinsic motivation: The myth continues. *Behavior Analyst, 24*, 1–44.

Cameron, J., & Pierce, W. (1994). Reinforcement, reward, and intrinsic motivation: A meta-analysis. *Review of Educational Research, 64*, 363–423.

Caprara, G., Barbaranelli, C., Pastorelli, C., Bandura, A., & Zimbardo, P. (2000). Prosocial foundations of children's academic achievement. *Psychological Science, 11*, 302–306.

Carr, E. (1993). Behavior analysis is not ultimately about behavior. *Behavior Analyst, 16*, 47–49.

Carr, E., & Durand, V. (1985). Reducing behavior problems through functional communication training. *Journal of Applied Behavior Analysis, 18*, 111–126.

Carr, E., Newsom, C., & Binkoff, J. (1980). Escape as a factor in the aggressive behavior of two retarded children. *Journal of Applied Behavior Analysis, 13*, 101–117.

Carr, E., Taylor, J., & Robinson, S. (1991). The effects of severe behavior problems in children on the teaching behavior of adults. *Journal of Applied Behavior Analysis, 3*, 523–535.

Catalano, R., Loeber, R., & McKinney, K. (1999). *School and community interventions to prevent serious and violent offending*. Washington, DC: U.S. Department of Justice, Office of Juvenile Justice and Delinquency Prevention.

Chance, P. (1998). *First course in applied behavior analysis*. Belmont, CA: Brooks/Cole.

Chandler, L., & Dahlquist, C. (2002). *Functional assessment*. Upper Saddle River, NJ: Merrill/Prentice Hall.

Christenson, S., & Godber, Y. (2001). Enhancing constructive family-school connections. In J. N. Hughes, A. M. LaGreca, & J. C. Conley (Eds.), *Handbook of psychological services for children and adolescents* (pp. 455–476). New York, NY: Oxford University Press.

Christenson, S., Reschly, A., Appleton, J., Berman-Young, S., Spanjers, D., & Varro, P. (2008). Best practices in fostering student engagement. In A. Thomas & J. Grimes (Eds.), *Best practices in school psychology V* (pp. 1099–1119). Bethesda, MD: National Association of School Psychologists.

Clarfield, J., & Stoner, G. (2005). The effects of computerized reading instruction on the academic performance of students identified with ADHD. *School Psychology Review, 34*, 246–254.

Cole, J., & Kupersmidt, J. (1983). A behavioral analysis of emerging social status in boys' groups. *Child Development, 54*, 1400–1416.

Colvin, G., & Sugai, G. (1988). Proactive strategies for managing social behavior problems: An instructional approach. *Education and Treatment of Children, 11*, 341–348.

Colvin, G., Sugai, G., Good, R. H., III,, & Lee, Y. (1997). Using active supervision and precorrection to improve transition behaviors in an elementary school. *School Psychology Quarterly, 12*, 344–361.

Colvin, G., Sugai, G., & Patching, B. (1993). Pre-correction: An instructional approach for managing predictable problem behaviors. *Intervention in School and Clinic, 28*, 143–150.

Conroy, M., Sutherland, K., Snyder, A., & Marsh, S. (2008, July/August). Classwide interventions: Effective instruction makes a difference. *Teaching Exceptional Children*, 24–30.

Cooper, J. O., Heron, T. E., & Heward, W. L. (2007). *Applied behavior analysis* (2nd ed.). Upper Saddle River, NJ: Pearson.

Copeland, S., & Hughes, C. (2002). Effects of goal setting on task performance of persons with mental retardation. *Education and Training in Mental Retardation and Developmental Disabilities, 37,* 40–54.

Cotton, K. (1999). *Research you can use to improve results* (4th ed.). Alexandra, VA: Association for Supervision and Curriculum Development.

Council for Exceptional Children. (1987). *Academy for effective instruction: Working with mildly handicapped students*. Reston, VA: Author.

Covington, M. (2000). Goal theory, motivation, and school achievement: An integrative review. *Annual Review of Psychology, 51,* 171–200.

Crone, D., & Horner, R. (2003). *Building positive behavior support systems in schools: Functional Behavioral Assessment*. New York, NY: Guilford Press.

Danielson, C. (2007). *Enhancing professional practice: A framework for teaching* (2nd ed.). Alexandria, VA: ASCD.

Darch, C., & Kame'enui, E. (2004). *Instructional classroom management: A proactive approach to behavior management*. Upper Saddle River, NJ: Pearson/Prentice Hall.

Dawson-Rodrigues, K., Lavay, B., Butt, K., & Lacourse, M. (1997). A plan to reduce transition time in physical education. *Journal of Physical Education, Recreation and Dance, 68,* 30–34.

Delquadri, J., Greenwood, C., Whorton, D., Carta, J., & Hall, R. (1986). Classwide peer tutoring. *Exceptional Children, 52,* 535–542.

Deno, S. (1985). The importance of goal ambitiousness and goal mastery to student achievement. *Exceptional Children, 52,* 63–71.

Deno, S. L., Espin, C. A., & Fuchs, L. S. (2002). Evaluation strategies for preventing and remediating basic skill deficits. In M. R. Shinn, H. M. Walker, & G. Stoner (Eds.), *Interventions for academic and behavior problems II: Preventive and remedial approaches*. Bethesda, MD: National Association of School Psychologists.

De Pry, R. L., & Sugai, G. (2002). The effect of active supervision and pre-correction on minor behavioral incidents in a sixth grade general education classroom. *Journal of Behavioral Education, 11,* 255–264.

Deshler, D. D., Schumaker, J. B., Lenz, B. K., Bulgren, J. A., Hock, M. F., Knight, J., & Ehren, B. J. (2001). Ensuring content-area learning by secondary students with learning disabilities. *Learning Disabilities Research and Practice, 16*(2), 96–108.

Detrich, R. (1999). Increasing treatment fidelity by matching interventions to contextual variables within the educational setting. *School Psychology Review, 28,* 608–620.

Dishion, T. J., & Stormshak, E. A. (2007). *Intervening in children's lives: An ecological, family-centered approach to mental health care*. Washington, DC: American Psychological Association.

Ellis, E. (1992). Perspective on adolescents with learning disabilities. In E. S. Ellis (Ed.), *Teaching the learning disabled adolescent: Strategies and methods*. Denver, CO: Love Publishing Co.

Ellis, E., & Worthington, L. (1994). *Research synthesis on effective teaching principles and the design of quality tools for educators* (Tech. Rep. No. 5). National Center to Improve the Tools of Educators, University of Oregon.

Emmer, E., & Evertson, C. (1981, January). Synthesis of research on classroom management. *Educational Leadership*, 342–347.

Emmer, E., Evertson, C., & Anderson, L. (1980). Effective classroom management at the beginning of the school year. *Elementary School Journal, 80,* 219–231.

Emmer, E. T., Evertson, C. M., & Worsham, M. E. (2002). *Classroom management for secondary teachers* (6th ed.). Needham Heights, MA: Allyn & Bacon.

Esler, A., Godber, Y., & Christenson, S. (2008). Best practices in supporting school-family partnerships. In A. Thomas & J. Grimes (Eds.), *Best practices in school psychology V* (pp. 917–936). Bethesda, MD: National Association of School Psychologists.

Evans, G., & Lowell, B. (1979). Design modification in an open-plan school. *Journal of Educational Psychology, 71,* 41–49.

Evertson, C., & Emmer, E. (1982). Effective management at the beginning of the school year in junior high classes. *Journal of Educational Psychology, 74,* 485–498.

Evertson, C., Emmer, E., & Worsham, M. (2003). *Classroom management for elementary teachers* (6th ed.). Boston: Allyn & Bacon.

Fairbanks, S., Sugai, G., Guardino, D., & Lathrop, M. (2007). Response to intervention: Examining classroom behavior supports in second grade. *Council for Exceptional Children, 73,* 288–310.

Farlow, L., & Snell, M. (1994). *Making the most of student performance data.* Washington, DC: American Association on Mental Retardation.

Farmer, T. W., Goforth, J., Hives, J., Aaron, A., Hunter, R., & Sigmatto, A. (2006). Competence enhancement behavior management. *Preventing School Failure, 50,* 39–44.

Feather, N. T. (Ed.). (1982). *Expectations and actions.* Mahwah, NJ: Erlbaum.

Ferguson, E., & Houghton, S. (1992). The effects of contingent teacher praise, as specified by Canter's assertive discipline programme, on children's on-task behaviour. *Educational Studies, 18,* 83–93.

Fielding, L., Kerr, N., & Rosier, P. (2007). *Annual growth for all students, catch-up growth for those who are behind.* Kennewick, WA: New Foundation Press.

Fisher, C., Berliner, D., Filby, N., Marliave, R., Cahen, L., & Dishaw, M. (1980). Teaching behaviors, academic learning time, and student achievement: An overview. In C. Denham & A. Lieberman (Eds.), *Time to learn.* Washington, DC: National Institute of Education.

Freeland, J., & Noell, G. (1999). Maintaining accurate math responses in elementary school students: The effects of delayed intermittent reinforcement and programming common stimuli. *Journal of Applied Behavior Analysis, 32,* 211–215.

Freer, P., & Watson, T. S. (1999). A comparison of parent and teacher acceptability ratings of behavioral and conjoint behavioral consultation. *School Psychology Review, 28,* 672–684.

Fuchs, L. S., Bahr, C. M., & Rieth, H. J. (1989). Effects of goal structures and performance contingencies on the math performance of adolescents with learning disabilities. *Journal of Learning Disabilities, 22,* 554–560.

Fuchs, L. S., Fuchs, D., & Deno, S. L. (1985). Importance of goal ambitiousness and goal mastery to student achievement. *Exceptional Children, 52,* 63–71.

Gettinger, M., & Ball, C. (2008). Best practices in increasing academic engaged time. In A. Thomas & J. Grimes (Eds.), *Best practices in school psychology V* (pp. 1043–1058). Bethesda, MD: National Association of School Psychologists.

Gettinger, M., & Stoiber, K. (1998). Excellence in teaching: Review of instructional and environmental variables. In C. Reynolds & T. Gutkin (Eds.), *Handbook of school psychology* (3rd ed., pp. 933–958). New York, NY: Wiley.

Good, R., & Brophy, J. (2000). *Looking in classrooms* (8th ed.). New York, NY: Longman.

Gortmaker, V., Warnes, E. D., & Sheridan, S. M. (2004). Conjoint behavioral consultation: Involving parents and teachers in the treatment of a child with selective mutism. *Proven Practice, 5,* 66–72.

Gottfried, A. E. (1983). Intrinsic motivation in young children. *Young Children, 39,* 64–73.

Greenwood, C. R., Hops, H., Delquadri, J., & Guild, J. (1974). Group contingencies for group consequences in classroom management: A further analysis. *Journal of Applied Behavior Analysis, 7,* 413–425.

Gresham, F. M. (1998). Social skills training with children. In T. S. Watson & F. M. Gresham (Eds.), *Handbook of child behavior therapy* (pp. 475–497). New York, NY: Plenum.

Gresham, F. M., Watson, S. T., & Skinner, C. H. (2001). Functional behavioral assessment: Principles, procedures, and future directions. *School Psychology Review, 30,* 156–172.

Grimes, L. (1981). Learned helplessness and attribution theory: Redefining children's learning problems. *Learning Disability Quarterly, 4,* 92–100.

Gunter, P., Hummel, J., & Venn, M. (1998). Are effective academic practices used to teach students with behavior disorders? *Beyond Behavior, 9,* 5–11.

Gunter, P. L., & Jack, S. L. (1993). Lag sequential analysis as a tool for functional analysis of student disruptive behavior in classrooms. *Journal of Emotional and Behavioral Disorders, 1,* 138–149.

Hall, R. V., & Hall, M. C. (1980). *How to select reinforcers.* Lawrence, KS: H&H Enterprises.

Hall, R. V., Lund, D., & Jackson, D. (1968). Effects of teacher attention on study behavior. *Journal of Applied Behavior Analysis, 1,* 1–12.

Hamre, B. K., & Pianta, R. C. (2001). Early teacher-child relationships and the trajectory of children's school outcomes through eighth grade. *Child Development, 72,* 652–638.

Harlan, J. C. (2002). *Behavior management strategies for teachers: Achieving instructional effectiveness, student success, and student motivation—every teacher and any student can!* Springfield, IL: Charles C Thomas.

Harniss, M. K., Stein, M., & Carnine, D. (2002). Promoting mathematics achievement. In M. R. Shinn, H. M. Walker, & G. Stoner (Eds.), *Interventions for academic and behavior problems II: Preventive and remedial approaches* (pp. 571–587). Bethesda, MD: National Association of School Psychologists.

Henderson, A., & Mapp, K. (2002). *A new wave of evidence: The impact of school, family, and community connections on student achievement.* Austin, TX: National Center for Family and Community Connections with Schools, Southwest Educational Development Laboratory.

Henderson, H. S., Jenson, W. R., & Erken, N. (1986). Variable internal reinforcement for increasing on-task behavior in classrooms. *Education and Treatment of Children, 9,* 250–263.

Hintze, J. M., Volpe, R. J., & Shapiro, E. S. (2002). Best practices in the systematic direct observation of student behavior. In A. Thomas & J. Grimes (Eds.), *Best practices in school psychology IV.* Washington, DC: National Association of School Psychologists.

Horcones, R. (1992). Natural reinforcements: A way to improve education. *Journal of Applied Behavior Analysis, 25,* 71–75.

Horner, R., Carr, E., Halle, J., McGee, G., Odom, S., & Wolery, M. (2005). The use of single-subject research to identify evidence-based practice in special education. *Exceptional Children, 71,* 165–179.

Horner, R. H., Vaughn, B. J., Day, H. M., & Ard, W. R. (1996). The relationship between setting events and problem behavior: Expanding our understanding of behavioral support. In L. Koegel, R. L. Koegel, & G. Dunlap (Eds.), *Positive behavioral support: Including people with difficult behavior in the community* (pp. 381–402). Baltimore, MD: Paul Brookes.

Howell, K. W., & Nolet, V. (2000). *Curriculum-based evaluation: Teaching and decision making.* Belmont, CA: Wadsworth/Thomson Learning.

Hudson, P., & Miller, S. P. (2006). *Designing and implementing mathematics instruction for students with diverse learning needs.* Boston: Allyn and Bacon.

Huston-Stein, A., Friedrich-Cofer, L. & Susman, E. J. (1977). The relation of classroom structure to social behavior, imaginative plan, and self-regulation of economically disadvantaged children. *Child Development, 48,* 908–916.

Iwata, B., Dorsey, M., Slifer, K., Bauman, K., & Richman, G. (1994). Toward a functional analysis of self-injury. *Journal of Applied Behavior Analysis, 27,* 197–209.

Iwata, B. A., Smith, R. G., & Michael, J. (2000). Current research on the influence of establishing operations on behavior in applied settings. *Journal of Applied Behavior Analysis, 33,* 411–418.

Jack, S., Shores, R., Denny, R., Gunter, P., DeBriere, T., & DePaepe, P. (1996). An analysis of the relationship of teachers' reported use of classroom management strategies on types of classroom interactions. *Journal of Behavioral Education, 6,* 67–87.

Jenson, W. R., Rhode, G., & Reavis, H. K. (2009). *The tough kid tool box.* Eugene, OR: Pacific Northwest Publishing.

Johnson, L., Graham, S., & Harris, K. (1997). The effects of goal setting and self-instruction on learning a reading comprehension strategy: A study of students with learning disabilities. *Journal of Learning Disabilities, 30,* 80–91.

Johnston, J., & Pennypacker, H. (1993). *Strategies for human behavioral research.* Hillsdale, NJ: Erlbaum.

Jones, V., & Jones, L. (2004). *Comprehensive classroom management: Creating positive learning environments and solving problems* (7th ed.). Needham Heights, MA: Allyn & Bacon.

Kame'enui, E. J., Carnine, D. W., Dixon, R. C., Simmons, D. C., & Coyne, M. D. (2002). *Effective teaching strategies that accommodate diverse learners* (2nd ed.). Upper Saddle River, NJ: Merrill/Prentice Hall.

Kame'enui, E. J., & Simmons, D. C. (1990). *Designing instructional strategies: The prevention of academic learning problems.* Englewood Cliffs, NJ: Macmillan.

Kauffman, J. (2005). *Characteristics of emotional and behavioral disorders of children and youth* (8th ed.). Upper Saddle River, NJ: Merrill/Prentice Hall.

Kazdin, A. (1987). *Conduct disorders in childhood and adolescence.* London, UK: Sage.

Kazdin, A. (2001). *Behavior modification in applied settings* (6th ed.). Belmont, CA: Wadsworth.

Kazdin, A., & Bootzin, R. (1972). The token economy: An evaluative review. *Journal of Applied Behavior Analysis, 5,* 343–372.

Keith, T., Keith, P., Quirk, K., Sperduto, J., Santillo, S., & Killings, S. (1998). Longitudinal effects of parent involvement on high school grades: Similarities and differences across gender and ethnic groups. *Journal of School Psychology, 36,* 335–363.

Keogh, B. (2003). *Temperament in the classroom: Understanding individual differences.* Baltimore, MD: Paul Brookes.

Kerr, J., & Nelson, C. (2002). *Strategies for addressing behavior problems in the classroom* (4th ed.). Upper Saddle River, NJ: Merrill/Prentice Hall.

Kounin, J. (1970). *Discipline and group management in classrooms.* New York, NY: Holt, Rinehart, & Winston.

Lalli, J. S., Vollmer, T. R., Progar, P. R., Wright, C., Borrero, J., Daniel, D., Hoffner Bartohold, C., et al. (1999). Competition between positive and negative reinforcement in the treatment of escape behavior. *Journal of Applied Behavior Analysis, 32,* 285–296.

Lam, T.C.M. (1995). *Fairness in performance assessment.* Greensboro, NC: ERIC Clearinghouse on Counseling and Student Services. (ERIC Document Reproduction Service No. ED391982)

Lampi, A. R., Fenty, N. S., & Beaunae, V. (2005). Making the three P's easier: Praise, proximity, and precorrection. *Beyond Behavior, 15,* 8–12.

Langland, S., Lewis-Palmer, T., & Sugai, G. (1998). Teaching respect in the classroom: An instructional approach. *Journal of Behavioral Education, 8,* 245–262.

Laraway, S., Snycerski, S., Michael, J., & Poling, A. (2003). Motivating operations and terms to describe them: Some further refinements. *Journal of Applied Behavior Analysis, 36,* 407–414.

Lembke, E., & Stormont, M. (2005). Using research-based practices to support students with diverse needs in general education settings. *Psychology in the Schools, 42,* 761–763.

Lerman, D., Iwata, B., Rainville, B., Adelinis, J., Crosland, K., & Kogan, J. (1997). Effects of reinforcement choice on task responding in individuals with developmental disabilities. *Journal of Applied Behavior Analysis, 30,* 411–422.

Lerman, D., Iwata, B., & Wallace, M. (1999). Side effects of extinction: Prevalence of bursting and aggression during the treatment of self-injurious behavior. *Journal of Applied Behavior Analysis, 32,* 1–8.

Lewis, T. J., & Sugai, G. (1999). Effective behavior support: A systems approach to proactive schoolwide management. *Focus on Exceptional Children, 31*(6), 1–24.

Lewis, T., & Sugai, G. (1996a). Functional assessment of problem behavior: A pilot investigation of the comparative and interactive effects of teacher and peer social attention on students in general education settings. *School Psychology Quarterly, 11,* 1–19.

Lewis, T., & Sugai, G. (1996b). Descriptive and experimental analysis of teacher and peer attention and the use of assessment based intervention to improve pro-social behavior of a student in general education setting. *Journal of Behavioral Education, 6*, 7–24.

Lohrmann, S., & Talerico, J. (2004). Anchor the boat: A classwide intervention to reduce problem behavior. *Journal of Positive Behavior Interventions, 6*, 113–120.

Lovitt, T. C. (1978). *Managing inappropriate behaviors in the classroom.* Reston, VA: Council for Exceptional Children.

Luiselli, J. K., Putnam, R. F., Handler, M. W., & Feinberg, A. B. (2005). Whole-school positive behavior support: Effects on student discipline problems and academic performance. *Educational Psychology, 25*(2–3), 183–198.

Lynn, S. K. (1994). Create an effective learning environment. *Strategies, 7*, 14–17.

Ma, X., & Willms, J. D. (2004). School disciplinary climate: Characteristics and effects on eighth grade achievement. *Alberta Journal of Educational Research, 50*, 169–188.

Madsen, C. H., Jr.,, Becker, W. C., & Thomas, D. R. (1968). Rules, praise, and ignoring: Elements of elementary classroom control. *Journal of Applied Behavior Analysis, 1*, 139–150.

Malone, B. G., & Tietjens, C. L. (2000). Re-examination of classroom rules: The need for clarity and specified behavior. *Special Services in the Schools, 16*, 159–170.

Marshall, M. (2001). *Discipline without stress, punishments or rewards: How teachers and parents promote responsibility and learning.* Los Alamitos, CA: Piper.

Martella, R. C., Nelson, J. R., & Marchand-Martella, N. E. (2003). *Managing disruptive behaviors in the schools.* Boston, MA: Allyn & Bacon.

Martens, B. K., Lochner, D. G., & Kelly, S. Q. (1992). The effects of variable-interval reinforcement on academic engagement: A demonstration of matching theory. *Journal of Applied Behavior Analysis, 25*, 143–151.

Martin, D. V. (1989, February). *Transition management: The student teacher's Achilles heel.* Paper presented at the annual meeting of the Association of Teacher Educators, St. Louis, MO.

Marzano, R. J. (2003). *Classroom management that works: Research-based strategies for every teacher.* Alexandria, VA: Association for Supervision and Curriculum Development.

Mayer, G. (1995). Preventing antisocial behavior in the schools. *Journal of Applied Behavior Analysis, 28*, 467–478.

McAllister, L., Stachowiak, J., Baer, D., & Conderman, L. (1969). The application of operant conditioning techniques in a secondary school classroom. *Journal of Applied Behavior Analysis, 2*, 277–285.

McCloud, S. (2005). From chaos to consistency: When one urban elementary school changed its culture from rowdy to calm, student achievement fell into place. *Educational Leadership, 62*(5), 46–49.

McGinnis, E., & Goldstein, A. (1994). *Skillstreaming the elementary school child* (Rev. ed.). Champaign, IL: Research Press.

McKinney, J., Mason, J., Clifford, M., & Perkerson, K. (1975). Relationship between classroom behavior and academic achievement. *Journal of Educational Psychology, 67*, 198–203.

McLean, E. (1993). Tips for beginners: Steps to better homework. *Mathematics Teacher, 86*, 212.

McLeod, J., Fisher, J., & Hoover, G. (2003). *The key elements of classroom management: Managing time and space, student behavior, and instructional strategies.* Alexandria, VA: Association for Supervision and Curriculum Development.

McNeely, C. A., Nonnemaker, J. A., & Blum, R. W. (2002). Promoting school connectedness: Evidence from the National Longitudinal Study of Adolescent Health. *Journal of School Health, 72*(4), 138–146.

Meece, J. L., Blumenfield, P. C., & Hoyle, R. H. (1988). Students' goal orientations and cognitive engagement in classroom activities. *Journal of Educational Psychology, 80*, 514–523.

Mendler, A. N., & Curwin, R. L. (1999). *Discipline with dignity for challenging youth.* Bloomington, IN: National Educational Service.

Mendler, A. N., & Curwin, R. L. (2008). *Discipline with dignity* . Bloomington, IN: Solution Tree.

Merrell, K. W., Ervin, R. A., & Gimple, G. A. (2005). *School psychology in the 21st Century: Introduction, principles, and practices.* New York, NY: Guilford Press.

Metzger, M. (2002). Learning to discipline. *Phi Delta Kappan, 84*, 77–84.

Miller, D., & Kraft, N. (2008). Best practices in communicating with and involving parents. In A. Thomas & J. Grimes (Eds.), *Best practices in school psychology V* (pp. 937–951). Bethesda, MD: National Association of School Psychologists.

Moran, C., Stobbe, J., Baron, W., Miller, J., & Moir, E. (2000). *Keys to the classroom: A teacher's guide to the first month of school.* Thousand Oaks, CA: Corwin Press.

Moskowitz, G., & Hayman, M. (1976). Success strategies of inner-city teachers: A year long study. *Journal of Educational Research, 69*, 283–389.

Murray, C., & Greenberg, M. (2006). Examining the importance of social relationships and social contexts in the lives of children with high-incidence disabilities. *Journal of Special Education, 39*, 220–233.

Murray, C., & Murray, T. (2004). Child level correlates of teacher-student relationships: An examination of demographic characteristics, academic orientations, and behavioral orientations. *Psychology in the Schools, 41*, 751–762.

National Research Council. (2000). *How people learn: Brain, mind, experience, and school.* Washington, DC: National Academies Press.

Nelson, J. R., Martella, R. M., & Marchand-Martella, N. (2002). Maximizing student learning: The effects of a comprehensive school-based program for preventing problem behaviors. *Journal of Emotional and Behavioral Disorders, 10*, 136–148.

Nelson, R. (1996). Designing schools to meet the needs of students who exhibit disruptive behavior. *Journal of Emotional and Behavioral Disorders, 4*, 147–161.

Niebuhr, K. (1999). An empirical study of student relationships and academic achievement. *Education, 9*, 679–681.

Northup, J. (2000). Further evaluation of the accuracy of reinforce surveys: A systematic replication. *Journal of Applied Behavior Analysis, 29*, 201–212.

O'Leary, K., & Becker, W. (1967). Behavior modification of an adjustment class. *Exceptional Children, 33*, 637–642.

O'Leary, K., & O'Leary, S. (Eds.) (1977). *Classroom management: The successful use of behavior modification* (2nd ed.). New York, NY: Pergamon Press.

O'Neill, R. E., Horner, R. H., Albin, R. W., Sprague, J. R., Storey, K., & Newton, J. S. (1997). *Functional assessment and program development for problem behavior: A practical handbook* (2nd ed.). Pacific Grove, CA: Brooks/Cole.

Orange, C. (2005). *Smart strategies for avoiding classroom mistakes.* Thousand Oaks, CA: Corwin Press.

Ortiz, S. O., & Flanagan, D. P. (2002). Best practices in working with culturally diverse children and families. In A. Thomas & J. Grimes (Eds.), *Best practices in school psychology IV* (pp. 337–351). Bethesda, MD: National Association of School Psychologists.

Ostrosky, M., Drasgow, E., & Halle, J. (1999). How can I help you get what you want? A communication strategy for students with severe disabilities. *Teaching Exceptional Children, 31*, 56–61.

Paine, S. C., Radicchi, J., Rosellini, L. C., Deutchman, L., & Darch, C. B. (1983). *Structuring your classroom for academic success.* Champaign, IL: Research Press.

Patrick, H., Turner, J. C., Meyer, D. K., & Midgley, C. (2003). How teachers establish psychological environments during the first days of school: Associations with avoidance in mathematics. *Teachers College Record, 105*, 1521–1558.

Pearson, A. (2009). *Guidance with good measure.* Chapin, SC: YouthLight.

Pedota, P. (2007). Strategies for effective classroom management in the secondary setting. *Clearing House, 80*, 163–166.

Phelan, P., Yu, H., & Davidson, A. (1994). Navigating the psychosocial pressures of adolescence: The voices and experiences of high school youth. *American Educational Research Journal, 31,* 415–447.

Pianta, R., Hamre, B., & Stuhlman, M. (2003). Relationships between teachers and children. In W. M. Reynolds & G. E. Miller (Eds.), *Handbook of child psychology: Vol. 7. Educational psychology.* Hoboken, NJ: Wiley.

Rader, L. (2005). Goal setting for students and teachers. *Clearing House, 78,* 123–126.

Reddy, R., Rhodes, J. E., & Mulhall, P. (2003). The influence of teacher support on student adjustment in the middle school years: A latent growth curve study. *Development and Psychopathology, 15,* 119–138.

Reinke, W., Lewis-Palmer, T., & Martin, E. (2007). The effect of visual performance feedback on teacher behavior-specific praise. *Behavior Modification, 31,* 247–263.

Repp, A., Nieminen, G., Olinger, E., & Brusca, R. (1988). Direct observation: Factors affecting the accuracy of observers. *Exceptional Children, 55,* 29–36.

Ridley, D. S., & Walther, B. (1995). *Creating responsible learners: The role of a positive classroom environment.* Washington, DC: American Psychological Association.

Rones, M., & Hoagwood, K. (2000). School-based mental health services: A research review. *Clinical Child and Family Psychology Review, 3*(4), 223–241.

Rosenshine, B. (1971). *Teaching behaviours and student achievement.* London, UK: National Foundation for Educational Research.

Rosenshine, B. (1983). Teaching functions in instructional programs. *Elementary School Journal, 83,* 335–351.

Rosenshine, B., & Stevens, R. (1986). Teacher behavior and student achievement. In M. C. Whitrock (Ed.), *Handbook of research on teaching* (3rd ed., pp. 376–391). New York, NY: Macmillan.

Royer, J. M., Cisero, C. A., & Carlo, M. S. (1993). Techniques and procedures for assessing cognitive skills. *Review of Educational Research, 63,* 201–243.

Scarborough, H. S., & Parker, J. D. (2003). Matthew effects in children with learning disabilities: Development of reading, IQ, and psychosocial problems from grade 2 to grade 8. *Annals of Dyslexia, 53,* 47–71.

Schell, L. M., & Burden, P. R. (1985). Working with beginning teachers. *Small School Forum, 7,* 13–15.

Scheuermann, B., & Evans, W. (1997). Hippocrates was right: Do no harm. A case for ethics in the selection of interventions. *Beyond Behavior, 8*(3), 18–22.

Scheuermann, B., & Hall, J. A. (2008). *Positive behavioral supports for the classroom.* Upper Saddle River, NJ: Pearson Education.

Schuldheisz, J. M., & van der Mars, H. (2001). Active supervision and students' physical activity in middle school physical education. *Journal of Teaching in Physical Education, 21,* 75–90.

Schumaker, J. B., Deshler, D. D., & McKnight, P. (2002). Ensuring success in the secondary general education curriculum through the use of teaching routines. In M. A. Shinn, H. M. Walker, & G. Stoner (Eds.), *Interventions for academic and behavior problems II: Preventive and remedial approaches* (pp. 791–823). Bethesda, MD: National Association of School Psychologists.

Scientifically based evaluation methods. (2005, January 25). *Federal Register, Notices, 70*(15), 3586–3589.

Sheridan, S. M., Kratochwill, T. R., & Bergan, J. R. (1996). *Conjoint behavioral consultation: A procedural manual.* New York, NY: Plenum Press.

Shinn, M., Ramsey, E., Walker, H., Stieber, S., & O'Neill, R. (1987). Antisocial behavior in school settings: Initial differences in an at-risk and normal population. *Journal of Special Education, 21,* 69–84.

Shores, R., Gunter, P., & Jack, S. (1993). Classroom management strategies: Are they setting events for coercion? *Behavioral Disorders, 18,* 92–102.

Silva, F. J., Yuille, R., & Peters, L. K. (2000). A method for illustrating the continuity of behavior during schedules of reinforcement. *Teaching of Psychology*, *27*, 145–148.

Silver-Pacuilla, H., & Fleischman, S. (2006). Technology to help struggling students. *Educational Leadership*, *63*, 84–85.

Simmons, D. C., Fuchs, L. S., & Fuchs, D. (1995). Effects of explicit teaching and peer tutoring on the reading achievement of learning disabled and low-performing students in regular classrooms. *Elementary School Journal*, *95*, 387–408.

Simola, R. (1996). *Teaching in the real world*. Englewood, CO: Teacher Ideas Press.

Simonsen, B., Fairbanks, S., Briesch, A., Myers, D., & Sugai, G. (2008). Evidence-based practices in classroom management: Considerations for research to practice. *Education and Treatment of Children*, *31*, 351–380.

Skiba, R., & Peterson, R. (2003). Teaching the social curriculum: School discipline as instruction. *Preventing School Failure*, *47*, 66–73.

Skinner, B. F. (1953). *Science and human behavior*. New York, NY: Basic Books.

Skinner, B. F. (1982). Contrived reinforcement. *Behavior Analyst*, *5*, 3–8.

Smith, B. (2000). Quantity matters: Annual instruction time in an urban school system. *Educational Administration Quarterly*, *35*, 652–682.

Spaulding, R. L. (1978). Control of deviancy in the classroom as a consequence of ego-enhancing behavior management techniques. *Journal of Research and Development in Education*, *11*, 39–52.

Spencer, V. G. (2006). Peer tutoring and students with emotional or behavioral disorders: A review of the literature. *Behavioral Disorders*, *31*(2), 204–222.

Sponder, B. (1993). Twenty golden opportunities to enhance student learning: Use them or lose them. *Teaching and Learning*, *15*, 18–24.

Sprick, R. S. (1994). *Cafeteria discipline: Positive techniques for lunchroom supervision* [Video program]. Eugene, OR: Pacific Northwest Publishing.

Sprick, R. S. (2003). *START on time! Safe transitions and reduced tardies* [Multimedia program]. Eugene, OR: Pacific Northwest Publishing.

Sprick, R. S. (2006). *Discipline in the secondary classroom: A positive approach to behavior management* (2nd ed.). San Francisco, CA: Jossey-Bass.

Sprick, R. S. (2009). *CHAMPS: A proactive and positive approach to classroom management* (2nd ed.). Eugene, OR: Pacific Northwest Publishing.

Sprick, R. S., Booher, M., & Garrison, M. (2009). *Behavioral response to intervention; Creating a continuum of problem-solving and support*. Eugene, OR: Pacific Northwest Publishing.

Sprick, R. S., Borgmeier, C., & Nolet, V. (2002). In M. A. Shinn, H. M. Walker, & G. Stoner (Eds.), *Interventions for academic and behavior problems II: Preventive and remedial approaches* (pp. 373–402). Bethesda, MD: National Association of School Psychologists.

Sprick, R. S., & Garrison, M. (2008). *Interventions: Evidence-based behavior strategies for individual students* (2nd ed.). Eugene, OR: Pacific Northwest Publishing.

Sprick, R. S., Garrison, M., & Howard, L. (1998). *CHAMPS: A proactive and positive approach to classroom management*. Eugene, OR: Pacific Northwest Publishing.

Sprick, R. S., Garrison, M., & Howard, L. (2002). *Foundations: Establishing positive discipline and school-wide behavior support* [Video program]. Eugene, OR: Pacific Northwest Publishing.

Sprick, R. S., Howard, L., Wise, B. J., Marcum, K., & Haykin, M. (1998). *Administrator's desk reference of behavior management* (Vol. 1). Eugene, OR: Pacific Northwest Publishing.

Sprick, R. S., Swartz, L., & A. Glang, A. (2007). *In the driver's seat: A roadmap to managing student behavior on the bus* [CD-ROM and DVD program]. Eugene, OR: Pacific Northwest Publishing and Oregon Center for Applied Sciences.

Sterling-Turner, H. E., Robinson, S. L., & Wilczynski, S. M. (2001). Functional assessment of distracting and disruptive behaviors in the school setting. *School Psychology Review*, *30*, 211–226.

Stone, R. (2002). *Best practices for high school classrooms: What award-winning secondary teachers do*. Thousand Oaks, CA: Corwin Press.

Stormont, M., Smith, S., & Lewis, T. (2007). Teacher implementation of precorrection and praise statements in Head Start classrooms as a component of a program-wide system of positive behavior support. *Journal of Behavioral Education*, *16*, 280–290.

Stronge, J. H. (2002). *Qualities of effective teachers*. Alexandria, VA: Association for Supervision and Curriculum Development.

Sugai, G., & Lewis, T. (1996). Preferred and promising practices for social skill instruction. *Focus on Exceptional Children, 29,* 1–16.

Sugai, G. M., & Tindal, G. A. (1993). *Effective school consultation: An interactive approach*. Pacific Grove, CA: Brooks/Cole.

Sugai, G., Horner, R. H., Dunlap, G., Heineman, M., Lewis, T., Nelson, C. M., et al. (2000). Applying positive behavior support and functional behavioral assessment in schools. *Journal of Positive Behavioral Interventions, 2,* 131–143.

Sutherland, K. S., Wehby, J., & Copeland, S. (2000). Effect of varying rates of behavior-specific praise on the on-task behavior of students with EBD. *Journal of Applied Behavior Analysis, 8,* 2–8.

Swann, W., & Pittman, T. (1977). Initiating play activity of children: The moderating influence of verbal cues on intrinsic motivation. *Child Development, 48,* 1128–1132.

Swift, M., & Swift, G. (1968). The assessment of achievement related classroom behavior: Normative, reliability, and validity data. *Journal of Special Education, 2,* 137–153.

Swift, M., & Swift, G. (1969a). Achievement related classroom behavior of secondary school normal and disturbed students. *Exceptional Children, 35,* 677–684.

Swift, M., & Swift, G. (1969b). Clarifying the relationship between academic success and overt classroom behavior. *Exceptional Children, 36,* 99–104.

Swift, M., & Swift, G. (1973). Academic success and classroom behavior in secondary school. *Exceptional Children, 39,* 392–399.

Sweeney, W., Ehrhardt, A., Gardner, R., Jones, L., Greenfield, R., & Fribley, S. (1999). Using guided notes with academically at-risk high school students during a remedial summer social studies class. *Psychology in the Schools, 36,* 305–318.

Sykes, S. (2002, October 24). Substitutes teach 6.4 percent of classroom time. *Salt Lake Tribune,* B3.

Tanner, B. M., Bottoms, G., Caro, F., & Bearman, A. (2003). *Instructional strategies: How teachers teach matters*. Atlanta, GA: Southern Regional Educational Board.

Teachers favor standards, consequences … and a helping hand. (1996). *American Educator, 20,* 18–21.

Thomas, D., Becker, W., & Armstrong, M. (1968). Production and elimination of disruptive classroom behavior by systematically varying teacher's behavior. *Journal of Applied Behavior Analysis, 1,* 35–45.

Thompson, R., Fisher, W., & Contrucci, S. (1998). Evaluating the reinforcing effects of choice in comparison to reinforcement rate. *Research in Developmental Disabilities, 19,* 181–187.

Troia, G., & Graham, S. (2002). The effectiveness of a highly explicit, teacher-directed strategy instruction routine: Changing the writing performance of students with learning disabilities. *Journal of Learning Disabilities, 35,* 290–305.

Trussell, R. (2008). Classroom universals to prevent problem behaviors. *Intervention in School and Clinic, 43,* 179–185

Udvari-Solner, A. (1996). Examining teacher thinking: Constructing a process to designing curricular adaptations. *Remedial and Special Education, 17,* 245–254.

U.S. Department of Education (2002a). Guidance for the Reading First Program. Retrieved from: www.ed.gov/programs/readingfirst/guidance.doc

U.S. Department of Education (2002b). *No Child Left Behind executive summary*. Washington, DC: Author.

U.S. Department of Education (2002c, November 18). *Report on scientifically based research supported by U.S. Department of Education* [Press release]. Retrieved from www.ed.gov/news/pressreleases/2002/11/11182002b.html

Van Acker, R., Grant, S., & Henry, D. (1996). Teacher and student behavior as a function of risk for aggression. *Education and Treatment of Children, 19,* 316–334.

Walker, H., & Bullis, M. (1990). Behavior disorders and the social context of regular class integration: A conceptual dilemma. In J. W. Lloyd, N. N. Singh, & A. C. Repp (Eds.), *The regular education initiative: Alternative perspectives on concepts, issues, and models* (pp. 75–93). Sycamore, IL: Sycamore Publishing.

Walker, H. M., & Holland, F. (1979). Issues, strategies, and perspectives in the management of disruptive child behavior in the classroom. *Journal of Education, 161*(2), 25–50.

Walker, H., Horner, R., Sugai, G., Bullis, M., Sprague, J., et al. (1996). Integrated approaches to preventing antisocial behavior patterns among school-age youth. *Journal of Emotional and Behavioral Disorders, 4,* 193–256.

Walker, H., & McConnell, S. (1988). *The Walker-McConnell scale of social competence and school adjustment: A social skills rating scale for teachers.* Austin, TX: Pro-Ed.

Walker, H., Ramsey, E., & Gresham, F. (2004). *Antisocial behavior in schools: Evidence-based practices* (2nd ed.). Belmont, CA: Wadsworth.

Walker, H. M., & Severson, H. H. (1992). *Systematic screening for behavior disorders* (2nd ed.). Longmont, CO: Sopris West.

Walker, H. M., Severson, H. H., Feil, E. G., Stiller, B., & Golly, A. (1998). First step to success: Intervention at the point of school entry to prevent antisocial behavior patterns. *Psychology in the Schools, 35,* 259–269.

Walker, H. M., & Shinn, M. R. (2002). Structuring school-based interventions to achieve integrated primary, secondary, and tertiary prevention goals for safe and effective schools. In M. R. Shinn, G. Stoner, & H. M. Walker (Eds.), *Interventions for academic and behavior problems: Preventive and remedial approaches* (pp. 1–26). Silver Spring, MD: National Association of School Psychologists.

Walker, H. M. & Sprague, J. (2007). Early, evidence-based intervention with school-related behavior disorders: Key issues, continuing challenges, and promising practices. In J. B. Crocket, M. M. Gerber, & T. J. Landrum (Eds.), *Achieving the radical reform of special education: Essays in honor of James M. Kauffman.* Mahwah, NJ: Erlbaum.

Ward, M., & Baker, B. (1968). Reinforcement therapy in the classroom. *Journal of Applied Behavior Analysis, 1,* 323–328.

Watson, L. (1967). Application of operant conditioning techniques to institutionalized severely and profoundly retarded children. *Mental Retardation Abstracts, 4,* 1–18.

Wehby, J., Symons, F., Canale, J., & Go, F. (1998). Teaching practices in classrooms for students with emotional and behavioral disorders: Discrepancies between recommendations and observation. *Behavioral Disorders, 24,* 52–57.

Weinstein, C. (1977). Modifying student behavior in an open classroom through changes in the physical design. *American Educational Research Journal, 14,* 249–262.

Wheeler, J., & Richey, D. (2005). *Behavior management.* Upper Saddle River, NJ: Merrill/Prentice Hall.

Winett, R. A., & Vachon, E. M. (1974). Group feedback and group contingencies in modifying behavior of fifth graders. *Psychological Reports, 34*(3), 1283–1292.

Wolf, D., Bixby, J., Glenn, J., & Gardner, H. (1990). To use their minds well: Investigating new forms of student assessment. *Review of Research in Education, 17,* 31–74.

Wolfgang, C. H., & Glickman, C. D. (1986). *Solving discipline problems: Strategies for classroom teachers* (2nd ed.). Boston, MA: Allyn & Bacon.

Woodward, J. (2001). Using grades to assess student performance. *Journal of School Improvement, 2,* 44–45.

Yawkey, T. D. (1971). Conditioning independent work behavior in reading with seven-year-old children in a regular early childhood classroom. *Child Study Journal, 2*(1), 23.

Ysseldyke, J. E., & Christenson, S. L. (1987). Evaluating students' instructional environments. *RASE, 8,* 17–24.

Ysseldyke, J., Murns, M., Dawson, P., Kelley, B., Morrison, D., Ortiz, S., et al. (2006). *School psychology: A blueprint for training and practice III.* Bethesda, MD: National Association of School Psychologists.

Ysseldyke, J., Thurlow, M., Wotruba, J., & Nania, P. (1990). Instructional arrangements: Perceptions from general education. *Teaching Exceptional Children, 22,* 4–8.

Name Index

Subject Index

e represents exhibit; *f* represents figure.

HOW TO USE
THE DVD

System Requirements

PC with Microsoft Windows 2003 or later
Mac with Apple OS version 10.1 or later

Using the DVD with Windows

To view the items located on the DVD, follow these steps:

1. Insert the DVD into your computer's DVD drive.
2. A window appears with the following options:

   Contents: Allows you to view the files included on the DVD.

   Links: Displays a hyperlinked page of websites.

   Author: Displays a page with information about the author(s).

   Exit: Closes the interface window.

If you do not have autorun enabled, or if the autorun window does not appear, follow these steps to access the DVD:

1. Click Start → Run.
2. In the dialog box that appears, type d:\start.exe, where d is the letter of your DVD drive. This brings up the autorun window described in the preceding set of steps.
3. Choose the desired option from the menu. (See Step 2 in the preceding list for a description of these options.)

In Case of Trouble

If you experience difficulty using the DVD, please follow these steps:

1. Make sure your hardware and systems configurations conform to the systems requirements noted under "System Requirements" above.
2. Review the installation procedure for your type of hardware and operating system. It is possible to reinstall the software if necessary.

To speak with someone in Product Technical Support, call 800-762-2974 or 317-572-3994 Monday through Friday from 8:30 a.m. to 5:00 p.m. EST. You can also contact Product Technical Support and get support information through our website at www.wiley.com/techsupport.

Before calling or writing, please have the following information available:

- Type of computer and operating system.
- Any error messages displayed.
- Complete description of the problem.

It is best if you are sitting at your computer when making the call.